Constituting Americans

......

New Americanists

A Series Edited by Donald E. Pease

Constituting Americans

Cultural Anxiety and Narrative Form

Priscilla Wald

Duke University Press   Durham and London   1995

Third printing, 2003

© 1995 Duke University Press

All rights reserved

Printed in the United States of America

on acid-free paper ∞

Designed by C. H. Westmoreland

Typeset in Bodoni Book

by Keystone Typesetting, Inc.

Library of Congress Cataloging-in-Publication Data

appear on the last printed page of this book.

Quotations from Mina Loy's poetry are from *The Last Lunar Baedeker*, ed. Roger L. Conover (Manchester, England: Carcanet Press Limited, 1982); reprinted by permission of Roger L. Conover.

Quotations from Gertrude Stein's personal correspondence are taken from the Yale Collection of American Literature, Rare Book and Manuscript Library, Yale University, and are used by permission.

For Audrey and Stanley, Evan and Nathaniel

Contents

· · · · · ·

Abbreviations

......

AA   Anthony Appiah, "The Uncompleted Argument: Du Bois and the Illusion of Race"

ABT   Gertrude Stein, *The Autobiography of Alice B. Toklas*

AL   *Abraham Lincoln: His Speeches and Writings*

BC   William Blackstone, *Commentaries on the Laws of England*

BG   Anzia Yezierska, *Bread Givers*

BS   Frantz Fanon, *Black Skin, White Masks*

BW   Barbara A. White, " 'Our Nig' and the She-Devil: New Information about Harriet Wilson and the 'Belmont' Family"

CAL   Evert A. and George L. Duyckinck, *Cyclopaedia of American Literature*

CMA   Gertrude Stein, "Cultivated Motor Automatism"

CN   *Cherokee Nation v. The State of Georgia*

COR   W. E. B. Du Bois, "The Conservation of Races"

CR   William Gilpin, *The Cosmopolitan Railway*

D   Theresa Hak Kyung Cha, *Dictée*

DB   *Downes v. Bidwell*

DD   W. E. B. Du Bois, *Dusk of Dawn: An Essay Toward an Autobiography of a Race Concept*

DLL   David Levering Lewis, *W. E. B. Du Bois: Biography of a Race, 1868– 1919*

DM   Deborah E. McDowell, "In the First Place: Making Frederick Douglass and the Afro-American Narrative Tradition"

DMP   Horace Kallen, "Democracy versus the Melting-Pot"

DR   *Democratic Review*

DS   *Scott v. Sandford*

EA   Gertrude Stein, *Everybody's Autobiography*

EAP	*The Works of the Late Edgar Allan Poe*
EH	Emil G. Hirsch, "The American University"
ER	Ernest Renan, "What Is a Nation?"
ES	Eric J. Sundquist, *To Wake the Nations: Race in the Making of American Literature*
F	Ralph Waldo Emerson, "Fate"
FB	W. E. B. Du Bois, "The Freedmen's Bureau"
FDP	*Frederick Douglass Papers,* series 1 (cited *FDP,* vol.: pp.)
FG	Franklin Giddings, *The Elements of Society*
FHU	Edgar Allan Poe, "The Fall of the House of Usher"
FM	Leon Katz, "The First Making of *The Making of Americans*"
FQ	Leon Katz, Introduction to *Fernhurst, Q.E.D.*
GM	Gertrude Stein, "The Gradual Making of The Making of Americans"
GS	Walter Benn Michaels, *The Gold Standard and the Logic of Naturalism*
GWFA	*Washington's Farewell Address*
HHM	Herman Melville, "Hawthorne and His Mosses"
HJ	Harriet A. Jacobs, *Incidents in the Life of a Slave Girl*
HOB	Lydia Maria Child, *Hobomok and Other Writings on Indians*
IA	Garry Wills, *Inventing America: Jefferson's Declaration of Independence*
IC	Benedict Anderson, *Imagined Communities: Reflections on the Origin and Spread of Nationalism*
JB	Houston Baker, *The Journey Back: Issues in Black Literature and Criticism*
JD	Janice Doane, *Silence and Narrative: The Early Novels of Gertrude Stein*
JM	*Johnson v. McIntosh*
JR	Jacob Riis, *The Making of an American*
JWJ	James Weldon Johnson, *The Autobiography of an Ex-Coloured Man, Three Negro Classics*
LDD	*Lincoln-Douglas Debates*
LG	Garry Wills, *Lincoln at Gettysburg*
LHA	Barrett Wendell, *A Literary History of America*
LR	Lisa Ruddick, *Reading Gertrude Stein: Body, Text, Gnosis*
LW	*Literary World*
MA	Gertrude Stein, *The Making of Americans*
MB	Frederick Douglass, *My Bondage and My Freedom*
MBV	Nathaniel Hawthorne, "The Minister's Black Veil"
MK	Nathaniel Hawthorne, "My Kinsman, Major Molineux"
ML	Jay Leyda, *The Melville Log*

MM   Homi Bhabha, "Of Mimicry and Man"

MN   Woodrow Wilson, "The Making of the Nation"

M-P   Israel Zangwill, *The Melting-Pot*

N   Ralph Waldo Emerson, "Nature"

NFD   Frederick Douglass, *Narrative of the Life of Frederick Douglass, an American Slave*

NMA   Gertrude Stein and Leon M. Solomons, "Normal Motor Automatism"

NS   N. S. Shaler, "European Peasants as Immigrants"

NSV   Thomas Jefferson, *Notes on the State of Virginia*

NWL   *Letters of Noah Webster*

NWS   Noah Webster Speller

ON   Harriet E. Wilson, *Our Nig, or Sketches from the Life of a Free Black*

OO   Otto H. Olsen, ed., *The Thin Disguise*

P   Herman Melville, *Pierre*

PF   *Plessy v. Ferguson*

PH   W. E. B. Du Bois, "The Propaganda of History" (in *Black Reconstruction*)

PL   Mary Antin, *The Promised Land*

PP   William James, *The Principles of Psychology*

PR   Gertrude Stein, "Portraits and Repetition"

RC   John W. Burgess, *Reconstruction and the Constitution*

RPE   William Archibald Dunning, *Reconstruction: Political and Economic, 1865–1877*

RW   Perry Miller, *The Raven and the Whale*

S   W. E. B. Du Bois, *The Souls of Black Folk*

SAH   Woodrow Wilson, "The Significance of American History"

SC   Otto Weininger, *Sex and Character*

SH   Emmet Starr, *Starr's History of the Cherokee Nation*

SLI   Arnold Rampersad, *Slavery and the Literary Imagination*

T   Ralph Waldo Emerson, "The Transcendentalist"

TA   Theodore Roosevelt, "True Americanism"

TJ   Thomas Jefferson, *Autobiography*

TP   Theodore Parker, "The American Scholar"

TR   Edmund Burke, "The Thirteen Resolutions"

U   Sigmund Freud, "The 'Uncanny'"

WA   William L. Andrews, *To Tell a Free Story: The First Century of Afro-American Autobiography, 1760–1865*

WAM   Gertrude Stein, *What Are Masterpieces*

WB   Walter Bagehot, *Physics and Politics*

WG   *Worcester v. Georgia*

WL   Wilson Lumpkin, *The Removal of the Cherokee Indians from Georgia, 1827–1841*

WM   William S. McFeely, *Frederick Douglass*

WW   Edgar Allan Poe, "William Wilson"

Y   Abraham Cahan, *Yekl and the Imported Bridegroom and Other Stories of the New York Ghetto*

YA   Ralph Waldo Emerson, "The Young American: A Lecture Read before the Mercantile Library Association, Boston, February 7, 1844"

Acknowledgments

Many thanks are in order to people and institutions that helped me complete this book. I would like to thank the Council for Research in the Humanities of Columbia University for summer grants and the Andrew W. Mellon Foundation for a fellowship at Stanford University that gave me the support necessary to begin this project.

I wish to thank Roger L. Conover for permission to quote from Mina Loy's poetry published in *The Last Lunar Baedeker* (Jargon Society Press, 1982). I also thank Patricia Willis, curator of the Yale Collection of American Literature, Rare Book and Manuscript Library, Yale University, for permission to quote from Gertrude Stein's personal correspondence. Grateful acknowledgment is made to all of the following for permission to reprint previously published work. A version of the first section of chapter 1 appeared earlier as "Terms of Assimilation: Legislating Subjectivity in the Emerging Nation," *boundary 2: an international journal of literature and culture*, vol. 19, special issues edited by Karl Kroeber (1992); it was reprinted in *American Indian Persistence and Resurgence*, ed. Karl Kroeber (Duke University Press, 1994) and, with slight revisions, in *Cultures of United States Imperialism*, ed. Amy Kaplan and Donald E. Pease (Duke University Press, 1994). The second section of chapter 2 was published in a different form as "Hearing Narrative Voices in Melville's *Pierre*," *boundary 2*, vol. 17, special issue edited by Donald E. Pease (1990); it was reprinted in *Revisionary Interventions into the Americanist Canon*, ed. Donald E. Pease (Duke University Press, 1994). Parts of chapter 4 were previously published as "A God Who Is Later a Terror: (En)countering the National Plot in Gertrude Stein's *The Making of Americans*," in *Prospects: An Annual of American Cultural Studies*, vol. 16, ed. Jack Salzman (Cambridge University Press, 1991).

I would also like to thank the editors and staff at Duke University Press, especially Reynolds Smith, Pam Morrison, and Mindy Conner, for their efforts, their patience, and their humor, as well as Janet Mazefsky and Tim Watson for the thorough indexing and proofreading, respectively.

I am grateful to the many friends, students, and colleagues at Columbia University, Stanford University, and elsewhere who prodded me to clarify and refine my ideas. There are too many of you to thank individually here, but please know that I deeply appreciate your interest and efforts. For valuable comments on drafts of this project, I wish to thank Akhil Amar, Jonathan Arac, Marcellus Blount, Carrie Tirado Bramen, Gillian Brown, David Damrosch, Andrew Delbanco, Kathy Eden, Jay Fliegelman, Elaine Freedgood, Susan Gillman, Jean E. Howard, Gordon Hutner, Karl Kroeber, Jonathan Levin, Kathryne V. Lindberg, Christopher Looby, Anne McClintock, Paul McNeil, Rob Nixon, Marjorie Perloff, Maggie Sale, Jack Salzman, James Shapiro, Michael Tratner, Gauri Viswanathan, Deborah Elise White, and the students who attended Richard Bushman's History/American Studies Discussion Group (especially Timothy P. McCarthy and Gary Stone), at which I presented chapter 1.

Sacvan Bercovitch offered important encouragement when I first began to formulate many of the questions that inform this book, and his comments on my work as well as his own work continue to challenge me in all the best ways. For the visions and endless revisions, for the cheerful willingness to read yet another draft and have yet another conversation, I thank Dale Bauer, Howard Horwitz, and Amy Kaplan. Both the process and the final product have benefited more than they know from their involvement. Robert Ferguson's detailed reading of the first draft, his ability to discern where I was going before I did and to ask exactly the right questions, brought me to a deeper understanding of my project. For that as well as for the ongoing conversations about the project, I thank him. Ann Douglas has offered unflagging support and indispensable critical insight. I am grateful for her detailed and perceptive responses to several drafts of this project, which improved the work at every level. In these responses, as in her own work in the classroom and on the page, she has inspired me to think beyond what I thought were my boundaries.

Finally, I am more than fortunate to have Joseph Donahue as a friend, interlocutor, and life companion. He has enriched my life intellectually and personally through his intelligence, his patience, his humor, and his decency. This book could not exist without him.

•••••

Until the missing story of ourselves is told, nothing besides told can suffice us: we shall go on quietly craving it . . . in the missing story of ourselves can be found all other missing stories.

—Laura (Riding) Jackson,
The Telling

Introduction

······

Strangers in Their Work

"How curious a land is this," wrote W. E. B. Du Bois of the Black Belt of Georgia, "how full of untold story, of tragedy and laughter, and the rich legacy of human life."[1] Du Bois, like the other four writers in this study, identified and tried to tell untold stories. In so doing, these authors came to understand why the stories they wanted to tell had remained so long untold. They confronted the limits of storytelling. In their different ways, these writers all discovered, as the modernist poet Laura Riding puts it, that the storytelling "self is implicated in the totality as a speaking self of it, owing it words that will put the seal of the Whole upon it."[2] Riding describes a debt: the conventions that enable the self to speak in turn require reinforcement. The storyteller confirms the terms of the story. My inquiries begin with the creative responses to that debt offered by Frederick Douglass, Herman Melville, Harriet Wilson, W. E. B. Du Bois, and Gertrude Stein, all of whom turned the limitations of their own stories into analyses of the limitations and possibilities of storytelling.

Social unacceptability and political censorship, personal prohibitions and cultural conventions, the literary market and language itself all contribute to the shaping of stories. Yet untold stories press for a hearing. My readings attend to disruptions in literary narratives caused by unexpected words, awkward grammatical constructions, rhetorical or thematic dissonances that mark the pressure of untold stories. The authors I consider arrived at their understanding of untold stories in response to the imperatives each experienced—in his or her way—to tell the story of the nation. My study explores how inquiries into the limitations of their stories became, in their works, analyses of the official stories through which a nation—"a people"—spoke itself into existence.

Official stories are narratives that surface in the rhetoric of nationalist movements and initiatives—legal, political, and literary—such as John Marshall's legislation of Indian Removal, Abraham Lincoln's program for a consolidated Union, and the efforts of literary Young America and the *Democratic Review* to shape an American literature. Official stories constitute Americans. I use the term "official" because of the authority they command, articulated, as they are, in relation to the rights and privileges of individuals. They determine the status of an individual in the community. Neither static nor monolithic, they change in response to competing narratives of the nation that must be engaged, absorbed, and retold: the fashioning and endless refashioning of "a people." Nation-builders in the nineteenth-century United States understood the importance of those stories to the project of nation-building. In the early- to mid-nineteenth century, jurists, politicians, and journalists all, in their fashion, competed to forge narratives that would instantiate their visions of the Union and define what the United States Constitution called "We the People." With the emergence of the United States as a world power at the turn of the twentieth century, educators and legislators evolved national narratives that could channel the challenge posed by the variously unassimilated people of the nation and its overseas territories into a rallying point for a self-conscious and exportable Americanism.

Their narratives reflect the different political and cultural visions and the different social and political roles of the nation-builders in this study, as well as the different historical periods in which they lived. Yet despite their differences, Supreme Court Justices like John Marshall and Roger Taney, politicians including Abraham Lincoln and Woodrow Wilson, critics and journalists such as John L. O'Sullivan, Evert Duyckinck, and Jacob Riis meet in my book because of their efforts to articulate a cultural identity, their passionate appeals for a recognizable America, and the stories they helped to tell about the nation. *Constituting Americans* studies the stories through which they sought to create memories of forgotten origins, to transform contestable geopolitical boundaries and plural ethnic and racial peoples into a community with origins that predate those contests. An allegedly latent cultural identity would legitimate the political entity of a United States nation, and an identifiably American literature would attest to an identifiably American culture. The nation-builders who appear in this study were especially aggressive in their efforts to tell an official story of America and in their attempts to press the nation's literati into service to that story.

In different ways, Douglass, Melville, Wilson, Du Bois, and Stein felt and recorded that pressure. They wrote many of their most challenging and self-reflexive works during, and in engagement with, debates about the constituting of America and Americans.[3] The works I consider manifest their writers' unsettling sense of not enjoying full authorial liberty in their texts, their uneasy awareness of a larger story controlling their stories. But these works also convey their authors' understanding that those larger stories constituted them as authors; they could not tell their stories without the conventions those larger stories provide. The works included in this study dramatize this dilemma by depicting narrators or characters who must choose between conforming to cultural prescriptions and refusing comprehensibility. For these authors, either option represented limits on the stories they could tell. Meditating on those limits, they refused the idea of a "free story" and the individualism implied by that idea. Instead, the oscillation between conformity and incomprehensibility proved strangely productive for them.[4] These authors used evidence of their own authorial struggles to reflect—and to reflect on—the relationship between literary production and cultural identity in the United States.

My investigation of literary responses to nationalist initiatives has led me to a grouping of writers that does not conform to the classifications of more familiar literary historical narratives, classifications according to historical period, genre, race, gender, or class. Those distinctions are important to my story, since they affect the access each writer had to the means of literary production, and therefore the writer's experience of authorship. Yet the resonances among these works have made clear to me that these concerns reached across historical and sociological boundaries—as well as genre classifications—through which current narratives of literary history have influenced not only what we read, but how we read, shaping our readings of individual literary works and of "American literature." The story of how and why these texts belong together is part of the story of *Constituting Americans*. These authors sought neither to reject, nor to flee from their culture, but, on the contrary, to engage it.[5] Through their literary narratives, they participated in the imagining of a community and transformed that imagining into a contemplation of the consequences and ambiguities of their own participation.

Anxiety and the Reformulation of Personhood

I am interested, in this study, in the anxiety surrounding the conceptualization of personhood that these authors confronted as they sought to tell, represent, and analyze untold stories: what had been suppressed and repressed by official stories of We the People. In describing that anxiety, I have applied, extended, and sometimes contested the concepts and terminology of contemporary theorists of the nation who address the relationship between personal and national narratives of identity, especially Benedict Anderson and Etienne Balibar.

My point of departure is the analogy Anderson posits between such narratives, both of which begin with "profound changes of consciousness." Experienced as "estrangement," these changes generate "a conception of personhood, *identity* . . . which, because it can not be 'remembered,' must be narrated."[6] For Anderson, the recognition of a discontinuity between past and present and the desire to make them continuous give rise to a narrative of identity, which in turn imparts the way people know, understand, and experience themselves—or, their selves. Yet an analogy between personal and national narratives can obscure their dynamic interaction. National narratives actually shape personal narratives by delineating the cultural practices through which personhood is defined. The role of married women or the rights of indigenous peoples are examples of how a culture, through its institutions and its conventions, defines individuals' existence—defines, that is, how they will experience and understand themselves as people and as part of a people.

For Balibar, any newly-formed community depends "on the projection of individual existence into the weft of a collective narrative, on the recognition of a common name and on traditions lived as the trace of an immemorial past (even when they have been fabricated and inculcated in the recent past)."[7] Since the idea of individual existence cannot preexist a group identity, Balibar suggests that the formation of a new community entails a deconstitution of the old: "individual existence" must first be dissociated from one collective identity (a tribe or region, for example) and then reimagined within another collective narrative. National narratives, for example, do not supply missing conceptions of personhood; rather, they forge one conception out of another to constitute an "individual" as a national subject with a new cultural identity.[8] They may not entirely replace, but they certainly reconstruct, regional, tribal, or other affiliations. At the same time, they obscure the reformulation of personhood that accompanies the constitution of a new community, which they present as a continuity rather than a disruption. In the official stories that concern me, for example, the discontinuity in government marked by the American Revolution was counterposed to a putatively universal conception of personhood that legitimated the Revolution as the necessary means to safeguard (and restore) the rights to which people and a people were inherently entitled.

Neither Anderson nor Balibar seems primarily interested in addressing the cultural anxiety generated by the reformulation of personhood. Such inquiries, as the work of Frantz Fanon suggests, are conventionally seen as the province of psychoanalysis, and Anderson and Balibar seem reluctant to introduce psychoanalytic concepts or even vocabulary directly into the study of the nation. Yet psychoanalytic formulations—in particular, the type of anxiety described by Sigmund Freud in the concept of the uncanny—hover as felt presences in their language: the "estrangement" that Anderson marks as the result of "profound changes of consciousness," for example, or Balibar's "trace of an immemorial past," the continuity with a forgotten moment (the stranger as self) and the sense of having forgotten (the self estranged). The uncanny helps us understand what inaugurates narratives of identity and what haunts them.

The uncanny is therefore central to my analysis of official stories of the nation. I have taken the term from Freud's own study of estrangement in his 1919 essay, "The Uncanny," written while the national boundaries of Europe were being redrawn. Freud sets out to explain the anxiety designated by the German *unheimlich* (literally, not homely or homelike).[9] That anxiety, he observes, grows out of the transmutation of something "known of old and long familiar" into something frightening (U, 220). Freud accounts for the change by turning to the process of repression, which alienates the familiar and returns any affect as anxiety. Linguistically, he tracks the "ambivalence" of the German word *heimlich* (homely)—and the related *heimisch* (native)—to its coincidence with its opposite, *unheimlich* (U, 226). Two definitions converge in *heimlich*, the familiar and the concealed, to produce the unsettling experience that results from the resurfacing of what is supposed to remain hidden, an experience named by *unheimlich*. Something reminiscent of "home" turns the unfamiliar into the disturbing. He develops his analysis through a reading of E. T. A. Hoffmann's *The Sandman*, and he locates the most prevalent causes of uncanniness in repressed castration anxieties and in disavowed beliefs in animism and the omnipotence of thoughts (the incursion of one system of beliefs into another).

A disjunctive moment in Freud's essay extends—or perhaps clarifies—the concept. The disjunction lies in a misalliance between a claim he makes in the essay and a footnote he uses to illustrate the claim. The note offers examples ostensibly supporting his assertion that anyone who has genuinely relinquished "primitive" beliefs in animism will prove impervious to experiences arising from that source, which include eerie encounters with one's double. In support of that observation, Freud summons several encounters with doubles that did not produce fear. Those encounters instead marked a failure of recognition. He offers first the account of German scientist Ernst Mach, who reports being startled to confront a presumed stranger of whom he had "formed a very unfavourable opinion" only to discover that the "stranger" was in fact his own mirror image. Following this account, Freud reports having been amused and dismayed to discover himself in "an elderly gentleman in a dressing-gown and a travelling cap" whom he had thought an accidental intruder in his railway compartment. And he remembers that he "thoroughly disliked [the intruder's] appearance." He ends the note by attributing his own and Mach's dislike of their mirror images to the possibility of "a vestigial trace of the archaic reaction which feels the 'double' to be something uncanny" (U, 248n).

The note is perplexing both in its contradictory claims and in its odd deployment of the uncanny. The example with which he intends to illustrate his and Mach's imperviousness to the experience of the uncanny becomes instead a depiction of their susceptibility ("vestigial traces"). But the deeper confusion lies in his use of their unrecognized mirror images to illustrate the uncanny: both he and Mach experience their unrecognized reflections as strangers rather than doubles. This note is important precisely because it does not fit, because it disrupts Freud's narrative of the uncanny: it is itself unsettling, and it signals an untold story.[10]

The story narrated in the note is about discovering the (inevitable) inaccuracy of one's experience of self. In the mirror image, the men confront reflections that do not correspond to their internalized ideas about themselves, which is to say they confront their own faulty images of themselves. They see themselves as though through the eyes of another.

The "intruder," for example, forces Freud simultaneously to recognize the stranger, whose appearance he dislikes, as himself and to mark the distance between a mirrored image and his experience and understanding of himself. Freud's *uncanny* recognition, in other words, turns on the discovery that the unfamiliar is really familiar (the stranger as self) but also that the familiar is unfamiliar (the self as stranger). The note locates uncanniness—identified through *discomfort*—in the experience of an altered self that calls the fundamental assumptions of what the self is and whence it derives into question.[11] Ultimately, as in Anderson's and Balibar's uses of estrangement, the uncanny sends us home to the discovery that "home" is not what or where we think it is and that we, by extension, are not who or what we think we are.

The changes in the consciousness of a group that, as Anderson notes, result in the reconceptualization of personhood broadly affect individuals' experiences of self and make them more susceptible to that disturbing sense of estrangement. That sense is registered, for example, in the words of Barrett Wendell, a prominent cultural commentator at the turn of the twentieth century, who, witnessing the emergence of the United States as a world power, worried that the corresponding demographic changes would make "the very name of us mean something not ourselves."[12] Wendell expresses the characteristic anxiety that accompanies challenges to the name "American"—to the nation's familiar (and dominant) narratives of identity and the conception of personhood they express. He articulates the fears of a dominant group that wants to protect its property, its own terms of inheritance, and, generally, its power. But the challenge to self-recognition that Wendell describes has a psychological dimension as well.

Constituting Americans attends to the anxiety evident in the language of legal, political, and social debates concerning personhood and national identity. There is a strikingly ontological cast to that language, as in Theodore Roosevelt's claim that "the man who does not become Americanized nevertheless fails to remain a European, and becomes nothing at all."[13] Roosevelt's assertion is more than a rhetorical flourish; the articulation of personhood through the language of being is a legal convention. The eighteenth-century English legal theorist Sir William Blackstone, whose *Commentaries on the Laws of England* formed the basis for legal education in the colonies while the revolutionary generation was setting the legal structure of the consolidated government in place, offers a vivid example of that deployment when he explains the law of *feme-covert:* "by marriage, the husband and wife are one person in law: that is, the very being or legal existence of the woman is suspended during the marriage, or at least is incorporated and consolidated into that of the husband: under whose wing, protection, and *cover*, she performs everything; and is therefore called in our law-french a *feme-covert*. . . . [A] man cannot grant any thing to his wife, or enter into covenant with her: for the grant would be to suppose her separate existence; and to covenant with her, would be only to covenant with himself."[14] The exclusion of the married (covered) woman from the terms of full personhood exemplifies the conventionality of personhood and the potential exclusion of other subject groups as well. Legal being—and I will develop this point at length in my analyses of the Supreme Court cases I discuss in Chapter 1—determines social being, and identity is experienced as essence. The ontological terms in which prominent spokespeople like Wendell and Roosevelt framed their political, social, and economic concerns, in other words, show that they experienced—or at least expressed—those concerns in terms of their very being. At stake, it seems, was their sense of their own meaningful existence.

No one better explains how national culture defines and disseminates a concept of personhood, and the anxiety generated by that process, than Frantz Fanon, the Antillean psychiatrist whose involvement in decolonization efforts led to his renovation of psychoanalysis. Revising Freud, Fanon shows that a psychoanalytic understanding of culture includes a rethinking of psychoanalytic assumptions. In his investigations, a psychoanalytic narrative of individual development is itself a national narrative. Fanon points to the structural similarities between the white European family, which is the basis for psychoanalytic inquiry, and the nation. The traditional Freudian psyhoanalytic narrative normalizes a (white) self that makes "a normal Negro child . . . abnormal on the slightest contact with the white world"—not only in the eyes of the white analyst or the white world, but in his or her own eyes as a result of an internalized definition of personhood derived from national culture.[15] For Fanon, analysis of the black man or woman can disrupt the psychoanalytic narrative, and that disruption in turn enables an analysis of the relationship between culture and the unconscious (and between national and personal narratives of identity). The analyst's task is to explain how a cultural language of personhood shapes a personal experience of self.

Fanon's analysis yields a black self economically and socially at odds with the language of personhood disseminated by cultural forms. He offers

by way of example French compositions written by Antillean school-
children in which "they reacted like real little Parisians," as in their descriptions of themselves during their summer vacations romping through
the fields and coming home "with *rosy* cheeks." Fanon's black Antilleans experience their bodies through the language of French personhood,
which is to say that they do "not altogether apprehend the fact of . . .
being . . . Negro[es]" (*BS*, 162n). These children, in other words, have
learned to think of themselves as French and to equate Frenchness with
personhood and both with whiteness. Their understanding of blackness
also comes through a prescribed narrative of identity, which shapes rather
than reflects their experiences. When they confront the white world,
which mirrors them as black, they experience themselves through that
understanding of blackness. The confrontation, for Fanon, leaves "a Negro . . . forever in combat with his own image," excluded from full and
equal personhood (*BS*, 194).

Conversely, the discrepancy between the "black skin" and "white
masks" of Fanon's title explains the haunting presence of colonized black
subjects within the French narrative of identity; they embody the possibility of exposing the normalizing use of whiteness in the definition of
French personhood and the experience of French selfhood. Fanon makes
use of that possibility, showing how whiteness is constituted and naturalized in relation to blackness: "The real Other for the white man is and
will continue to be the black man. And conversely. Only for the white man
The Other is perceived on the level of the body image, absolutely as
the not-self—that is, the unidentifiable, the unassimilable" (*BS*, 161).[16]
Fanon's analysis of the fear of black corporeality—in particular of black
(male) sexuality—implicitly demonstrates how French personhood is gendered as well: the mischaracterization of Antillean men is accompanied
by the erasure of Antillean women. (Of "the woman of color" he writes, "I
know nothing about her" [*BS*, 180].) Personhood is white, and whiteness is
gendered and sexualized according to the relationships of the naturalized
white family which is Fanon's point of departure. Black subjects embody a
disjunction in their experience of French personhood marked by the discrepancy between their language of selfhood and the cultural representations of their bodies ("rosy cheeks," for example). That disjunction signals
the return of a cultural repressed—the return, that is, to the reformulation
(in language) of personhood according to cultural practices specific to
French nationalism. This return transforms the memory of a *forgetting*

that, in Anderson's terms, motivates a narrative of identity into a memory of *what has been forgotten* (the reformulation of personhood); the disturbance signaled by the uncanny, in other words, can generate or disrupt the narrative.

National narratives of identity seek to harness the anxiety surrounding questions of personhood, but what they leave out resurfaces when the experiences of individuals conspicuously fail to conform to the definition of personhood offered in the narrative. The untold stories that concern me represent such disruptions. They must therefore be reabsorbed by the official stories they challenge. Yet the extra work required by that reabsorption threatens to expose the discontinuity it is supposed to obscure. Thus the uncanny continues to haunt the narrative, drawing attention to its obscured origin in the reformulation (hence to the conventionality) of personhood. Intrinsic to the narrative of identity is the ongoing possibility of a return to its own genesis in the uncanny (the unrecognized self)—in its efforts, that is, to establish continuity where there has been a rupture. In the following chapters, I explore the sense of estrangement expressed as ill-fitting selfhood by individuals excluded from the terms of full and equal personhood and the uncanniness they represented within the official stories.

Uncannily American

The authors I consider in this study encounter, experience, and depict cultural anxieties that inform their meditations on their authorship, anxieties generated by the reformulation of personhood first as the United States struggled to define itself as a nation in the mid-nineteenth century and later as it contended with the difficulties of its emergence as a world power at the turn of the twentieth century. Of course the nature of those conflicts varied among these writers, and the contexts in which I read their works in each chapter reflect the different aspects of their encounters with cultural anxiety and the different arenas in which those encounters took place. Although their struggles resonate with each other, they were not identical. These writers understood and used their crafts differently and struggled with different narrative genres, each with its attendant conflicts and prescriptions. Yet from among these many differences, authorship—

the process of writing—emerges consistently as a means of exploring the internalized frontiers that constituted them as Americans.

Frederick Douglass wrote *Narrative of the Life of Frederick Douglass, an American Slave* (1845) and *My Bondage and My Freedom* (1855) as personal accounts of a political figure. His concern with the implications of a black man's assumption of a public American self found expression in the constraints placed on the stories he could tell about this experience, constraints placed explicitly by abolitionist sponsors and less obviously by the conventions of American personhood. In Chapter 1, I read Douglass's narratives in the context of the uncanniness of nonwhite subjects depicted in the Supreme Court cases of *Cherokee Nation v. Georgia* (1831) and *Scott v. Sandford* (1857) and in the speeches of Abraham Lincoln.

Fiction writers, as Herman Melville and Harriet Wilson knew, were not immune from the imperatives that circumscribed Douglass's stories. In Melville's *Pierre; or, the Ambiguities* (1852) and Wilson's *Our Nig; or Sketches from the Life of a Free Black* (1859), the censorship imposed by an editorial establishment and the less conspicuous arbitrations of a literary market attest to the anxieties generated by an author who attempts to tell a culturally unauthorized story. In both works, characters' internalization of cultural conventions and imperatives further limit the tales they can tell as it conspicuously structures their sense of being. I begin Chapter 2 with a discussion of how the tensions evident in the legal and political documents discussed in Chapter 1 shaped the calls for a national literature issued by the literary nationalists known as the Young Americans and shaped as well the doctrine of Manifest Destiny espoused by their colleagues at John L. O'Sullivan's *Democratic Review*. While Melville's work responds directly to the Young Americans, with whom he was well-acquainted, Wilson's work addressed a more abstract northern white editorial establishment. Yet both works show authors determinedly working to understand and represent the precepts of literary acceptability.

Official revisions of We the People following the Civil War mandated a national citizenship and universal male suffrage. With those changes, and with the emergence of the nation as a world power and the arrival of immigrants in unprecedented numbers, came the need for new (and renewed) stories of American identity. For the statesman historian, a role valorized and exemplified by Woodrow Wilson at the turn of the century, telling the proper story about the nation constituted a political triumph.

For W. E. B. Du Bois, deconstituting the dominant turn-of-the-century narrative of American history and American identity was a political necessity. Chapter 3 considers Du Bois's representations of his authorial struggles in *The Souls of Black Folk* (1903), a narrative comprised of chapters representing different genres and different efforts to tell the story of being black in America. The "sense of always looking at one's self through the eyes of others" that Du Bois calls "double-consciousness" finds literary expression as the sense of always telling one's story through the narratives of others.[17] Such is the price, he suggests, of being comprehensible, but "the price of culture is a Lie" (*S*, 504).

No one explores the consequences of refusing comprehensibility more dramatically than Gertrude Stein in *The Making of Americans* (completed 1911, published 1925), a work legendary for its unreadability and therefore a fitting subject for my concluding consideration, in Chapter 4, of what and how we read. My inquiry begins with why this "Curie / of the laboratory / of vocabulary," as the modernist poet Mina Loy called her, has been read in all kinds of aesthetic contexts but almost never in a cultural context, almost never in terms of her own relentless efforts to tell a story in and about America.[18] Illustrating how the aesthetic experimentation of *The Making of Americans* grows out of Stein's interest in representing the untold story of the making of Americans and in applying insights garnered from her training in psychology to an analysis of the cultural prescriptions manifested in immigrant narratives, I offer a context in which Stein's work may be read as the magnum opus she thought she was writing and not the botched precursor of later and greater (and shorter) masterpieces.

Although I have made personhood rather than race the central term of my investigation, my project has benefited greatly from recent work in the study of American literature that has stressed conversations among black and white authors and shown the structural importance of race both to individual texts not typically thought to be about race and to the constitution of "American literature." As Fanon's theories so clearly demonstrate, the ambiguous and fluctuating meanings of race are central aspects of the formulation of personhood during the periods that concern me. And Toni Morrison's provocative claim that "American literature," like American identity, derives its coherence from an Africanist presence, an "unsettled and unsettling population," in particular makes it impossible not to think about how as well as what we read.[19] Recent work on race and literature has helped me understand not only the terms in which personhood is constituted in the United States but also the indirect ways through which a variety of departures from a normative "American" personhood find expression. Such work has accordingly helped me shape my method of inquiring into the structural importance of those departures to literary works.

The power of the five principal literary works I consider derives in part from the risky, complicated, and engaging strategies through which they confronted cultural anxieties: in order to be psychologically unsettling, they had to be formally unsettled. In the pages that follow, I explore how the uncanny structured writers' experiences of their authorship and led them to both literary innovations and analyses of We the People. In the relationships among their experiences, their innovations, and their analyses lies a story of the overlapping and sometimes contradictory cultural practices through which personhood is formulated.

Neither Citizen nor Alien

National Narratives, Frederick Douglass, and
the Politics of Self-Definition

From the vantage point of his 1855 autobiography, *My Bondage and My Freedom*, Frederick Douglass expressed resentment toward his former associates, the abolitionist William Lloyd Garrison and his colleagues, who had commissioned Douglass's first written account of his enslavement, *Narrative of the Life of Frederick Douglass, an American Slave* (1845). The abolitionists needed Douglass, and they knew it, although a number of them privately lamented their dependence on the articulate, dashing fugitive slave who, to their minds, manifested a dangerous intractability.[1] The impassioned and ambitious Douglass was reluctant to circumscribe his account of his experiences as a slave in accordance with the story his associates wanted him to tell. They wished to use his testimony to win converts to a political cause that they defined; he wanted the liberty to interpret and condemn as well as to represent the anguish of a man in chains. "It did not entirely satisfy me to *narrate* wrongs," he recalled in 1855; "I felt like *denouncing* them."[2] Eager to offer his oratorical gifts to the abolitionist cause, he was nonetheless troubled by the constraints imposed upon his authorship by white abolitionists.

Ironically, the abolitionists were troubled by Douglass's gifts. By all accounts a man on fire, Douglass gave speeches alive to the nuances of words and timing. They are tactile, gripping. Yet the dazzling speaker was hard to reconcile with the degraded protagonist he was forced to portray. Douglass reports in *My Bondage and My Freedom* that, at the behest of his associates, he put aside his frustration and wrote the 1845 *Narrative* in order to demonstrate how Frederick Douglass, lowly slave, became Frederick Douglass, commanding orator, thereby establishing his authenticity for a doubting public.

The *Narrative,* however, does not entirely confirm the description of the author's obedience and acquiescence offered in *My Bondage and My Freedom.* Despite his commitment to his cause and his admiration and affection for his white antislavery brethren, Douglass could not suppress his discomfort with the curtailments of his story, nor with the conception of a dependent black self that this account required. Douglass, in other words, never fully acceded to the prescripted abolitionist narrative. His discomfort surfaces, as I shall demonstrate, in textual disruptions: a revealing word, a surprising juxtaposition, an awkward sentence through which the repressed—or the suppressed—returns. These disruptions shape his narrative, as they tell an alternative story about his enslavement and his authorship.

Douglass's partial mischaracterization of the *Narrative* in the later work is not surprising. *My Bondage and My Freedom* also tells two stories, and his parallel struggle for authorial control in that work is evident in similar textual disruptions, some of which are produced by his use of passages from the earlier work itself. The freer and more comfortably American self to which the author of *My Bondage and My Freedom* lays claim is still struggling with a story not fully his own. In both personal narratives, the bid for authorial control corresponds to the quest to become a more integrated and accepted American. But the tale of a descendant of Africans claiming a place within the constituted body of "We the People" was an especially disturbing and perplexing one for a mid-nineteenth-century white audience. The status of the descendants of Africans—and of other nonwhite subjects—in the emerging nation was inseparable from other unresolved issues surrounding the Constitution. Debates on the status of indigenes and descendants of Africans could not avoid addressing whom the founders had intended to include in "We the People," what entity they had legislated into existence with the Constitution, and the very role of that Constitution in the ongoing governance of the United States. Douglass's *desire* to address those questions was as troubling to many antebellum audiences as the actual content of any story that he might tell. He wished to make those audiences experience the anguish not only of a man in chains, but of a man *thinking* in chains. He insisted that they recognize him for what he was: a rational human being deprived of natural rights and conventionally defined as property. In effect, Douglass embodied a human being excluded from personhood. Explicitly, he asked his audiences to recognize the incompatibility of the practice of slavery and the principles of equality and liberty laid forth in the Declaration of Independence. Implicitly, his personal narratives addressed curtailments of liberty less visible than enslavement, curtailments made evident in his struggle to tell his story.

The story of a freer American self told in *My Bondage and My Freedom* itself emerges as part of the narrative of American personhood with which he struggles. The "freedom" of that story, and of the self to which it attests, overlooks the conventions that limit even as they enable any writer's story (and experience of selfhood). For Douglass, the limitations of those conventions are especially significant, since they prevent in particular the story that he as a black man wishes to tell about the relationship of enslavement and racism to personhood in the United States. Douglass shows not only how the freer story is only partially available to him, but also how it contributes to his lesser status, to the subordinate black selfhood that he cannot accept.[3] The cultural importance of that story, and the free selfhood that it articulated, made indirection an important part of an alternative story. Accordingly, Douglass represents his self as a story that could not be fully told.

This chapter contextualizes Douglass's narratives within both the anxious responses to the efforts of nonwhite subjects to tell their stories in two Supreme Court cases and the use Abraham Lincoln made of a similar anxiety in his speeches. The Courts of two politically-divergent Supreme Court justices, John Marshall and Roger Taney, addressed the indeterminate status of indigenous tribes and descendants of Africans, respectively, in *Cherokee Nation v. the State of Georgia* (1831) and *Scott v. Sandford* (1857), more commonly known as *Dred Scott*. Recognizing the importance of definition as a function of the law, both Courts legislated the unrecognizability of the nonwhite claimants by labeling them "neither citizens, nor aliens."[4] Both the Marshall and the Taney Courts thereby adjudicated the inability of those subjects to tell their stories officially in the highest court of the land.

In the stories they sought to tell and in their desire to tell them, the Cherokee plaintiffs and Dred Scott asked for recognition by the law of the United States. Yet in both cases, the stories and the very presence of these subjects troubled "the constituted 'we'" that James Boyd White calls "the great achievement of the law."[5] The law constitutes a "we" through an official story, beginning with a founding moment that generates a code of laws and principles expressive of the spirit of the "we." The Constitution's

"We the People," for example, spontaneously speaks itself into existence, and the law at once articulates and performs its spirit. Radically differing versions of the official story, therefore, pose a threat to its authority. Since the new government claims to derive its authority from the consent of the governed, then anything that calls into question the nature of that consent or what is meant by the governed could seriously challenge the authority of the government. The stories and the presence of the Cherokee people and of the descendants of Africans constituted such a challenge. Neither group was unambiguously included among the people by and for whom the Constitution was framed, and such an inclusion would make the "we" altogether unrecognizable to themselves. These groups represented human beings who had not consented to the laws by which they were bound, human beings, that is, excluded not only from citizenship, but also from certain basic natural rights and thereby from the personhood defined by those rights.

Exclusions troubled the new republic from its founding moments and posed an ongoing problem in the emerging nation. Race was a significant but certainly not the only factor limiting legal representation and existence. A playful yet revealing exchange between leading political figure and future president John Adams and his wife Abigail in the spring of 1776 discloses another such exclusion and ostensible motivation for it. Anticipating a declaration of "independancy," Abigail Adams hoped that the inevitable "new Code of Laws" would be more inclusive than its predecessor. She cautioned her husband to "Remember the Ladies, and be more generous and favourable to them than your ancestors. Do not put such unlimited Power into the hands of the Husbands," she advised. "Remember all Men would be tyrants if they could. If perticuliar care and attention is not paid to the Laidies we are determined to foment a Rebelion, and will not hold ourselves bound by any Laws in which we have no voice, or Representation."[6] Abigail thus extended the logic of revolutionary rhetoric.

John's response, although patronizing, speaks to the complex anxiety raised by groups to whom the full rights of personhood did not extend. John "cannot but laugh" at his wife's "extraordinary Code of Laws," but his words express concern. "We have been told that our Struggle has loosened the bands of Government every where. That Children and Apprentices were disobedient—that schools and Colledges were grown turbulent—that Indians slighted their Guardians and Negroes grew insolent to their Masters. But your Letter was the first Intimation that another Tribe more numerous and powerfull than all the rest were grown discontented."[7] Beneath his teasing tone, he expresses a general fear of uprisings, concern over how to establish a new code of laws with authority and how to keep claims of rights violations made by British colonists leading the rebellion from extending to those groups not included among their ranks. To distinguish white women from their male counterparts, for example, Adams turns them into "another Tribe," a phrase suggestive of the "Indians" who threaten to slight "their Guardians." Abigail herself had concluded her letter with a declaration of dependency, asking her husband to "Regard us . . . as Beings placed by providence under your protection and in immitation of the Supreem Being make use of that power only for our happiness." Her words echo a rhetoric of guardianship deployed by the British colonists to mark at once their benevolence toward and their superiority to many excluded groups, among them white women, children, slaves, and indigenous tribes.

More than half a century after John and Abigail's exchange, John Marshall would label indigenous tribes "domestic dependent nations" under the guardianship of the state. Although wards cannot lay equal or immediate claim to the status and rights of their guardians, they can expect to grow into independence. Not so for many of the wards of this state, however, be they white women, Indians, or any of a number of groups variously excluded. In particular, lawmakers summoned conceptual differences concerning the nature of personhood when dealing with the indigenous tribes or the descendants of Africans. Yet despite the potency of those arguments, as *Cherokee Nation* and *Dred Scott* made clear, no task put a greater strain on the fragile authority of "We the People" than the need to explain why certain groups were deprived of the natural and conventional rights that justified nineteenth-century American government. Government policies that removed tribes from their land or that enslaved Africans and their descendants challenged the language of liberty through which the colonies had sanctioned their rebellion and the Constitution founded its "more permanent Union." The presence of people obviously excluded from the "inalienable rights" to "life, liberty and the pursuit of happiness" enumerated by the Declaration of Independence bore witness both to the conventionality of natural rights and to the vulnerability of persons subject to that conventionality. In question was the right of the government to disfranchise human beings who had committed no crime.

Their presence invoked an anxiety evident in a query posed with increasing frequency in the political oratory of the Jacksonian and antebellum periods: what keeps the government from making white men slaves?

Disfranchised human beings represented more than the Union's inadequate protection of rights. Those deprived of natural rights in particular embodied—or disembodied—a challenge to the conception of personhood articulated in the founding texts. Understanding how the presence of enslaved people represented such a challenge, Thomas Jefferson had worried about the security of liberties viewed as other than "the gift of God . . . not to be violated but with his wrath."[8] Those liberties were God-given because the self was a gift from God. Despite his devotion to the ideals of a rational Enlightenment ideology, Jefferson here expresses pragmatic concern for the permanence of ideas premised on reason rather than divine authority. Even when secularized, the belief in natural rights retained the fervency—and authority—of the religious conviction from which they had derived. "Being is a right inherent in us by birth," wrote William Blackstone in the 1760s, "and one of the gifts of God to man at his creation, when he endued him with the faculty of free will." But rights have no practical meaning independent of their enforceability, which is the role, and the sacred trust, of government. "Every man, when he enters into society," Blackstone continues, "gives up a part of his natural liberty, as the price of so valuable a purchase" (BC, 121). Embodying the alienability of natural rights—and the consequent denial of the personhood defined by those rights—the disfranchised pointed to the power of government to violate its sacred trust. The bestowal of citizenship and protection of liberties that were the recognized tasks of the law seemed to collapse into a *conferral* of personhood from which even a white native-born American man might well worry that he may one day be excluded as other groups were already excluded.[9] The decisions in *Cherokee Nation* and *Dred Scott* exhibited that process of exclusion and, as I shall argue, amplified rather than resolved the uncanniness of the litigants for a white American public.

In the triumphant Unionist narrative he shaped, Abraham Lincoln made rhetorical use of that uncanniness. His speeches presented a narrative of Union—specifically, *his* narrative of Union—as a prerequisite for social existence. Through careful rhetorical maneuvering, social existence in turn became the mark of *any* meaningful existence. Lincoln, in other words, made meaningful existence contingent upon his narrative of

Union, and he used the uncanniness of human beings excluded from personhood to demonstrate the fate of any subject excluded from that Union. But he never resolved the question of the status of descendants of Africans within that Union. They remained haunting presences, symbols of exclusion at once necessary to his narrative and threatening to disrupt it.

My discussion of Lincoln precedes my discussion of Douglass in this chapter because I want to underscore what is at stake in Douglass's efforts to tell his own story. By the time he wrote *My Bondage and My Freedom*, Douglass had begun to subscribe to a Unionist narrative similar, in general terms, to the one Lincoln later brought to the White House. As his nomination and election suggest, Lincoln's version of the Union, one less radical than Douglass's, was probably the most radical version acceptable to the voting American public, and even that version precipitated a war. Lincoln's narrative and responses to it thus make clear the strength of the forces Douglass sought to challenge. The constraints on the story that Douglass can tell even in *My Bondage and My Freedom* correspond to the limitations placed on the experiences and expressions of personhood by a Unionist narrative. Those constraints, although made most obvious by a descendant of Africans, nonetheless had more widespread implications; they bore uncanny witness not only to the shaping (and misshaping) of the selfhood available to Douglass, but to the legislating of personhood in general by a national narrative.

Legislating Personhood in the Emerging Nation

Together, *Cherokee Nation* and *Dred Scott* represent a contest of narratives each trying to legitimate a version of the official story of the nation, and each complicated by the presence of human beings who embody its unresolved contradictions. The more the Courts attempted to evade or explain those contradictions, the more apparent they made them. I am suggesting, and I shall demonstrate in what follows, that these cases made apparent how much an official story actually determines the shape of the nation and how difficult it is, therefore, to tell a markedly different version of that story. Central to each official story is a carefully circumscribed conception of personhood.

While on the bench, Marshall and Taney saw themselves first and foremost as jurists rather than politicians. Marshall advocated an independence from the executive and legislative branches of government in keeping with the checks and balances set in place by the Constitution. So seriously did he take this separation that he refused to vote in presidential elections during his tenure. Taney, a Virginia Federalist turned Jacksonian Democrat, promised to put aside the politics through which he had received his appointment and devote himself " 'to the calm but high duties of the station with which [he was] honored.' "[10] Nevertheless, their political commitments shaped their readings of the Constitution. From his thirty-four years as Chief Justice, Marshall, appointed in 1801 by President John Adams and working especially with his revered colleague Justice Joseph Story, bequeathed a determinedly Unionist Constitution and accompanying legal precedents that the Taney Court (which included Story for its first decade) could not entirely challenge. Taney, in turn, despite his secessionist sympathies, remained on the bench during the Civil War in order to contest the constitutional legitimacy of Lincoln's war policies.

Cherokee Nation and *Dred Scott* presented the Courts with the most divisive political issue of Jacksonian and antebellum America, the very issue that most clearly expressed Marshall's and Taney's political differences: the conflict between federal and state sovereignty. Fundamental to both arguments was the safeguarding of the rights, and thereby of the personal liberty, of the citizens and potential citizens of the Union. The question of how the Union could best guarantee that liberty was at the forefront of legal and political debate in its formative years. For those who believed that the Constitution affirmed a social compact among smaller units, such as legal theorist St. George Tucker and South Carolina's most prominent political figure, John C. Calhoun, a centralized government made adequate representation of the people an impossibility and threatened the liberty that defined Enlightenment personhood. For those who believed it brought a consolidated entity into being, including Supreme Court Justice John Marshall and later, lawyer-turned-politician Abraham Lincoln, on the other hand, liberty could best be ensured by the consolidation and preservation of the Union. The primacy of the safeguarding of rights to both arguments explains why human beings deprived of natural rights challenged the consistency of each political argument and its accompanying narrative.

Despite disagreements over whether federal or state sovereignty better ensured natural rights that occurred within as well as between the Marshall and Taney Courts, the paramount importance of the stable conception of personhood rooted in natural rights is evident, and challenged, in both *Cherokee Nation* and *Dred Scott*. The antecedence of certain natural rights was as fundamental to Marshall's vision of the Constitution as to Taney's, and their narratives were never more taxed than when natural rights came into conflict with each other. Writing the opinions of the Court in *Cherokee Nation* and *Dred Scott*, each of the Chief Justices offered a tortured and even inconsistent narrative that attested to contradictions in the definitions and regulations of life, liberty, and especially property—of personhood itself, no less than sovereignty. In the name of those inalienable rights the Union had been called into existence, since the states had united for their protection. The basic rights were most vociferously invoked when the stability of the Union was in question: when political debates, increased immigration, and territorial expansion following the War of 1812 made the heterogeneity of "the people" harder to deny, or when the publication of James Madison's notes on the Constitutional Convention in 1840 replaced the story of consensus with a view into the compromises and resulting ambiguities of the Constitution. The obvious conventionality of inalienable rights would further strain the already tenuous bonds that turned a population into a people, into We the People.

The connection between a troubling cultural diversity and the Union's uncertain status comes across in both Supreme Court cases: both cases came to the Court as a result of confusion generated by the extension of the federal law into unincorporated territory. *Cherokee Nation* was brought by a group of Cherokees against the state of Georgia for violating federal treaties that recognized the sanctity and sovereignty of the Cherokee Nation. The case concerned Georgia's right to extend its legislation into Cherokee territory that lay within the state's borders, territory that federal treaties had made exempt from state law. In *Dred Scott*, the Supreme Court heard an appeal of Dred Scott's unsuccessful suit for his liberty. Scott's counsel argued that extended residence in free territory had entitled Scott to freedom under federal law. *Dred Scott* considered the claims of state and federal authority in legislating territorial government and slavery. Both cases involved a conflict between state and federal law, and both preceded federal crises—the Nullification Crisis of 1832–33 entailing South Carolina's right to nullify the federal tariff of 1832, and the secession that led to the Civil War.

The cases could almost have predicted those crises, since both cases made plain the uncertain bases, hence the instability, of the Union, rights, and personhood. Neither case could be adequately resolved because sovereignty disputes, natural rights conflicts, and questions of personhood were at once inseparable and at odds. The source of the tension in both legal narratives was the mutual contingency of the Union and "We the People." Presumably called into existence by We the People, the Union arose to protect the people's natural rights. A challenge to a natural-rights-based conception of personhood, such as *Cherokee Nation* and *Dred Scott* alternatively posed, therefore, rocked the basis of the Union. Conversely, the identity of "We the People" was contingent on the stability of the Union: there could be no "Americans" without "America." The narratives could neither ignore, nor explain the logical inconsistencies by which both were therefore troubled. What it meant to exist outside the law was made all too apparent by the subjects of the two cases, the Cherokee people and Dred Scott. And both cases disclosed the contingency of personhood on the law as they revealed the metaphysical void wherein excluded subjects dwelled: persons de jure and de facto without natural rights, human beings whom the law would not fully and equally represent.

Of utmost concern in the case that came before Marshall's Court was the status of the Cherokee Nation. William Wirt, defense counsel for the Cherokee Nation, sought to establish the unconstitutionality of Georgia's violation of the federal treaties between the United States and the Cherokee Nation. But in order to bring the case to the Supreme Court, Wirt had also to establish the "foreign nation" status of the Cherokee Nation since the Supreme Court lacked the jurisdiction to hear a case brought by citizens of a state against the state itself. Ironically, for the predominantly nationalist Marshall Court to find for the Cherokee Nation, and thereby to uphold federal over state sovereignty, the Court had to uphold the principle of coexistent sovereignties within common boundaries (both Cherokee and Georgia, and Cherokee and United States), a principle closer to that of the social compact theorists than to that of consolidationists like Marshall. At deeper issue, then, was just what kind of entity the "Cherokee Nation" described, and how it could be positioned in relation to We the People.

Marshall, in the end, did not find for Cherokee sovereignty. Instead, he responded with a decision that turned on the unique "condition of the Indians in relation to the United States [which] is, perhaps, unlike that of any other two people in existence." He rejected the designation "foreign," which characterized "nations not owing a common allegiance," when

defining the "relation of the Indians to the United States." Marshall by-
passed the potentially conflictual sovereignty issues—between the Cherokee and Georgia, the Cherokee and the United States, and the United
States and Georgia—when he domesticated indigenous tribes: "Indian
territory *is admitted* to compose a part of the United States. In all our
maps, geographical treatises, histories, and laws, it is so considered. In
all our intercourse with foreign nations, they are considered as within
the jurisdictional limits of the United States, subject to many of those
restraints which are imposed upon our own citizens. . . . [I]t may well
be doubted whether those tribes which reside within the acknowledged
boundaries of the United States can, with strict accuracy, be denominated
foreign nations."[11] The representational bind herein expressed grew out of
the expanding borders of the United States, an expansion that brought the
Declaration's "merciless savages" on "our frontiers" within the nation's
boundaries.[12] Once used to delineate geographic boundaries, these "savages" now threatened to define the limits of the law. In response, Marshall
redefined the indigenes, removing them from the discourse of nationhood
as effectively as his political and military counterparts would remove
them from their homes within the Union's expanding borders. With the
passive construction of the phrase "is admitted," Marshall elided the
subject authorizing this redefinition. He assumed a consensus that had
already refused representation to the tribal nations: "In all *our* maps . . .
it is so considered."

Ostensibly reading Constitutional law, he was in fact writing it. Just as
the Cherokee Nation was circumscribed by Georgia's boundaries, so too
were the "Indians" comprehended within an "American" discourse. This
entailed a two-step process that Marshall enacted rhetorically. With the
consolidationist precepts of a collective identity and a geographic totality
in mind, he translated the Cherokee Nation into something other than a
sovereign entity. Marshall followed a logic common to assimilationists
both in the government and among many of the Christian missionaries.
Refusing to recognize the sovereignty of the Cherokee Nation, he effectively promoted the consolidation of tribes that federal treaties had previously ordained to be discrete. This implied merging was consistent with
the strategy that brought forth "Indians" who, as individuals, could then
(like immigrants) be assimilated into the Union.[13] Marshall could confirm
the jurisdictional authority of a Georgia state court without explicitly
ruling on the question of federal sovereignty, without, that is, capitulating

to a states' rights narrative. But Marshall could still—and did—recast in a distinctly Unionist narrative the often contradictory government policies toward indigenous peoples, policies that veered between removal and an assimilation that secured the appropriation of their land and identity.[14]

Much of the confusion of the case was rooted in a contradictory Indian policy. The characteristic ambivalence of that policy was amplified by the differing attitudes among presidents and across state lines, and it surfaced most dramatically as the nation expanded. The importance of the land to Indian policy is evident even in Thomas Jefferson's progressive view. Writing to Indian agent Benjamin Hawkins of the importance of promoting "agriculture" and "household manufacture" among the Indians for their own preservation, Jefferson noted, in 1803, that these developments would "enable them to live on much smaller portions of land," rendering "vast forests useless . . . and even disadvantageous."[15] Jefferson genuinely believed in the superiority of European-style cultivation and in the "civilized" society to which it would inevitably give rise, but the interests of the United States government in the "disadvantageous" land were not inconsiderable: "While they are learning to do better on less land," explained Jefferson, "our increasing numbers will be calling for more land, and thus a coincidence of interests will be produced between those who have lands to spare, and want other necessaries, and those who have such necessaries to spare, and want lands." The president thus urged the Indian agent "to promote among the Indians a sense of the superior value of a little land, well cultivated, over a great deal, unimproved." Most disturbing in this letter, however, is his injunction that the "wisdom of the animal which amputates & abandons to the hunter the parts for which he is pursued should be theirs, with this difference, that the former sacrifices what is useful, the latter what is not." The violence that would come to pass, and the exclusion from personhood that would justify that violence, are both implicit in the metaphor.

Nonetheless, Jefferson believed that the Indians and the settlers should, and in "the natural progress of things" would, "meet and blend together, . . . intermix, and become one people." He assured the Chiefs of the Upper Cherokee, those who expressed an interest in United States citizenship, that the United States was prepared to welcome them to that citizenship if the Cherokees were prepared to become individual landowners, living in family units with the men farming and the women engaged in the domestic pursuits of spinning and weaving.[16] Reformulations of personhood through an adoption of American gender roles as well as conceptions of property were a prerequisite to citizenship. In return for these changes, Jefferson offered the benefits of United States citizenship, "the rights and privileges" that would allow them to live "without anyone to make them afraid, to injure their persons, or to take their property without being punished for it according to fixed laws." Once having established the primary laws of ownership and inheritance, he explained to the "Delawares, Mohiccons, and Munries," the indigenes would be welcome to "be Americans." Eventual intermarriage was part of his vision: "You will mix with us by marriage," he assured them, "your blood will run in our veins and will spread with us over this great island." Jefferson is clear about the choice they face: assimilate through this intermarriage— to which, like white women, they must surrender their names, homes and (group) property—or face "total disappearance from the face of the earth."[17] The President takes no responsibility for that disappearance, which would ostensibly come not at the hands of rapacious settlers, but as an inevitable result of a faulty civilization and bad land management. The Indians will not prosper because hunters invariably cannot. In none of these addresses does Jefferson acknowledge the alternative cultivation practiced by many tribes, including the Cherokees.

In fact, the Cherokees willing to adopt white ways and remain on their land posed more of a threat to white culture than those who chose to remain in the old ways and remove west. *Cherokee Nation* was finally about the incomprehensible hole in the map within the perimeters of Georgia. Marshall's narrative of the Union could make no sense of it, and the Cherokee bid for nationhood American style only further complicated that narrative. An increasing Cherokee nationalism evinced the Cherokees' plan to remain indefinitely in possession of the disputed territory, thereby precipitating both Georgia's controversial legislation and, in the end, the Marshall Court's decision. Debates within the Cherokee community had entailed whether their own nationalism could best be expressed in traditional Cherokee terms or in United States terms, but it was the traditionalists' defeat, and the adoption of a Cherokee constitution, to which Georgia most blatantly responded. The 1827 Constitution of the Cherokee Nation, spearheaded by the mainly interracial (mixed Cherokee and white parentage) elite, signaled a victory for a Cherokee nationalism simultaneously modeled on and opposed to United States nationalism.[18] The political ascendancy of the "Indian-hating" Andrew Jackson in the

1820s encouraged, and was even largely predicated on, a federal policy that replaced the ambiguous policies of assimilation and removal with a new and more determined program of removal.[19] The victorious Cherokee nationalists hoped that a demonstration of their "civilization"—through, for example, this parallel constitution—would ensure their right to remain on their land. Although changes in United States policy guaranteed their ultimate removal, the trends signified by the Cherokee Constitution triggered events that may actually have expedited it.

The "Americanized" Cherokees, many of whom had become European-style farmers and even slaveholders, evoked anxious responses in their white neighbors, as typified by the reformist superintendent of the Office of Indian Affairs at this time, Thomas L. McKenney, who opined, "They seek to be a People. . . . It is much to be regretted that the idea of Sovereignty should have taken such a deep hold of these people."[20] Likewise Georgia Congressman Wilson Lumpkin, who would become governor of Georgia in 1831, later reported that the Cherokee situation in Georgia had become untenable when "a portion of the Cherokee people, composed mostly of mixed breeds and white bloods, had advanced in all the various arts of civilization to an extent that rendered it altogether impracticable to enforce the Laws of the United States passed by Congress for regulating intercourse with Indian Tribes within the United States, and for governing and restraining such tribes."[21] Evidence of those advances, for Lumpkin, consisted of "their own written and printed Constitution, and code of laws" (WL, 42). For McKenney and Lumpkin, outrage stemmed from anxieties that were exacerbated by the profound threat of Cherokee separatism to the collective identity. The Cherokee Nation's becoming like but not of the United States political entity, mirroring without acceding to its conditions, seemed to jeopardize the terms of a United States national identity. And the threat of Cherokee nationalism was literally embodied by the "mixed-bloods," who represented the mixing of bloods referred to by Jefferson, but who did not fully accede to the terms of assimilation that the President had delineated, who had, that is, remained Cherokees.

Georgia's claims on Cherokee territory were registered in an 1802 compact with Jefferson when Georgia ceded western territory to the federal government in exchange for the government's extinguishing Indian titles to the land within the state "as early as the same can be obtained, on reasonable terms."[22] Certainly the discovery of gold on Cherokee land in the late 1820s was not an inconsiderable motivation for Georgia to push its claim to Cherokee land, but the first issue of the *Cherokee Phoenix*, the Cherokees' first newspaper, in 1828, published the Cherokee Constitution, which attested to the Cherokees' intention to remain on the "lands solemnly guaranteed and reserved forever to the Cherokee Nation by the Treaties concluded with the United States."[23] The particular nature of the threat posed by the Cherokee Constitution was complicated in precisely those ways in which, as Homi Bhabha suggests, "mimicry is at once resemblance and menace."[24] As a colonial strategy, an imposed mimicry mandates "a reformed, recognizable Other, as a subject of a difference that is almost the same, but not quite," which is to say, "almost the same, but not white" (MM, 126, 130). In response to an ideology envisioning Americans as cultivators, Cherokee nationalists took up plows and crosses, purchased looms and slaves, and adopted a constitution, hopefully preserving whatever indigenous culture could elude the disciplinary gaze. But the nationalist Cherokees, by imitating rather than assimilating or otherwise disappearing, recontextualized the logic of United States nationalism.

A Cherokee nation posed an important symbolic threat to the Union. Cherokee sovereignty would validate a permanent Cherokee presence on lands considered by Georgia to belong to the state. Such a presence would challenge the integrity of the state and of the Union. A Cherokee nation would thereby recapitulate the prerevolutionary colonies' relation to England: "'imperium in imperio' (a state within a state)," conceptually complicating ideas of American exceptionalism, absorptiveness, and republicanism.[25] As the indigenous tribe played America to the federal government's Great Britain, the government's removal of the Cherokee people could come dangerously close to reenacting, in reverse, the founding moment of the United States. The Cherokee Constitution insisted on the legitimacy of a Cherokee conception of property and on the compatibility of that conception with the founding principles of the United States. But in using the familiar language of the United States Constitution to sanction a communal rather than individual right to land ownership, the Cherokee Constitution brought distinctly into focus tensions involving the natural right to property.

The first section of Article 1 spells out the "boundaries of this nation," differentiating the Cherokee Nation not only from the United States, but also from the Cherokee people who had migrated west in accordance with United States government colonization programs—who had, that is, allowed themselves to be translated out of Georgia's boundaries and displaced from their traditional homeland. The second section defines the land as the Cherokee Nation's exclusive property:

> The sovereignty and Jurisdiction of this Government shall extend over the country within the boundaries above described, and the lands therein are, and shall remain, the common property of the nation; but the improvements made thereon, and in the possession of the citizens of the Nation, are the exclusive and indefeasible property of the citizens respectively who made; or may rightfully be in possession of them; Provided, that the citizens of the Nation, possessing exclusive and indefeasible right to their respective improvements, as expressed in this article, shall possess no right nor power to dispose of their improvements in any manner whatever to the United States, individual states, nor individual citizens thereof; and that whenever any such citizen or citizens shall remove with their effects out of the limits of this Nation, and become citizens of any other Government, all their rights and privileges as citizens of this Nation shall cease. (*SH*, 55–56)

The passage articulates the Lockean concept of entitlement ("ownership") based on work ("improvements"). As in England and the United States, where aliens were not entitled to own land, this proprietorship is contingent upon membership in the community. Although this land is "indefeasible" (almost the same as the Declaration's "inalienable," but not quite) for any member of the community, its disposition is regulated by the Cherokee government.[26] Cherokee property could not be indiscriminately bequeathed by its owners, and it could, under certain circumstances, be alienated from its owner by the Cherokee government. No mention is made of natural rights in the Cherokee Constitution, an expression omitted in the United States Constitution as well. But in the United States, the natural rights of the people were assumed to be the basis of their government, part of the fabric of American society.[27] The Cherokee Constitution either signaled the entitlement to the full natural rights of the Cherokee people or it underscored the authorization of a government for which natural rights were not necessary. In either case, it posed representational problems for the United States. If it accepted the Cherokee Constitution, the United States government would have to acknowledge either the consistent violations of the Cherokees' natural rights or the possibility of a government that defined rather than was authorized by natural rights—a government that distinctly resembled the United States government. The Cherokee Constitution in effect mimicked de facto United States policy.

The natural right to property had already proved an especially vexed question in cases involving indigenous tribes that came before the Court. In *Johnson and Graham's Lessee v. William McIntosh* (1823), the Court ruled on the right of the Piankeshaw tribe to sell land that a United States treaty recognized as under their occupancy. The case came before the Court because of a dispute over the title to land that the white plaintiffs had purchased from the Piankeshaw and the United States government had granted to the white defendants. The Marshall Court—Marshall in particular—was consistently troubled by how far to take the abstract laws of nature into account in deciding upon the law of the land. In *Johnson,* Marshall upheld the appeal of the defense counsel to "the uniform understanding and practice of European nations, and the settled law, as laid down by the tribunals of civilized states, [that] denied the right of the Indians to be considered as independent communities, having a permanent property in the soil, capable of alienation to private individuals."[28] The brief report of the defense repeats "alienation" two more times: "the extent of their right of alienation must depend upon the laws of the dominion under which they live" and "the Indian title to lands [is] a mere right of usufruct and habitation, without power of alienation" (*JM*, 568, 569). The Piankeshaw, in other words, could not "alienate"—that is, sell—their land because they did not own it. Actually, they could not own it, being prevented, ironically, not by their status as aliens but by natural law: "By the law of nature, they had not acquired a fixed property capable of being transferred" (*JM*, 569).

The Marshall Court distinguished between the natural right to property and the conventionality of its definition when it upheld the defense's claim that "as grantees from the *Indians,* [the plaintiffs] must take according to *their* laws of property, and as Indian subjects. The law of every dominion affects all persons and property situate within it . . . ; and the Indians never had any idea of individual property in lands" (*JM*, 568). The defense here betrays a geometric logic in which concentric circles contain tribal property relations within an American discourse of property: the plaintiffs are within Indian dominion for the sake of their purchase, but the Indians are, in turn, circumscribed by United States definitions of property and rights. But from within that circle, the Piankeshaw tribe functioned, like the Cherokee territory within Georgia, to show the priority of cultural convention over the natural rights on which it depended: they lacked the concept of and therefore the entitlement to the right to property in land.

In *Johnson,* Marshall ruled on precisely that priority, which was perfectly consistent with his consolidationist narrative. However natural the right to own might be, regulations governing the definition and disposition of property were an expression of the law of nations rather than nature:

> As the right of society to prescribe those rules by which property may be acquired and preserved is not, and cannot be drawn into question; as the title to lands, especially, is and must be admitted to depend entirely on the law of the nation in which they lie; it will be necessary, in pursuing this inquiry, to examine, not singly those principles of abstract justice, which the Creator of all things has impressed on the mind of his creature man, and which are admitted to regulate, in a great degree, the rights of civilized nations, whose perfect independence is acknowledged; but those principles also which our own government has adopted in the particular case, and given us as the rule for our decision. . . . [I]f the principle has been asserted in the first instance, and afterwards sustained; if a country has been acquired and held under it; if the property of the great mass of the community originates in it, it becomes the law of the land, and cannot be questioned. (*JM*, 572, 591)

The use of passive voice at once insists on and begs the question of the authority of positive law. Natural law derives its authority from universal truth; positive law, from the kind of reasoning that is inscribed in a written constitution. Where the former is impressed on the mind of man by the Creator, the latter, not intrinsically beyond challenge, is made so by reason, by the need to maintain order through the guidance of a code of rules. Marshall's passive voice elides the subject of the sentence to place the authority of these laws beyond question.

The Cherokee Constitution in effect called the bluff of the United States government by demonstrating, through a written constitution, a conception of property found lacking in indigenous cultures by the Marshall Court in *Johnson.* The Cherokee Constitution articulated a code of laws compatible with a traditional conception of property. If the Cherokee had been told repeatedly, as by Thomas Jefferson, that a code of laws grew out of land ownership, then the Cherokee Constitution showed how a recognizable code of laws could grow out of a combination of tribal and (contingent) individual ownership, the latter a Lockean ownership of improvements. The Cherokee Constitution registered the influence of European civilization in certain particulars. Inheritance, for example, passed through men rather than women, indicating a significant move away from matrilineal kinship relations. The Constitution challenged claims such as Marshall's in *Johnson* that the indigenes were at once "a people with whom it was impossible to mix, and who could not be governed as a distinct society," and it brought government policy to an impasse (*JM*, 590). Removal of a people with a developed conception of ownership justified by a code of laws attested more to the power than to the rights-based claims of the United States. But the Cherokee Nation itself would complicate the geographic integrity of the Union. Once Andrew Jackson was elected president in 1828, the Marshall Court, despite such decisions as *Johnson*, offered the Cherokees their only possibility, however remote, for a fair hearing.[29]

Cherokee Nation ruled on the possibility of Cherokee nationalism and the representational dilemma it posed. The case raised legal, political, and moral conflicts for the Court and especially for Marshall. Despite his pronouncements in *Johnson*, he remained troubled by the "plight of the Cherokee." Contrary to his usual preference for—and the Court's usual practice of—a united front, he encouraged the two dissenters, Justices Smith Thompson and Joseph Story, to file their dissenting opinions. Thompson believed that the Cherokee Nation constituted a sovereign—and foreign—government entitled to the recognition and respect of the United States government. Story concurred in Thompson's dissenting opinion, and Marshall subsequently collaborated with both of them, and with Court Reporter Richard Peters, in a pamphlet that publicized the case.[30] "If courts were permitted to indulge their sympathies," he had noted at the beginning of his official opinion, "a case better calculated to excite them can scarcely be imagined" (*CN*, 15). Nonetheless, his opinion represented the policy of the Court, and his efforts to legislate an unambiguous relationship between the tribal nations and the United States government reflected that policy. An advocate of the colonization—in Africa—of descendants of Africans living in the United States, the chief justice seemed as unwilling to assimilate as to grant sovereignty to "a people once numerous, powerful, and truly independent . . . gradually sinking beneath our superior policy, our arts and our arms" (*CN*, 15). Morally, however, he was perplexed by Jackson's aggressive removal policy and called instead for the tribal nations to "be denominated domestic dependent nations" since "they are in a state of pupilage. Their relation to the United States resembles that of a ward to his guardian. They look to our government for protection; rely upon its kindness and its power; appeal to it for relief to their wants; and address the president as their great father" (*CN*, 17). Marshall's rhetoric represented a logical extension of United States Indian legislation, which, as the defense had pointed out in *Johnson*, "treat[ed] them as an inferior race of people, without the privileges of citizens, and under the perpetual protection and pupilage of the government" (*JM*, 569). Although the chief justice was trying to soften Andrew Jackson's aggressive removal policy, he offered instead only a paternalism that ironically withheld the father's name from his adopted children.[31]

Marshall's domestic fantasy had been effectively dramatized, and anticipated, by future abolitionist Lydia Maria Child in *Hobomok* (1824), a literary work in which she played out a scenario that Marshall could only imply in a legal decision. Set in colonial New England, the novel uses its white female protagonist's ill-advised marriage to Hobomok, chief of a neighboring tribe, to secure her Americanization. The fate of Charles Hobomok Conant, son of Hobomok and Mary Conant and adopted son of Charles Brown, accomplishes for a fictitious individual what Marshall rhetorically tried, unsuccessfully, to do for the tribal nations. The novel conscientiously depicts Mary's consent to marry Hobomok as the unfortunate outcome of her grief at reports of the death of her Royalist fiancé, Charles Brown, and anger at her father's unrelenting fanaticism. When she awakens to the consequences of her impulsive behavior, Mary redeems herself for her early nineteenth-century audience by accepting her exile and renouncing her inheritance. Although her father "conjure[s] her not to consider a marriage lawful, which had been performed in a moment of derangement" and enjoins her to return both to him and to the inheritance bequeathed to her by a beloved paternal grandfather, Mary "urg[es] him to appropriate her property to his own comfort" since "her marriage vow to the Indian was [no] less sacred, than any other voluntary promise."[32] Mary must stay married to Hobomok because of a contract that cannot be declared illegal by British law. Only Hobomok can release her from her contract. Her inheritance, on the other hand, is invalidated when she relinquishes a legal identity that is contingent on her (consensual) membership in a community in which those laws apply. Those property laws do not extend to Mary when she leaves English domain.

Hobomok, however, turns out to be an appropriately cooperative noble savage. When Charles Brown appears, almost as though reborn, Hobomok concedes his entitlement to both Mary and the land and selflessly agrees to " 'go far off among some of the red men in the West. They will dig him a grave, and Mary may sing the marriage song in the wigwam of the Englishman' " (*HOB*, 139). His emigration and death speak more to the need to resolve the dilemmas of an ambiguous government policy than to express the deep wish of migrating tribes, but, most importantly, his self-abnegation Americanizes those it leaves behind. Mary can no longer return to England as she had wished because, she explains, " 'my boy would disgrace me, and I never will leave him; for love to him is the only way that I can now repay my debt of gratitude' " (*HOB*, 148). Instead, she must remain in the New World to construct the American family both by reconciling with her Puritan father and by reconstituting Charles Hobomok.

The significance of Hobomok and his son inheres in the family's reconstitution according to the ideology of the early nineteenth century. Mary and Hobomok's amalgamation reconciles the austere Mr. Conant to Charles Brown, and her return reforms her rigid father into an affectionate patriarch and, "partly from consciousness of blame, and partly from a mixed feeling of compassion and affection," a doting grandparent (*HOB*, 149). Hobomok's erasure is signaled rhetorically through Charles Hobomok's assimilation: "he departed to finish his studies in England. His father was seldom spoken of; and by degrees his Indian appellation was silently omitted" (*HOB*, 150). The tacit agreement, denoted by passive voice, that whitewashes Mary's son attests to a faith in consensus and the ability of the community to absorb a dash of Indian blood. In fact, that blood seems to be just the seasoning necessary to deanglicize, or nativize, the fledgling national culture. But Charles (Hobomok) Conant Brown's Indianness can metaphorically occasion his family's Americanization only if his father departs, a contingency that recalls the appropriating of tribal names, insignia, dress, customs, and even bastardized ceremonies as badges of "Americanness." (The Indians, in absentia, ironically would mark the *integrity* of the continent—and the nation-to-be.) Hobomok occasions a transformation of the Conant family that symbolically links colonial and early nineteenth-century America as it distinguishes both from England. Hobomok's son can even be schooled in England precisely because he can never be Anglicized, only further Americanized. As an Indian, however, Charles Hobomok gradually ceases to exist.

Like the assimilation imagined by Child, the assimilation presented in Americanization initiatives, such as Jefferson's, as early as the second decade of the nineteenth century assumed the dissolution of tribal affiliations. Only disaffiliated individuals could become Americans. Justice William Johnson, a North Carolinian appointed to the Court by Jefferson to counter the known federalism of the Marshall Court, offered a consenting opinion in *Cherokee Nation* in which he pointedly excluded the "Indians" from "the family of nations" and, consequently, from representation within the United States legal system—and even, by implication, from the human family (*CN*, 21, 25, 26). The heterogeneity that would be introduced by the inclusion of the indigenes troubled Johnson, who deconstituted "Indians" back into tribal affiliations when he contended that "every petty kraal of Indians, designating themselves a tribe or nation, and having a few hundred acres of land to hunt on exclusively. . . . should indeed force into the family of nations, a very numerous and very heterogeneous progeny" (*CN*, 25). His use of the word "kraal," an Afrikaner term for an enclosed village or the animal pen within the village (like the English "corral"), shows just how loath Johnson was to claim human kinship with indigenes. In view of Johnson's kinship metaphors and Child's depiction of Mary Conant's marriage to Hobomok, one wonders how long even the most ardent advocates of assimilation, like Jefferson, would have held their ground if significant numbers of indigenes had been willing to "individualize," to marry in. Mary herself was ashamed to return home with an indigenous husband, and ashamed to return to her beloved England with the evidence of their coupling in the form of Charles Hobomok. In any case, the Cherokee Constitution was a bid for the coexistence between cultures rather than the assimilation of individuals, an option not written into the American script.

While Marshall lacked the fictional alternatives of a novelist, the jurist did have textual options. The law is centrally concerned with naming and defining. Marshall's "domestic dependent nation" named the Cherokees into a legal status (of nonpersonhood) made apparent by Justice Henry Baldwin, a Jackson appointee who concurred in Marshall's *Cherokee Nation* opinion, in his ominous (and prophetic) declaration that "there is no plaintiff in this suit" (*CN*, 31). Marshall found the textual justification for his decision in "the eighth section of the third article" of the United States Constitution which empowers congress to 'regulate commerce with foreign nations, and among the several states, and with the Indian tribes.'

In this clause they are as clearly contradistinguished by a name appropriate to themselves, from foreign nations, as from the several states composing the Union. They are designated by a distinct appellation; and as this appellation can be applied to neither of the others, neither can the application distinguishing either of the others be in fair construction applied to them. The objects, to which the power of regulating commerce might be directed, are divided into three distinct classes—foreign nations, the several states, and Indian tribes. (*CN*, 18)

When Smith Thompson, in a dissenting opinion, labeled the Court's reading of this passage "mere verbal criticism," he exposed the rhetorical foundation of the Union. Thompson returned to the original act of naming to counter the "argument . . . that if the Indian tribes are foreign nations, they would have been included without being specially named, and being so named imports something different from the previous term 'foreign nations'" (*CN*, 62). He offered two alternative readings of the phraseology of the document: stylistic, "avoid[ing] the repetition of the term nation"; and practical, allowing Congress to deal separately with each tribal nation. Yet the very textuality of the debate underscored the power of rhetorical representation. Anticipating the anxious question of what keeps a government from making white men slaves, the Court's rhetorical erasure of the Cherokee plaintiffs offered the equally anxious (if not overtly articulated) query of what keeps a government from making white men (legally) disappear.

But the Cherokees could only be excluded from full personhood in the eyes and within the bounds of the law of the United States. In effect, the Cherokee bid for recognition by the United States as a foreign nation was a bid for full personhood within those bounds. Subject to the laws of Georgia, the Cherokees would otherwise be entitled only to the limited rights and privileges of free descendants of Africans. The decision of the Marshall Court did not bring them within those bounds. Nonetheless, John Ross, the Chief who spearheaded the legal initiatives, was not entirely displeased by the decision. Concerned that the result of *Cherokee Nation* would fuel removal efforts from within the Cherokee Nation as well as from the United States government, Ross urged the Cherokees not to be disheartened by the Court's decision. In an address following the decision,

Ross cited the Court's admission of the Cherokee Nation as "a distinct political society, separated from others, capable of managing its own affairs and governing itself" and insisted "that the denial of the injunction has no bearing whatever upon the true merits of our cause," but only upon "the limited powers of the Supreme Court." Ross assured his constituency that the Cherokees' rights will be recognized "whenever a case between proper parties may be brought before it."[33] With that assurance, Ross seems to have read Marshall's intentions correctly. The Chief Justice had himself explained that the Court could only rule on the constitutionality of Georgia's interventions on Cherokee land "in a proper case with proper parties" (*CN*, 20).

That case, *Samuel A. Worcester v. the State of Georgia* (1832), was brought before the Court by Cherokee sympathizers in the following year. Significantly, the federal intervention called for by the plaintiffs in *Cherokee Nation* was conferred by the Court in *Worcester,* where the case involved "the personal liberty of a citizen."[34] The case ruled on the claim of the plaintiffs, Reverend Samuel A. Worcester and Dr. Elizur Butler, both missionaries, of rights violations—including wrongful detainment— on the part of the state of Georgia, and it revolved around the constitutionality of an act passed by the Georgia legislature on December 22, 1830, claiming state jurisdiction over tribal territory. Georgia required all white citizens residing in Cherokee territory to sign an oath of allegiance to the state of Georgia. Of the missionaries residing in the Cherokee territory within the boundaries of Georgia, only those two both chose and received permission from their superiors—in their case, the Boston-based American Board of Commissioners for Foreign Missions—to contest Georgia's legislation. Both were arrested and convicted by the state of Georgia, and both refused a pardon from the state in order to allow their counsel, *Cherokee Nation* attorneys William Wirt and Thomas Sergeant, to bring the case before the Supreme Court. Wirt and Sergeant called forth the federal treaties that upheld Cherokee sovereignty within established boundaries. Not only was there now a "plaintiff in this suit," but the case, which linked the "personal liberty" of an American citizen to tribal land rights, came dangerously close to demonstrating a correlation between the legal representational invisibility of the mixed-blood Cherokees and the necessary self-abridgment of even the most apparently representative Christian white male within a collective identity. While the case was really about the constitutionality of Georgia's legislation, in other words, the prosecution pointedly turned attention to the personal liberty of white male citizens. Could the Court make white men disappear? Marshall now had his "proper case with proper parties" and accordingly declared Georgia's legislation unconstitutional.

The question of the Cherokees' Americanization resurfaced in *Worcester*. Justice John McLean, for example, argued that their "Americanization" entitled the Cherokee people to federal protection but, in turn, required their complete acquiescence. "By entering into" treaties with them, he asked, "have we not admitted the power of this people to bind themselves, and to impose obligations on us?" (*WG*, 582). Although McLean recognized that the United States assimilation policies had Americanized the tribal nations into certain entitlements, that recognition did not depart significantly from Marshall's paternalism. Indeed, that paternalism was the basis for programs such as the Indian Civilization Fund, first managed by McKenney for agricultural instruction and Indian schools, and alluded to by McLean as "the means adopted by the general government to reclaim the savage from his erratic life, and induce him to assume the forms of civilization." Such programs, he argued, tended "to increase the attachment of the Cherokees to the country they now inhabit" (*WG*, 588). McLean clearly did not advocate a permanent Cherokee nation within Georgia's boundaries, although he did maintain that "the abstract right of every section of the human race to a reasonable portion of the soil, by which to acquire the means of subsistence, cannot be controverted" (*WG*, 579). The tribal nations were not to define their own rights; rather, *as* Americans, they were to submit to the authority of the United States government to define rights: "The exercise of the power of self-government by the Indians, within a state, is undoubtedly contemplated to be temporary. . . . [A] sound national policy does require that the Indian tribes within our states should exchange their territories, upon equitable principles, or, eventually, consent to become amalgamated in our political communities" (*WG*, 593).

The use of "amalgamated," although conventional, subtly articulates the subtext of such legislation, very much like "domestic dependent nations." Reconfigured as children, but without the possibility of coming of age as citizens, Indians were amalgamated into a surrender of any property held in the name of a tribal affiliation. The link between their domestication and their dispossession found expression in their emblematic connection to white women in some of the literature of this period.[35] Even the most enlightened official policies, and the narratives that supported them, did no more than advocate a national forgetting such as the tacit agreement that allows Charles Hobomok to pass in the name of his adopted father. Of course, the exception of an individual could certainly not extend into policy for an entire tribe. By the 1830s, the unfeasibility of wide-scale assimilation—the result of both American and indigenous reluctance—made removal virtually inevitable. Hence, the national fairy tale of *Hobomok* and the failure of the Marshall Court's efforts to find a tenable legal solution.

A national crisis, rather than the Court's decision, finally resolved the stand-off between the Marshall Court and both Georgia and Andrew Jackson. Worcester and Butler remained in custody while Georgia refused to attend to the Court's ruling and Governor Lumpkin continued only to offer to pardon them. The attorneys' plan to bring Georgia's inaction officially before Jackson promised only a showdown between the Marshall Court and the president, which boded ill for the Court. But when South Carolina's threat to nullify a federal tariff brought consolidationists and states' righters again into conflict, the politically opportunistic South Carolinian John Calhoun drew parallels between the two cases, making secession and Civil War serious possibilities. The fate of the Union proved more important to the missionaries and their supporters than the plight of the Cherokees, and the missionaries accepted Lumpkin's pardon.[36]

My reading of the Cherokee cases and surrounding documents may help to explain some of the motivations of their decision. I have sought to explain the anxiety manifested in these cases through an analysis of the uncanniness of human beings excluded from personhood. According to legal historian G. Edward White, the Marshall Court demonstrated the contingency of liberty and equality in America to oppressed racial groups, and the meaninglessness of "natural law . . . as a set of abstract, extra-constitutional principles of justice" to students of American law.[37] To this analysis I would add that the cases in fact demonstrated what they tried to obscure: that the government more than protected but actually conferred putatively *natural* rights, hence the personhood defined by those rights, upon subjects recognized by the government. That lesson was available, if only intuitively, to anyone witnessing Cherokee Removal, African enslavement, or married (white) women's property laws. It was even embraced—in a modified form—as a tenet of republicanism by some important political theorists in the formative years of the Union. Educator, medical doctor, and statesman Benjamin Rush, a signer of the Declaration of Independence, expressed the hope, in "Of the Mode of Education Proper in a Republic," that an American system of education would teach the white male student "that he does not belong to himself, but that he is public property."[38] It is interesting to imagine the subtle psychological implications of such a lesson in view of human beings who could be literally dispossessed, or turned into possessions, by that very government.

The Cherokee cases demonstrated a correlation between legally-sanctioned personhood and the stories that could be told in the nation's courts. The white male missionaries *could* tell their stories (significantly, the female missionaries were not compelled by Georgia to sign the oath), but they chose to retract them when those stories might damage the Union. Perhaps the lesson of the cases—the intrinsic contingency of their own personhood on the Union and the fate of those excluded from that personhood—made the meaninglessness of their "personal liberty" without that Union too difficult to contemplate.[39] In any case, the Union was more important to the missionaries than their version of the Cherokee saga.

If Marshall's narrative had to account for human beings who could become dispossessed, Taney's decision in *Dred Scott* had to explain how human beings could become possessions. Both narratives involved the conflicts embodied by human beings excluded from the rights of personhood. For Taney and the majority of his Court, however, rights of citizenship and personhood were defined, interpreted, and safeguarded by the states rather than the Union. Nonetheless, that difference did not affect the anxious efforts to explain the exclusion of descendants of Africans manifested in the official narrative of *Dred Scott*. Many tensions faced by the Marshall Court were exacerbated by the late 1850s, when the Taney Court ruled on *Dred Scott*. Stronger divisions along sectional lines made the possibility of Civil War more immediate. Since *Dred Scott* concerned the legislation of slavery in the territories, the case entailed the unresolved sovereignty conflicts at play in *Cherokee Nation*. The Taney Court's decision to consign Dred Scott to the same status to which the Marshall Court consigned the Cherokees, neither citizens nor aliens, could have allowed Taney, like Marshall in *Cherokee Nation*, to refuse to rule on the conflict between federal and state sovereignty. But Taney did not wait for "a proper case with proper parties." Instead, he declared the federal legislation of the Missouri Compromise unconstitutional and sought to establish the priority of state over federal sovereignty.

Although Taney was typically less textually based in his rulings than Marshall, he, like his predecessor, returned to the text of the Constitution to establish narrative continuity for his decision to maintain the legal unrepresentability of nonwhite subjects.[40] Asserting that descendants of Africans were rhetorically excluded from We the People, Taney insisted that the Constitution prohibited their holding state, and therefore federal, citizenship. Nor, however, were they eligible for alien status. Dred Scott consequently could not sue for his freedom in the state of Missouri, where the suit had originated, because he was not and could never be a citizen of that state. Taney's majority opinion, moreover, describes a Constitution that prevents the federal government from prohibiting slavery in a territory and gives states rather than the federal government jurisdiction over the regulation of domestic institutions, including slavery. Even if Dred Scott could sue in a state or federal court, neither his master's sojourn in the free state of Illinois, nor his stay in the territory designated free under the Louisiana Purchase could legitimate his suit for freedom in Missouri, a slave state.

Taney's narrative nevertheless carefully distinguishes between Indians and descendants of Africans. By the late 1850s, the government's aggressive removal policy had substantially diminished any significant physical or representational challenge from the tribes. Writing in 1857, Taney *contrasted* the legal status of "that class of persons . . . whose ancestors were negroes of the African race, and imported into this country, and sold and held as slaves" with that of "Indian Governments [that] were regarded and treated as foreign Governments, as much so as if an ocean had separated the red man from the white."[41] One must either question Taney's legal scholarship or interrogate his willful misremembering of *Cherokee Nation*. His opinion reveals a deliberative shift of emphasis that elucidates an important difference between these groups:

It is true that the *course of events* has brought the Indian tribes within the limits of the United States under subjection to the white race; and it has been found necessary, for their sake as well as our own, to regard them as in a state of pupilage, and to legislate to a certain extent over them and the territory they occupy. But they may, without doubt, like the subjects of any other foreign Government, be naturalized by the authority of Congress, and become citizens of a State, and of the United States; and if an individual should leave his nation or tribe, and take up his abode among the white population, he would be entitled to all the rights and privileges which would belong to an emigrant from any other foreign people. (*DS*, 404; emphasis added)

Their lack of proximity seemed to mean that the "Indians" could now constitute an alien nation, and their reluctance to assimilate as individuals had always permitted suggestions that they could be thus amalgamated.[42] By contrast, each side of the slavery debate invoked the mulatto to depict the gruesome consequences of the institutions of the other side: the threat from within. Descendants of Africans were more intricately involved in the economy of the nation—especially in the South—than the indigenous tribes had been. Despite colonization initiatives, the "removal" of descendants of Africans posed greater complications than the expulsion (or extermination) of separatist tribes. Black subjectivity evidently presented the more serious danger in the antebellum United States.

The Chief Justice used the specter of amalgamation to articulate the Court's most unambiguous and provocative stand on black subjectivity and government authority in *Dred Scott*.[43] Beginning his majority opinion with a catalogue of anti-amalgamation laws (originally directed as much against "Indians" as "descendants of Africans"), Taney pointedly excluded black subjects from "the whole human family, . . . civilized Governments and the family of nations" (*DS*, 410). With the common currency of body and family tropes, he made use of as vivid a language of kinship as that with which Justice William Johnson anxiously imagined a figuratively miscegenated "family of nations" created by the admission of "every petty kraal of Indians": "citizens in the several States, became also citizens of this new political body; but none other; it was formed by them, and for them and their posterity, but for no one else. . . . It was the union of those who were at that time members of distinct and separate political communities into one political family, whose power . . . was to extend over the whole territory of the United States" (*DS*, 406). Taney's metaphors suggest a threat posed by blacks to the genealogy of a white "family of independent nations" (*DS*, 407), and they justify the anti-amalgamation laws, which "show that a perpetual and impassable barrier was intended to be erected between the white race and the one which they had reduced to slavery" (*DS*, 409). The passive construction through which Taney presented his appeal to the will of the founders and their cohort demonstrates the strategy that Robert Ferguson calls "the rhetoric of inevitability," a strategy that paradoxically establishes history as at once a justification for and an outgrowth of the laws of nature.[44]

Taney used a rhetoric of inevitability to inscribe Indian Removal within the progressive movement, the Manifest Destiny, of the American people. With phrases like "course of events" and "found necessary," he loosely echoed the Declaration of Independence in a narrative that located the subjection of tribes within the terms of the American Revolution, although emigration of these "nations and tribes" (the distinction was no longer so crucial) had removed the immediate risk of analogy between the United States and England that the Cherokee resemblance to the revolutionary colonies in *Cherokee Nation* had promoted.[45] The prosperity of the Union had resulted, inevitably, in the civilization or removal of the tribal nations (either way, in the passing of tribal cultures). That same prosperity, however, extended slavery, which, he implied was consequently as inevitable and as beneficial to all concerned as Indian Removal. Both grew out of what Marshall and Taney each called "civilization" in their narratives. Hence, the familiar paternalistic rhetoric that enslaves Africans and their descendants, as it effaces tribal cultures, "for their sake as well as our own."

Whereas Indian Removal made it possible to emblematize (and thus, as in *Hobomok*, to Americanize) tribal culture, the slave remained within United States culture as a visible symbol of legal nonpersonhood: neither *potential* citizen nor alien. A descendant of Africans thereby registered the uncanniness of the legally unrepresentable subject more forcefully than a member of a tribal nation in Taney's historical narrative. "Indian governments" had represented the threat offered by the proximity of an alternative collectivity. A descendant of Africans, in Taney's narrative, embodied the individual threat of a human being deprived of choice and self-possession within (but not of) the Union. Taney's reconstructed historical narrative thus had to legitimate—and moralize—slavery by distinguishing *individual* black from *individual* white human beings and excluding the former from potential citizenship *and* from the natural rights of personhood. At stake was the states' rights claim that the state rather than the federal government protects the liberties of *all* of its citizens. The majority opinion in *Dred Scott* had to establish the priority of both the master's property rights over the slave's right to self-possession and of the state's right to regulate slavery over federal legislation.

White Americans' self-ownership was evidently at issue in *Dred Scott*. The confused language and circular arguments of two proslavery Southern Supreme Court Justices, John A. Campbell and Peter V. Daniel, both of whom concurred in Taney's opinion, evinced concern that the issues of the case somehow challenged the "status of [white] persons" in the United States. Campbell saw the inalienable rights of individuals in conflict with federal sovereignty; he argued that those rights curbed the power of Congress to "determine the condition and status of persons who inhabit the Territories" (*DS*, 509). Campbell differed from a consolidationist like Marshall in seeing the federal government not as the source of but as a potential threat to inalienable rights. To make his point, he imagines "an American patriot" who might contrast the European and American systems by affirming " 'that European sovereigns give lands to their colonists, but reserve to themselves a power to control their property, liberty, and privileges; but the American Government sells the lands belonging to the people of the several States (i.e., United States) to their citizens, who are already in the possession of personal and political rights, which the Government did not give, and cannot take away' " (*DS*, 513). Largely on the basis of this distinction, Campbell's "patriot" suggests, the colonies had declared their independence. For Campbell, the "American Government" merely transfers *property* that is already *collectively* owned by the people to individuals. He begs the question—by appealing to convention—of who is empowered to decide exactly who is entitled to "the possession of personal and political rights, which the government did not give, and cannot take away."

Justice Daniel manifests concern in his opinion that the concept of inalienable rights, improperly construed, can lead to the conceptualization of people as property. He insists that "the power of disposing of and regulating" property "vested in Congress . . . did not extend to the personal or political rights of citizens or settlers . . . inasmuch as *citizens* or *persons* could not be property, and especially were not property *belonging* to the United States" (*DS*, 489). Daniel's reasoning is tautological: the status of enslaved people as property makes their citizenship unthinkable; conversely, the status of anyone designated "citizens or persons" makes their designation as property unthinkable. "In the establishment of the several communities now the States of this Union, and in the formation of the Federal Government," he argues, "the African was not deemed politically a person" (*DS*, 481). He associates the power of disposing and regulating personal and political rights with proprietorship. Like Campbell, he defers to convention to answer the question of who distributes property rights, of who is to decide who *is* and who *owns* property. Moreover, while Daniels implicitly equates federal sovereignty with the possible enslavement of white Americans, he does not explain how state sovereignty avoids that potential. Unarticulated but everpresent is the nagging question that arises with any challenge to the universal status of natural rights and with the issue of their distribution: what keeps a government from making white men slaves?

The counternarratives offered by the two dissenters, Justices McLean and Benjamin Curtis, a conservative New Englander known as a defender of property rights, explicitly articulated the anxiety most fundamental to the case. Their arguments demonstrate the threat that slavery posed to the rights and liberties of everyone. Neither jurist was an extremist, and both sought to maintain the legality of slavery and to suggest the challenge to the law constituted by the peculiar institution. Curtis's conservatism is evident in his reluctance to contest the legality of slavery, and his lengthy and thorough dissent displays a committed legal mind, one dedicated to upholding rather than challenging the law.[46] McLean, on the other hand, demonstrates a politician's equivocating—and his own presidential ambition—when summoning the danger of the Union's dissolution posed by the legal institution while never explicitly advocating abolition. Whether as a political strategy or an intellectual commitment, both dissenters argued that the *Dred Scott* decision, in all of its manifestations, threatened the personal liberty of all Americans.

For McLean, slavery laws throughout history "show that property in a human being does not arise from nature or from the common law, but, in the language of this court, 'it is a mere municipal regulation, founded upon and limited to the range of the territorial laws.'" Ominously, he evoked the crux of impending national crisis, further expressed in his labeling "this decision . . . the end of the law" (*DS*, 549). To enslave a person was, for him, to push the law to its extreme: if a law that turns a human being into property does not arise from nature, McLean *explicitly* asked, then what stops a government from making "white men slaves?" (*DS*, 542).

No less apocalyptically, if somewhat less dramatically, Curtis pointed to the meaninglessness of natural law principles in the absence of government. In response to Taney's questioning the legitimacy of the regulatory powers of Congress in the territories, the dissenter noted that: "Without government and social order, there can be no property; for without law, its ownership, its use, and the power of disposing of it, cease to exist, in the sense in which those words are used and understood in all civilized States" (*DS*, 615). Curtis spelled out the most radical implications of a positive law argument, showing how the law names property into existence by standardizing linguistic structures if not language itself.[47] The material fact of property is a function of owning and bequeathing, actions and relations that the law governs. The "law," in turn, refers to the terms that make experience comprehensible. By implication, the subject's desire to comprehend, to make experience meaningful, underwrites his or her obedience to the law. Curtis's articulation depicts the law as a discourse defending the subject against an always encroaching anarchy that threatens both the physical body and meaningful experience. Despite their theoretical priority, neither rights nor personhood makes sense in the absence of the law.

Curtis did not intend to deconstruct the law. On the contrary, this passage follows not only the logic of Blackstone, but also that of the Constitution's regulation of commerce, currency, and naturalization to bring the individual states of the Union within the terms of a uniform law. The conservative New Englander argued for a common vocabulary of private property that would assimilate all who accepted its terms into an American discourse. But *Dred Scott*, no less than *Cherokee Nation*, suggested that such assimilation—even if possible—required a significant degree of cultural erasure. For people from non-European cultures, such an erasure was more dramatic and the rights guaranteed less inclusive— overall, the exchange was less desirable—than for their European counterparts. Even Curtis's and McLean's dissenting arguments concerned whether or not, rather than how, non-Europeans could and ought to become Americans. Curtis sought to apply and preserve, not to reform, the law, and his opinion must be understood as a response to Taney's demonstration, through an appeal to the anti-amalgamation laws with which the chief justice opened his majority opinion, that the father was not willing to give his name to his darker skinned progeny.[48]

Curtis attested to what *Cherokee Nation* and *Dred Scott* demonstrate: the importance of words, and of a narrative that could turn words into law, to the project of nation-building. These cases ventured to tell a story, a narrative of cultural identity that would define personhood and standardize the terms of assimilation. But they equally manifested the difficulties intrinsic to that process. Designed to be fluid, responsive to a changing world, the law had also to establish a basis for continuity and stability in that changing world. The troubling presence of nonwhite subjects reflected the unresolved discord that would result in Civil War and the need for a reformulation of personhood—in sum, the inadequacy of contemporary terms of assimilation. But the very disruptions that marked that inadequacy could also be productively harnessed by a narrative that sought to correct it.

Plotting the Nation

The relationship between law and language articulated by Curtis informed the political strategy of another prominent lawyer. "The world has never had a good definition of the word liberty," Abraham Lincoln told the participants in a Sanitary Fair in Baltimore, one year before his assassination, "and the American people, just now, are much in want of one. We all declare for liberty; but in using the same *word* we do not all mean the same *thing.*"[49] Thus Lincoln explained the war of words that raged in an embattled Union. It was a war that had preceded and, Lincoln suggested, to some extent caused the armed conflict, and the president had fought it with great skill. Lincoln knew that it made all the "difference whether the . . . movement at the South be called 'secession' or 'rebellion,'" and he told Congress so in a special session on July 4, 1861 (*AL,* 4:602). He knew that a "civil war" was not a "revolution," and he fashioned a narrative that would implement his vision of Union and standardize his definition of "liberty." Through that narrative, which began with the Declaration of Independence and used the slave's uncanniness to promote the white American's investment in the Union, Lincoln plotted a new story of the American nation.

Garry Wills convincingly argues that the most potent official story of the United States—the narrative of the American nation that begins on July 4, 1776—is the legacy of Abraham Lincoln and a product of the Civil War.[50] As a lawyer, Lincoln had learned to construct legal narratives that continually invoked and obscured origins in order to establish the "categorical authority" of the law.[51] These legal narratives, in other words, authorized their claims by retroactively but obscurely choosing a point of departure and making a sequence of events lead naturally and inevitably to a particular interpretation of the present. Such narratives derived—as they continue to derive—their authority from the rhetoric of inevitability that Lincoln freely deployed. With the logic supplied by that rhetoric, a narrative could transcend the origins of American legal discourse and turn the founders' words into law. The self-evident truths of the Declaration provided Lincoln with that origin.

In February 1861, shortly before his inauguration, Lincoln told a crowd assembled in Philadelphia's Independence Hall that he had "never had a feeling politically that did not spring from sentiments embodied in the Declaration of Independence" (*AL*, 4:24). Lincoln's brilliant oratory—his meticulous sense of timing and genius for sensing and using to advantage the mood of a crowd—made reference to the Declaration in Independence Hall inevitable. But by 1861 Lincoln also undoubtedly believed this claim. During the 1850s, he had increasingly turned to the Declaration to represent the founding of the nation, a strategy culminating in Gettysburg's "four score and seven years." Lincoln was hardly the first political figure to return to the Declaration rather than the Constitution. The strategy was especially common among groups who believed themselves excluded from the great principles therein articulated. Alternative Declarations that borrowed the language and sought to capture the spirit of Thomas Jefferson's document were plentiful in the first half of the nineteenth century, representing, for example, workingmen and trade unionists, antimonopolists and industrialists, nonrenters and nonproducers, and, perhaps the most widely remembered, advocates of the rights of women.[52] But no such return was more influential than Abraham Lincoln's, and his success in authorizing that return, in beginning the nation with the Declaration, was the result of a forceful narrative. Where other groups adopted the language of the document to assert their rights, Lincoln had the power to reclaim the spirit of 1776 in order to re-establish the nation.

The rhetoric of Lincoln's speeches manifests renewed vigor in 1854, when the passage of the Kansas-Nebraska Act repealed the Missouri Compromise of 1820. This act, which was at the center of controversy in the antebellum United States, addressed the organization of the Nebraska territory in preparation for statehood. The terms of the Missouri Compromise prohibited slavery in all the territory in question, but the Kansas-Nebraska Act legislated the right of the population of the territory—and of the future state(s) to be formed from it—to decide on all issues concerning slavery. Proponents of popular sovereignty called the constitutionality of the Missouri Compromise into question, as did Taney and most of the concurring justices in the *Dred Scott* decision. The challenge to federal authority in the territories actually prompted Benjamin Curtis's remarks, cited above, concerning the meaninglessness of property in the absence of government. Instrumental in the drafting and enactment of the Kansas-Nebraska Bill was the man who would become Lincoln's most celebrated political rival and in response to whom Lincoln would develop his most prescient narrative and political strategies, Senator Stephen A. Douglas of Illinois, chairman of the Senate Committee on Territories. Douglas's public support of the act inspired an impassioned Abraham Lincoln to retort with what was for him a new order of political speech. The future president appealed to "the logic of history" to bring forth a vision of a Union beset with dangers and badly in need of both renovation and reinvestment. In his Peoria, Illinois speech on the repeal of the Missouri Compromise (1854), the "spirit of seventy-six" rather than the Constitution is most pressingly imperiled by "the spirit of Nebraska." Lincoln calls upon his audience to "re-adopt the Declaration of Independence" (*AL*, 2:275).

By the 1850s the Constitution was viewed by many as a compromise document, whereas the Declaration expressed the principles that had united the colonies and legitimated their rebellion. Assuming a consensus on those principles, Lincoln had to construct a narrative that would unobtrusively offer his own vision as the sole expression of the spirit of seventy-six. In the Repeal speech, Lincoln follows the logic of the genre of the judicial opinion when he summons "history," like precedent, in place of a more appropriate grammatical subject: "In order to [get?] a clear understanding of what the Missouri Compromise is, a short history of the preceding kindred subjects will perhaps be proper" (*AL*, 2:248).[53] The uncertain verb (get?) makes it difficult to know whether the grammatical subject of the sentence should be the speaker or the general audience. If the verb were actually "give," for example, then "I" should follow the comma. In either case, the history itself occupies the place of the subject, as though authorizing—and authoring—itself. This history appears as truth, not a version, and it features a "confederacy" that "owned no country at all" to characterize the state of the union prior to the agreement to cede territory to the "general government." The slaveholding states' righter Thomas Jefferson, whom Lincoln calls "the most distinguished politician of our history," comes into this history in favor of government-owned territory and as the originator of the idea of "prevent[ing] slavery [from] ever going into the north-western territory" (*AL*, 2:249).[54]

Almost a year later, Lincoln lamented, in a letter to George Robertson, a Kentucky judge who also opposed the extension of slavery, that the "spirit which desired the peaceful extinction of slavery, has itself become extinct with the occasion and the men of the Revolution" (*AL*, 2:318). Ominously, he observes that the prosperity of the Union has resulted in a departure from its principles: "When we were the political slaves of King George, and wanted to be free, we called the maxim that 'all men are created equal' a self-evident truth; but now when we have grown fat, and have lost all dread of being slaves ourselves, we have become so greedy to be *masters* that we call the same maxim 'a self-evident lie'" (*AL*, 2:318). To reclaim the self-evident truth was the task of Lincoln's narrative, and with that reclamation came a renewed sense of the possibility of one's own enslavement in the absence of an enlightened government.

That government, for Lincoln, was the Union, and slavery was the great enemy not only of liberty, but of the Union. So necessary was the Union to liberty, in fact, that Lincoln would accept slavery for as long as he could rather than risk a serious threat to the Union. The Repeal speech makes clear that Lincoln opposes the extension of slavery although he tolerates its existence. Nonetheless, in the Repeal speech, Lincoln presents the institution of slavery as fundamentally un-American and a threat to white personhood even while he explicitly enjoins his audience to uphold all the laws of the land, including the fugitive slave law. The institution of slavery makes it possible for a human being to be reduced to property, and it also reduces a white man in the North "to a . . . smaller fraction of a man" (*AL*, 2:269). The question of legal representation, Lincoln explains, returns to the compromise that the Articles of Confederation bequeathed on the Constitution; states' representation in the House of Representatives will be "determined by adding to the whole number of free persons, including those bound to service for a term of years, and excluding Indians not taxed, three fifths of all other persons."[55] Using Maine and South Carolina as examples, Lincoln shows how a northern state with more than twice the number of white males as a southern state was nevertheless entitled to exactly the same number of representatives and presidential electors. Thus slavery entitled white male South Carolinians to a disproportionate representation in the Union. But Lincoln hinges his very being on legal representation when he quips "that whether I shall be a whole man, or only, the half of one, in comparison with others, is a question in which I am somewhat concerned" (*AL*, 2:269). This rhetoric could have an especially dramatic impact on audiences even remotely familiar with the legislated disappearance—and the social consequences of the legal invisibility—of nonwhite subjects.

Lincoln's narrative conferred personhood in conjunction with allegiance to his version of the Union. Having infused his audience's sense of injustice with a hint that their representation—political and social—was at stake, he urges obedience to the legal corollary of his Union:

> Stand with anybody that stands RIGHT. Stand with him while he is right and PART with him when he goes wrong. Stand WITH the abolitionist in restoring the Missouri Compromise; and stand AGAINST him when he attempts the repeal of the fugitive slave law. In the latter case you stand with the southern disunionist. What of that? you are still right. In both cases you are right. In both cases you expose the dangerous extremes. In both you stand on middle ground and hold the ship level and steady. In both you are national and nothing less than national. This is the good old whig ground. To desert such ground, because of any company, is to be less than a whig—less than a man—less than an American. (*AL*, 2:273–74)

Here Lincoln defines the meaning of his political affiliation, but he also links manhood and Americanness to his vision of the Union. The fullest expression of identity inheres in upholding *a* national law that Lincoln represents as *the* national law. The hallmark of his reconstructive national narrative, the uncanny (nonwhite) subject, was most effective when Lincoln could suggestively make his listeners wonder what—and whether—they would be if they were not Americans. He needed his audience to imagine their own nonpersonhood (nonmanhood) and to understand that possibility as the outcome of the dissolution of the Union that he depicted in his narrative. Although it is hard to imagine any audience that consciously considers the possibility of its own actual nonexistence, this possibility could remain a suggestion, lingering beneath consciousness, subtly tying existence to sociolegal representation and essence to identity, strengthening their allegiance to the Union that Lincoln offered them. Significantly, however, his unself-consciously conventional use of "man" makes clear how even someone as sensitive to the dynamics and strategies of exclusion as Lincoln could, from the outset, overlook the exclusion of half the population, enslaved and free, from the terms of full personhood.

The Repeal speech demonstrates the basic elements of the strategy that Lincoln would develop first in response to Stephen Douglas and subsequently as president during the nation's most dramatic crisis—and the modern nation's (re)formative moment. His use of the uncanniness of the slave and of slavery promoted the investment of his enfranchised constituents not just in the Union but in the Union envisioned by Lincoln. By turning the debate over the Constitution into a contest over the principles of the Declaration, Lincoln returned to a time when colonists who were united against a tyrant confirmed their moral imperative by insisting on their own consolidation. But, as the canny Lincoln knew, his very insistence on colonial bonds in the eighteenth century spoke to the tenuousness of those bonds. Lincoln thus held before his audience the need to reaffirm those bonds and—a point he would push in later speeches—the apocalyptic consequences of their severance.

The presence of Stephen Douglas is the remaining element of the Repeal speech critical to the shaping of Lincoln's narrative. Douglas emerged, even before the celebrated debates between the incumbent senator and his folksy Republican challenger in 1858, as the embodiment of the political threat summoned by Lincoln. The "Little Giant," as Douglas was called, set concrete terms for an ongoing debate through which Lincoln sharpened an argument as he subtly fashioned a narrative. In June 1857, Lincoln delivered a speech on the *Dred Scott* decision in response to Douglas's speech on the same subject two weeks before. Speaking, like Douglas, in the state capital, Lincoln positions himself carefully in relation to his opponent by an elaborate rhetorical maneuvering that extends the themes of the Repeal speech. In especially colorful language, Lincoln indicts Douglas's commitment to popular sovereignty as an assault on the Declaration—rather than, as Douglas claimed, a reading of the Constitution: "now, to aid in making the bondage of the negro universal and eternal, [the Declaration] is assailed, and sneered at, and construed, and hawked at, and torn, till, if its framers could rise from their graves, they could not at all recognize it" (*AL*, 2:404). The material defacement of the document offered by Lincoln's rhetoric coarsens the more refined Douglas. And the senator's alleged debasement of the principle of equality is turned into the threat of despotism. Lincoln had written to George

Robertson about the danger in forgetting what it felt like to be a political slave, and Lincoln's Douglas embodies that danger.

The master rhetorician most pointedly evokes the essence of that danger in a literal extension of Douglas's claim that the founding fathers never intended the Declaration to include descendants of Africans, that " 'they were speaking of British subjects on this continent being equal to British subjects born and residing in Great Britain!' " (AL, 2:407). In an observation that he would effectively expand upon a year later, a wry Lincoln protests that "the French, Germans and other white people of the world are all gone to pot along with the Judge's inferior races" (AL, 2:407).[56] It is Douglas the *judge*, in this context, rather than Douglas the *senator* who threatens white Americans with the kind of unrepresentability to which the Supreme Court had just consigned black Americans. In Lincoln's narrative, that disappearance is the inevitable consequence of slavery.

But while his narrative relied upon the specter of the enslaved person, Lincoln had to imagine a place for the liberated slave in his Union. He found that task difficult, since a growing mulatto presence, especially in the slaveholding South, showed a changing face of the population of the United States, and each side accused the other of darkening the white face. In the speech on the *Dred Scott* decision, Lincoln summoned the "natural disgust in the minds of nearly all white people, to the idea of an indiscriminate amalgamation of the white and black races" to turn a tactic that he attributed to Douglas into his own (AL, 2:405). Where Douglas, according to his opponent, had hoped "to appropriate the benefit of this disgust to himself," Lincoln used statistics to "show that slavery is the greatest source of amalgamation" (AL, 2:405, 408). Aware of the aversion of white Americans to amalgamation, Lincoln knew he had to find a way to include the descendants of Africans in his vision of Union without marrying them into a national "family" or making them part of a body politic.

What changed during the 1850s was not so much Lincoln's vision as his symbolization of the Union, and the change allowed him to argue for coexistence without the implication of amalgamation. In his 1852 eulogy on Henry Clay, "Honors to Henry Clay," Lincoln had praised Clay, who "knew no North, no South, no East, no West, but only the Union, which held them all in its sacred circle" (AL, 2:123). The Great Compromiser "exorcised the demon which possessed the body politic, and gave peace to a distracted land" (AL, 2:123). The metaphor of the body politic naturalizes the Union and demonizes the threat of secession, the perpetrators of which have unnaturally entered into and are threatening the body of which they are not a part. The image of a demonic possession turns a political struggle into a theological one that threatens both the life and the soul of the nation. But Taney's *Dred Scott* opinion stepped up anti-amalgamation rhetoric and problematized the metaphor of the body politic.

When Lincoln spoke again in Springfield, in June 1858, a year after his speech on the *Dred Scott* decision, he offered the new symbol and a fully developed narrative strategy. "A House Divided" invoked the Bible, Thomas Paine, and, less directly but most powerfully, George Washington to authorize the house as a symbol of the Union. The Biblical metaphor of a house divided was a conventional one in early America, having been popularized by Thomas Paine in *Common Sense* when he observed that the bicameral government of the English Constitution described "all the distinction of a house divided against itself."[57] Since that time, it had been used as an emblem of division and unproductive conflict. In his introduction to the first issue of *The United States Magazine and Democratic Review* (1837), for example, editor, publisher, and literary nationalist John L. O'Sullivan dedicated his periodical to the investigation of "how the relation between majorities and minorities, in the frequent case of a collision of sentiments and particular interests, is to be so adjusted as to secure a mutual respect of rights, to preserve harmony and good will, and save society from the *malum extremum discordia,* from being as a house divided against itself."[58] With this conventional metaphor Lincoln could invoke but not insist on the family bonds. The "house" shifted the emphasis from blood kinship to coexistence, while it reinforced the need for cooperation among political factions.

Whether the symbol of the house grew out of Lincoln's need for a new emblem or incidentally provided a more accommodating metaphor, the house had an important precedent in the edifice of Washington's celebrated and widely disseminated 1796 Farewell Address. The first president's speech ranked among the most widely circulating documents of the period; it was not only cited extensively or printed in full in works ranging from textbooks, histories, and biographies to emigrant manuals and novels, but it was also frequently reprinted in pamphlet form along with the Declaration of Independence and the federal or a state constitution and even read annually in Congress. The address pursued the federalist strategy of mandating the federal government rather than the state governments as the most reliable guardian of individuals' rights and liberties, not surprisingly, since James Madison originally drafted it at Washington's request in 1792, and Washington reworked it with Alexander Hamilton, coauthor, with Madison and John Jay, of the Federalist Papers. Washington enjoined his readers to remember that "the unit of government, which constitutes you one people . . . is a main pillar in the edifice of you[r] real independence," and he stressed the importance of "your national union to your collective & individual happiness."[59] For Washington, the mutual dependence of the geographical regions and the gains promised by the united strength and resources of "an indissoluble community of interest" turns "the Union" into "one nation" (GWFA, 143). But by far the largest advantage that the Union offers to the different regions in this speech is freedom from border conflicts and therefore from "overgrown military establishments, which under any form of Government are inauspicious to liberty, and which are to be regarded as particularly hostile to Republican Liberty" (GWFA, 144). Still hoping to institute his version of the Union peacefully, Lincoln returned to the very speech that Mason Locke Weems, author of The Life of George Washington, had reprinted in his best-selling biography with the prefatory hope that "it may check for a while the fatal flame of discord which has destroyed all the once glorious republics of antiquity, and here now at length in the United States has caught upon the last republic that is left on the face of the earth."[60]

Its obvious consolidationist sentiments made the Farewell Address an especially appropriate pretext for Lincoln's first major political inauguration, his Senate race. But Lincoln had to account for important differences in the Union he had inherited. Washington could tell the members of his late eighteenth-century audience that "the name of American, which belong[ed] to [them], in [their] national capacity," was rooted in cultural uniformity: "With slight shades of difference, you have the same Religion, Manners, Habits & Political Principles" (GWFA, 142, 143). Whatever fictions lent credibility to Washington's claim, however, had been sufficiently challenged by the 1850s so as not to be available to Lincoln. In fact, even in the early 1780s Jefferson's Notes on the State of Virginia had registered his fear of the disruptive influence of heterogeneity, in particular that immigrants would disrupt social harmony, "infuse into [the legislation] their spirit, warp and bias its directions, and render it a heterogeneous, incoherent, distracted mass" (NSV, 211). National expansion and an increase in immigration gave rise to sentiments powerful enough to support the "Know-Nothings," a nativist political party, which was most active in the early 1850s. Although Lincoln thought "little better" of the principles of the Know-Nothings than he did "of those of the slavery extensionists," the group included many of his former and would-be allies whom he needed for his anti-extensionist coalition. He therefore hoped to avoid "the painful necessity of taking an open stand against them."[61] In any case, the antiforeign bias in the antebellum United States joined the stepped-up anxieties about amalgamation to make Washington's edifice a fitting structure for Lincoln's breakthrough speech.

Lincoln delivered "A House Divided" at the close of the Republican State Convention in acceptance of the nomination for the United States Senate. The genre of such a speech required the candidate's alignment with national heroes. "A House Divided" had to turn the sectional Republican party (formed in 1856) into the heir apparent of a national legacy. Toward that end, Lincoln predicted a crisis in the Union that would turn the task of upkeep into a heroic labor. After citing the biblical line "A house divided against itself cannot stand," the candidate ventures an ominous opinion: "I believe this government cannot endure, permanently half *slave* and half *free*" (*AL*, 2:461).[62] The sentiment, with nearly the same phrasing, had begun as a question in the aforementioned 1855 letter to George Robertson, which concluded with the words, "Our political problem now is 'Can we, as a nation, continue together *permanently—forever—* half slave, and half free?" (*AL*, 2:318). Three years later, Lincoln answered his question in the negative: the nation cannot endure as a house divided. This was never quite a revolutionary statement. "A House Divided" follows the prediction with a qualification: "I do not expect the Union to be *dissolved*—I do not expect the house to *fall*—but I *do* expect it will cease to be divided. It will become *all* one thing, or *all* the other" (*AL*, 2:461). The hint of a threat reminded Lincoln's audience of the tenuousness of an edifice that needed their upkeep. But secession murmurings made it dangerous to call the permanence of the Union too much into question; the qualification suggests an inevitability of unity that somewhat attenuates the threat.

What was impermanent, Lincoln argued, was actually the founders' compromise. The nation could not endure permanently half slave and half free, but the dissolution of the Union was unthinkable. Thus, slavery had either to be abolished or nationalized. The founders had set in motion a program over which he and his opponents contested. At the same time,

Lincoln had to discredit any attempts by his opponents to claim the legacy. The founders had to have intended ultimate abolition. To that end, Lincoln turns the events surrounding the *Dred Scott* decision into a proslavery plot authored by Presidents Franklin Pierce and James Buchanan, Justice Roger Taney and Senator Stephen Douglas. But he cleverly makes the conspirators architects rather than authors, and their conspiracy is the framing of an *alternative* house:

> We cannot absolutely *know* that all these exact adaptations are the result of preconcert. But when we see a lot of framed timbers, different portions of which we know have been gotten out at different times and places and by different workmen—Stephen, Franklin, Roger and James, for instance—and we see these timbers joined together, and see they exactly make the frame of a house or a mill, all the tenons and mortises exactly fitting, and all the lengths and proportions of the different pieces exactly adapted to their respective places, and not a piece too many or too few—not omitting even scaffolding—or, if a single piece be lacking, we can see the place in the frame exactly fitted and prepared to yet bring such piece in—in *such* a case, we find it impossible not to *believe* that Stephen and Franklin and Roger and James all understood one another from the beginning, and all worked upon a common *plan* or *draft* drawn up before the first lick was struck. (*AL*, 2:465–66)

Where Lincoln wants to attend to the house divided—to keep up the national edifice—the conspirators are constructing one anew. The repetition of "frame" could not fail to alert his listeners to the constitutional activity of the conspirators, since it is the verb most commonly associated with the authorship of that document: its drafters are typically referred to as "framers." Lincoln demonizes his political opponents by virtue of their inherently un-American activity of opposing We the People. Where Washington made his "fellow-citizens" responsible for the general upkeep of their "edifice," Lincoln's opponents destroy the (joint) inheritance by building their own alternative house. The Republicans are not the newcomers; rather, they safeguard a legacy threatened by the Democrats. Douglas fares especially badly in the speech. The Little Giant advocated popular sovereignty as the clearest expression of individual liberty. Lincoln's binarism turns Douglas's popular sovereignty into an effort to nationalize slavery only months after Douglas had opposed Kansas's proslavery Lecompton Constitution on the grounds that it did not represent the will of the people (voters) of Kansas.[63]

Lincoln's strategy is to represent himself as within a narrative already written, in contrast with the alternative framers—or plotters. Unlike them, he favors "the course of ultimate extinction" of slavery, which, like "the course of human events," brooks no natural opposition. It is as inevitable as the Union itself. In opposing this course, the unnatural framers oppose that Union. The ominousness and the inevitability combine to make those false framers at once menacing and ineffectual. And the conspiracy diverts the attention of the audience away from the contested power of the federal government.

Douglas proved himself a worthy foe in his response to Lincoln's charges. Resisting his opponent's efforts to draw him into a discussion of slavery, Douglas kept the issue of popular sovereignty before his audience as the source of the candidates' disagreement. The framers' intent, he argued, was to take the "separate and distinct interests" of each section into account rather than to make them subject to the same laws.[64] "Uniformity is the parent of despotism the world over," he told a Chicago audience in July 1858, "not only in politics, but in religion." Lincoln's controversial phrase about the Union's durability occasioned the accusation that the Republican nominee had asserted, "as a fundamental principle of this government, that there must be uniformity in the local laws and dominant institutions of each of all the states in the Union" and had advocated "boldly and clearly a war of sections" (*LDD*, 29). According to Douglas, Lincoln mandated "one consolidated empire," while Douglas supported "diversity, dissimilarity, variety in all our local and dominant institutions" (*LDD*, 18, 20).

The incumbent pointedly opposes racial equality in this speech. Favoring the preservation of "not only the purity of the blood, but the purity of the government from any mixture or amalgamation with inferior races," Douglas goes south of the United States border to show the "degeneration, demoralization, and degradation below the capacity for self-government" in Central and South America. His language vivifies the body politic, precisely the metaphor replaced by Lincoln with "the house divided," as it insists on "a people composed of European descendants" (*LDD*, 23).

Each candidate amplified an anxious rhetoric to identify the other with a threat to the framers' Union. Where Douglas summoned the integrity of the body and the nation to that end, Lincoln, in a speech delivered on the following night, again called forth the tenuousness of a Union all too susceptible to Douglas's challenge. By 1858, Lincoln's Union, as we have seen, was definitely not a body politic. The Republican candidate carefully distinguished the ties of kinship from the bonds of Union in a meditation on the July Fourth ritual, worth quoting at length:

> We hold this annual celebration to remind ourselves of all the good done in this process of time, of how it was done and who did it, and how we are historically connected with it; and we go from these meetings in better humor with ourselves—we feel more attached the one to the other, and more firmly bound to the country we inhabit. In every way we are better men in the age, and race, and country in which we live, for these celebrations. But after we have done all this we have not yet reached the whole. There is something else connected with it. We have besides these men—descended by blood from our ancestors—among us perhaps half our people who are not descendants at all of these men, they are men who have come from Europe—German, Irish, French and Scandinavian—men that have come from Europe themselves, or whose ancestors have come hither and settled here, finding themselves our equals in all things. If they look back through this history to trace their connection with those days by blood, they find they have none, they cannot carry themselves back into that glorious epoch and make themselves feel that they are part of us, but when they look through that old Declaration of Independence, they find that those old men say that "We hold these truths to be self-evident, that all men are created equal," and then they feel that that moral sentiment taught in that day evidences their relation to those men, that it is the father of all moral principle in them, and that they have a right to claim it as though they were blood of the blood, and flesh of the flesh, of the men who wrote that Declaration, and so they are. That is the electric cord in that Declaration that links the hearts of patriotic and liberty loving men together. (*AL*, 2:499–500)

When he replaces "blood ties" with an "electric cord" of shared political beliefs, Lincoln confounds Douglas's amalgamation imagery and charges of sectionalism, evoking the communications and transportation initiatives connecting the regions of the Union. Beneath the tenuousness of this collective identity and the threat of its impending decomposition lurks the fate of an enslaved man, evoked to emblematize the fate of any subject not attached to the electric cord: "If one man says it does not mean a negro, why may not another say it does not mean some other man?" (*AL*, 2:500). Lincoln misrepresents his opponent, returning to the much earlier statement that "the people" of the Declaration "were equal to the people of England" in order to accuse Douglas of excluding all non-Anglo-

Americans from the collective identity (*AL*, 2:500). The judge is depicted as wanting to restrict, and thus deconstruct, the Union. One can imagine with what effectiveness Lincoln turned to his audience to say: "According to [Douglas's] construction [of the Declaration], you Germans are not connected with it" (*AL*, 2:500). Descendants of Swedes, Irish, or any of the other immigrant groups could not miss their own implication.

And yet Lincoln's pronouns show evidence at least of confusion, if not of the exclusionism of which he accuses Douglas. The threat of decomposition haunts his reconstructed genealogy as it resurfaces in his shifting "we." The "*we*" who are "descended by blood from our ancestors" face off against the "*they* . . . who have come from Europe." Despite the claims for unity, the pronoun "our" changes as a referent, distinguishing between descendants of the original colonists and more recent immigrants: the "our" in "our people" ("among us perhaps half our people . . . are not descendants of" the founders) is not equivalent to the "our" in "our equals" ("finding *them*selves *our* equals in all things"). Lincoln's rhetoric often comes dangerously close to its own undoing, but his genius inheres in his ability to channel those risks into rhetorical power.

Although such pronominal inconsistencies probably reflect confusion, Lincoln also makes good use of an uncertain "we." His return to the Declaration rather than the Constitution permitted him more easily to exclude proponents of slavery (and, by implication, secession) from "American" identity. The "we" who inherited the Declaration's legacy are the "we" who, later in the speech, "could not get our Constitution unless we *permitted* . . . slavery" (*AL*, 2:501; emphasis added). The proslavery founding fathers are erased from history as the Constitution becomes the legacy of antislavery Unionists. Thus Lincoln forcefully and self-consciously reconstitutes We the People in accordance with his fervently consolidationist political goals. His "we" ranges from those "descended by blood" from the founding fathers to the immigrants connected by "the electric cord"; "it does not stop with the negro," but it pointedly excludes proponents of slavery (*AL*, 2:500).

In Lincoln's narrative of the Union, Douglas emerges as a subversive who "promises to rub out the sentiment of liberty in the country, and to transform this Government into a government of some other form." His arguments "that the inferior race [sic] are to be treated with as much allowance as they are capable of enjoying; that as much is to be done for them as their condition will allow," cast Douglas as King George to Lincoln's Jefferson. And in the person of the Little Giant, Lincoln summons the anxious rhetoric of the Declaration, the threat of becoming political slaves: "What are these arguments? They are the arguments that kings have made for enslaving the people in all ages of the world. You will find that all the arguments in favor of king-craft were of this class; they always bestrode the necks of the people, not that they wanted to do it, but because the people were better off for being ridden" (*AL*, 2:500). Not content to espouse only the principles of Jeffersonian liberty, Lincoln borrowed this image from the last letter written by the third president. On June 24, 1826, Jefferson wrote to decline Roger C. Weightman's invitation to join the surviving signatories of the Declaration for a July Fourth celebration in Washington. He regretted that ill health would prevent his attendance but expressed his satisfaction that "the general spread of the light of science had already laid open to every view the palpable truth, that the mass of mankind has not been born with saddles on their backs, nor a favored few booted and spurred, ready to ride them legitimately."[65] A conventional revolutionary rhetoric of enslavement links monarchy metaphorically to slavery.

But in a sleight of hand no less impressive than Lincoln's, Jefferson had once before made that connection. In an excised passage of the Declaration, the drafter of the original document had charged King George III with "wag[ing] cruel war against human nature itself, violating it's [*sic*] most sacred rights of life and liberty in the persons of a distant people who never offended him, captivating & carrying them into slavery in another hemisphere, or to incur miserable death in their transportation thither" (TJ, 22). Lincoln's audience may well have been familiar with this passage, since Jefferson had included the original document, with the congress's emendations, in his published *Autobiography*.[66] Onto the king, Jefferson had placed responsibility for all the dangers besetting the colonies: for encouraging the hostility of "the merciless Indian savages," for inciting "treasonable insurrections of our fellow-citizens, with the allurements of forfeiture & confiscation of our property," and for inspiring slave rebellion ("exciting those very people to rise in arms among us, and to purchase that liberty of which he has deprived them, by murdering the people on whom he also obtruded them" [TJ, 21–22]). The excised passages disclose a Jefferson in *principle* against the peculiar institution, and indeed he consistently advocated gradual emancipation policies. But his reasoning in the excised passages manifests confusion. As Garry Wills has pointed out, Jefferson charged the king with enslavement in a "tor-tuous preamble" that covers up "the real onus of the charge [which] is that the King has been freeing slaves to fight against their American owners" (*IA*, 72). Slavery confounds the logic of Jefferson's argument as it challenges the principle that justifies the experiment of Union. It must, there-fore, be excised from the Union, Lincoln suggests, as it was from the document. The excised passages of the Declaration hover to evoke the danger of compromise and the risk of the Union's disintegration in a Lincolnian narrative that ostensibly advocates the former and disavows the latter.

The possibility of a slave uprising, haunting emblem of a guilty nation's collective fantasy, is accordingly central in that narrative. In September 1858, an Edwardsville, Illinois audience heard Lincoln summon that threat:

> when . . . you have succeeded [by "the logical consequences of the Dred Scott decision"] in dehumanizing the negro; when you have put him down, and made it forever impossible for him to be but as the beasts of the field; when you have extinguished his soul, and placed him where the ray of hope is blown out in darkness like that which broods over the spirits of the damned; are you quite sure the demon which you have roused *will not turn and rend you?* . . . Familiarize yourselves with the chains of bondage, and you are preparing your own limbs to wear them. Accustomed to trample on the rights of those around you, you have lost the genius of your own independence, and become the fit subjects of the first cunning tyrant who rises. And let me tell you, all these things are prepared for you with the logic of history, if the elections shall promise that the next Dred Scott decision and all future decisions will be quietly acquiesced in by the people. (*AL*, 3:95–96)

Oppression creates the threat of an uprising. That had been established "with the logic of history." But that threat paled before the metaphysical threat to liberty posed by the Union's own peculiar institution. Sermon-esque, this speech envisions the punishments that await the unfaithful, notably the loss of liberty. Compromise with proslavery interests seemed increasingly untenable to Republicans, and Lincoln's language became increasingly vivid and dramatic. By 1858, by mere acquiescence in the institution of slavery, the free subjects of an ideology of liberal selfhood risked becoming the captive subjects of a cunning tyrant. Keeping the vivid image of the literally enslaved always in mind, Lincoln implicitly asks: What indeed keeps a tyrant, no less than a government, from making white men slaves?

Lincoln quoted a letter from Henry Clay, written in 1849, in this speech to demonstrate that the Great Compromiser shared that sentiment. Clay's response to those who would sanction slavery based on the " 'alleged intellectual inferiority of the black race. . . . proves that among the white races of the world any one might properly be enslaved by any other which had made greater advances in civilization. And, if this rule applies to nations there is no reason why it should not apply to individuals; and it might easily be proved that the wisest man in the world could rightfully reduce all other men and women to bondage' " (*AL*, 2:93).[67] Neither Clay nor Lincoln doubted the "advances in civilization" with which, for example, Chief Justice Roger Taney justified Indian Removal and slavery in the *Dred Scott* case. And Clay, like Lincoln, politically favored colonization in Africa or Latin America of the descendants of Africans living in the United States, an analogue rather than contrast to Indian Removal.[68] Yet this passage offers a Clay perhaps more comfortable in the role of abolitionist than with the title Great Compromiser. Lincoln's depiction is less inaccurate than selective, evidence of his seeking ever harder to establish himself as the heir apparent to the founders and their most distinguished successors as he tried alternately to counter and capitalize on mounting perceptions of his radicalism. Indeed Lincoln and Douglas contended specifically for the mantle of the Great Compromiser throughout their campaigns, even directly challenging each other's right to the benediction of "our old leader Henry Clay." Even more important to the strategy of Lincoln's national narrative, however, were those prominent Virginians, Washington and Jefferson.

The monument of Mount Rushmore attests to the status Lincoln sought through his use of those political forefathers—and to his success in eventually achieving it. But their national stature only partly explains the Illinois politician's use of the southern statesmen. Lincoln's political ambitions and personal convictions made a direct appeal to the South impossible. An appeal through its most prominent citizens—safely dead—was certainly expedient. Jefferson's opposition to the precepts of consolidationism, for example, need not arise. Even more astutely, Lincoln identified with those two slaveholders who, in speech and in gesture, renounced the institution of slavery and expressed their wish for its passing. Thus Lincoln indirectly addressed the appeal made by proslavery advocates among his contemporaries to the slave-owning founders. More subtly, however, he deliberately chose ambiguously antislavery predecessors.

Ambiguity bordering on contradiction is the most salient feature of Lincoln's narrative. Its ambiguity responds to a prominent characteristic of antebellum political culture: the conflict between being at once good, obedient sons and worthy competitors of heroic fathers. As George Forgie demonstrates, Lincoln was an especially representative "son," and Forgie sees the Civil War as the inevitable outcome of the need of this "post-heroic generation" to prove their heroism by safeguarding the legacy of the fathers.[69] Certainly Lincoln's narrative shows evidence of that conflict—in particular, the ambiguity of antislavery slaveholders left space for a heroic act of interpretation: Lincoln the hero could actively construct a narrative in which Lincoln the dutiful son passively inherited an intact Union.

The appeal of Lincoln's narrative lay in the opportunity it offered his audience simultaneously to be creative and to re-present their creativity as dutiful obedience. I have represented Lincoln's turning to the Declaration rather than the Constitution as an effort to bypass the legal ambiguities of the compromise. And so it did. But the Declaration has ambiguities of its own. It celebrates an event that was at once a severing and a joining. The Declaration converted kinship ties with England into "political bands" that could be "dissolved." Yet, the Declaration had also to point the way to an ongoing association—an ideological rather than a biological connection—among the "one people" who were renouncing their former ties. The principle of liberty might seem beyond question, but the Declaration did not resolve whether that equality was more effectively preserved through aggregation or separation—the making or breaking of political bands. These political bands, after all, were made to be dissolved.

Lincoln depicted the formation of those bands as an intrinsically interpretive and even textual act. Citing Proverbs, he calls "the assertion of that *principle,* at *that time.* . . . *the* word, '*fitly spoken*' which has proved an 'apple of gold' to us. The *Union,* and the *Constitution,* are the *picture* of *silver,* subsequently framed around it [and] . . . made, not to *conceal,* or *destroy* the apple; but to *adorn,* and *preserve* it" (*AL,* 4:169).[70] The italicized words in the first sentence stress the timing and context—the presentation—of the Declaration. The addition of the word "framed" nicely links the Biblical image of a picture to the Constitution. The framers were engaged in presentational, contextual, and interpretive acts, the same kind of activity in which Lincoln is himself engaged. If the political bands were themselves textual, so must be their perpetuation.

Nowhere did Lincoln spell out the textual obligations of Americans more explicitly than in his celebrated "Address Delivered at the Dedication of the Cemetery at Gettysburg." And nowhere were words more needed. Created to bury the rotting corpses of an especially bloody battle, the cemetery built on the battlefield offered a potentially important symbol of transformation. The famous orator Edward Everett, not Lincoln, was invited to perform the dedicatory oration; yet it is Lincoln's brief three paragraphs that made history at Gettysburg. "The power of words," notes Garry Wills, "has rarely been given a more compelling demonstration" (LG, 20). In substance, the speech is sparse. Lincoln observes, conventionally, that the soldiers who fought the battle had done more to consecrate the ground than the participants in the ritual could possibly do. He contrasts saying and doing in the oft-quoted line: "The world will little note, nor long remember what we say here, but it can never forget what they did here" (AL, 7:23).[71] The inadequacy of words comes through the admission that "in a larger sense, we can not dedicate—we can not consecrate—we can not hallow—this ground" (AL, 7:23). The emphatic repetition of the same concept with different words shows only that no word, no matter how it is said, is sufficient to describe what transpired on the battlefield. And Lincoln, of course, enjoins his audience to "take increased devotion to that cause for which [the dead soldiers] gave the last full measure of devotion" (AL, 7:23). The real drama of the Gettysburg Address is not in the explicit message of the speech, not in the meaning of the words, but in their performance.

When Lincoln calls for a "new birth of freedom" at the end of the speech, he constructs an analogy between the founders and the soldiers, and between the audience and the nation itself (AL, 7:23). The nation was "brought forth" by the founders in an opening birth metaphor that insists on a consolidationist Union: "Four score and seven years ago our fathers brought forth on this continent, a new nation, conceived in Liberty, and dedicated to the proposition that all men are created equal. Now we are engaged in a great civil war, testing whether that nation, or any nation so conceived and so dedicated, can long endure" (AL, 7:23). The "nation" began with the Declaration and, as a nation, expressed the intention of the fathers. The war is a "civil war" rather than a "revolution" or even "rebellion." Yet the *new* birth urged by Lincoln upon his audience is neither just a safeguarding nor even a *re*birth. Gettysburg almost seems to promise a break from the fathers, especially when the audience is encouraged "to be dedicated . . . to the unfinished work which they who fought here have thus far so nobly advanced" (*AL,* 7:23). Of course Lincoln means the upkeep of the nation, the perpetuating of the Union. But the soldiers have replaced the fathers in imparting this legacy—the "new birth of freedom." Most immediately, however, the soldiers have created a battlefield by fighting and dying in a particular place, and the task at hand is the dedication of a cemetery. As the continent bore a nation, so must this land give birth anew. The "unfinished work" seems most immediately to be the transformation of the battlefield into a symbol. Without words to supply meaning, the battlefield is just a place where men fought and died. Words turn it into a symbol, and when Lincoln called the dedication "altogether fitting and proper" (*AL,* 7:23), he may have had the "word fitly spoken" of Proverbs 25:11 in mind.[72]

At Gettysburg, the word fitly spoken is "dedicate." The nation is *dedicated* to a proposition. The audience has come to *dedicate* a cemetery, which it cannot successfully do, but the audience can be *dedicated* to the soldiers' unfinished work and "to the great task remaining before us": the new birth of freedom (*AL,* 7:23). The people cannot dedicate the ground (a transitive verb), but they can dedicate themselves (an intransitive verb) and be, like the nation itself, dedicated to a proposition. In effect, Lincoln urges his audience to become symbols of the nation—before America, Americans. The fathers declared their independence from England; Lincoln, offering an internalized nation, declares a partial independence from the fathers. They had had to turn a treaty, which applied the law, into a constitution, which embodied as it theorized that law. At Gettysburg, each individual "American" was obliged to constitute the nation-state, which had now become a state of mind.

Lincoln used the metaphysical self rather than the body as the symbol of his Union, which allowed him more convincingly to link the disintegration of the Union to the disappearance of that self. The "great task" of dedication for which Lincoln called anticipated that disappearance by making the ultimate act of self-assertion a self-surrender, a *dedication* of the self. In turn, the Union sanctified each self. If the wrong kind of Union might lead to despotism, and to the self's enslavement, the disintegration of the Union was even more metaphysically ominous. For founding fathers such as Washington and Jefferson, the law marked the boundary between liberty and monarchy. By Lincoln's time, however, anarchy had become the more immediate threat. Lincoln used the possibility of anarchy (posed, he argued, by secessionists) to emphasize the risk to Union and thereby to the conceptual identity of "the people"—and of people.

Delivered almost exactly between Lincoln's two inaugural addresses in March 1861 and 1865, the Gettysburg Address put into play the symbolic strategy that had added latent force to the First Inaugural Address and is most fully and exquisitely executed in the Second. The first Republican president joined the threat of anarchy to a rhetoric of self-surrender in a last hopeful Union-saving measure. Preceding the address at Gettysburg by more than two and one-half years, the First Inaugural Address shows a Lincoln still working to avoid conflict and still searching for the most dramatic symbol of Union. The president-elect had drafted the speech in January, a month before a congress representing seven southern states met in Alabama to form the Confederate States of America, and he delivered it a month before the attack on Fort Sumter that initiated violent conflict.

The speech works alternately through reassurance and ominous innuendo, self-effacement and self-assertion. Promising to uphold the Constitution, Lincoln also speaks to the wisdom of obeying the law and safeguarding the Union. A map replaces the divided house as Lincoln insists that the survival and prosperity of the parts of the Union are contingent upon the whole. "Perpetuity is implied, if not expressed, in the fundamental law of all national governments," and, conversely, "the central idea of secession, is the essence of anarchy" (AL, 4:264, 268). The "great body of the people" that Lincoln invokes in the First Inaugural Address is no longer the inseparable "body politic," but a group that must obey the law precisely because of the possibility (and consequences) of its divisibility (AL, 4:269). The Union, the outgrowth of a permanent geographical condition, ensures the states' survival as separate entities:

Physically speaking, we cannot separate. We cannot remove our respective sections from each other, nor build an impassable wall between them. A husband and wife may be divorced, and go out of the presence, and beyond the reach of each other; but the different parts of our country cannot do this. They cannot but remain face to face; and intercourse, either amicable or hostile, must continue between them. Is it possible, then, to make that intercourse more advantageous or more satisfactory, *after* separation than *before?* Can aliens make treaties easier than friends can make laws? Can treaties be more faithfully enforced between aliens than laws can among friends? (*AL*, 4:269)

The reality of secession and the power of anti-amalgamation sentiment prompt Lincoln to reject the marriage contract as an emblem of the bond of Union. The marriage contract grows out of a choice; the contract of Union, although also a choice, emerges from necessity: the inevitability of "broils and wars" and the impending threat of "overgrown military establishments" cautioned against by Washington in his Farewell Address and demonstrated, Lincoln implies, by nineteenth-century Europe. Lincoln pushes past the contested site of the law and instead evokes the map of the Union, the geographical reality of shared boundaries. Here he summons the iconic geographical representation of "these United States" employed by both the Articles of Confederation and the Constitution, in which the list of ratifying states moves down the Atlantic seaboard in a southerly direction from Maine: a *geography* of inevitability.[73]

In the common sense and goodwill of the people, Lincoln rests one defense of the Union. The "political bands" of the Declaration had become the "bonds of affection" with which the speech concludes (*AL*, 4:271). But current events could not have failed to make those affective ties suspect. Just exactly what constituted those bonds was in question, and to many on both sides they evoked more of bondage than of bonding. To that uneasiness, Lincoln responded with his usual rhetorical flair. The president's appeal to the law makes the Constitution a more fitting pretext for this speech than the Declaration, and "the history of the Union itself" with which he confirms the perpetuity of the Union begins with a treaty, the Articles of Association of 1774 (*AL*, 4:265). The colonies' aggregation thus historically precedes their separation from England. With "the logic of history," the Constitution is the outgrowth and perfection of that aggregation and to it, the president subordinates himself. That subordination is communicated through the rhetorical and grammatical manipulations of which Lincoln was master. Passive constructions, third-person pronouns, and quotations from the Constitution, Lincoln's campaign speeches, and the Republican Party Platform create the sense of a performer more than an enactor, an executor more than an executive.

His rhetoric subordinates the subject—himself—to national destiny: "In compliance with a custom as old as the government itself, I appear before you to address you briefly, and to take, in your presence, the oath prescribed by the Constitution of the United States, to be taken by the President 'before he enters on the execution of his office'" (*AL*, 4:262). The subject assumes representative dimensions and speaks not as "himself" but for the Constitution; Lincoln attempts to reassure both the secessionists and his allies that he will act not as an individual or even Republican self, but will uphold the Constitution: "Apprehension seems to exist among the people of the Southern States, that by the accession of a Republican Administration, their property, and their peace, and personal security, are to be endangered. . . . [A]ll the protection which, consistently with the Constitution and the laws, can be given, will be cheerfully given to all the States when lawfully demanded, for whatever cause—as cheerfully to one section, as to another" (*AL*, 4:262–63). Even the terms of his reassurance—"It ["reassurance to the contrary"] is found in nearly all the published speeches of him who now addresses you" (*AL*, 4:262)—rhetorically erase subjectivity; passive voice and third person self-reference are compounded by the grammatical slippage that replaces subject ("he") with object ("him"), as Lincoln projects a public persona ("published speeches") who will entirely, and appropriately, efface himself. Lincoln insists on his simple caretaking role: "the executive['s] . . . duty is to administer the present government, as it came to his hands, and to transmit it, unimpaired by him, to his successor" (*AL*, 4:270).

Not only Lincoln, but all "the people" are bound by the Constitution in precisely the ways that he articulates more fully in the Gettysburg Address. Has "any right, plainly written in the Constitution, . . . been denied?" Lincoln asks. And he answers, "I think not. Happily the human mind is so constituted, that no party can reach to the audacity of doing this" (*AL*, 4:267). With the verb *constituted*, Lincoln suggests that human minds—individuals—as well as "the people" have been formed by the Constitution. No one is audacious enough to challenge the ideology that informs his or her consciousness, he suggests. Rather, the Constitution is part of each individual's fabric of being. The passive construction of "the human mind is so constituted" implies that the Constitution is grounded in universal human truths, but it could also suggest that the Constitution shapes *social* being. The Constitution is inseparable from identity.

The two arguments of the address, that the Union must be upheld by the initiative of individuals and that the Union is inevitably upheld by individuals whose essence is entwined with it, come together in the gorgeous last sentence of the address: "The mystic chords of memory, stretching from every battle-field, and patriot grave, to every living heart and hearthstone, all over this broad land, will yet swell the chorus of the Union, when again touched, as surely they will be, by the better angels of our nature" (*AL*, 4:271). Lincoln had originally concluded the speech with "the guardian angel of the nation" rather than "the better angels of our nature," and the change is significant. The people rather than a higher authority must save the Union. But "better angels" implies internalized forces, within and yet not within. And the image equivocates, as does the phrase "surely they will be," about whether Union-saving measures call for conscious action or are inevitable. By Gettysburg, the dedication of the self would require an *act* of self-surrender, a gesture enacted in the rhetoric of the Second Inaugural Address.

By March 1865 when Lincoln delivered the Second Inaugural Address, reconstruction of the nation had replaced impending war as the major problem facing the nation. The Union was not out of danger just because the Unionists had won the war. Wounds had to be healed and the exact nature of the Union determined before "the Union" could become a nation. Lincoln still had a vision to realize, *a* Union that had to be equated with *the* Union. Nothing could better deflect attention from the particularity of his vision than the fragility of the Union, which called, therefore, for rallying rather than questioning. The triumph of his Republican ideology is evident in Lincoln's focus on each individual's personal stake in the Union in the Second Inaugural Address. But he tempers the triumph with an anxious uncertainty when he ends the first paragraph of the address with an effaced subject and an uncertain future for the Union:

> At this second appearing to take the oath of the presidential office, there is less occasion for an extended address than there was at the first. Then a statement, somewhat in detail, of a course to be pursued, seemed fitting and proper. Now, at the expiration of four years, during which public declarations have been constantly called forth on every point and phase of the great contest which still absorbs the attention, and engrosses the energies of the nation, little that is new could be presented. The progress of our arms, upon which all else chiefly depends, is as well known to the public as to myself; and it is, I trust, reasonably satisfactory and encouraging to all. With high hope for the future, no prediction in regard to it is ventured. (*AL*, 8:332)

In the last sentence, dangling modifier and passive voice defer subjectivity as Lincoln refuses to predict the fate of the Union. The two seem somehow connected, as though the "I" cannot exist without the certainty of a reconstructed Union. The first person—singular or plural—appears only once in this excessively passive passage, embedded within a clause: "I trust." In the wake of a crisis concerning the collective identity, the subject, which certainly cannot act, can barely even exist—can only "trust." The threat of nonexistence lingers ominously in the rhetoric. In contrast with the "fitting and proper" details of the First Inaugural Address (and the words of Gettysburg), no word fitly spoken will adequately serve this occasion. No Declaration of Independence, that is, but a Declaration of Dependence, will complete the task of unification. And the self hangs (rhetorically) in the balance.

The deferred subject of this passage also begged a central question of the conflict: whom would We the People include, and, more pointedly, who would speak in their (its?) name? Would the United States itself be a plural or singular subject? Lincoln's rhetoric articulates his stand: the American subject cannot exist without the Union, in the name of which social existence is held in trust. With the contingency of that subject, he promoted a personal investment in the fate of the Union, now unobstructedly on the way to nationhood, as the triumph of individual rights gave way to the heroism of self-subordination. But Lincoln never got the chance to turn to the task of reconstructing a more inclusive Union.

In particular, Lincoln's narrative displaced but did not resolve the question of the positioning of black subjects within We the People. An insistently domestic rhetoric had resurfaced with the war. In his annual message to Congress on December 1, 1862, Lincoln had proclaimed that the "portion of the earth's surface which is owned and inhabited by the people of the United States, is well adapted to be the home of one national family" (*AL*, 5:527). There is no "line . . . suitable for a national boundary," and "reunion" is inevitable (*AL*, 5:528, 529). To promote that family reunion in the Second Inaugural Address, Lincoln subordinates all other conflicts to slavery, an "interest" which "all knew [to be] . . . , somehow, the cause of the war" (*AL*, 8:332). With slavery abolished, he suggests, all cause of conflict has ceased and the nation can again unite, literally, as an adopted family, "car[ing] for him who shall have borne the battle, and for his widow, and his orphan" (*AL*, 8:333). But Frederick Douglass significantly complicated that image when he spoke at the dedication of the Freedmen's Monument, which was erected by descendants of Africans in 1876 to commemorate the Great Emancipator. Calling Lincoln "the white man's President," Douglass distinguishes between the white Americans who "are the children of Abraham Lincoln" and the black Americans who "are at best only his step-children, children by adoption, children by force of circumstances and necessity."[74]

Lincoln's familial metaphor only expressed, and even aggravated, the tensions of reconstruction. The man who, however motivated by political expediency, had in 1854 denied the political and social equality of blacks and whites (AL, 2:255–56) and in 1858 had assured his audience that "as God made us separate, we can leave one another alone. . . . There are white men enough to marry all the white women, and enough black men to marry all the black women, and in God's name let them be so married" (AL, 2:498), would hardly be unambivalently prepared, in 1864, to legitimate mulatto heirs to the house. On the other hand, the separate co-existence of races that he advocated would merely replace the Mason-Dixon line with a color line. Lincoln did not cease advocating removal as a solution even after the colonization of American descendants of Africans in Liberia, South and Central America, and Haiti had all proved untenable.

As Lincoln had omitted free blacks from his head count of Maine's male population when tallying representation in his Repeal speech, so he glossed over the black presence in his reconstructed American family. Lincoln's narrative depended on uncanny black subjects—enslaved persons and free descendants of Africans—to emblematize the fate of any subject without a Union that guaranteed liberty for all its subjects. He used black subjects, in other words, to emblematize the contingency of social existence on his nation. His narrative demanded the acquiescence of subjects, black and white, in the terms of his narrative and their disappearance without those terms. But Lincoln never fully worked out an equal place for black subjects within a reconstructed narrative. His terms were designed for and suited to white subjects. For black subjects, that meant acquiescing in a legislated inequality within that narrative. The uncanniness of black subjects used by Lincoln, of human beings not fully included in the terms of personhood, also troubled his own narrative. As slavery compromised the liberty of all of the subjects in Lincoln's narrative, the representational constraints on black subjects in that very narrative manifested its prescriptedness: the terms of personhood legislated by Lincoln. Biographer Stephen B. Oates shows a Lincoln eagerly soliciting Frederick Douglass's opinion of his Second Inaugural Address.[75] Well might the president have done so; the two antebellum narratives of that most prominent spokesperson of the mid-nineteenth century offered important insight into the strategies and limitations of Lincoln's national narrative.

The Authorship of Frederick Douglass, an American Slave

Frederick Douglass was a logical choice for orator at the unveiling of the monument financed entirely by liberated slaves. He had been a surreptitious teacher of fellow slaves and, on coming North, had quickly become an ex officio preacher for the congregation of an African Methodist Episcopal church in New Bedford, Massachusetts.[76] That experience served him well first in his work with the Garrisonians and later, after his dissent, in his crusades for equality and in support of a more consolidationist Union, one more in concert with, although not identical to, Lincoln's vision. Despite his stringent criticisms of the sixteenth president, Douglass professed strong affection for him. An ambivalence more pronounced than, but nonetheless reminiscent of, Lincoln's own depiction of the founders characterizes the portrait of Lincoln drawn by Douglass at the unveiling of the Freedmen's Monument on Good Friday, eleven years to the day following the assassination. Douglass criticizes a Lincoln to whom "the Union was more . . . than our freedom or our future," but commemorates the same man under whose "wise and beneficent rule we saw ourselves gradually lifted from the depths of slavery to the heights of liberty and manhood" (*FDP*, 4:434). An astute political strategist, Douglass recognized the power of Lincoln as a symbol and, even more, the power of Lincoln's narrative.

Douglass developed his own narrative of Union during his eventful early career. As a protégé of the celebrated abolitionist William Lloyd Garrison, he had condemned slavery as an expression of the intrinsic corruption of the Union and the founding documents. But by the early 1850s, he had begun to articulate a nationalist narrative in which he identified as an *American* and considered himself already included among We the People. The institution of slavery, in this version, corrupted the

Union and defamed its most sacrosanct principles expressed in its founding texts. The speech at the Freedmen's monument shows a Douglass characteristically critical of the unequal status accorded descendants of Africans in Lincoln's narrative but supportive of the fundamental vision of the Union so central to that narrative.

Douglass's conversion from Garrisonian to political abolition resulted in a dramatic rewriting of his account of his experiences as a slave. He would revise this account four times before his death in 1895, but a comparison between the first two, both written in the antebellum period, most clearly demonstrates the relevance of formal literary strategies to his political concerns. Textual disjunctions in the 1845 *Narrative of the Life of Frederick Douglass, an American Slave,* for example, show a narrator compelled to tell a story different from the story he wishes to tell.[77] Through disruptions of the narrative, Frederick Bailey surfaces as the embodiment of what Douglass must repress in his effort to represent himself as an American, more than a decade prior to the *Dred Scott* decision. A more nationalist Douglass reshapes that portrait of an ill-fitting self into the story of a more comfortably and recognizably American self in the 1855 *My Bondage and My Freedom.* The revised account does away with the authorizing prefatory documents by prominent white sponsors and the stock language of heroism of the *Narrative,* some of the more noteworthy conventions of the slave narrative.[78] Douglass instead authoritatively assumes the status of "representative American" in line to inherit the legacy, and intrinsic heroism, of the founding fathers. Yet that legacy comes at great cost to Douglass and to his story. Douglass's new status still imposes constraints on the story he can tell, and those constraints correspond to and express conventions of personhood in which he remains unequally and thus inadequately represented. Manhood and, less explicitly but no less forcefully, whiteness are interlocking terms of the Americanness that Douglass inherits from the fathers ("the heights of liberty and *manhood*" to which he claims Lincoln had lifted the slave). While he will not accept an unequal status overtly assigned to descendants of Africans, he necessarily inherits a concept of personhood marked by race and gender as by nation.

Much of the contemporary debate about Douglass's narratives turns on whether the reader believes that Douglass's embrace of an American identity in *My Bondage and My Freedom* compromises or better enables his account of his experiences as a slave. Houston Baker points to the absence of a conventional vocabulary of individuated black selfhood in the mid-nineteenth century to offer a Douglass trapped into fashioning himself publicly in the terms of white selfhood. Baker summons the perplexing relationship between literacy and authenticity when he sees the narrator's ability to convey the "lived (as opposed to represented) slave experience" as contingent "upon the keenness of the narrator's skill in confronting both the freedom and the limitations resulting from his literacy in Prospero's tongue."[79] Douglass, as Baker sees him, moved increasingly away from authenticity as he assumed a more public role. But the political strategy that motivated *My Bondage and My Freedom* interests critics such as William L. Andrews, Eric J. Sundquist, and biographer William S. McFeely, all of whom see the 1855 text as a better book.[80] Douglass's more confident authorship, they argue, tells a freer story than the more obviously prescripted *Narrative*. And Sundquist, who contends that "*My Bondage and My Freedom* tells us far more about Douglass as a slave, and about slave culture generally, than does the *Narrative*," is troubled by claims that Douglass was "enslaved to the hypocritical discourse of American equality." The view that the more mature Douglass was "incarcerated" by an appropriative liberalism is, to Sundquist, a "paranoid reading . . . [that] belittles both his intelligence and his craft" (ES, 89–90).

I am not arguing for either of Douglass's accounts as a more effective critique or more accomplished work than the other. Rather, I am concerned with how each work in its way represents an author engaged with the terms of his authorship and with how the insights into the conventions of authorship correspond to insights into the conventionality of personhood and the terms of his oppression in the United States. Together, the two narratives seem to chart Douglass's movement from a matrilineal inheritance of enslavement (the condition of the child follows the mother) to a patrilineal (and patriarchal) inheritance of freedom. But even the revised account cannot completely repress Douglass's discomfort with the new inheritance, a discomfort expressed by the unsettling presence of Frederick Bailey. The *Narrative* itself announces that presence in *My Bondage and My Freedom,* both in evident revisions that Douglass makes in the later work and in some passages from the earlier work that he marks with block quotations. Evidence of a suppressed text surfaces both in references to the *Narrative* and in other allusions to an untold story of Frederick Bailey, a descendant of Africans. The *Narrative* had sold well, and Douglass was a prominent public figure whose story was well known. In *My Bondage and My Freedom,* he was writing against—and within—a literary narrative written by himself as well as a cultural narrative. In the later work, Douglass uses the tension between his own narratives to represent the struggle with authorizing conventions through which he expressed and analyzed his position as an American of African descent. In both works, his self-conscious attention to his own authorship discloses the fate of the black self—which is also to say, as he demonstrates, the *American* self—within an American narrative.

Douglass's political conversion was certainly genuine, and the narrator of *My Bondage and My Freedom* partially mischaracterizes the *Narrative* in the service of his more pro-Union vision. In the revised account, Douglass blames the obviously prescribed self of the *Narrative* on his first abolitionist mentor, William Lloyd Garrison. It was as an idealistic and ambitious young man in his early twenties that Douglass had first addressed the Massachusetts Anti-Slavery Society, and his susceptibility to the dynamic and impassioned Garrison is not surprising. Garrison was himself a brilliant speaker and a committed activist who fought against slavery and colonization and for the assimilation of the descendants of Africans. But Garrison opposed the effort to abolish slavery through political or legal means. Abolition was, for him, a moral issue. The Constitution, he told his many audiences, was a proslavery document, and the courts legitimated the peculiar institution. Garrison went so far as to advocate the dissolution of the Union. His ideas and strategies appealed to the gifted young orator, but the equally impassioned Douglass could not long sustain a mentor.

The break was inevitable. Ambition and resentment toward Garrison at once contributed to and amplified the change in Douglass's politics, as the palpable disappointment in his earliest allies registered in *My Bondage and My Freedom* makes clear. An introduction to that work written by Dr. James McCune Smith, an African-American colleague from the post-Garrison period, implies that Douglass's "self-relying and independent character" had always prevented his total commitment to Garrison's "strictest sect."[81] But the strength of Smith's language, which derived from rather than sought to shape Douglass's narrative, conveys an anger born of disappointment: "Bitter and vindictive sarcasm, irresistible mimicry, and a pathetic narrative of his own experiences of slavery, were the intellectual manifestations which they encouraged him to exhibit on the platform or in the lecture desk" (*MB*, 14). Douglass himself recalls resenting the associates who turned his testimonials into an abolitionist ritual in which he was asked "to repeat the same old story month after month" (*MB*, 220). He recognized the importance of his abolitionist sponsors' plot, the story he must tell in accordance with their strategies to captivate audiences in the service of their larger program. But he was critical of their injunctions against his analyses and their attempts to shape his demeanor and choose his words. The repetition characteristic of the ritual they called for compromised his intellectual and performative growth as an orator.

Racism was also a factor. Even before his trip to Great Britain in 1845, Douglass felt belittled by some of the white abolitionists who did not always treat him with the spirit of equality that they professed. Having escaped from slavery into both freedom and "manhood," Douglass found himself re-presented "as a '*chattel*'—a '*thing*'—a piece of southern '*property*'" (*MB*, 220), an *American slave*. This sense was exacerbated while Douglass was abroad. But the trip also brought renown and patrons to the young orator as well as converts to the cause. In England, Douglass received the encouragement and financial backing necessary to develop his own analyses and interpretations and to publish his own newspaper. Both continued on his return to the United States, where Douglass also found a new intellectual interlocutor, political ally, and financial patron in white philanthropist Gerrit Smith.

Douglass's interaction with Smith no doubt encouraged his shift in thinking that turned former cohorts into bitter political opponents. Smith argued that participation in politics was not, as Garrison averred, immoral; on the contrary, it was the only effective means to abolish Dixie's cherished domestic institution. Douglass increasingly agreed. In his 1847 London address, "Farewell to the British People," Douglass, still following Garrison, had proclaimed that the institution of slavery was inscribed in the United States Constitution, and that "every man who pledges himself to raise his hand in support of the American constitution—every individual who swears to support this instrument—at the same time swears that the slaves of that country shall either remain slaves or die" (*FDP*, 3:22). By the time of his return to Great Britain in the fall of 1859, Douglass had long since changed his beliefs and his strategy. In 1860 he delivered "The American Constitution and the Slave" to a Glasgow audience, calling that same instrument a "great national enactment, done by the people" and insisting that "the text and only the text . . . is the constitution of the United States" (*FDP*, 3:347). The text that he had previously construed as deliberately ambiguous had now become "a plainly written document" in which "sound rules of interpretation all drive us to the words of the law for the meaning of the law" (*FDP*, 3:349). *My Bondage and My Freedom*, written in accordance with this conversion, registers Douglass's conviction that he is already included in a correctly interpreted We the People, an interpretation that white Americans had to acknowledge if they wished to be true to America.

Douglass devalues the *Narrative* in the language he uses to describe his displeasure with his Garrisonian associates in *My Bondage and My Freedom:* "It did not entirely satisfy me to *narrate* wrongs; I felt like *denouncing* them" (*MB*, 220). Narrating, for Douglass, is a kind of ritualized repetition, and the 1845 *Narrative* in this representation, is an accordingly prescribed text. Yet the drama and power of the narrator's deep engagement in a struggle for self-expression hardly accords with this characterization. While Douglass undoubtedly felt constrained by the abolitionists under whose sponsorship he produced his first book, the *Narrative* depicts constraints on Douglass's story intrinsic more generally to broader cultural and authorial conventions. His subsequent attribution of the curtailment of his story entirely to abolitionist prescriptions was in keeping with his personal break with Garrison and with his revised politics, which combined to propel him toward the premises of a more affirmatively nationalist narrative. Between the first two versions of his experiences, a politically seasoned Douglass retreated from his obvious discomfort with a politically expedient narrative, moving in the process from a broadly social to a more particularly institutional critique: the *Narrative*'s critique of the nation that fosters slavery became *My Bondage and My Freedom*'s criticism of the institution as a corrupting force. With that shift came a corresponding change in his depiction of authorship; a freer story expressed a freer self, the revised self of *My Bondage and My Freedom*. Any evident discomfort with the master's tools gave way to their exploitation for a more pragmatic end. The critique offered in *My Bondage and My Freedom* is even more indirect than the already subtle critique of the *Narrative*. It is ironic but not surprising that as Douglass became more visible and more vocal, he had ever to suppress evidence of his struggle for self-expression. Seeking to become, in every sense, an American spokesperson, he had to disavow his discomfort with the limitations on his story.

The very title of *My Bondage and My Freedom* suggests an author who has achieved his freedom and can comfortably claim his voice rather than a narrator subjected to (and by) a preconceived plot. James McCune Smith even introduces Douglass as a man who belongs, "a Representative American man—a type of his countrymen" who can write "an American book, for Americans, in the fullest sense of the idea" (*MB*, 17, 23). Unitarian minister and antislavery activist Theodore Parker had asserted the importance of narratives such as Douglass's for a general United States audience in a commencement address, delivered four years after the publication of the *Narrative*, that excoriated American literary scholars for not discharging their debts to the nation by creating an "indigenous and original" literature. Only "the Lives of Fugitive Slaves," he contended, constituted a "series of literary productions that could be written by none but Americans, and only here. . . . All the original romance of America is in them, not in the white man's novel."[82] Parker redefines an America that begins with rather than excludes the descendants of Africans. But there is an irony involved in the transformation of the slave narrative into a national(ist) genre. By appropriating the genre as an emblem of an indigenous American culture, Parker obscures the actual divisiveness of the peculiar institution. And the literal slave becomes the emblem of American freedom rather than evidence of American slavery. These ironies had not escaped the fugitive slave who penned the *Narrative*, and they certainly did not pass by the free man who authored *My Bondage and My Freedom* even as he appeared to minimize the struggle with an authorizing narrative—and with the haunting resonance of metaphors of enslavement such as Parker uses when he describes American authors as "the slaves of public opinion" (TP, 41). While the self-conscious narration of the *Narrative* shows a writer struggling to tell a story against narrative conventions and cultural prescriptions, the more comfortable authorship of *My Bondage and My Freedom* demonstrates how conventions and prescriptions can transform that story into a national narrative.

Nonetheless, the different demands of the genres account for Douglass's more overt chafing against conventions in the *Narrative* than in *My Bondage and My Freedom*. Whether in the immediate political service of abolitionist and northern Unionist sponsors or the ideological service of those calling for a uniquely American literature, the popularity of the slave narrative underwrote the emergence of a genre with conventions that often, as Douglass complained, not only shaped the narrator's experiences, but even encouraged fictional accounts by nonslave, sometimes white, authors. Financially, politically, and ideologically, slave narratives could be profitable. But profitability of any kind implied meeting externally generated demands, and those demands in turn prescribed a certain kind of text. Whatever their moral imperatives, Garrisonian abolitionists could not afford to ignore what appealed to the audience. Neither, for that matter, could an ambitious young orator. So if the audience expected "an American slave" and awaited a "slave narrative," it was incumbent upon the orator or narrator to provide just that.

Despite the blame he placed upon his abolitionist sponsors, Douglass knew the difficulties involved in meeting audience expectations and market demands. A self-conscious Douglass implicates himself as author in this process in a scene he calls "the blood-stained gate, the entrance to the hell of slavery," in which he recounts witnessing the beating at the hands of his master of a woman he calls Aunt Hester (NFD, 42). The allusion to the entrance to hell locates Douglass's Narrative in the familiar literary tradition of the epic. It was a tradition that others had also evoked. As Unitarian minister and abolitionist Ephraim Peabody noted, "We know not where one who wished to write a modern odyssey could find a better subject than the adventures of a fugitive slave."[83] In the famous epic journeys to the underworld—Odysseus's, Aeneas's, and Dante's—the hero assumes a new identity or resumes a lost one and finds the way home or founds a new home. Aunt Hester's beating inaugurates just such a journey for the young slave, but also for the young author; both are initiated into the terms of their identities in a journey that filters the experience of slavery through the conventions of a literary genre.

Consistent with the premises of Garrisonian abolitionism, the scene offers an ideological critique of American institutions, the family as well as slavery. A concealed and frightened child watches his master beat a woman because she had "happened to be absent when [her] master desired her presence" and because she "had been found in company with Lloyd's Ned," a man whom her master, Captain Anthony, had refused to allow her to marry, "which circumstance . . . was the chief offence" (NFD, 42). Aunt Hester "disobeys" as an enslaved woman, and the language and imagery of the passage describing her beating figuratively suggest a rape. Captain Anthony took her into the kitchen, and stripped her from neck to waist, leaving her neck, shoulders, and back, entirely naked. He then told her to cross her hands, calling her at the same time a d——d b——h. After crossing her hands, he tied them with a strong rope, and led her to a stool under a large hook in the joist, put in for the purpose. He made her get upon the stool, and tied her hands to the hook. She now stood fair for his infernal purpose. Her arms were stretched up at their full length, so that she stood upon the ends of her toes. He then said to her, 'Now, you d——d b——h, I'll learn you how to disobey my orders!' and after rolling up his sleeves, he commenced to lay on the heavy cowskin, and soon the warm, red blood (amid heart-rending shrieks from her, and horrid oaths from him) came dripping to the floor. (*NFD*, 43)

Douglass conveys his ambiguous relation to the scene when he observes, "I was doomed to be a witness and a participant. It struck me with awful force" (*NFD*, 42). Like Aunt Hester, he is a victim, figuratively beaten ("It struck me"). But Douglass also participates in the scene by witnessing it, in the active sense of testifying rather than the more passive observing.

Douglass the author brings the scene before a public whom he hopes to turn into a jury. The scene is a "bloody transaction," in part a business deal for the slave-owning master, but also perhaps one for the witnessing slave. Both Douglass and his antislavery sponsors knew that sensational scenes such as this one would sell both books and the cause because the audience would be titillated by it. This scene does not appear in *The Liberator*, Garrison's antislavery newspaper, with other extracts advertising the "great sensation" that Douglass's *Narrative* "cannot fail to produce."[84] But it is probably one of the scenes foremost in the mind of one letter writer who, comparing Douglass's work with Charles Dickens's *Oliver Twist* and Eugène Sue's *Mysteries of Paris*, testifies to the power of Douglass's work by noting that she was moved *beyond* tears: "For I am an American woman, and for American women I bleed. I groaned in the agony of my spirit. . . . never before have I been brought so completely in sympathy with the slave—never before have I felt myself so completely bound with them."[85] The language of her response indeed indicates a titillated identification with Aunt Hester. Douglass has produced a "great sensation." The eroticized violence of this scene is fueled by and in turn reproduces the enslaved woman's commodified personhood. As an author, Douglass participates in the representation, perpetuation, and reproduction of these dynamics. Feeling himself "doomed to be a witness and a participant," Douglass is afraid that for him as an author, no less than for Captain Anthony, slavery itself has become a commodity.

The eroticized language is also in keeping with the Garrisonian view of the institution of slavery that Douglass shared. Slavery in this scene evinces more than causes the corruption of the Union, and that deeper corruption is manifested in other institutions, including the family. A family dynamic is implicit in the interrelations of the scene's participants: master Captain Anthony, Aunt Hester, and young Frederick. Like many slave narrators, Douglass suggests, at the beginning of his narrative, the "whispered opinion" that Captain Anthony is his father. The death of his mother, also reported at the beginning of the *Narrative*, leaves open the maternal relation, which can be filled by a female relative such as Aunt Hester, whom Douglass describes as "an own aunt of mine" (*NFD*, 42). The eroticized beating witnessed by the concealed and frightened child becomes a perverse primal scene.[86] The narrator dwells on Aunt Hester's comeliness and remarks on Captain Anthony's refusal to allow her to marry her handsome slave lover, Ned.

Slavery allows Captain Anthony literally to disrupt a family. But the metaphoric primal scene offers another kind of proprietorship, that of a husband/father for a wife/mother. Both slavery and the traditional family are enabled by the intrinsically corrupting commodification of personhood.[87] The ambiguous relationships among all of the scene's participants allow Douglass to present the metaphoric dimensions of family relations; thus he underscores the proprietary terms supplied by American patriarchy that allow the institution of slavery to exist. An analogy between wives and slaves ("the slavery of women and the slavery of the colored race"), similarly articulated by numerous proponents of woman suffrage and abolition (Douglass was a celebrated speaker for both movements), turned on their statuses, respectively, as disfranchised persons and personal property.[88] The act of legal naming that turned a woman into a "wife" or a human being into a "slave" transferred natural rights of property and the personhood they defined to a "husband" or conferred them on a "master." Aunt Hester's beating dramatizes the consequences of legal entitlements that arise from a definition of personhood that is marked by race and gender, categories that enable the exclusion of human beings from the right to own and therefore from the liberal ideology of self-ownership. Slavery is no more un-American in this scene than the American family:

both are based on a concept of ownership that troubles the ideology from which it derives. The suggestion of more literal relations among the participants in Douglass's scene attests to the deeply intertwined institutions of slavery and the family in the South. Of course, Douglass knew that implications of slavery's encouragement of interracial coupling would play well to an audience of antislavery racists.

The depiction of the beating of Aunt Hester, one of the most thoroughly revised scenes in the second book, changes with the narrator's political convictions. The representative author of *My Bondage and My Freedom* is no longer implicated in any "bloody transaction." For him, moreover, the institution of slavery does not exemplify corruption but itself corrupts the Union and the family. Temporal distance insufficiently accounts for the more measured tone, the greater detail but greater detachment, evident even as Douglass introduces the scene: "The circumstances which I am about to narrate, and which give rise to this fearful tempest of passion, are not singular nor isolated in slave life, but are common in every slaveholding community in which I have lived. They are incidental to the relation of master and slave, and exist in all sections of slaveholding countries" (*MB*, 57). This scene is one of many scenes that he recounts to illustrate the barbarism of slavery and its corruption of the American family. The beating is no longer seminal for the narrator, no longer an "entrance to the hell of slavery." In fact, the young Douglass of *My Bondage and My Freedom* is "first introduced to the realities of slavery" not through the beating but through his grandmother's surrendering him to his master, through the disruption of his family (*MB*, 37).

Most noticeably, Douglass has replaced the eroticized language and familial subtext with a more sedate reportage. He downplays the sexual and familial relationships among the scene's participants. Aunt Hester is now "Esther," one of many female relatives and no longer singled out as a maternal stand-in. Although "Hester" and "Esther" are variants of the same name, the Hester of the 1845 *Narrative* may even have become "Esther" to avoid any association with the adulterous "Hester" of Nathaniel Hawthorne's 1850 *The Scarlet Letter*.[89] Although Douglass mentions Esther's beauty, he does not dwell on Captain Anthony's desire for her and Anthony's interference in her relationship with Ned Roberts (now Edward rather than Lloyd's Ned) is less explicable in this version. It is now an "unnatural and heartless order" (*MB*, 57–58). As an arbitrary master rather than "father," Captain Anthony interferes with the slave family, consistent with Douglass's indictment earlier in the text of slavery's "obliterating from the mind and heart of the slave, all just ideas of the sacredness of the family, as an institution" (*MB*, 29). Douglass no longer wants to equate the institutions of slavery and the family. In *My Bondage and My Freedom*, slavery pollutes *any* country, and *throughout* the country, in which it is found. It is a challenge to rather than a failure of an enlightened republic, and it threatens the Union, the legacy of the fathers.

Yet not all revisions of the *Narrative* were as thorough as the Aunt Hester scene. In some cases, small details remain in the revised text, signaling a Douglass who chafes at the limitations even as he celebrates the political possibilities intrinsic to the role of American spokesperson. An attention to what he cannot tell in both works broadens into complementary analyses of what it meant to be enslaved in America. That complementarity is evident in the differences between his account of how he got his name in each work. Douglass makes clear that he was named into an American identity in the act of writing the *Narrative*, when, toward the end of that work, he recounts how he got the name Frederick Douglass. In substance, the story is simple. Named by his mother Frederick Augustus Washington Bailey, Douglass had to rename himself several times both on his journey North and as a fugitive slave living in New Bedford. From the moment of that naming begins the narrative of Frederick *Douglass*, an *American* slave—not Frederick *Bailey*, a *southern* one. The narrative of Frederick Douglass is a public account that reconstructs the life of Frederick Bailey, a point deemphasized but lingering in *My Bondage and My Freedom*, which stresses the continuity rather than the rupture between Frederick Bailey and Frederick Douglass.

In both accounts, the name Douglass is bestowed on the fugitive slave by Nathan Johnson, an African-American abolitionist who gives him shelter and helps him settle into New Bedford. Johnson, who had been reading Sir Walter Scott's *The Lady of the Lake*, chooses for the fugitive the name of the hero of the poem, an unjustly exiled Scottish chief. Expressing pride in his heroic name, the author of *My Bondage and My Freedom* protests only that his host, Nathan Johnson, would have been more deserving of it. The narrator of the earlier account has more profound reservations about his change of name: "I gave Mr. Johnson the privilege of choosing me a name, but told him he must not take from me the name of 'Frederick.' I must hold on to that, to preserve a sense of my identity" (*NFD*, 101). Ten years later, he would refer to "the comparatively unimportant matter, as to what should be my name" and call the name given him by his mother "pretentious" (*MB*, 209). The younger Douglass, writing his narrative precisely to establish that he is who he claims to be, attends more explicitly to the fragility of his identity and the importance of a name. The language of the earlier work conveys more of a struggle and sense of loss in the act of naming.

My Bondage and My Freedom downplays the discomfort that concludes the naming scene in the *Narrative*. In the earlier work Douglass leaves a gap between the name and the first-person subject: "From that time until now I have been called 'Frederick Douglass;' and as I am more widely known by that name than by either of the others, I shall continue to use it as my own" (*NFD*, 101). Quotation marks around the name signal that the narrator has been spoken into existence.[90] "Frederick Douglass" is a public name that the narrator *uses* as he accepts his public identity—that of "American slave." Even the title preserves the distinction; *Narrative of the Life of Frederick Douglass, an American Slave* is "Written by Himself," not by "Frederick Douglass." "Written by Himself," a convention of slave narratives, of course underscores the narrator's literacy, an important part of his story of liberation, and it asserts his authenticity to a characteristically dubious white audience. Yet "Written by Himself" might also indicate what "Frederick Douglass" leaves out, an unknown individual whose isolation resurfaces in the discomfort of an ill-fitting public self. The younger narrator who wants to preserve a sense of his identity fears disappearing into a historically reconstructed unrecognizability, a fear that finds expression in his struggle for control of his own narrative, his apparent effort "to tell a free story."[91]

The altered role of Douglass's mother in the two scenes also marks an important difference. In the first, he must hold on to a part of the identity that she has conferred on him with his name. In the second, the name she has given him is "pretentious," and he accordingly shows no particular attachment to his name. Significantly, when he gives up the name *Bailey*, he gives up *her* name, the mark of his matrilineal identity and of his enslavement. While Harriet Bailey's bestowal of her son's name represents a positive impact on the fashioning of his identity in the earlier work, in the later work she embodies Douglass's need for self-representation. His name is not important in *My Bondage and My Freedom*, Douglass suggests, because an enslaved person does not control the categories marked by, and privileges dispensed according to, names. His naming, in fact, is bound up with his enslavement.

Yet the apparently less conflictual name change in *My Bondage and My Freedom* may itself be more complicated than it initially seems. The complication comes through a detail that Douglass offers as an aside, without commentary or evident concern. In both accounts, he arrives as Johnson only to find the Johnson family in New Bedford sufficiently numerous so as "to produce some confusion in attempts to distinguish one from another" (*MB*, 209). But he expands this account in *My Bondage and My Freedom*, noting that the popularity of the name Johnson among slaves arriving in New Bedford was "much to the annoyance of the original 'Johnsons,'" and that Nathan Johnson was himself "unwilling to have another of his name added to the community in this unauthorized way" (*MB*, 209). The Johnsons' "annoyance" stands out in this account of his warm reception by and gratitude toward the African-American community of New Bedford, and "unauthorized" is striking because the name he receives—Douglass—is no more authorized than the name with which he had arrived. Johnson himself chooses Douglass's name from Scott's popular literary work. Nathan Johnson is evidently troubled by the addition of another Johnson rather than the lack of authorization for Bailey's name change.

The naming indeed marks a new status. The Douglass of *My Bondage and My Freedom* recalls, "It was necessary to have a name in my new relations" (*MB*, 209). The "annoyance" of the Johnsons may be nothing more than an acknowledgement of the importance of a name to a free person, an individual. But it could equally express the precariousness of a name and of the identity marked by that name. The African-American Johnsons' reluctance to share their patronym with the fugitive slaves may point allegorically to a deeper anxiety concerning the place of the slaves, and of all descendants of Africans, within the nation. The migration to the North of freed or fugitive slaves presages the representational dilemma perceived by a white native-born population when faced with the influx of a distinct (nonwhite) group of people whose deracination emblematizes historical dislocation and uncertain status. For white America, a small black American population could be a useful margin against which to imagine a center, but a large free black population, as opponents of abolition and proponents of colonization regularly argued, would challenge an already tenuous We the (White) People. Douglass's celebration of freedom coexists in *My Bondage and My Freedom* with his recognition that his American identity is complicated.

Douglass cannot suppress that message despite his expurgations in an account of his first experience of Northern racism, an account that follows the naming scene in both works. The *Narrative* itself presents an indirect critique; the narrator follows the decision to use the name Frederick Douglass as his own with the sentence, "I was quite disappointed at the general appearance of things in New Bedford" (*NFD*, 101). The word "disappointed" is a dramatic irony, turning on the expectation of the fugitive slave that nonslaveholding whites must be poor, as such a class is in the South. He is "disappointed" to discover the splendor of New Bedford, including the superiority of his black host to "nine tenths of the slaveholders in Talbot county Maryland" (*NFD*, 103). But the narrator quickly recounts his inability to find employment among the white practitioners of his trade, ship caulkers, who refuse to work alongside a black man. The word "disappointed" lingers as an echo, a whispered critique of northern racism just under the surface of the text. The narrator hastens to add in a qualifying footnote, "I am told that colored persons can now get employment at calking in New Bedford—a result of anti-slavery effort" (*NFD*, 103n). But whatever the historical validity of this statement, it remains an unincorporated addition to the narrative, suggesting the possibility of editorial direction, self-imposed or otherwise.

In *My Bondage and My Freedom*, the narrator introduces the scene with anticipation of the reader's fond condescension: "The reader will be amused at my ignorance, when I tell the notions I had of the state of northern wealth, enterprise, and civilization" (*MB*, 209). A joke shared between reader and author at the indulgent expense of the inexperienced fugitive slave replaces the momentary edge gained through irony by the narrator of the previous text. And for "disappointed" the older narrator substitutes "amazement and joy" to describe his response to New Bedford (*MB*, 210). Where the earlier *Narrative* begins the fugitive's impressions of New Bedford with his confrontation of the town's wealth—a slightly claustrophobic sense of being "walled in by granite warehouses of the widest dimensions" filled with luxuries (*NFD*, 102)—the later version starts with the sight of Quakers, which "greatly increased" the author's "sense of freedom and security" (*MB*, 210). In this context, the very same sentence about the warehouses conveys protection and well-being rather than anxious enclosure. When Douglass goes in search of work, he does so with the full joy of a self-owner; "I was now my own master," he proclaims (*MB*, 212). When white caulkers threaten to strike if Douglass is employed, he responds by reaffirming his freedom—"I was free, and free to work, though not at my trade" (*MB*, 213)—despite the difference in wages resulting from this prohibition.

These revisions do more than smooth out the choppy style of an inexperienced writer; they proclaim an alternative ideology. Douglass does not minimize the importance of his freedom. Nor, however, does he neglect to report this experience of northern racism. As in the *Narrative*, this account summons a similar experience in the Baltimore shipyards. In *My Bondage and My Freedom*, however, Douglass accompanies the earlier account with an analysis of how the slaveholders "with a craftiness peculiar to themselves" have set white laborers against black slaves, thus "making the said white man almost as much a slave as the black slave himself" (*MB*, 188). He predicts that the wage slavery of white laborers in competition with legally enslaved labor will inspire the white laborers to overthrow slavery.[92] Yet his analysis is contradicted by his experience in the North. Evidently the craftiness is not "peculiar" to the slaveholders. Either he did not notice the contradiction or (which I find more likely) he offers an implied critique of the slaveholding nation that complicates his professed political views. This complication is especially troubling since many advocates of slavery offered critiques of northern capitalism—of wage slavery—to justify their more "benevolent" institution. Douglass's experience of northern racism, which could extend into a class analysis, compromises as it complicates his analysis of slavery in *My Bondage and My Freedom*. The experience remains an unacknowledged but troubling detail in his account.

My Bondage and My Freedom registers Douglass's ongoing effort to transform Frederick Bailey, a Maryland slave, into Frederick Douglass, an American author. A change in relation to the rituals of the nation marked this metamorphosis, although similar rhetorical strategies among Garrisonians, consolidationists, and confederationists in the antebellum period make it hard to pinpoint the change. Likewise, it is impossible to locate exactly the border between political strategy and personal analysis. Like Lincoln, Douglass the American invoked the founders—especially Washington and Jefferson—as he turned increasingly to the principles of the

Declaration of Independence. But Garrison no less than Roger Taney invoked the same founders and the Declaration of Independence. The change is most evident in Douglass's self-representation. The theology of an imagined community required a heroic self-surrender such as Lincoln enacted in his rhetoric. For the converted self of *My Bondage and My Freedom*, that would mean having to consign Frederick Bailey entirely to the past.

The first July Fourth oration delivered by the liberated slave in 1852, three years before the publication of *My Bondage and My Freedom*, offers evidence of the political conversion-in-process, although the break with Garrison had already taken place over these issues. "What to the Slave Is the Fourth of July?" presents slavery as a *national* institution and ends with a poem by Garrison. Yet their estrangement pervades the rhetoric of the speech, and where the young orator would previously have invoked his first mentor, the seasoned speaker summons Gerrit Smith in defense of the Constitution, which, "interpreted as it *ought* to be interpreted, . . . is a GLORIOUS LIBERTY DOCUMENT" (*FDP*, 2:103). The replacement of father Garrison with new ally and friend Smith was one step in the reconfiguration of the national family that Douglass was beginning to assay. Anxiety about the future of the Union was harnessed in this project as in this oration. Delivering the speech on the fifth instead of the fourth of July, Douglass marked the exclusion of black subjects as un-American, a threat to the national ritual and a challenge to "the first great fact in your nation's history," the Declaration of Independence (*FDP*, 2:363). Freedom inheres in the Union, and any threat to the Union, such as the nationalization of slavery instituted by the Fugitive Slave Law, puts "the liberty and person of every man . . . in peril" (*FDP*, 2:375). By a process of inversion, the slave becomes a representative American. Five years before the *Dred Scott* decision, Douglass wonders what allows the nation to concede the "manhood" and "the natural right[s] of" the slave and still affirm the legality of slavery (*FDP*, 2:369–70). And what, he asks implicitly, keeps the government from making white men slaves?

The orator of this speech deliberately presents a self in transition. He insists on his separation from white Americans, calling the United States "*your* nation"; the Fourth, a holiday commemorating "*your* National Independence" and "*your* political freedom," and the founders, "*your* fathers." On the other hand, although he is "identified with the American bondman" and stands "with God and the crushed and bleeding slave on this occasion," he is separate from the slaves for whom he speaks (*FDP*, 2:368, 369). Having been purchased and then liberated by patrons in Great Britain, he is, strictly speaking, no longer an American bondman. Yet his language bespeaks more import in his distinctness. As a free black man, Douglass has a preferable but less definable place in the nation than he had had before. Here is a self betwixt and between, poised to be named into an identity not yet available to him, a self suspended no less than the first-person subject of Lincoln's Second Inaugural Address. And a self similarly contingent upon and embodying the fate of an uncertain and unstable We the People.

The nation is also—and similarly—suspended in this oration. The founders are dead—and symbolically dying. Dating its birth from the Declaration, Douglass describes a nation "now 76 years old . . . a mere speck in the life of a nation," an orphan in search of fatherly guidance, having survived the biblical lifespan "alloted . . . for individual men": "three score years and ten" (*FDP*, 2:360). Those founders can still guide through example, however, having themselves been orphaned by their refusal to tolerate the "parental prerogatives" imposed by "England as the fatherland" (*FDP*, 2:361). In a significant twist, the orphaned slave becomes the true heir of the regenerated founders, who "were peace men; but . . . preferred revolution to peaceful submission to bondage" (*FDP*, 2:364–65). In the post-heroic language of antebellum America, Douglass calls upon the "American bondman" to salvage the ambiguous legacy of an "America . . . false to the past, false to the present, and solemnly bind[ing] herself to be false to the future" (*FDP*, 2:369). There were a very few presidential hopefuls who called themselves abolitionists and embraced positions as radical as Douglass's. Lincoln, of course, was not one of them. Not all consolidationists envisioned the same consolidation. But Lincoln shared with a converted Douglass a narrative strategy: both summoned the uncanniness of the slave to show how a corrupt institution threatened the Union. The resemblance was drawn upon (and reinforced) by Stephen Douglas, who labeled Lincoln one of the "new converts" whom "Fred. Douglass, the negro, helped to baptize" (*AL*, 3:175).

The slave as representative symbol was important to abolitionists as well. Garrison and prominent fellow-abolitionist Wendell Phillips had already clothed the fugitive slave in the robes of the nation's founders in the prefatory documents with which they authorized the *Narrative* of their protégé. Drawing repeatedly on a pantheon of national heroes—from the

Pilgrims through the Declaration's signatories to Patrick Henry—they sought at once to establish Douglass's heroism as familiarly American and to enlist the founders in the cause of abolition. Garrison recalled that, after hearing Douglass give an impassioned address at a New Bedford antislavery convention, "I rose, and declared that Patrick Henry, of revolutionary fame, never made a speech more eloquent in the cause of liberty, than the one we had just listened to from the lips of that hunted fugitive" (*NFD*, 30). Phillips returned to 1776 when "the fathers . . . signed the Declaration of Independence with the halter about their necks" to avow that Douglass, too, publishes his "declaration of freedom with danger compassing [him] around" (*NFD*, 37). Thus they wrote Douglass into a national narrative as, in Garrison's words, "a fugitive slave, in the person of Frederick Douglass" (*NFD*, 31). Douglass had use value to the abolitionists, and to the North in general, *as a fugitive slave*. Hence the title that insists on being the narrative of the life of Frederick *Douglass* (not of Frederick Bailey), "an American slave."

But a subtly recalcitrant Frederick Bailey expressed discomfort with this iconography in the *Narrative* by invoking the slaveholding Virginian only to surpass him: "In coming to a fixed determination to run away, we did more than Patrick Henry, when he resolved upon liberty or death. With us it was a doubtful liberty at most, and almost certain death if we failed. For my part, I should prefer death to hopeless bondage" (*NFD*, 86). Refusing to plagiarize a prewritten narrative, he instead insists on his difference from the "fathers": his action is more heroic than Patrick Henry's because descendants of Africans have only a "doubtful liberty" in the United States. But a change in his understanding of the nation and of his place in it, both personally and politically motivated, called for a revision of his relationship to the founders.

A reconstituted national family in the July Fourth oration is the result of this change. While "the fathers of this republic" (*FDP*, 2:364) remain "your [white Americans'] fathers" throughout, the Constitution that they wrote makes Douglass their spiritual heir. In language anticipating that which Lincoln would use in his Second Inaugural Address, Douglass invokes Isaiah to enjoin true Americans to "judge for the fatherless; plead for the widow" (*FDP*, 2:378).[93] With no one more "fatherless" than American slaves, their inclusion in the reconstituted family is all but literally specified in the national legacy of the fathers. Only when his white "fellow-countrymen" have faced their hypocrisy, Douglass suggests, will he be able to "unite with" the children of their common fathers, literally and figuratively. He has not chosen, but is "compelled" (*FDP*, 2:364) by those who "dispute" his "claim to have been regularly descended" from the fathers to pronounce his exclusion, an exclusion that threatens the unity of the nation (*FDP*, 2:366). Douglass depicts a monstrous creation that menaces its progenitors: the "horrible reptile" of slavery "is coiled up in [the] nation's bosom" like the serpentine Orestes of Clytemnestra's guilty dreams, a "venomous creature . . . nursing at the tender breast of [the] youthful republic" (*FDP*, 2:383–84).

The former slave presents himself as truer to the founding principles than his countrymen; they—not he—have departed from the founders' spirit. In thus reversing the terms of his exclusion, he positions himself centrally within the national ritual from which the speech putatively pronounces his exclusion. That ritual finds formal expression in what Sacvan Bercovitch calls "the American jeremiad," a genre that recasts opposition to a current government as a reenactment of the founders' rebellion and critique of the present state of society as affirmation of the nation's founding ideals.[94] William Andrews reads the *Narrative* as the more jeremiadic of Douglass's accounts, and certainly the text has features of a jeremiad (WA, 124–25). But, as I have suggested, Douglass manifests discomfort with the (American) self imposed upon him by Garrison and Phillips in the prefatory documents of that work. His ignorance of his birth date with which Douglass begins the *Narrative* marks the exclusion of Bailey from historical representation. It is his sponsors who want the native-born narrator to enter into "American" history with the declaration of independence by which he decides to go North. Garrison and Phillips are the Jeremiahs. Bailey chooses to remain outside of that narrative, a spectral reminder of what "the person of Frederick Douglass" must repress.

By contrast, in the July Fourth oration, Douglass more explicitly adopts the language of the American jeremiad. He professes a profound faith in the national founding documents and invokes "the name of the constitution and the bible, which are disregarded and trampled upon" to "dare to call in question and to denounce . . . everything that serves to perpetuate slavery—the great sin and shame of America!" (*FDP*, 2:369). He condemns the *corruptions* of a particular historical American Church and State, a "nation [that] never looked blacker to me than on this 4th of July!" (*FDP*, 2:368). The indictment of this "black America" deploys even as it challenges the terms—black and white—of his own unequal status within We the People.

Yet reservations about his inheritance and uncertainty about the place of descendants of Africans in the reconstructed family complicate his jeremiad. The matricidal image of a coiled reptile nursing at the breast of the youthful republic indirectly expresses Douglass's uneasiness. On the surface, the metaphor is simply a vivid and not uncommon condemnation of slavery. Lincoln, too, in an 1860 speech on the slave question, depicts slavery as a rattlesnake, this one in bed with sleeping children. He argues that as he would not dare strike such a snake for fear of harming the children, so he does not "dare strike at [slavery] where it is," but nor would he "carry it to bed where there are children" (*AL*, 4:5). The states and territories of the Union are, in this image, the children of the patriarchs, and slavery threatens them with infanticide. Douglass also describes a nation "still lingering in the period of childhood," which makes his subsequent image of the Union-as-mother all the more striking (*FDP*, 2:360). This nursing mother nourishes her own doom; she is thereby more implicated in that doom than the progeny in Lincoln's metaphor, and this image evinces a trace of Douglass's earlier politics.

But a deeper uneasiness also finds expression in the image of matricide, which, obliquely and indirectly, summons another possible matricide: where is Harriet Bailey—or any black woman—in this new order? The Union-as-mother is surely not his own "sable, unprotected, and uncultivated *mother*" (*MB*, 42). And when Douglass, speaking as the heir apparent of the fathers, conventionally claims his legacy of liberty and manhood, when he insists that from concessions of "the manhood of the slave" the slave rightly claims his liberty, what place has he left his mother, his wife, his sisters and daughters (*FDP*, 2:369)? More than conventional rhetoric is involved in this omission. In this oration, Douglass radically and unmistakably affiliates himself with the "solid manhood" of the "peace men" and with the priorities of their masculinist assumptions "that man is entitled to liberty[,] that he is the rightful owner of his own body" (*FDP*, 2:364–65, 370). The masculine pronoun is accurate here, since the law did not necessarily entitle even a free woman to hers.

His life had surely taught him that freedom was racialized and gendered. That lesson is recorded in his *Narrative*. In the Aunt Hester scene, for example, the intertwined roles of slave and wife and of master and husband reinforce for the witnessing child that freedom and power—like father—are white and male. Later, Douglass reports that his defeat of the infamous Mr. Covey, a stern and brutal master, in hand-to-hand combat "rekindled the few expiring embers of freedom, and revived within [him] a sense of [his] own manhood" (*NFD*, 79). As Douglass embarks on his journey to manhood and liberty, to representative Americanness, he must struggle to overcome not only Covey, but also, it seems, the matrilineal inheritance of his identity. Hence the identity still conferred upon him by Harriet Bailey in the 1845 *Narrative* becomes, in the 1855 *My Bondage and My Freedom,* nothing more than a "pretentious" name.

Yet a haunting question lingers in the displaced image of matricide, an uneasiness with the terms of liberty to which Douglass lays claim. After all, if there is no place for Harriet Bailey, then what place is there for Frederick Bailey *as her son,* as a descendant of Africans? The question surfaces only in innuendos and implications in this oration; it is never explicitly—or perhaps consciously—formulated. Nonetheless, while Douglass asserted his patriotic belief in the ideals of the founders and insisted on his right to assume a place among them, the metaphor of matricide expressed an ambivalence about the nature of that Union and about the place of black women and of black men—of himself—within it. The challenge implicit in the dramatic serpentine metaphor of "What to the Slave Is the Fourth of July?" itself sucks at the tender breast of Douglass's reformulated political vision.

My Bondage and My Freedom picks up on that challenge. Despite Harriet Bailey's diminished role in bestowing her son's identity in the revised work, she has a slightly larger (yet still cameo) appearance. Douglass still confesses that he barely knew her, but she is more "distinct," and Douglass recounts how she defended him against "the sable virago" who ruled the master's kitchen and punished enslaved children by withholding food from them (*MB*, 38, 41). That defense taught the young Douglass that he "was not only a child, but *somebody's* child" (*MB*, 41). From that one incident, she is able to occupy the cultural space of mother. Douglass's memory of his mother is complicated. Although "her face is imaged" on his memory, and he ever feels "her presence," he can only remember the "side view of her face" (*MB*, 41–42). Compounding this sign of indirection, Douglass turns for her image to *"Prichard's Natural History of Man"*—specifically, to "the head of a figure—on page 157—the features of which so resemble those of my mother, that I often recur to it with something of the feeling which I suppose others experience when looking upon the pictures of dear departed ones" (*MB*, 39). The figure, as several readers have noted, seems to be the head of a princely man, possibly white.[95] That slippage might, as Deborah E. McDowell suggests, capture "emphatically the discursive priorities of masculinity and its gendered relation to the feminine" (DM, 199). Yet it is also possible that Douglass *means* to depict just how mediated his experience of her has been. The image of a possibly white man superimposed upon his memory of his mother offers insight into *her*, and by implication *his*, inadequate representation within the (white) natural history of man—and into their exclusion from full personhood.[96]

The work continues to denounce Douglass's exclusion from the rights and ideals of the United States, from the law and from patrilineal inheritance, but that exclusion as well as the institution responsible for it are now unnatural as well as un-American. Slavery challenges civilization by destroying the American family—in particular, the father and the genealogies that preserve his name:

> Genealogical trees do not flourish among slaves. A person of some consequence here in the north, sometimes designated father, is literally abolished in slave law and slave practice. . . . Slavery does away with fathers, as it does away with families. Slavery has no use for either fathers or families, and its laws do not recognize their existence in the social arrangements of the plantation. When they do exist, they are not the outgrowths of slavery, but are antagonistic to that system. The order of civilization is reversed here. The name of the child is not expected to be that of its father, and his condition does not necessarily affect that of the child. (*MB*, 28–38)

Here slavery threatens to be patricidal as well as matricidal. Douglass carefully establishes slavery as the outgrowth of *laws* endangering the premises and assumptions of the laws of the Union. Plantation law is a law unto itself—not the *natural* law of civilization or even the *positive* law of the United States. Slavery is anarchic, reversing the order of civilization and challenging the terms that govern property: the patronym that determines ownership and inheritance. And it is a crime against nature, diverting "the tenderest affection [mother/child] which a beneficent Father allows . . . from its true and natural object"—an unnatural act against God and the family of man (*MB*, 39). A pointedly orphaned Douglass suffers the severing of those bonds more than his 1845 counterpart. But the passage also makes apparent the significant extent to which laws create identities and social existence. The orphaned Douglass embodies the fate of any American if plantation law becomes too literally the law of the land.

Arguing that Douglass's break with "'American Garrisonianism' . . . allowed him to see signs of 'oppression' in the very 'form' of the fugitive slave narrative that he had written in 1845," William Andrews aptly reads *My Bondage and My Freedom* as "a quiet but thorough revision of the significance of the life of Frederick *Douglass*" (WA, 216–17; emphasis added). This story is told as much through formal as through substantive changes, and the narrator of *My Bondage and My Freedom* claims that authenticity requires his departure from presumed reader expectations in the longer and more detailed version of his experiences. Following his account of the deception through which his grandmother deserted him at the house of his master, he remarks: "The reader may be surprised that I narrate so minutely an incident apparently so trivial, and which must have occurred when I was not more than seven years old; but as I wish to give a faithful history of my experience in slavery, I cannot withhold a circumstance which, at the time, affected me so deeply. Besides, this was, in fact, my first introduction to the realities of slavery" (*MB*, 37). With "in fact," Douglass issues a subtle corrective to the earlier narrative, which locates its entrance to hell in the eroticized beating of Aunt Hester. The reader of *My Bondage and My Freedom* "may be surprised" because, Douglass suggests, this narration departs from the expected pace and details of the genre. But the expected narratives generated by those formal constraints fail to "give a faithful history." In place of the fast-paced sensationalized account of the horrors of slavery is a more speculative study of the impact of slavery on the culture of the United States as well as a more measured stock-taking of the development of a public figure.

Yet Douglass explains his departure from the stylistic conventions of the slave narrative as the need to satisfy one of its most basic requirements: authenticity, which is itself, paradoxically, prescribed. The claim to authenticity, in other words, is itself conventional. As we have seen, the changes in *My Bondage and My Freedom* correspond to changes in political allies, vision, and strategy. The familiar details delimiting the conversion of this "representative American" (such as the conventions of the jeremiad) authorize his story every bit as much as—and, it seems, more smoothly than—the prefatory documents of his earliest associates in the abolitionist movement. Explicit injunctions such as Garrison lays out are more readily recognized and resented than the conventions of language and form that express and perpetuate culture.

Douglass never became fully at ease in his conversion, and he used his authorship to represent his uneasiness. The author of *My Bondage and My Freedom* summons the writer of the *Narrative* by marking off long citations from the *Narrative*. In those passages, the earlier work surfaces as evidence of an incomplete conversion and of the story of the authorization of a fugitive slave. Because *My Bondage and My Freedom* frequently retains the exact wording of the *Narrative* without acknowledging the debt, the few lengthy block quotations stand out. Douglass uses such strategically placed passages to call attention to his ongoing struggle with an authorizing narrative.

The first such citation is especially rich, offering a way to read subsequent citations as well as both narratives. The passage describes the narrator's early experience of the songs sung continuously by the slaves to keep the masters and overseers apprised of their whereabouts and their progress. The discussion that introduces the passage is itself largely drawn from the *Narrative*, but it is not marked as such. Douglass underscores the explicitly cited passage:

> I have sometimes thought, that the mere hearing of those songs would do more to impress truly spiritual-minded men and women with the soul-crushing and death-dealing character of slavery, than the reading of whole volumes of its mere physical cruelties. They speak to the heart and to the soul of the thoughtful. I cannot better express my sense of them now, than ten years ago, when, in sketching my life, I thus spoke of this feature of my plantation experience:
>
> > "I did not, when a slave, understand the deep meanings of those rude, and apparently incoherent songs. I was myself within the circle, so that I neither saw nor heard as those without might see and hear. They told a tale which was then altogether beyond my feeble comprehension; they were tones, loud, long and deep, breathing the prayer and complaint of souls boiling over with the bitterest anguish. Every tone was a testimony against slavery, and a prayer to God for deliverance from chains. The hearing of those wild notes always depressed my spirits, and filled my heart with ineffable sadness. The mere recurrence, even now, afflicts my spirit, and while I am writing these lines, my tears are falling. To those songs I trace my first glimmering conceptions of the dehumanizing character of slavery. I

can never get rid of that conception. Those songs still follow me, to deepen my hatred of slavery, and quicken my sympathies for my brethren in bonds. If any one wishes to be impressed with a sense of the soulkilling power of slavery, let him go to Col. Lloyd's plantation, and on allowance day, place himself in the deep, pine woods, and there let him, in silence, thoughtfully analyze the sounds that shall pass through the chambers of his soul, and if he is not thus impressed, it will only be because 'there is no flesh in his obdurate heart' " (*MB*, 65–66)

Small editorial changes made in the passage from the earlier version show a writer attentive to his prose. The *Narrative*'s "while I am writing these lines, an expression of feeling has already found its way down my cheek" (*NFD*, 47), for example, becomes the more crisp "while I am writing these lines, my tears are falling." Such changes, however small, complicate Douglass's use of direct quotation. "I cannot better express my sense of them now, than ten years ago," he writes, yet the slight alterations belie that claim. Authorship entails endless revision, searching for the right words, writing within and chafing against conventions. Pointedly returning to the *Narrative*, Douglass conveys his sense of his own limitation at this moment in the later text. Was his work ten years ago perfectly expressed, or are some feelings, some stories, beyond expression? No one knows better than the seemingly comfortable author of *My Bondage and My Freedom* that he can never tell his whole story.

An analogy emerges between the slaves whose melodies express what they cannot speak and the writer who uses textual performance—here the intrusion of citation—when he finds words limited. The choice of where to mark the quotation seems especially curious to readers familiar with both works, since, as I have noted, earlier (unmarked) sentences are also taken from the *Narrative*. Yet, for some reason, the author marks the symbolic inability of the young slave to understand the songs of the older ones. "Within the circle," he could not understand. Only now, from "without" looking in, can he be an interpreter. The songs are evidently comprehensible only with a change of status. But what of the slave singers themselves? What distinguishes them from the young Douglass? The implied comparison suggests a perspective that comes with age or perhaps with their own change of state. The older slaves can remember or at least imagine the lost liberty of their African past, either first hand or through a communication that the reader is never privileged to witness or learn of in any of Douglass's narratives: an oral culture keeping alive the memory of the past, of Africa and liberty. The songs emanate from between worlds, from a consciousness deepened by or even born of the contrast implied by an important transformation.

With the citation, Douglass evokes his own metamorphoses—as a liberated slave, but also as an author. Sundquist reads the passage as offering an analogy between the author of the *Narrative* and the young, uncomprehending slave: his "recognition that in the *Narrative* he stood 'within the circle' . . . of Garrison's radical antislavery and the defined self of the platform storyteller it provided" (ES, 92). Indeed, that analogy would accord with the depiction of the *Narrative* presented elsewhere in *My Bondage and My Freedom*. But why, then, point to this passage as a description on which he cannot improve? Why evoke an authorship that he finds so deeply flawed? And, most importantly, why call attention to a narrative that his current work revises—unless he wants to call attention to himself as a writer in the *act* of revision? This is an undeniably self-conscious moment. Douglass was clearly writing with a copy of the *Narrative* before him, and he must have assumed that some readers would—or, at least, could—be reading that way as well. A careful writer, he must have been prepared to have them discover traces of his revision and, in some cases, to think about those traces. To those readers, he made available both the authorial strategies of the earlier work and the strategy behind the depiction of the younger author in *My Bondage and My Freedom*. The analogy forged in the passage is not so much between the author of the *Narrative* and the young uncomprehending slave as between the author of both narratives and the older slaves. The author of both texts is aware of Bailey, aware that he is himself still partly Bailey and that from that liminal status, that betwixt and between, comes the real force of his own authorship. No conversion, he suggests, is ever complete. *Narrative of the Life of Frederick Douglass, an American Slave* is itself a slave song, a haunting melody that says more through form than its author can express directly.

The writer of the *Narrative* emerges from this depiction as an author no less self-aware than the writer of *My Bondage and My Freedom*. The quoted passage ends with another citation, "there is no flesh in his obdurate heart," taken from a passage denouncing bias on the basis of skin color in William Cowper's *The Task*. A man imprisoned in his own melancholic madness, Cowper wrote *The Task* in response to the suggestion that writing about a mundane object, a sofa, might help him regain his mental composure. The title refers to the task of discovering how to live one's life, and to the task of writing in order to do so—of writing himself out of his metaphysical enslavement. The free white English poet is not an authorizing presence so much as a companionate one grappling with constraints intrinsic to authorship. The citation shows Douglass as an author fully alive, in both narratives, to the possibilities of writing as itself a heroic task. But the task of the representative American author is compounded by his sense of having been enlisted to tell a certain story. By citing the *Narrative,* the author of *My Bondage and My Freedom* calls attention to the task of the authorship of both narratives, to writers engaged in narrativizing their lives through conventional plots and stock scenes that make them recognizable as slaves (fugitive or liberated) and Americans.

The author of *My Bondage and My Freedom* does not so much undermine his claim to the title "representative American" as make available the implications of that status. The circumstances of the *Narrative* recounted in *My Bondage and My Freedom* disclose the complexity of authorship as they correlate Douglass's authorship with his enslavement. Frederick Douglass became an author to prove he was Frederick Bailey, a fugitive slave, that although he "did not talk like a slave, look like a slave, nor act like a slave," he "had . . . been south of Mason and Dixon's line" (*MB,* 221). In this act, Frederick Douglass both authorized Frederick Bailey and exposed him(self) to recapture. "The writing of my pamphlet, in the spring of 1845," he recalls ironically, "endangered my liberty, and led me to seek a refuge from republican slavery in monarchical England" (*MB,* 223). The *Narrative,* in other words, had undone the concealment that the name had been chosen to ensure. Frederick Douglass was useful to his antislavery sponsors particularly when he demonstrated an authenticity that threatened his freedom. Conversely, however, as *My Bondage and My Freedom* makes clear, his celebrity status saved him from, as it exposed him to, recapture. With the purchase of his legal liberty by friends in Great Britain, he became an emblem of what it meant to be threatened by enslavement, entrapped within a symbolic identity. Unquestionably, he preferred being a symbol to being a slave, but the suggestive analogy complicates the "freer story" of *My Bondage and My Freedom.*

In that later work, Douglass is willing to risk the consequences of using the slave as a symbol. The danger of minimizing the horrors of literal enslavement are nevertheless evident in a formulation that follows the first citation from the *Narrative:* "The slave is a subject, subjected by others; the slaveholder is a subject, but he is the author of his own subjection. There is more truth in the saying, that slavery is a greater evil to the master than to the slave, than many, who utter it, suppose" (*MB*, 69). Philosophically (as in Hegel's formulation) the slave is freer than the master, although surely not free; the slave can escape, while the master carries his enslavement with him. Particularly striking, however, is the use of the word *author.* Authorship here is at once the emblem of the master's freedom and the means of his self-subjection. By implication, the master can only work toward freedom if he recognizes himself as the author of his subjection. Douglass does not pursue the analysis. "Let others philosophize," he demurs, "it is my province here to relate and describe; only allowing myself a word or two, occasionally, to assist the reader in the proper understanding of the facts narrated" (*MB*, 69). Yet that is precisely the role he ostensibly rejects in writing *My Bondage and My Freedom,* the role forced on him by Garrison and his cohort: " 'Let us have the facts,' said the people. So also said Friend George Foster, who always wished to pin me down to my simple narrative. 'Give us the facts,' said Collins, 'we will take care of the philosophy' " (*MB*, 220). As elsewhere in *My Bondage and My Freedom,* Douglass stops short of extending an analysis that would in any way complicate his condemnation of slavery and minimize the plight of the slave. He does not push the association of authorship with both subjection and oppression. Yet his analyses linger in the "word or two," hints that offer glimpses into authorship as the activity through which Douglass demonstrates how current constraints on the story he can tell resemble the constrictions imposed by the abolitionists.

Douglass dramatizes the complications of his authorship in both texts in his account of how he learned to read and write, skills that bear with them, in Houston Baker's words, "both the freedom and the limitations resulting from literacy in Prospero's tongue" (*JB*, 43). He learned to read in Baltimore, where he lived for a time with the inlaws of his mistress. His first teacher was the wife of that Baltimore couple, until her husband interrupted her lessons with admonitions about the incompatibility of education and enslavement. Douglass marks this conversation between the Aulds, in both works, as the genesis of his understanding of "the white man's power to enslave the black man" (*NFD*, 58; *MB*, 93).[97] He resolves to learn to read and write as a way of achieving a spiritual liberty. To that end he enlists the unwitting help of white neighborhood children and completes his lessons by copying the letters previously copied by his young master from *Webster's Spelling Book,* the nation's most widely used speller. An American slave copies his master's text, which is in turn a copy of a master text. Simple on a literal level, this moment is symbolically complex. Webster's speller supplies him with the letters—more broadly, the conventions—that make his written story possible. But the symbolism of the act makes Webster's speller a fitting predecessor to the sponsors who simultaneously enable and restrict his speaking. When Douglass uses his hard-won literacy to write down his story, he fully and painfully confronts the ambiguity of a liberty that he had dreamed of, that he had survived in the hope of achieving, while he was still a slave. His account is less ambiguous about his liberty than it is only ambiguously liberating.

Webster's speller emblematizes that ambiguity. Noah Webster was known for his consolidationist sentiments and for the role he envisioned for his spelling and grammar texts in the promotion of a national American identity. Douglass and his young master learn to write not only from the most commonly used speller, but also from a text that grew out of its author's conviction that writers in the United States ought to participate in the development of the nation. Douglass and young Tommy Auld are similarly initiated into the mysteries of both literacy and American identity by a writer who, in a 1783 letter to Connecticut legislator John Canfield, mandated an "America . . . as independent in *literature* as she is in *politics,* as famous for *arts* as for *arms.*"[98] Webster's letter accompanied a petition to the Connecticut Assembly in which he requested exclusive rights to the production, sale, and profit of his spelling and grammar books. And he justified his request by explaining the potential contribution of his work to the state and to the emerging confederation. For Webster, all literary works—among which he included his speller—ought to articulate a cultural identity that reflected and justified, and also therefore promoted, union among the components of the fledgling Republic. The multivolume work that he proposed to call *The American Instructor,* for example, began with "a proper Spelling Book" designed to challenge the dominance of the English Thomas Dilworth's *Spelling Book* in the United States schools (*NWL*, 1). The speller, as he explained in the petition, could serve both as a guide to *American* "Orthography and Prosody" (NWS, 4)— toward internal standardization of American English—and as an emendation to the content of Dilworth's speller, some of which Webster found "totally useless in America" (*NWL*, 1).[99] The profit from and control over textual production allowed the would-be author "to promote [both] the interest of literature and the honor and dignity of the American empire" (*NWL*, 2). The Connecticut Assembly could encourage literary production with promises of the authors' profit from and control over their texts, and in turn the rights and privileges of authorship attested to the power of a governing body that could confer and safeguard them.

A speller may seem an unusual choice for such a task, but Webster's letter and petition insist on the centrality of that text to the federal project, as indeed one of its most fundamental items. Webster repeatedly refers to himself as the assembly's "memorialist," a word meaning both letter-writer and historian. By the eighth repetition of "memorialist" in three paragraphs (five in the last paragraph alone), a word that in this context had begun by meaning "letter-writer" increasingly suggests "historian." The transformation that he hoped the assembly would accomplish is thus rhetorically performed: the letter-writer (the petitioner) is turned into a historian, an author. This metamorphosis would at once depend upon and attest to the power of the assembly, but only the memorialist could help consolidate that power. Webster's urgent declaration of literary independence stressed one of two tasks that faced the confederation: declaring cultural independence from an empire that had supplied the majority of the colonies' early colonists as well as their language, social forms, and political institutions. The other task was the unification of these colonies. When Webster penned his request to the Connecticut Assembly, the federated states were not yet constituted as a nation as they would be in the nineteenth century, and distinguishing the recently liberated colonies from England marked a critical step in their redefinition. Without calling explicit attention to the lack of unity, he implied the Union's need for common memorials and for the standardized rhetorical and grammatical conventions, "Orthography and Prosody" (spelling and pronunciation) that would promote a unified cultural identity: the collective authorship subsequently figured in the Constitution's We the People.

Webster explicitly offered his speller "to diffuse an uniformity and purity of *language*—to add superior dignity to this infant Empire and to human nature"—to reproduce and disseminate cultural identity.[100] But it was also very consciously a memorial, a combination historical text and testament to the new confederation, an effort to create a past for something that did not yet exist in the present. The petition explains that *The American Instructor,* which would conclude with the "discovery" and "settlement" of America, was "designed to diffuse a political knowledge of this grand confederation of republics among that class of people who have not access to more expensive means of information" (*NWL,* 2)—a "political knowledge" of a legal entity and a corresponding cultural identity not yet in existence among a rising middle class that would embody it by believing in it.

Because *Webster's Spelling Book* increasingly propagandized the nation in the nineteenth century, it was both an obvious and a complicated site for the genesis of Douglass's authorship. Webster offered his text in the service of participatory democracy, and Douglass took it in exactly that spirit: liberty through literacy. Hugh Auld's objections to Douglass's literacy attest to the challenge he thus poses. Literacy, Auld explains to his wife, will make a slave less content. But Douglass's account of his acquisition of literacy is also emblematic of his "Americanization." Both Douglass *and* his young master learn by copying from *Webster's Spelling Book;* the same process creates both as authors—and subjects. They are thus strangely familiar. That familiarity interferes with the assumptions about personhood that allow Hugh Auld to accept the enslavement of Africans but assume his own exemption from the possibility of enslavement. Douglass's copying—in effect, an act of mimicry—repeats the master's copying, but with a difference that makes the terms of the master discourse more conspicuous.[101] Objecting to Douglass's literacy, Hugh Auld articulates America's fear not only of what literate slaves might do with their literacy, but also of the larger implications they embody when they refute white America's assumptions about the differences between white and black personhood—of the conventionality (the prescriptedness) of whiteness and blackness and of personhood. In turn, Douglass learns to read by copying a master—and a master's—discourse, a scenario emblematic of the complexities of his authorship.

The national narrative called for a heroic self-subordination, and to that call Frederick Douglass responded. But that act had consequences, and the author embodied what was risked by and lost in the suspended self of the national conversion. Even when his political strategy called for his successful conversion, even when, that is, the public figure sought to represent himself as already a representative American, Douglass did not—surely could not—fully repress that prescriptedness. Harriet Bailey, for instance, disappears from her son's language as her image fades from his mind, but her exclusion is neither as effective, nor as unnoticed by her son as many readers have suggested. Douglass continued, throughout his career, to be troubled by the implications of disappearances and erasures, and to work to call attention to untold stories. In both the *Narrative* and *My Bondage and My Freedom*, writing is not only a medium but also an analogue through which Douglass depicts the rhetorical and formal aspects of his struggle to negotiate, on one hand, a legislated exclusion from full personhood and, on the other hand, a heroic self-subordination to a national narrative that offered only unequal representation to Frederick Bailey.

Douglass's analogue calls attention to both the literariness of United States nationalism and the importance of literature to the project of nation-building. That was also the explicit and resounding message of self-proclaimed literary nationalists who called upon authors to articulate a cultural identity for the imagined community. The forceful articulations of literary nationalists gave shape and an explicitly nationalist inflection to the characteristically amorphous pressures exerted by literary markets or even less avowedly political editorial establishments, sensitizing some writers—such as the two considered in the next chapter, Herman Melville and Harriet Wilson—to the cultural concerns that necessarily shaped their stories. The presence of editors and literary markets in both works signal authorial constraints, but most striking in each, as in Douglass's narratives, is the telltale textual evidence of a struggling authorial presence.

2

"As From a Faithful Mirror"

Pierre, *Our Nig*, and Literary Nationalism

America was a story that needed telling, or so claimed the publishers and editors of a variety of periodicals in the early-to-mid decades of the nineteenth century dedicated to the telling of that tale. Different visions of the nation of course prompted different versions of the tale, but these tellers agreed on the importance of literature to the project of nation-building. Differences among them notwithstanding, these periodicals worked to convince a generation of authors to tell a story of America and to do so simply—or not so simply—by being American. This chapter explores the literary nationalism of a small but particularly aggressive group of New York-based literati known as the Young Americans and the efforts of two writers from very different backgrounds to understand the impact of the pressures of a nationalist imperative on their writing—the stories they could tell—and on themselves as national subjects.

No group of literary nationalists more passionately advocated the importance of a cultural declaration of independence from England than the Young Americans. Despite their size, this group formed powerful literary and editorial alliances, finding a forum for their views in journals such as *The United States Magazine and Democratic Review*, more commonly known as the *Democratic Review*, a journal founded in 1837 and dedicated to the promotion of United States nationalism. Preceded and outlasted by the prestigious Boston-based *North American Review*, the *Democratic Review* typically lacks the status of its rival in the literary histories of the United States. Yet the *Democratic Review* is particularly relevant for this study because of its association with the concept of "Manifest Destiny," a term coined by the founding editor of the *Democratic Review*, John L. O'Sullivan, within three years of the first issue.[1] The importance of this concept to the nation's self-definition explains the representative importance of this relatively short-lived group. While the Young Americans did not bestow a major literary legacy on the nation, they forcefully articulated prevalent assumptions about the literariness of the nation and the role of literature in nation-building. Significantly, in their delineation of a program for a relationship between literature and politics and their insistence on the importance of a uniquely "American" literature, the Young Americans helped to define the occupation of literary critic as explicator of original genius. It was the critic, they argued, who would make the nation see and know itself in its most original men of letters.[2]

For O'Sullivan, a truly American literature had to work toward defining the "Manifest Destiny" of the nation. In making the destiny of the nation manifest, literature at once attested to and promoted an American cultural identity through a national narrative that obscured even as it celebrated the author. In *Pierre* and *Our Nig*, Herman Melville and Harriet Wilson consider the strategies of that narrative: how it works and what it leaves out. Melville's *Pierre* directly addresses the literary nationalist program of Young America, showing how cultural conventions determine a young author's beliefs and shape the story that he can tell. Those internalized conventions doom the would-be author to plagiarism and ultimately, if circuitously, lead to his self-destruction; Pierre's suicide parodies a heroic self-surrender to a national narrative. Melville's Pierre is the archetypal American subject, and metaphors of his enslavement and feminization make apparent his dependence on the national narrative for his sense of himself as a presentable and representable person. Pierre literally cannot survive a challenge to that narrative.

Although the literary nationalists had no direct impact on Harriet Wilson, her analyses of the pressures of nationalism on an aspiring author show an engagement with, and the pervasiveness of, these concerns. *Our Nig* recounts the difficulty of an author, "Our Nig," to tell the story of a mulatta child's illegal indentured servitude—effectively, her enslavement—by a northern white family. Wilson superimposes the story of "Our Nig's" authorship on the allegory of Frado's struggle to find representation within a national narrative. She thereby demonstrates how the conventions of that narrative at once circumscribe the stories that can be told and empower white men and women, in different ways, to name and determine the fate of a black woman.

Between them, these works demonstrate how a range of sources—from self-proclaimed literary nationalists to a more amorphous literary market—participated in the fashioning of a cultural identity in the emerging nation. Issues on which critical readings of both works have centered obscure the resemblance between Pierre Glendinning, a scion of the American aristocracy, and Frado, a mulatta indentured servant, as well as between a professional white male author and an impoverished and deserted black mother writing for her life. *Pierre* has been typically, although not exclusively, read as the failed experiment of a (more or less grudgingly acknowledged) tortured genius; the distance between author and character has been collapsed in an autobiographical reading of this work, "the draught of a draught in a desperate sense."[3] *Our Nig*, too, has been read autobiographically, but for different reasons and to different ends. Readers have summoned the resemblance between Frado and Wilson to prove the existence of an African-American woman author who was almost forgotten. In both cases, the autobiographical readings, while convincing, have nonetheless minimized the thematic treatment of authorship.[4] I do not mean, in turn, to downplay the formal and stylistic differences between these narratives. No African-American woman in the antebellum United States had the same access to the literary establishment that Melville had, despite the difficulties of his reception. That did not mean that she could not hope to sell her work, but rather that it would be received differently, as a curiosity rather than a literary achievement, and would therefore require a different presentation. It is thus hardly surprising that *Pierre* and *Our Nig* are very different. More striking are their strategic and thematic similarities, which attest to the inseparability of political and aesthetic concerns for both authors.

Both works evince and address the difficulty of telling the story of exclusion. In what, speaking of *Pierre*, he called his "rural bowl of milk," Melville examines the fate of the national subject within, and without, the law.[5] The only son of an aristocratic American family, descendant of heroes of the Indian and Revolutionary Wars, Pierre stands poised to inherit the nation. But unable to tolerate his discovery of his prescriptedness, he leaves his divided house without an heir. Although neither Frado nor "Our Nig" shares the fate of Pierre, Frado is figuratively enslaved by a depiction of herself, painted by the Bellmont family, that she internalizes. She cannot imagine herself without the terms of their national narrative. Her enslavement becomes an analogue for the financial and political considerations that circumscribe "Our Nig's" analysis of the national narrative. In Pierre's alienation and in Frado's enslavement, Melville and Wilson explore the cultural anxieties that made their stories, like those of the Cherokee and slave litigants, so difficult to tell.

Conspiring with the Design

O'Sullivan founded the *Democratic Review* with his brother-in-law, Samuel Langtree. A Jacksonian Democrat, O'Sullivan envisioned a nation that was neither Douglass's nor Lincoln's nation. In fact, his Young American collaborators at the *Democratic Review* did not share his politics.[6] Yet they shared a commitment to the development of a national culture and fashioned a narrative of literary nationalism that for their brief association in the 1840s transcended specific political differences and offered a program notable for its insistence on the literary promotion of an American identity. Most importantly, they agreed that the articulation of a national culture required the development of a recognizable national literature. In the Introduction to the first issue of the *Democratic Review*, the writer, almost certainly O'Sullivan, proclaims, "it is only by its literature that one nation can utter itself and make itself known to the rest of the world"; hence the importance of a literature that would be uniquely and recognizably American.[7] Yet the literary prescriptions offered in the pages of the *Democratic Review* were typically confusing; they fashioned a literature that paradoxically reflected and created a national identity, an ambiguity that also characterized the concept of Manifest Destiny. Significantly, writers interested in learning to write like Americans could find less guidance in the reviews of particular literary works than in manifestos about the nation itself, essays like O'Sullivan's "The Great Nation of Futurity" (1839) or Evert Duyckinck's "Nationality in Literature" (1847).

The nation of O'Sullivan's "The Great Nation of Futurity" was at once extant and imminent; the diverse origins of "the American people" and the basis of the Declaration in "the great principle of human equality" marked the "disconnected position" of the nation from "the past history of any [other nation], and still less with all antiquity, its glories, or its crimes" (6.23:426). That "disconnected position" at the same time constituted and called for a tradition that the literature of the nation had to supply. But only a literature that had itself broken from tradition could adequately express the identity of that nation. "The Great Nation of Futurity" found a paradigm for that literature in "the Declaration of National Independence."

Whether summoned by Noah Webster or Frederick Douglass, Abraham Lincoln or Stephen Douglas, the Declaration of Independence marked both a distinction between the colonies and England and a new conjunction among the colonies. An American literature modeled on "the Declaration of National Independence" had similarly to express at once independence (distinction) and nationhood (conjunction). "All history has to be re-written" from an *American* perspective, argues O'Sullivan in his introductory essay, which is to say "in light of the democratic principle" (1.1:14). And in "The Great Nation of Futurity," he heralds the "national birth" of the United States as "the beginning of a new history," the genesis of a narrative of identity (6.23:426). With the Declaration as a paradigm, O'Sullivan posits a reciprocity between a text and the material world in which the Declaration utters a nation into existence and actually becomes its tradition, a tradition of group authorship and its corollary, the disappearance of the speaking subject into the group.

O'Sullivan's new history differs from Lincoln's logic of history in its *evident* textuality, its *emphasis* on the act of authorship. Lincoln had to distinguish his particular version of history from other versions within the United States. O'Sullivan and the literary nationalists had a different goal. They wanted to fashion an American story that would express the uniqueness as well as the coherence of the United States, a national culture distinct, especially, from English culture. They emphasized the telling of that story, an authorship which attested to that distinct culture, more than the tale itself. Yet, as I shall demonstrate, the literary nationalists insisted on prescriptions for that storytelling that authorized their (often contradictory) political vision. Melville and Wilson register the nature and consequences of those prescriptions.

The narrative fashioned by the literary nationalists was shaped by the contradictions and demands of the doctrine of Manifest Destiny, a doctrine espoused by O'Sullivan and in principle opposed—but in practice acquiesced in—by his Young American associates. They urged American writers to breathe the spirit of the American landscape, invariably an expansive western landscape, into their indigenous literature. "The expansive future is our arena," O'Sullivan intones in "The Great Nation of Futurity," "and for our history. We are entering on its untrodden space" (4.23:427). O'Sullivan, like his literary allies, explicitly enjoined the nation's writers not to define the nation by the priority of the material continent, but consciously and conspicuously to turn that landscape into a symbol of the nation, what Myra Jehlen terms an "American Incarnation," something very much like what I earlier called Lincoln's geography of inevitability.[8]

Rewriting history and symbolizing the landscape were to be conscious, and consciously national, projects. Implicit in that symbolization, in other words, was an awareness of the transformation enacted in the incarnation. The writer of "The Great Nation of Futurity" insists that "American patriotism is not of soil; we are not aborigines, nor of ancestry, for we are of all nations; but it is essentially personal enfranchisement," an ideal (6.23:429). Like Justice Benjamin Curtis in his *Dred Scott* decision, O'Sullivan implies that the law—government, the "American experiment" (1.1:1)—creates as it demarcates the territory. "America" inheres not in the physical space of the continent, but in how the collectivity transforms that landscape—and in how that newly politicized landscape attests to the presence of "the American people."

For O'Sullivan, the diverse European peoples populating the new continent require a group story to express a collective identity, and that story is about the idea that has brought them together as a group, the common commitment to a government instituted to attest to the advantages of governance according to the divine principles of liberty and equality: "in its magnificent domain of space and time, the nation of many nations is destined to manifest to mankind the excellence of divine principles" (6.23:427). That common commitment replaces identification by land or lineage. The identity of those who share it precedes but is also manifested by the story, and they exist as a group in order to broadcast that story. At the same time, the story reinforces, shapes, and in its way, creates the group. Their destiny inheres in the principles, but it is their transformation of the landscape that manifests their existence as a group and thus witnesses their enactment of their destiny.[9] While the continent does become a symbol of the nation, the symbolizing process more importantly attests to a national spirit, although even the architects of Manifest Destiny themselves frequently confused the symbol with the process.

O'Sullivan was not alone in his belief that the symbolic use of the land could minimize sectional and political divisions within the Union. In an 1844 oration entitled "The Young American," an epithet intended to refer to the general population rather than the particular movement, Ralph

Waldo Emerson calls for gardens, since they make "it indifferent where you live. A well-laid garden makes the face of the country of no account."[10] Emerson's gardens avoid divisive disputes as they show the transformative power of an idea. "Americanness" inheres in the transforming—or symbolizing—*process* rather than in any material fact of the land. That land, especially in the context of the expansionism of the 1840s (the much disputed annexation of Texas, which Emerson opposed, for example) could foster disunity unless made "of no account" by its metamorphosis—into a garden as into a symbol. The garden calls attention to the agents of change rather than to the contested property. Even in his anthropomorphic claim that "the nervous, rocky West is intruding a new and continental element into the national mind," Emerson makes clear that the land intrudes as an idea (YA, 216).

The garden is the dialectical conceptualization of the material presence of the land and its meaning: "How much better when the whole land is a garden and the people have grown up in the bowers of a paradise" (YA, 216). Here the garden is less an efflorescence than the manifestation of a transformation of—conceived as a conspiring with—nature. In this "country of beginnings, of projects, of designs, and expectations," Emerson posits "a sublime and friendly Destiny by which the human race is guided" (YA, 217), a Destiny manifested, again, not in the landscape, but in its metamorphosis—and in the gardens that mark the translation of a national vision (an idea) into national vision (perception). Emerson's gardens act as a text, like the national literature that "the rapid and impetuous orator of New England" Rufus Choate had advanced before a Massachusetts audience in 1833.[11] Common books would unite a reading public into a "national character" with a literature that would be "common property," Choate—who was also a lawyer—explained, "and, unlike that land, it would be indivisible. It would be as the opening of a great fountain for the healing of nations."[12] By turning the land itself into such a text, Emerson turns the American people into common authors as well as common readers. As in O'Sullivan's formulation, gardens *express* and *reinforce* more than *create* a national character, although neither Emerson nor O'Sullivan and his associates consistently held to that distinction.

According to the Young America literary nationalists, a coherent body of literature such as Choate argued for could and should promote the process of manifesting the nation and its destiny. The injunction with which Emerson concludes "The Young American" elegantly and concisely (although not intentionally) summarizes their program: "If only the men are employed in conspiring with the designs of the Spirit who led us hither, and is leading us still, we shall quickly enough advance out of all hearing of other's censures, out of all regrets of our own, into a new and more excellent social state than history has recorded" (YA, 230). Yet literary Young America never claimed Emerson's Young American. The *Democratic Review* did hail "Nature" and rank Emerson among the "minds of the highest order of genius" (1.3:319). And the Duyckincks and their cohort admired Emerson as a writer, but they found him, finally, too obscure and Transcendentalism too arcane for their purposes, a choice that further clarifies their own vision of an American author. In their 1855 *Cyclopaedia*, the Duyckincks described his work as "some of the most subtle, airy, eloquent, spiritual products of American literature," telling praise for critics who valued substantiality and hardiness (*CAL*, 365). In the end, Emerson's Young American was more exuberantly self-authorizing and spontaneous than the Young Americans of *The Democratic Review*. Where Emerson advocated a break with tradition, the Young Americans conspicuously claimed a tradition. Emerson's Young American challenged and revivified a fossilized government, while the Young Americans' author expressed and developed the greatest national story ever told. And Emerson reveled in the inconsistencies that troubled Young America.

The *Democratic Review*'s call for a national literature recruited writers to conspire with the designs of the Spirit, but theirs was a national plot that entailed the creation both of American narratives and of *an American narrative*. The job of a national literature, as they articulated it, was to make manifest the design of a national destiny by representing a diverse group of European peoples as a distinct culture, a culture rooted in a shared vision rather than a shared past.[13] The symbolizing process that very obviously converts a changing land mass into a nation, making its shifting boundaries seem coherent, attests to a definable cultural presence. My reading differs from accounts of Manifest Destiny in which adherents of that doctrine intended to obscure the act of symbolizing beneath a putative act of discovering. It is certainly true that just as the erased distinctions signified by the term "Indians" retroactively helped to posit a pre–United States homogeneity, "the continent" of Manifest Destiny rhetoric helped to image and ground coherence. But the coherence itself was authorized by an articulated set of beliefs—an acknowledged, indeed a celebrated, ideology—evident in the act of authorship performed by We the People.

The national vision created by the narrative of Manifest Destiny had to resolve (or obscure) the contradictions and representational and political difficulties of an imperial nation. If the transformation of the land signaled the presence of a coherent people, then expansion should not trouble coherence. Expansion, instead, had to express rather than challenge that coherence, had indeed to become a defining characteristic of the nation. O'Sullivan associate and chief propounder of the doctrine of Manifest Destiny, William Gilpin, reported to the United States Senate, in 1846, that "the untransacted destiny of the American people is to subdue the continent, to rush over this vast field to the Pacific Ocean."[14] National growth, in this report, demonstrates the efficacy of the nation's democratic principles: "from nothing we have become 20,000,000. . . . we are grown to be in agriculture, in commerce, in civilization, and in natural strength, the first among nations existing or in history" (CR, 230). These principles justify the subduing of the continent. In turn, that subduing rather than the continent emblematizes the nation. The nation begins with a principle that is uttered into a culture (a way of being and of symbolizing); the culture becomes a political entity, a nation, by establishing boundaries. But the professed imperialism of the proponents of Manifest Destiny demonstrates a missionary zeal that physical boundaries would bely. Gilpin's exuberant catalogue, worth quoting in full, pushes past the Pacific Ocean

> to animate the many hundred millions of its people, and to cheer them upward—to set the principle of self-government at work—to agitate these herculean masses—to establish anew order in human affairs—to set free the enslaved—to regenerate superannuated nations—to change darkness into light—to stir up the sleep of a hundred centuries—to teach old nations a new civilization—to confirm the destiny of the human race—to carry the career of mankind to its culminating point—to cause stagnant people to be reborn—to perfect science—to emblazon history with the conquest of peace—to shed anew resplendent glory upon mankind—to unite the world in one social family—to dissolve the spell of tyranny and exalt charity—to absolve the curse that weighs down humanity, and to shed blessings round the world! (CR, 230)

The problems that would, by the Civil War, make national unity an impossibility are evident in Gilpin's metaphors. The assertion that the nation's destiny is "to set free the enslaved," as we have seen, eventually could no longer coexist with the fact of an enslaved population, and the union of any people in "one social family" had to contend with the hint of miscegenation intrinsic to that metaphor. These and related conflicts exacerbated by expansion consistently troubled assertions of national coherence.

Although the Young Americans opposed the national expansion for which Manifest Destiny stood, the glorious symbol of an expanding nation proved irresistible to them. In his own manifesto, "Nationality in Literature," Evert Duyckinck celebrated national expansion. His professed concerns about material expansion gave way before his obvious delight in the prospect of the global influence (ideological expansion) of the United States.

> there are many persons who have not yet tasted of death, who were living when Edmund Burke, on the floor of the British Parliament, described America as having been, within the life-time of the then Lord Bathurst, "a little speck, scarce visible in the mass of the national interest; a small seminal principle, rather than a formed body." That infant people, then "but in the gristle, and not yet hardened into the bone of manhood,"—struggling with the vicissitudes of life in a new country, and subduing the wilderness and the savage tribes who peopled it,—thirteen feeble colonies, "growing by the neglect of their parent state, ["] *have* . . . achieved their National Independence, . . . erected new institutions of government, a new civil polity and social condition,—become the first political power in the Western hemisphere, and the second commercial power in the world,—and *is* beginning to exert an influence upon human affairs, which, if wisely directed, seems likely to change the destinies of our race, through all future time, and over the entire surface of the globe. (20.105:264; emphasis added)

Duyckinck's assumptions and his confusion about the nation and national expansion emerge in the rhetoric of the passage. For instance, he asserts the consolidation of the colonies into the Union, a precondition for global influence, in a grammatical inconsistency. He shifts from the third-person plural auxiliary verb "have" ("that infant people, . . . thirteen feeble colonies, . . . have") to the third-person singular "is." This grammatical slip reflects irresolution about whether "that infant people" is a plural or a singular subject, an irresolution that Young America set out to address. Here Duyckinck's shift corresponds to—and rhetorically enacts—a consolidationist victory, in which the people (and the colonies) unite to form a nation: *these* United States become *the* United States. There may even be something willful in this error, as though a grammatical sleight of hand (metaphorically, an act of authorial choice) can perform the transformation: the contraction (from plural to singular) enables the expansion of national growth.

The expansion figured here does not seem to threaten consolidation, as the Young Americans feared; rather, the essence—and the destiny—of the nation is expansion. And an expanding *nation* implies the triumph of the democratic principle. Yet Duyckinck's language belies this triumph. Something is lost in the emergence of the nation, a loss played out in the language between the two auxiliary verbs, "have" and "is": "Thirteen feeble colonies . . . have . . . *achieved* their National Independence, . . . *erected* new institutions of government, . . . *become* the first political power in the Western hemisphere . . . and is beginning to exert an influence upon human affairs." The verbs between "have" and "is" mark a shift from the colonies' actions ("achieved," "erected") to the existence of the nation ("become"), and the nouns move from the *object* of transitive verbs ("National Independence") to the *subject* of an intransitive verb (political and economic growth). The rhetorical logic of this passage progresses from what the nation has done—its uttering itself into existence— to what it has become (utter*ance* rather than utter*ing*). Political and economic growth, intended as evidence of the superiority of the democratic principle, instead demonstrate only national influence. We see the independence and the new institutions, but the "influence upon human affairs" is vague, in need of "wise direction" and of definition.

The metaphors Duyckinck borrows from Burke gender both the nation and the dissemination of national influence.[15] And against the "savage tribes," this descendant of Europeans (Duyckinck's ancestors were Dutch) asserts the whiteness of "that infant people." A white male body becomes the emblem—the governing body—of the nation, and expansion becomes an expression of its very essence, its white masculinity. In Chapter 1, I showed the legal and social fate of bodies not in conformity with this body image in an expanding nation. Those exclusions similarly troubled the formulations and haunted the metaphors of Young America. Later in this chapter, we will see them resurface in *Pierre* and *Our Nig*.

In this passage, however, the metaphor is supplied from overseas, and it attests to the kinship between Great Britain, "the parent state," and the former colonies. The passage shows Duyckinck claiming more of a kinship with Great Britain than the Young Americans typically acknowledged. The words of Conservative Irish member of Parliament Edmund Burke, from "The Thirteen Resolutions" (one of his two speeches "On Conciliation with America"), seem oddly out of place in a description of the nation's uttering itself into a cultural and political independence. Duyckinck both cites and paraphrases Burke, interweaving Burke's words with his own phrases in a description of America that appears to fulfill the prophecy of the British statesman. Burke offers not only the metaphor of the young male body and of an "American spirit" in this speech, but also the principle of an empire that governs by influence, by the superiority of the liberty offered in and embodied by the English Constitution, rather than by violence.[16] "It was not English arms, but the English Constitution, that conquered Ireland," writes Burke; "you never touched the form of the vital substance of free government" (TR, 120–21). And Burke even posits the "love of freedom [which] is the predominating feature" of the "character of the Americans" as an English legacy: "the people of the colonies are descendants of Englishmen" (TR, 121). English echoes resound throughout Duyckinck's nationalist paean, adding some force to the charge, leveled by critics and political rivals, that Young America was a fundamentally derivative movement.[17] National expansion itself seems to be a familial inheritance from the British empire.

The unexamined confusion and contradictions concerning national growth, expansion, and American exceptionalism made Young America and its associates call all the more urgently for an American literature to force the nation from what Duyckinck calls its "colonial and provincial dependency on the old world" (20.105:265). Literature becomes, for him, not just a means for the expression of this challenge, but a medium for its enactment as well: "When the colonies finally asserted their independence, it was only against the political power of the mother-country. They retained her language, her letters, and the fame of her great writers, as their birthright as Englishmen, or the descendants of Englishmen; their young career in letters was commenced under all the influences of old habits, old associations, and old prejudices in favor of English models, and the mind of the country has not yet cast off this old literary domination" (20.105:266). Duyckinck here summons the "birth-right" that Burke used to advocate English conciliation with the colonies, but for Duyckinck the family metaphor underscores the importance of renouncing rather than reconciling; his is the child's rather than the parent's—in this case, the *mother's*—perspective. As in Lincoln's speeches, manhood—synonymous, as the metaphor makes clear, with personhood—is itself at stake in national independence; a (pro)generative culture replaces mother and birthright. Literature must be a *manly* endeavor.

Characteristically, in the *Democratic Review*, the metaphor of enslavement describes a culture still dependent on the mother country, a culture not yet distinctively national, but sufficiently cohesive to allow the first-person plural pronoun: "our mind is enslaved to the past and present literature of England" (1.1:14). The metaphor of enslavement, not an uncommon one, was a conventional trope of Revolutionary rhetoric and was even used by Burke in his "Conciliation with America" speeches.[18] But it appears in the pages of the *Democratic Review* with a remarkable insistence, often as an adjective, "slavish imitation" (O'Sullivan, 1.1:14), or an adverb, "slavishly adhere to old and foreign models" (E. Duyckinck, 20.105:271). Duyckinck even argues that "overmastered by the literature of England, we have consented to remain in a *state of pupilage*, instead of aspiring to be masters in the vocation of letters"—the metaphor employed as well by the defense in *Johnson v. McIntosh* (20.105:266; emphasis added).[19] Familiar demons that trouble United States nationalism, threats to manhood and liberty, are herein summoned to insist on the importance and the immediacy of the national task of literature. Those metaphors reinforced what the literary nationalists of the *Democratic Review* characteristically suggested: the government designed to ensure the liberty of "the people" was itself at risk without the cultural independence reflected in the nation's literature. Implicitly, they also expressed who was constituted by "the American people" by implying who was not included therein—domestic dependents, the enslaved. Yet political events—and antislavery activists—were making those metaphors increasingly difficult to summon in this fashion.

As the contradictions in their vision of America become increasingly evident in their calls for a national literature, the less literary among the affiliates of the *Democratic Review* in particular turned more forcefully to textual metaphors. William Gilpin, for instance, introduced his messianic catalogue of what the nation was destined to achieve with a celebratory phrase that emphasized the pre-scriptedness of America: "From this threshold we read the future" (*CR*, 230). The future is evidently prewritten, but by whom? The Puritans, similarly underscoring the textuality of their world, would have said God, but for Gilpin, O'Sullivan, and Duyckinck, to name a relevant few, it is a godhead abstracted in a social principle. O'Sullivan from the beginning called "the democratic princi- ple . . . the sister spirit of Christianity" (*DR* 1.1:8). Gilpin's use of the growth and prominence of the nation as evidence of divine sanction cer- tainly resembles Puritan rhetoric. But there is a key difference involving authorship: the Declaration expresses, and the Constitution is authored by, the (alleged) will of "the People." Through the act of writing these texts by which they literally authorize themselves, "the People" demonstrate their worthiness to enact a national destiny. Here is Emerson's conspiracy with the ambiguously named Spirit, a deity reconceived as the articulation of the inherent principle through which the group already coheres. Man- ifest Destiny looks to the past—what the nation has become—to "read the future." The Puritans themselves unquestionably dwell in the metaphors of Manifest Destiny—such as in O'Sullivan's piously entoned "bearing forward the ark of democratic truth, entrusted to us as a chosen people, towards the glorious destiny of its future" (1.1:13)—inhabitants of a signif- icantly mediated vision, the attempt to reclaim a much revised "national" past. "America" emerges in the dynamic tension between reading and writing—or expressing and creating—an identity.

In this formulation, which celebrates the sense of telling a prewritten story, literary works are supposed to retell—or discover—the story of America. Duyckinck simultaneously advocates a mirroring and a generat- ing role for literature in his prescriptive essay "Nationality in Literature":

> Something will be gained for the cause of an indigenous literature by a clear development of the idea and the necessity of nationality. First and foremost, nationality involves the idea of home writers. Secondly, the choice of a due proportion of home themes, affording opportunity for descriptions of our scenery, for the illustration of passing events, and the preservation of what tradition has rescued from the past, and for the exhibition of the manners of the people, and the circumstances which give form and pressure to the time and the spirit of the country; and all these penetrated and vivified by an intense and enlightened patriotism. The literature of a country should, as from a faithful mirror, reflect the physical, moral and intellectual aspects of the nation. (20.105:267)

Indigenous literature and nationality coexist in a mutually-defining rela- tionship in this passage. The metaphor of the faithful mirror appears to suggest that literature is to reflect national greatness. But Duyckinck also wants to assign literature a more actively creative task; nationality, which "involves the idea of home writers," itself rests on the demonstrable presence of a preexisting indigenous literature. Explicitly following prominent French woman of letters Mme. de Staël, Duyckinck suggests that reflecting is also a way of shaping the nation. Mme. de Staël, he writes, "concludes, that the form of government, the laws, the private manners and pursuits, and the religion of a people, are reflected by, and characterize their literature; and that these circumstances, in their turn, re-act upon the form of the government, the spirit of the laws, and the temper and condition of the people" (20.105:267). The mirror has a clearly formative effect on political and cultural identity, a dialectical process that literature perpetuates; here is the activity of symbolizing conceived as a perpetual (re)constituting.

Duyckinck turns to the law to represent the simultaneously creative and reflective role that he envisions for a national literature. It was the Enlightenment French philosopher Montesquieu, he explains, who elucidated the relationship between "the political and civil laws of each nation" and "the Spirit of laws" (20.105:268). For Montesquieu, laws had to reflect the conditions of the group, from landscape to life style. "The Spirit of laws" expresses the relationship between the laws and the particular factors from which they are derived and by which they are therefore justified. Where the laws turn the group into a society, "the Spirit of laws" explains the appropriateness—the inevitability—of those laws for that society. "The Spirit of laws," in other words, expresses a preexisting collectivity governed by the laws. When Duyckinck asks, "Do not these relations just as essentially enter into, and characterize, the spirit of a national literature?" (20.105:268), he gives a national literature a governing role that he bases in the ability of that literature to articulate a latent identity. Such an identity exists, but it is unrealized until given expression by a national literature—as, for Montesquieu and de Staël, it was expressed by the law.

Critics of Young America charged the group with prescriptiveness, contending that the movement would circumscribe the very independence and originality for which it called. Duyckinck cites a critic who, writing in the rival *North American Review*, characteristically complains "that 'an intense national self-consciousness, though the shallow may call it patriotism, is the worst foe to the true and generous unfolding of national genius'" (20.105:267).[20] And James Russell Lowell, who would eventually become editor of the *North American Review,* insisted that no literature could, strictly speaking, be called national; he equated nationalism in literature with provincialism.[21] Responding to accusations that they compromised the *independence* of authors, Young Americans countered by defining true American authorship as independence. Young American William Alfred Jones declares in his own manifesto, "Democracy in Literature," that "of all men the author and the scholar, should come nearest to the ideal of the Patriot" and that "every true writer is an independent," assertions he finds synonymous (*DR,* 11.50:196). And Duyckinck proclaims, "We would set no limits to the subjects on which our authors should write. We would leave to them the whole range of nature and humanity. We would wish them to strike every key in the grand scale of human passion. *But we would have them true to their country"* (20.105:271; emphasis added). An assertion earlier in that essay best demonstrates the role he imagines for literature and what he means by "true to their country": "We would not restrict the empire of thought," he insists, "but annex our noble domain to it" (20.105:269). In 1847, the metaphor of annexation would surely evoke the annexation of Texas, a potentially divisive political issue. But Duyckinck's metaphor reconceives the empire as a state of mind, as an ideological rather than geographic entity, which can therefore be endlessly expanded. Once the geopolitical annexation has happened, it falls to literary nationalism to perform the work of absorption, which it accomplishes through redefinition. To that end, the authors free to write as they please must nonetheless continually (re)constitute "America" and "Americans."

For Young America, the literary critic stood in relation to literature as writers generally stood to culture. Duyckinck concludes "Nationality in Literature" with a promise subsequently to "point out the American writers and writings most deeply imbued with a national spirit," to create what in the parlance of contemporary academia is called a literary canon (20.105:272).[22] The reviewer of Emerson's "Nature," in the *Democratic Review,* calls critics "the priests of literature" (1.3:320), and Jones calls "the critic . . . the advocate of the poet, the exponent of the feelings of the people towards him, the middle-man between the two" (19:198). According to Young American Cornelius Mathews, himself a prolific writer, the critic should discern "the author's design" as the nationalist author should discern the "Spirit's."[23] The Young Americans were typically explicit about their political role—exuberantly so. "In behalf of this young America of ours," Mathews told a New York audience, "I insist on nationality and true Americanism in the books this country furnishes to itself and to the world."[24] Through its various manifestations, as well as implicitly through anthologies, Young American critical journalism avowedly created as much as it reflected a national literature. Yet they never forgot that the literary critic was also a writer, and they dwelled in the contradictions of a manifest destiny that alternately celebrated and obscured their critical activity. Implicitly, Young America asked authors to perform the kind of heroic self-surrender that Lincoln would call for in the Second Inaugural Address, and with a similar reward: self-realization through self-sacrifice. Expectations that opponents of the movement saw as constraints placed upon the "American author" became, in the eyes of Young America, an opportunity for greatness. But, finally, their program called more for critics than for writers, and it created as it relied on a distinction between them. Such was the discovery of the author of *Typee* (1846), in whom they thought they had found just the kind of author they sought.

Unlike Emerson, Melville enjoyed an intimate relationship with Young America in the late 1840s. Unlike his Young American associates, however, Melville was also drawn to Emerson because, he wrote to Evert Duyckinck in 1849, "I love all men who dive."[25] In *Pierre, or the Ambiguities* (1852), Melville at once explores a young American author's efforts to dive and marks his break with Young America. Melville's novel analyzes the effect of the prescriptions of Young America's nationalist narrative on a would-be author who has internalized those terms. But an earlier work, written in conjunction with prominent Young Americans, anticipates *Pierre* as it suggests, through parody, a growing discomfort with the terms through which Young America authorized the American writer.

In 1850, writing as "a Virginian Spending July in Vermont," Melville penned a review of Nathaniel Hawthorne's *Mosses from an Old Manse* for consecutive August issues of George and Evert Duyckinck's *Literary World*, Young America's critical review.[26] Biographical accounts of the circumstances of the composition of the review posit its genesis in Melville's response to an assertion of British superiority in letters made by Oliver Wendell Holmes during the course of a Berkshire outing that also included Hawthorne, prominent Young Americans Evert Duyckinck and Cornelius Mathews, and other notable literati.[27] The language of the "Virginian" is certainly compatible with the presumption of an empassioned response to Holmes. The reviewer condemns belief in British literary supremacy ("Shakespeare's unapproachability") as inappropriate "for an

American, a man who is bound to carry republican progressiveness into Literature as well as into Life."[28] He also declaims that "while we are rapidly preparing for that political supremacy among the nations which prophetically awaits us at the close of the present century, in a literary point of view, we are deplorably unprepared for it; and we seem studious to remain so" (HHM, 1164). With such assertions the review had no trouble passing the notorious censorship of Duyckinck and Mathews, who reputedly helped Melville edit it after the celebrated Berkshire revels. Duyckinck's voice seems to blend with Melville's in the sentiments, rhetoric, and style of much of the review. Characteristic of Duyckinck is the claim that "it is not meant that all American writers should studiously cleave to nationality in their writings; only this, no American writer should write like an Englishman, or a Frenchman; let him write like a man, for then he will be sure to write like an American" (HHM, 1164). The assumptions that a writer in the United States who writes from experience rather than literary imitation—who writes, that is, like a man—is very much in keeping with Young America's assumptions of a cohesive identity waiting to be expressed, as well as with their equation of Americanness and manhood. A *Literary World* review of Melville's *Mardi* written in 1849, for example, asks, "Is not this sign of a true manhood, when an American author lifts his voice boldly to tell the truth to his country people?" (*ML*, 299). At the same time, however, "Hawthorne and His Mosses" subtly registers Melville's break with his Young America affiliates, a break they would not recognize until its more obvious articulation in *Pierre*.

Evidently, the editors of the *Literary World* did not find Melville's meditation on the manhood of "Nathaniel of Salem" troubling. The Virginian claims no acquaintance with the author, who, he feels, "has dropped germinous seeds into [his] soul . . . and further, and further, shoots his strong New England roots into the hot soil in [his] Southern soul" (HHM, 1167). The passage is in keeping with the tone of the essay and New Yorkers Duyckinck and Mathews might well have enjoyed the playfulness with which Melville feminized the Virginian. Moreover, the usages of manhood and germination in this context are sufficiently conventional to escape notice. Not particular to Manifest Destiny, that language was certainly characteristic of it, as in O'Sullivan's "We feel safe under the banner of the democratic principle, which is borne onward by an unseen hand of Providence, to lead our race toward the high destinies of which every human soul contains the *God-implanted germ*" (*DR*, 1.1:9; emphasis added) or his insistence that "the vigorous national heart of America, propelling the onward march of the multitude, propagating and extending" the Puritan emigrants' "powerful purpose of soul . . . was the seed that produced individual equality, and political liberty, as its natural fruit" ["Great Nation," 6.23:429]). Nonetheless, Melville's eroticized rhetoric depicts Hawthorne as a seducer more nearly than the patriot-writer heralded by the literary nationalists and anticipates the "lipographs" with which the author-hero autographs ladies' albums in *Pierre.* In his hands, such glorious expostulations of national destiny as O'Sullivan's or as Duyckinck's seminal principle hardening into the bone of manhood to erect new institutions of government become seduction—even an implicit sodomy—of the feminized Virginian/South by the aggressively masculine Hawthorne/New England: the author as national expansionist. Two years later, he would conspicuously feminize Pierre Glendinning in a passage reminiscent of the Virginian's germination allusion in order to mark Pierre's exclusion from a narrative of American (masculine) identity and his consequent inability to conceive of himself as an author.

Melville was sincere in his admiration of Hawthorne, and I do not read these images as critical of him. Rather, Melville extends the implications of Young America's paradigm of authorship. His critique surfaces through unexpected turns, such as an odd one that follows a comparison of Hawthorne and Shakespeare. Anticipating the reader's doubt that Hawthorne approaches the Bard of Avon, the reviewer notes the inappropriateness of the belief in Shakespeare's superiority "for an American, a man who is bound to carry republican progressiveness into Literature, as well as into Life" (HHM, 1161). He concludes with a somewhat disjunctive meditation on the discovery of America the continent in 1492 rather than America the principle of 1776: "You must have plenty of sea-room to tell the Truth in; especially, when it seems to have an aspect of newness, as America did in 1492, though it was then just as old, and perhaps older than Asia, only those sagacious philosophers, the common sailors, had never seen it before; swearing it was all water and moonshine there" (HHM, 1162). The American *bound* to carry republican progressiveness wherever he goes brings a narrative like the one that created "America," a narrative that determines what can and what cannot be seen. Thus far he does not depart from Young American precepts, and he genuinely does not, with Holmes, cede superiority in letters to the British. But neither could he ignore—and, in this passage, he evokes—what was overlooked in the name of "discovery" and by the rhetoric of Manifest Destiny: the idea of "America" did indeed predate the continent, but it was not new with "America." And the continent, far from being synonymous with the nation, was itself frequently overlooked and had certainly been overrun by it.

The Virginian expresses his most powerful depiction of Hawthorne's departure from Young American precepts in his observation that "Hawthorne's soul . . . is shrouded in a blackness, ten times black." This blackness, again a conventional trope, refers to Hawthorne's Calvinism, and it expresses his unfathomability: "He is immeasurably deeper than the plummet of the mere critic" (HHM, 1159), a line that echoes Melville's reference to Emerson in the 1849 letter to Evert Duyckinck: "it takes a great whale to go down stairs 5 miles or more; & if he dont attain the bottom, why, all the lead in Galena can't fashion the plummet that will" (*ML*, 292). With Hawthorne's "blackness," the Virginian returns to Shakespeare, through whose "dark characters"—Hamlet, Timon, Lear, Iago— the Bard expresses truths that it would be "madness for any good man, in his own proper character, to utter" (HHM, 1160). In marking the insights of Hawthorne that have apparently eluded the critics and that demonstrate his greatness, the trope suggests an additional meaning. The greatness of Hawthorne as an author is what is inaccessible to the literary nationalists (the critics), what their vision of an American author (and an American people) does not include. In *Pierre*, Melville uses both blackening and feminization to mark the fate that awaits the author who, from within the influence of the literary nationalists, tries to reach past the terms of their narrative. In turn, that author's fate contributes to an analysis of the gendered and racialized personhood at once manifested in and obscured by the metaphors of literary nationalism.

The Virginian looks forward to Pierre Glendinning in an implied critique that will blossom into *Pierre*. Young America, and literary nationalism in general, confers upon the American author the task of creating, largely through rhetoric, a cohesive American culture that corresponds to—ostensibly reflects—a political entity: to "breathe the spirit of our republican institutions . . . [to] assert *its* national independence, and speak the soul—the heart of the American people" (O'Sullivan, 5.23:428). The authors were called upon to make Americans culturally just as the founders had made America and Americans politically. Since that political identity was generated by a *textual* uttering, a declaration of independence with a *textual* paradigm, the author was a fitting analogue of as well as an agent for promoting Americanism. As a collective, Americans had purportedly declared themselves into existence. Surely the author whose task was to declare independence from previous literary conventions emblematized that declaration of national affiliation and cultural identity. "From the very nature of things," writes William Alfred Jones, "every true writer is an independent" and "the true poet is inherently and almost necessarily a republican" (11.50:196–97). But the constraints upon the terms of that authorship, the limitations on the story that could be told, disclosed the exclusions from the narratives of literary nationalism.

Melville's figure, in turn, risked obscuring the blackness with which Frederick Douglass and Harriet Wilson concerned themselves. While Pierre's "independence" is compromised by internalized cultural constraints that prevent him from telling his story, Harriet Wilson's Frado faces external as well as internal prohibitions. She is denied access even to the language of republicanism and the forms of independence. Yet Pierre shows how an analysis of that figure can explain rather than obscure the material conditions of social inequities—the specification of the full rights of personhood according to race, gender, and class, for example. Reading *Pierre* and *Our Nig* together enriches the context of this discussion. Both texts, as the Virginian says of Hawthorne, "avail [themselves] of this mystical blackness as a means to the wondrous effects [they make] it to produce in [their] lights and shades" (HHM, 1158). Both reflect on the culture that would mirror them.

The Stranger in the Mirror

In an oft-quoted passage of a letter to Hawthorne, written in 1851 while he was finishing *Moby-Dick*, Melville complains: "Dollars damn me; and the malicious Devil is forever grinning in upon me, holding the door ajar. . . . What I feel most moved to write, that is banned,—it will not pay. Yet, altogether, write the other way I cannot. So the product is a final hash, and all my books are botches."[29] What initially appears to be a critique of the market's censorial powers in fact articulates a deeper and more poignant psychological insight into the dialectic between internal and external censorship. Melville stages precisely this drama in *Pierre*. The young Pierre Glendinning is at once a beloved author, darling of critics and public alike, and a dutiful son. But with his discovery of an alleged half sister, hence of his father's purported adultery, Pierre is compelled to tell a story that no one wants to hear. His declaration of independence from the values of his childhood home finds expression in his vow "to gospelize the world anew," but it also leaves him with the task of supporting himself and a makeshift family of female dependents.[30] As a writer, Pierre hopes to do both. Yet, as Melville laments, these are contradictory tasks: the prerequisites for financial success are not, to his mind, compatible with Pierre's intention to gospelize the world anew. Pierre's own ambivalence leads indeed to the "final hash" of a botched book.

In the end, a prescribed story of American identity that Pierre has internalized compromises the story he wishes to tell.[31] Pierre casts his attempt to reject the hypocritical values of his upbringing as a declaration of independence, but the premise of his rejection is fundamentally contradictory. His declaration is itself the source of those values. Any rethinking of those values, therefore, is recast in their terms. The editors who arbitrate taste in Pierre's world wield a power at once psychological and cultural. Popular writer Fanny Fern indicts a male editorial establishment for its malevolent and ill-deserved control of the literary market in *Ruth Hall* (1855), a novel in which the work of a woman author is censored by such an establishment dominated by her brother. Fanny Fern was the alias of Sara Parker Willis, sister of poet and influential editor Nathaniel P. Willis, and she makes her author heroine triumph because she speaks for a public that unites with her in overturning arbitrary editorial judgments. Not so in *Pierre*, in which editors at once dictate and exemplify—can dictate because they do exemplify—public taste. Writers, in turn, must contend not only with editors and with the public, but with values they share with those arbiters. They write not in opposition to, but coterminously with the reading public. Pierre struggles with the terms of a story— and a selfhood—that he finds confining, yet he lacks both understanding of and control over his discomfort. As a result, he writes a ludicrous work that neither conforms to nor effectively challenges the preconditions of an American tale. Pierre is as much emblem as victim of Young America. His suicide follows logically from his failed authorship; he cannot imagine himself without the narrative of identity that he has sought to renounce.

Psychological and cultural factors are aligned in *Pierre* as Melville recasts a boy's struggle for autonomy in the representative dimensions of the movements for cultural and literary independence under way in the mid-nineteenth century. George Forgie's "post-heroic generation" meets Young America in Pierre Glendinning, who is ambivalent about a paternal inheritance that typically troubled his post-heroic cohort. His father's alleged misstep gives him a way out: he can declare independence from the deeds of his father, but do so in the name of his father. As Lincoln sought to make good on the claims of his forefathers, Pierre could strive to fulfill the legacy left by the good name (and name only, it seems) of his own father. In the gap between deed and name lies Pierre's story, a new story expressive of a new generation intent upon a "new birth of freedom" and a mad dash across the continent. Vowing to "gospelize the world anew," Pierre frames that story in the language of Young America. Between the name and the deed lies the symbolizing process, and therein the story of America. Pierre refracts the post-heroic generation through the lens of Young America's literary nationalism. Emergent is a confusion and ambivalence characteristic of the Duyckinck circle. Melville's critique is bold: Pierre, like most of his generation, is unquestionably more prepared to read than to write. In *Pierre*, Melville articulates the darker implications of his injunction, in "Hawthorne and His Mosses," to "let [an American writer] write like a man, for then he will be sure to write like an American" (HHM, 1164). Writing like an American, Pierre marks his doom.

An author's writing about an author's writing about an author certainly asks for the autobiographical reading that *Pierre* often gets. In the *Melville Log,* for example, Jay Leyda juxtaposes particularly relevant passages from *Pierre* with Melville's correspondence, such as a letter to Evert Duyckinck lambasting the practice of daguerreotyping authors, or a letter complaining of problems with his eyes that interfere with his writing (*ML,* 408). Both passages indeed found their way into *Pierre*. And Pierre's authorial failure is frequently seen as Melville's as well. Two central chapters, "Young America in Literature" and "Pierre as a Juvenile Author," have occasioned particular attack and are often summoned as evidence of Melville's loss of control. Perry Miller, for one, argues that Melville "put a private letter to [Evert] Duyckinck into the middle of his romance, thus destroying its last pretense to regularity" (*RW,* 306), and Nina Baym contends that Melville's "fiction got in the way of the direct statement that [he] was seeking to make."[32] For Richard Brodhead, *Pierre* is a "draught of a draught, in a . . . desperate sense . . . [that] trace[s] its author's discovery of the impossibility of his own creative project . . .

[and] rule[s] out even the minimal faith in his own work that the task of revision would require of him."[33]

From another perspective, however, the placement of these two chapters demonstrates a carefully plotted analysis that an autobiographical reading obscures. Authorship was at once activity and metaphor for Melville; the scene of writing metaphorically enacts the drama of familial identity. Writing and identity were linked by the Young American literary nationalists who called upon literature to articulate a cultural identity, and Melville investigated that relationship in the chapters about Pierre's authorship. Melville did not arbitrarily append "Young America in Literature" and "Pierre as a Juvenile Author" to the events of the text; rather, they immediately follow Pierre's confrontation of the world's refusal to recognize him according to the familiar terms of his cultural identity. Pierre, in other words, confronts the consequences of declaring independence from the terms of that identity, a decision that generates his resolve to be an author. By following this confrontation with a conceptualization of authorship, Melville foregrounds the metaphoric implications of authorship for Pierre. In the revisioning of the narrative, Pierre's authorship does not evince the "originality" of which "the world is forever babbling" (*P*, 302). It is not a declaration of independence. Instead it expresses the inscription of that declaration within a cultural discourse that silences as it emplots (and characterizes) Pierre.

The review of *Pierre* in the *Literary World* leaves no doubt about Young America's reception of the work. The reviewer, probably one or both of the Duyckincks, is troubled because Melville has "constructed his story upon some new theory of art to a knowledge of which we have not yet transcended; he evidently has not constructed it according to the established principles of the only theory accepted by us until assured of a better, of one more true and natural than truth and nature themselves, which are the germinal principles of all true art."[34] Melville's "new theory of art" was surely not in accordance with the literary nationalism of Young America. The reviewer is haunted by Pierre's "leering demoniacal spectre of an idea," by its "spectral, ghost-like air" and by the "unreal nightmare-conceptions, [the] confused phantasmagoria of distorted fancies and conceits, ghostly abstractions and fitful shadows" that turn the writer into "a spectre of the substantial author of 'Omoo' and 'Typee,' the jovial and hearty narrator of the traveller's tale of incident and adventure" (*LW*, 119). The reviewer's metaphors astutely, if perhaps unwittingly, read *Pierre* as a kind of ghost story. And indeed this comic horror tale traces Pierre's thwarted attempts at authorship and his subsequent suicide to his disappearance within an authorizing cultural discourse from which he believes he has declared independence. Evidently unaware "that all the great books in the world . . . are but the mirrors, distortedly reflecting to us our own things," Pierre "directly plagiariz[es] from his experiences to fill out the mood of his apparent author-hero, Vivia" (*P*, 331, 352).

Pierre's plagiarism of his own experiences suggests that those experiences are not only prewritten, but also owned by another. *Plagiary,* the root of *plagiarize,* originally referred to the theft of a slave or child, both considered property, gradually encompassed any kidnapping, and eventually included the theft of ideas and creations. This last application, which the *Oxford English Dictionary* dates from the seventeenth century, indicates the emergence of the concept of a self-ownership that extends to creative production.[35] Pierre's *own experiences,* however, evidently do not belong to him. He cannot confer them at will even on his *own* (and *owned*) literary creation. Melville expresses Pierre's lack of self-ownership through the metaphor of the young writer's textuality, the script he seems to be enacting rather than writing. But although Pierre's efforts at authorship, his attempts to "gospelize the world anew," will be thwarted by whatever has prewritten, makes sense of, and "possesses" his experiences, that authorship will encounter, and hence make visible, the dynamics of that possession in a cultural narrative that constructs personhood through ownership.

Even his discovery of a woman claiming to be his illegitimate half sister, a discovery that prompts Pierre to question his cultural inheritance, is suspiciously prewritten:

> So perfect to Pierre had long seemed the illuminated scroll of his life thus far, that only one hiatus was discoverable by him in that sweetly-writ manuscript. A sister had been omitted from the text. He mourned that so delicious a feeling as fraternal love had been denied him. Nor could the fictitious title, which he so often lavished upon his mother, at all supply the absent reality. This emotion was most natural; and the full cause and reason of it even Pierre did not at that time entirely appreciate. For surely a gentle sister is the second best gift to a man; and it is first in point of occurrence; for the wife comes after. He who is sisterless, is as a bachelor before his time. For much that goes to make up the deliciousness of a wife, already lies in the sister.

"Oh, had my father but had a daughter!" cried Pierre; "some one whom I might love, and protect, and fight for, if need be. It must be a glorious thing to engage in a mortal quarrel on a sweet sister's behalf! Now, of all things, would to heaven, I had a sister!" (*P*, 11–12)

The passive voice depicts a character, even a reader, but surely not a consciously controlling author. Someone (or thing) else is scripting the "sweetly-writ manuscript" of Pierre's life. Half the plot of *Pierre* is in keeping with the wish herein expressed: Pierre will find himself, or be found by, a sister—his father's daughter, no less—on whose behalf he will indeed "engage in a mortal quarrel." This fantasy goes a long way toward explaining why Pierre so readily believes Isabel's questionable claims on his fraternity—and on his father's paternity.

Pierre seems to be reenacting a familiar plot, and for Melville's audience that sense is reinforced by literary resonances. For instance, the narrator's suggestion "that this strange yearning of Pierre for a sister, had part of its origin in that still stranger feeling of loneliness he sometimes experienced, as . . . the only surnamed male Glendinning extant" (*P*, 12) sounds very much like Roderick Usher's lamentation of the imminent demise of his sister, which " 'would leave him . . . the last of the ancient race of the Ushers' " in Poe's "The Fall of the House of Usher" (1839).[36] Common elements in the plot of Poe's story and the events of *Pierre* might warn the reader not to trust Pierre's "exultant swell" at the thought of "capping the fame-column, whose tall shaft had been erected by his noble sires" (*P*, 12); the mutual affection of Roderick and his sister Madeline brings on the fall of the house of Usher as well as of the Ushers' house. In Poe's morbid tale, a susceptible narrator recounts the strange events of an apparent ghost story wherein he helps Roderick bury the supposed corpse of Madeline in a vault in the house only to have her arise on a stormy night to embrace the trembling Roderick in a mutual death clasp. Following this fall of the house of Usher, the fleeing narrator witnesses the collapse of the literal house.

As "The Fall of the House of Usher" presages the devastation in *Pierre*, the narrator of Poe's story anticipates Pierre in his susceptibility to a prewritten script. The chary reader must at least question the reality of Madeline's return. The narrator, albeit in hindsight, describes his susceptibility to the gloom of the house from the outset. He confesses to being virtually compelled to visit his old school friend after receiving a powerful letter and recalls being influenced by "the terms, and the general manner of the narration" of Usher's account of his circumstances (FHU, 322). Moreover, at the climax of the tale, the sounds of Madeline's approach directly echo the sounds described in the book he reads in an effort to soothe an obviously mad Roderick. The tale offers a mutual delusion, Roderick's infectious madness and the narrator's evident suggestibility, as an alternative explanation for the putatively supernatural events.

I am claiming here less a direct literary echo than Melville's effective use of the Gothic, and of psychological terror, the characteristics of which would have been familiar to readers of Poe's work. Beginning with Charles Brockden Brown's *Wieland*, the genre was quite popular in the United States and especially intrigued Poe and Hawthorne. Characteristically, these authors recast the supernatural as a richly ambiguous authorship in which characters produce specters, from an unacknowledged (internalized) script, that haunt and often destroy them.[37] In *Pierre*, Melville uses these dynamics to suggest cultural specters, dissociated ideas and values that haunt as they circumscribe the beleaguered author. In effect, Pierre, Roderick, and Roderick's visitor are possessed by such specters of their own making but reproduced in accordance with cultural demons.

Pierre's idea of heroism, which ultimately produces his specters, extends from a domestic ideal—defense of the home, an ideal seconded by his mother, who hopes he will "show his heroicness in some smooth way of favoring fortune, not be called out to be a hero of some dark hope forlorn" (*P*, 27). Such was the paradoxical legacy of the founding fathers to their mid-nineteenth-century descendants, the post-heroic generation, a cohort constantly reminded figuratively of what Mrs. Glendinning reminds Pierre literally: their descent from, and obligation to, almost epic heroes.[38] Mason Locke Weems enjoins the readers of his celebrated *Life of George Washington* not only to be like Washington, but also to preserve his legacy, the Union—hence the inclusion of the Farewell Address in the text of the biography, beginning with editions put out in the early nineteenth century. But as Mrs. Glendinning muses, "It must be hard for a man to be an uncompromising hero and a commander among his race, and yet never ruffle any domestic brow" (*P*, 27). Housekeeping, so to speak, offers at best dubious possibilities for heroism.

As a literary pre-text, Poe's story establishes Pierre's self-proclaimed sister, Isabel, as the specter Pierre creates according to the cultural plot of his domestic fantasy. Isabel, like Madeline, precipitates the fall rather than the preservation of the house of her "father" and her "brother." Indeed, as Melville notes, a century before Sigmund Freud would make a similar observation, "if there be any thing a man might well pray against, that thing is the responsive gratification of some of the devoutest prayers of his youth" (*P,* 12). In wishing that his *father* had had a daughter, Pierre hopes for precisely what he gets (or creates): discovery of his father's transgression, which allows Pierre to reject his paternal inheritance in the name of his father. This paradox establishes absolutely Pierre's credentials for membership in the post-heroic generation, for which the Civil War itself would become the proving ground. Pierre, however, loses the battle, disappearing, not unlike Roderick Usher, into his own (and his culture's) delusions.

Pierre's other desire, to gospelize the world anew, seems to answer Emerson's call, in "Nature" (1836), for a religion by revelation rather than tradition. But a Pierre ill-suited to heroism finds his discoveries and the insights to which they lead intolerable. His immediate discovery of the (alleged) hypocrisy of his father pushes Pierre toward insights into the constructedness of legitimacy and, eventually, the prescriptedness of cultural identity. Pierre cannot tolerate that insight and its implications for the status of his own personhood. He is comfortable with a declaration of independence not from, but, on the contrary, prescribed by cultural discourse.

Pierre is never really a willing rebel. The reader's first introduction to Isabel is an allusion to a face that "had been visibly beheld by Pierre" (*P,* 54). The passive construction again undermines Pierre's agency. And the description of their first encounter, at a sewing circle, begins by establishing Pierre as a "target for the transfixing glances of those ambushed archers of the eye" (*P,* 57). It is as a potential lover, then, rather than a brother that "Pierre's glance is palely fixed" on "that face" from which "wonderful loveliness, and a still more wonderful loneliness, have with inexplicable implorings, looked up to him" (*P,* 57, 58). Pierre is drawn in, passive and conquered: "A wild, bewildering, and incomprehensible curiosity had seized him, to know something definite of that face. To this curiosity, at the moment, he *entirely surrendered himself;* unable as he was to combat it, or reason with it in the slightest way" (*P,* 58; emphasis added). His susceptibility to Isabel combines with his childhood wish for a sister to prevent his ability to question her subsequent claim to be that father's daughter of his fantasy. The "mystic tyranny" of a face that "had first and fully possessed [Pierre] for its own" is a troubling pretext for a declaration of independence (*P,* 63, 66).

Pierre's crisis actually precedes his discovery of his father's alleged transgression. A messenger mysteriously delivers a letter to him one night, literally at the threshold of Lucy Tartan's door, just as Pierre, who "now possessed his soul in joyful mildness and steadfastness," is about to set their marriage date (*P,* 75). Without knowing the contents of the letter, Pierre responds to the unusual circumstances of its delivery with an intensity that suggests his predisposition to melodrama. On arriving home, still not having read the letter, "Pierre . . . started at a figure in the opposite mirror. It bore the outline of Pierre, but now strangely filled with features transformed, and unfamiliar to him; feverish eagerness, fear, and nameless forebodings of ill! He threw himself into a chair, and for a time vainly struggled with the incomprehensible power that possessed him" (*P,* 76). Pierre's apparent self-possession is readily overturned, and his uncanniness as readily established. In the mirror, Pierre sees the stranger who embodies his own lack of self-knowledge. Thoughts of his upcoming marriage rather than the contents of Isabel's letter precipitate the crisis foretold by the stranger in the mirror.

Pierre's disturbing mirror image accompanies, and surely reflects, the change in social status signified by his impending marriage. "According to the order and constitution of the divine government," says Reverend Matthew Sorin in his 1840 *The Domestic Circle,* "man is appointed to rule in the affairs of this life. It is his prerogative to hold the reins of domestic government, and to direct the family interest, so as to bring them to a happy and honorable termination."[39] In Sorin's conventional language, the implied analogy between the family and the nation aptly expresses the apparent source of Pierre's crisis: marriage will transform the romantic youth into an *American man.* Even Mrs. Glendinning pauses over the consideration that "Pierre is but a boy; but when his father wedded . . . — why, his father was turned of five-and-thirty years" (*P,* 74). Marriage means that Pierre must assume and prepare to pass on the inheritance and the patronym, at once a familial and a national duty. Having already established the elder Glendinning's legacy as resonantly national, Melville carefully allegorizes Pierre's psychological crossroads. The youth who begins to cross Lucy Tartan's threshold comes face to face with the unresolved contradictions between inheriting and creating a national legacy—with the role, that is, that his generation is asked to assume—

contradictions obscured by Young America's authors. Does Manifest Destiny, in other words, call for a nation of writers or of readers?

Melville frames the question in the difference between Pierre's possessing and being possessed, and the uncanny unfamiliarity of his mirror image accompanies his experience of himself as possessed. Pierre lives in a world that defines his personhood in terms of his rights to own and inherit, his preparation to receive and transmit a patriarchal legacy, yet he is evidently not prepared for his inheritance. The morning following Pierre's disturbing discovery, Mrs. Glendinning will confirm by seeing the transformation of her son: " 'What haggard thing possesses thee, my son?' " she asks. "Speak, this is incomprehensible' " (*P,* 115). Both mother and son seem to agree that what cannot be comprehended—understood and contained—cannot be possessed. Conversely, Pierre is possessed by what he cannot comprehend. Variants on both words resurface continually, often together, throughout *Pierre;* generically, they evoke a literary preoccupation evident in the gothic tales of the period.

Typically in American gothic tales, the incomprehensible is first and foremost the deep recesses of the self, the unacknowledged personal motivations that come under the rubric of the conscience. In Hawthorne's "Young Goodman Brown" (1836) and Poe's "William Wilson" (1839), to name two particularly vivid examples (to both of which Melville alludes in *Pierre*), characters are possessed by forces beyond their comprehension, although not necessarily beyond their own creation. The newly married Goodman Brown displays an overactive conscience when he leaves his wife, Faith, one evening to go on an errand into the wilderness. Nevertheless, the story does not determine whether he dreams or experiences his own and Faith's attendance at a Black Sabbath that includes not only the professed enemies of the Puritan village, but its most pious inhabitants as well.

Similarly, the profligate protagonist of "William Wilson," one of whose dupes is a young man surnamed Glendinning, is haunted by a real or imagined double throughout his life. The ambiguity intensifies at the end of the story, when the protagonist, having stabbed his well-meaning double, asks, "But what human language can adequately portray *that* astonishment, *that* horror which possessed me at the spectacle then presented to view?"[40] Human language fails in the presence of a scenario that is finally incomprehensible; Wilson can merely represent the "spectacle" to the reader's view as it has been (passively) "presented" to his own:

A large mirror,—so at first it seemed to me in my confusion—now stood where none had been perceptible before; and, as I stepped up to it in extremity of terror, mine own image, but with features all pale and dabbled in blood, advanced to meet me with a feeble and tottering gait.

Thus it appeared, I say, but was not. It was my antagonist—it was Wilson. . . . Not a thread in all his raiment—not a line in all the marked and singular lineaments of his face was not, even in the most absolute identity, mine own!

It was Wilson; . . . and I could have fancied that I myself was speaking while he said:

"You have conquered, and I yield. Yet, henceforward art thou also dead— dead to the World, to Heaven and to Hope! In me didst thou exist—and, in my death, see by this image, which is thine own, how utterly thou hast murdered thyself!" (WW, 356–57)

The mirror figures an utter (and uttered) confusion of identities, a confrontation between selves—or experiences of "selves"—that tears the fabric of cultural identity and may thereby permit a rare glimpse into its constructing mechanisms. The protagonists of both stories, William Wilson and Young Goodman Brown, susceptible from the outset, appear to be driven mad by the stories' events. But the irresolution of the stories' conclusions prevents the reader from totally dissociating from these characters. The reader is drawn into precisely the perceptual conundrum of a William Wilson or a Goodman Brown, a world of uncertainty that may be either supernatural or psychological. And that uncertainty extends to the boundaries of the self.

In both stories the confusion is fueled by guilt brought on by the disjunction between what the character does and what the character believes he is supposed to do. This misalignment is a psychological analogue to Frederick Douglass's ill-fitting selfhood, the sense of not being who he is supposed to be. The self-condemned "criminals" of Poe's and Hawthorne's stories experience (and embody) a crisis of selfhood akin to that of the nonwhite subjects of the same period. The haunted protagonists lack the self-awareness of a Douglass, of course, but even he must fight the self-doubt occasioned by his difference from the prevailing norms.

Conscience, after all, marks an internalized social acceptability, a recognizing in social terms. Insofar as Young Goodman Brown and William Wilson deviate from social norms, they become as unrecognizable to themselves as Douglass, or as the litigants of *Cherokee Nation* and *Dred Scott* are before the law. It is the experience of alienation. With this analogue, I mean not to collapse the experiences of social and psychological alienation, but to superimpose them in order to explain displacements: how an exclusion from whiteness, for example, may be reconfigured in terms of mental or physical illness or deviance and, conversely, how deviance may be represented through metaphors of *social* exclusion. For both fictional protagonists, and for the readers of both tales, that alienation finds expression as the inability to distinguish between reality and hallucination. For the reader, this experience, duplicated but at a remove, can make visible the terms that constitute recognizability and that thus construct a coherent self. In these mirrors or figurative mirrorings the "self" confronts its own problematic recognition. Melville interrogates as he reproduces this experience in *Pierre*.

Pierre refuses such a confrontation. Before he reaches the threshold of marriage, he is comfortably mirrored by the women in his life. In an early scene, Pierre and Lucy stand "silently but ardently eying each other, beholding mutual reflections of a boundless admiration and love" (*P,* 7). Almost immediately, the narrator explains the equally ardent mutual love of mother and son; Mrs. Glendinning "in the clear-cut lineaments and noble air of the son, saw her own graces strangely translated into the opposite sex. There was a striking personal resemblance between them" (*P,* 9). Pierre, who knows himself as he is reflected by others, is "companioned by no surnamed male Glendinning, but the duplicate one reflected to him in the mirror" (*P,* 12). As long as he conforms to internalized cultural expectations, the image and the original are indistinguishable. But when his pliancy—Mrs. Glendinning calls it "docility"—is disturbed by the stirrings of passion evoked by Isabel's face, he becomes unrecognizable both to himself and to those who mirror him. Passion threatens to inspire his deviation from the role he is supposed to play. With Pierre's unrecognized passion, the repressed returns as a disjunction between experience and expectation that results in a denial of agency. Pierre refuses responsibility; he experiences himself as "possessed" by sensations and, later, by actions that he will not own.

Isabel's letter, which announces her sororial relationship to Pierre, allows him to divert his passion into heroism; "Henceforth," he vows, "I will know nothing but Truth; glad Truth, or sad Truth; I will know what *is,* and do what my deepest angel *dictates*" (*P,* 80). Again, the idea of dictation undercuts an apparent declaration of independence. Pierre's "deep-est angel," as will become increasingly clear, "dictates" in accordance with the values of a cultural identity. Moreover, Pierre's susceptibility to an internalized script—the prewritten manuscript of his life—corresponds to his susceptibility to the rumors generated by his aunt, his father's sister. Isabel's resemblance to a portrait of a seated Glendinning Senior, known as the chair portrait to distinguish it from another portrait favored by Mrs. Glendinning, substantiates her claims in Pierre's mind. This portrait has already occasioned the aunt's recollection of her brother's unaccountable behavior and her speculations as to its origin in an amorous affair with a mysterious French immigrant, a hypothesis that conveniently comple-ments Isabel's memories. A series of coincidences makes *sister* Isabel believable. The narrator casually remarks on Pierre's propensity for "an impulsive subservience to the god-like dictation of events themselves" (*P*, 107), continuing to underscore Pierre's proclivity for subordinating in-quiry to the desire for comprehension. This subordination prepares the reader for Pierre's plaintive observation that, having "but piled up words; bought books, and bought some small experiences, and builded me in libraries; now I sit down and *read*" (*P*, 110; emphasis added). Although Pierre means to contrast amassing books with thinking about them in this declaration, he also makes apparent, inadvertently, his susceptibility to others' thoughts. Pierre is more prepared to read than to write.

Similarly, Pierre seems more prepared for a passive, receptive role, one conventionally associated with mid-nineteenth-century views of mater-nity, than for the governing paternal role that Reverend Sorin mandates. In language reminiscent of the Virginian's description of Hawthorne's effect on him in "Hawthorne and His Mosses," the narrator describes Pierre's response to Isabel as "foetally forming in him. Impregnations from high enthusiasms he had received" (*P*, 128). Isabel, by contrast, describes herself as "too full without discharge," and Pierre resolves not to interrupt the flow of her strange tale, but "to sit passively and receive its marvelous droppings into his soul" (*P*, 136, 142). This feminized depiction could still be compatible with authorship; pregnancy and gestation metaphors were conventional in descriptions of authorship and coexisted with assertions of the author's manliness. Poe, for example, in a review of Hawthorne's *Mosses from an Old Manse* that preceded Melville's "Hawthorne and His Mosses" by four years, uses a birth metaphor—"giving birth to some universal sentiment or instinct in embryo"—to define "true originality."

And James Russell Lowell, in a *North American Review* essay that attacked Young American literary nationalism, offers the metaphor of gestation to describe a literature that "should be national to the extent of being as . . . thoroughly impregnated with humane and manly sentiment, as is the idea on which our political fabric rests."[41] For Pierre, authorship was supposed to generate a (manly) challenge to all cultural categories, which could lead to his transgressing gendered subjectivity. But Pierre is more reader than writer, and he gives over his authorial role to Isabel—and his aunt. Here the reversal of reproductive roles marks Pierre's unwitting rather than willful reluctance to assume a conventional paternal role.

Isabel appears to implant and govern Pierre's perception of her. The story she tells about herself represents a child as close as is humanly possible to the original relation to the universe Emerson advocates in "Nature." Illegitimate and orphaned, Isabel is mirrored by a world to which she is representable only in exclusion—in effect, neither citizen nor alien. Since she dwelled in that world as a stranger—and for a long time without language—she believes she has particular access to, and can describe, her own socialization. Isabel was not positively mirrored—that is, she found no positive reflection of herself—until the relatively late appearance of Glendinning Senior. When Isabel meets her putative father, she looks "into the smooth water behind the house, . . . [and sees] the likeness—something strangely like, and yet unlike, the likeness of his face" (*P*, 148). At the same time, she first hears the word "father" whispered into her ear. To that word, Isabel traces her conscious entrance into the social order—her entrance into the cultural symbolic of self-representation that seems to begin with a literal mirroring and with the literal name of the father—but it is a word she learns slowly.[42] As she explains to Pierre,

> I did not then join in my mind with the word father, all those peculiar associations which the term ordinarily inspires in children. The word father only seemed a word of general love and endearment to me—little or nothing more; it did not seem to involve any claims of any sort, one way or the other. I did not ask the name of my father; for I could have had no motive to hear him named except to individualize the person who was so peculiarly kind to me; and individualized in that way he already was, since he was generally called by us the gentleman, and sometimes my father. (*P*, 173–74)

The linguistic terms of Isabel's legal status mark her exclusion from conventional representations of personhood such as the law expresses and perpetuates. It is not, however, until Mr. Glendinning's visits cease—presumably with his death—that Isabel feels the need to decipher "the mysterious writing" on the handkerchief that he had dropped at his last visit. Isabel resolves to learn to read and write in order to learn "the meaning of those faded characters." Of course, "the talismanic word" proves to be the name of the father, Glendinning (*P,* 175).

The father's absence, then, makes his name important as it motivates Isabel's literacy. The logic of her discovery, read allegorically, suggests that the name of the father, in which the law symbolically governs genealogy and inheritance, arises to make present, or re-present, what is absent. Or, to follow the implications of Justice Curtis's observation in the *Dred Scott* case, the law creates rather than reflects genealogical and property relations. Without the law, for instance, parent/child relations do not *meaningfully* exist. Isabel's literacy inducts her into her identity, an identity represented *in relation to* the name of her father. Her stories position her on the margins of culture; even her exclusion locates her, and enables her to know herself, in cultural terms. But until her father's mirroring and subsequent absence she cannot name her desire to participate in a meaningful way. " 'I cannot speak coherently here,' " she tells Pierre while narrating the events prior to her father's appearance (*P,* 147). Her "thoughts well up in" her, she explains, and "as they are, they are, and I can not alter them, for I had nothing to do with putting them in my mind, and I never affect any thoughts, and I never adulterate any thoughts; but when I speak, think forth from the tongue, speech being sometimes before the thought; so, often, my own tongue teaches me new things" (*P,* 147). But in entering into a meaningful relation with the name of the father, she begins the search that leads her to Pierre and, significantly, allows her presumably for the first time to claim her inheritance and to tell her story.

Isabel's lack of conformity to a narrative that Pierre can recognize makes her interlocutor uncomfortable. True to form, he strives "to condense her mysterious haze into some definite and comprehensible shape. He could not but infer that the feeling of bewilderment, which she had so often hinted of during their interview, had caused her continually to go aside from the straight line of her narration; and finally to end it in an abrupt and enigmatical obscurity. But he also felt assured, that as this was entirely unintended, and now, doubtless, regretted by herself, so their coming second interview would help to clear up much of this mysteriousness" (P, 162). Pierre wants Isabel to be comprehensible, which is precisely what his wished-for fraternal relationship to her allows. For him, too, the name of the father shapes Isabel's narration. He is drawn to Isabel because he "seemed to see that it was not so much Isabel who had by her wild idiosyncrasies mystified the narration of her history, as it was the essential and unavoidable mystery of her history itself, which had invested Isabel with such wonderful enigmas to him" (P, 165). She authors the story, but he immediately reconstructs the plot, and thus comprehends Isabel, in accordance with his own internalized script.

A discrepancy emerges in the text between how Pierre sees Isabel and how he thinks he sees her. He thinks he finds her mysterious: " 'In her life there was an unraveled plot; and he felt that unraveled it would eternally remain to him" (P, 168). And the mystery of Isabel, "the unraveled plot," makes him dissatisfied with the novels he had previously enjoyed. Isabel is a better read, and in contrast with her "plot," novels, with "their false, inverted attempts at systematizing eternally unsystemizable elements; their audacious, intermeddling impotency, in trying to unravel, and spread out, and classify, the more thin than gossamer threads which make up the complex web of life . . . over Pierre had no power now" (P, 168). Pierre believes his sister has made him a deep reader, one who pierces "straight through" the "helpless miserableness" of novels: "the one sensational truth in him, transfixed like beetles all the speculative lies in them. He saw that human life doth truly come from that, which all men are agreed to call by the name of God; and that it partakes of the unravelable inscrutableness of God" (P, 168). Unlike novels, experience is a series of "imperfect, unanticipated, and disappointing sequels (as mutilating stumps)" (P, 169). But the narrative glosses over an important discrepancy that is apparently unavailable to Pierre. The "unravelable inscrutableness of God" is not synonymous with, and is actually the opposite of, the "*unraveled* plot" of Isabel's history; "unraveled plot" is an image of clarity rather than, as Pierre seems to intend, of obscurity. Evidently, Pierre recognizes neither the script nor his need to comprehend Isabel within it. In fact, she becomes so emblematic—as opposed to enigmatic—that "to him, Isabel wholly soared out of the realms of mortalness, and for him became transfigured in the highest heaven of uncorrupted Love" (P, 170). Isabel is neither imperfect, nor unanticipated for Pierre, and she is certainly not disappointing.

Isabel Banford is not central to Pierre's script. Rather, a sister is, and not just a sister but specifically his father's daughter. With sister Isabel comes his belief in his father's transgression, a belief that enables him to challenge and ultimately decide to preserve his father's (good) name. Isabel embodies precisely the discrepancy between experience and representation, the father's actions and his "good name," articulated in an elaborate fantasy by a portrait of Pierre's father, the same portrait in which Pierre's aunt discerns evidence of her brother's alleged love affair with a French immigrant. The portrait seems to speak to Pierre, to second the young American's efforts at insight: "we, as it were, abdicate ourselves, and take unto us another self, Pierre; in youth we are, Pierre, but in age we seem. Look again. I am thy real father, so much the more truly, as thou thinkest thou recognizest me not, Pierre" (*P,* 101). In the thirty-three repetitions of Pierre's name during this brief fantasy, the portrait seems to suggest Pierre's contingency on this discrepancy between the selves of youth and age, as though Pierre is named into existence by it. Pierre's opportunity for heroism certainly is, and, as a member of the post-heroic generation, he needs such an opportunity to demonstrate his worthiness to inherit the national legacy, to bear and pass on the name of the father(s).

Isabel also fleshes out the earlier fantasy in which Pierre manifests an unacknowledged insight into a related aspect of cultural symbolism. His wish for a sister explicitly conjoins sister and wife: after all, "he who is sisterless is as a bachelor before his time." According to this fantasy, man is drawn into society through his female kin. So important is the sororial relationship to Pierre that he reproduces it rhetorically with his mother, whom he playfully calls "sister." But it is odd that Pierre should imagine that a sister would better serve that social function than a mother. And not just a sister, but, again, a *father's daughter,* a woman whose relationship to Pierre is defined in relation to—in the name of—the father. In the combined uncertainty and emphatic importance of that kinship relation, ongoing efforts to perpetuate a given culture are evident.[43]

Isabel embodies the unraveled plot of the cultural symbolic, and it is in that incarnation that she poses the most significant threat to Pierre. Her exposure promises not only to divide the Glendinning house—not to mention the Glendinning legacy—but also to interrogate the foundations on which that home is constructed. Through *sister* Isabel, however, Pierre preserves the *status quo.* On one hand, she allows him to reenact the inherited drama of his identity. On the other, she enables him to renounce his unacknowledged passion for a working girl of unknown parentage and to cover up the intolerable discrepancy between his experience and his and others' expectations of him. He outdoes his father by resisting the temptations to which Glendinning Senior had allegedly succumbed.

As Pierre's sister, however, Isabel also embodies the possibility of another cultural threat, the threat of incest, a possibility that already hovers in Pierre's and his mother's playful mutual appellations of "brother" and "sister."[44] Thus flirting with the forbidden, Mrs. Glendinning and Pierre contain one of the most powerful and dangerous cultural threats within a rhetorical game. The cultural symbolic, which creates meaningful genealogical relations such as are governed by the patronym, names "incest" into a cultural (emphatically not natural) transgression: "incest" defies cultural prohibitions; it names—and marks as transgressive—the act of sexual intercourse between two people who share a biological genesis. But with the alleged actions of Pierre's father, unwitting "incest," such as sex between siblings who do not recognize each other as such, is an ongoing possibility. By embodying Glendinning Senior's sexual transgressions, Isabel makes visible both the cultural constructions that make experience comprehensible, and the continual threat to those constructions—and, therefore, to *meaningful* experience. Sister Isabel *means* that unwitting "incest" is always possible and that the symbolic foundation of the culture is always tenuous. Sister Isabel really does afford Pierre the opportunity to "gospelize the world anew."

Confronted with his father's putative daughter, Pierre faces conflicting desires and responsibilities. The narrator chides him for his contradictory "grand resolutions"—publicly to acknowledge Isabel and yet "charitably" to withhold her existence from his mother and dutifully to safeguard the name of his father. Together, cautions the narrator, "they all mutually expire" (*P*, 203). And that mutual expiration entails Pierre's pretending to marry Isabel while fleeing to New York City with her and an adulteress named Delly Ulver. Thus he intends to legitimize Isabel, removing any evidence of transgression—his father's or Delly's—from the gaze of Saddle Meadows. His fictitious marriage elaborately covers up the challenge he embraces. What is more, it prevents him from ever again having to approach the threshold of Lucy Tartan with matrimonial intent. Protecting his father's name, Pierre ironically fails to reproduce it. He replaces the perpetuation of the patronym with a fictitious marriage, one kind of fiction with another. In spite of himself, the unwilling (and unwitting) rebel precipitates the fall of the House of Glendinning rather than gospelizes the world anew.

Pierre replays that conflict in his decision to write. As an author, he wants simultaneously to expose and to obscure the perpetuation of the patronym as a cultural plot. Paternity seems to be something Pierre believes he can deny, but, typically, he confuses representation with materiality. Burning the incriminating portrait, Pierre seeks to banish the memory and influence of his father. " 'Henceforth,' " he declaims, " 'cast-out Pierre hath no paternity, and no past; and since the Future is one blank to all; therefore, twice-disinherited Pierre stands untrammeledly his ever-present self!' " (*P*, 235). To Isabel, he can even doubt—or, better yet, disregard—their kinship: " 'I am Pierre, and thou Isabel, wide brother and sister in the common humanity,—no more' " (*P*, 319). The irrelevant patronym and the deeds done in its name constitute the gospel he will offer from his sparsely furnished and underheated rooms in the Church of the Apostles: " 'I will write such things—' " he vows, " 'I will gospelize the world anew, and show them deeper secrets than the Apocalypse!—I will write it, I will write it!' " (*P*, 319).

Pierre's revelation, as he explains it to Isabel, borders on nihilism:

> "a nothing is the substance, it casts one shadow one way, and another the other way; and these two shadows cast from one nothing; these, seems to me, are Virtue and Vice."
>
> "Then why torment thyself so, dearest Pierre?"
>
> "It is the law."
>
> "What?"
>
> "That a nothing should torment a nothing; for I am a nothing. It is all a dream—we dream that we dreamed we dream." (*P*, 319)

"It is the law," he explains, in an apparently conventional reference to the way things are. But in this carefully chosen language, Pierre's expostulation is not accidental. The "law" is the nothing-substance that names cultural values—Virtue and Vice—into existence. And Pierre imagines that he has transcended the law. " 'Call me brother no more!' " he had begun, and when Isabel insists on the epithet, enjoining, " 'Let us sit down again, my brother,' " Pierre responds forcefully, " 'I am Pierre' " (*P*, 320). His insistence on his first name refuses at once the epithet "brother" and the patronym, Glendinning; Pierre stands before Isabel unaccommodated man, or so he thinks. But the ambiguous "no more" that follows Pierre's assertion of "common humanity" prophetically undercuts his newfound insights. They are, as he insists, *no more* than "brother and sister in the common humanity." But they are also *no longer* simply thus in the sequence of events, the plot, that Pierre has already set in motion. The conventions represented by the law never cease to govern his actions. In another prophetic statement, Isabel claims, " 'now, when thou wouldst be lunatic to wise men, perhaps—now doth poor ignorant Isabel begin to comprehend thee' " (*P,* 319–20). Pierre is indeed comprehended—and possessed—by the ideas that Isabel embodies to him, too much so, in fact, to return physically or psychologically. "I am Pierre" he insists, in a phrase at once too resonant with and empty of meaning to be challenged. And his authorship must ultimately serve his desperate need to comprehend.

The two chapters on authorship interrupt the chronological progression of the narrative, surfacing between Pierre's arrival in the city and his settlement in the aptly named Church of the Apostles. Thematically, the strategically placed chapters connect Pierre's recognition that he is without the law to his authorial efforts. His need to comprehend and to be comprehended is exacerbated precisely by the declaration of independence that precedes his resolve to write but that also makes him most incomprehensible to his mother, to the Saddle Meadows community in general, and most willfully uncomprehended by his last refuge, his cousin, Glendinning Stanly. Before leaving Saddle Meadows, Pierre seeks to provide for his alternative ménage, Isabel and Delly, by appealing to his cousin to proffer the New York hospitality that he has already offered to Pierre and his approved fiancée, Lucy Tartan. But on his arrival, archetypally at "that preluding hour of the night when the shops are just closing, and the aspect of almost every wayfarer . . . speaks of one hurrying not abroad, but homeword," a disbelieving Pierre finds himself homeless (*P,* 268).

Even the cherished scion of aristocratic America finds himself dispossessed of and by the law when his loss of faith in the name of his father prompts him to renounce his home. Pierre makes the Lear-like discovery through an exchange with a suspicious stage-driver that the deference to which his upbringing has accustomed him is a function of his position rather than his person. In New York City, divested of the manifestations that would identify him as a gentleman, the Saddle Meadows refugee can make no sense of his surroundings. In an "unconscious transfer to the stage-driver," a frustrated Pierre provokes the driver's whip (*P,* 271). When a policeman interrupts the ensuing scuffle, the driver protests, "though you're an officer, I'm a citizen for all that," and forces Pierre and his companions to remove their belongings since, he gloats, "I'll have my rights . . . I've the law now" (*P,* 273). Pierre as he knows himself does not exist without the law. He is unrecognizable, and without the law he will find his story untellable.

Pierre does not fully face the implications of his exclusion until he confronts Glendinning Stanly. The name Glendinning Stanly literally inverts the name Pierre Glendinning ("pierre," French for "stone"; "stan," Anglo-Saxon), and Glen accordingly had in his boyhood served as a kind of mirror for Pierre. This early mutual affirmation of the cousins took the shape of "a much more than cousinly attachment" in which a "spontaneous self" pours out "the generous impulsiveness of youth [prior] to the provident circumspectness of age" (*P,* 253, 255)—prior, that is, to Pierre's transference of his love to the object of Glen's thwarted romantic attentions, Lucy Tartan. In New York, however, the orphaned and "Europeanized Glen" refuses to mirror his self-exiled cousin (*P,* 256). When Pierre bursts into a party in Glen's chambers, the cousins instantly know each other despite the intervening "years peculiarly productive of the greatest conceivable changes in the general personal aspect of human beings" (*P,* 278–79). As the narrator explains, "the eye seldom alters. The instant their eyes met, they mutually recognized each other. But both did not betray the recognition" (*P,* 279). Pierre, whose recent actions have defamiliarized his world and alienated him from his community, looks to Glen to be recognized within a familiar social context. He longs to be known. Subjectivity itself seems to hold its breath in this passage, as Pierre shouts his cousin's name. But "the superb-eyed" (*P,* 279), as the narrator designates Glen, declines to recognize his cousin; he refuses, that is, to "betray the recognition."

The awkwardness of the phrase "both did not betray the recognition" captures the complexity of the moment. Pierre acknowledges Glen by betraying/manifesting his recognition of his cousin, while Glen betrays his cousin by refusing to acknowledge him. But in another sense, Glen's betrayal is also a compliance. His refusal to recognize Pierre leaves his cousin standing "erect, and isolated," precisely the heroic posture he covets (*P,* 279). After all, Pierre has supposedly chosen to reject his father's name, to live without legal recognition. For his part, Pierre, in pronouncing Glen's name, acknowledges his orphaned cousin's choice to live within legal recognition. Their formative mutual mirroring turns into a substitution when the early death of Pierre's mother, precipitated by Pierre's actions, leaves Glen Stanly the heir of the Saddle Meadows estate. Replacing Pierre, Glen inherits the name of the renounced father. But the replacement turns into a mutual destruction as both "stones" prove equally unyielding, and the monuments of early friendship become, ironically, each other's tombstone.

The reader is more prepared for Glen's rebuff than is Pierre. Built-up resentments unrecognized by the more petted and beloved Pierre find expression in the obvious hostility of Glen's overly aggressive gift-giving, a potlatch of sorts. The orphaned cousin is more than prepared to displace the scion of Saddle Meadows, and Glen's refusal to recognize Pierre here constitutes an act of psychic violence, a metaphoric murder that foreshadows their mutual destruction. The orphan disrupts the scion's narrative of identity, the continuity that allows "the prompt-hearted boy . . . to be recognized in [the] matured man" (*P,* 255). In effect, he disestablishes the selfhood of his overreliant cousin. Any narrative of identity may be similarly disrupted, and Melville prefigures this disruption in *Pierre* with an allusion to another of Hawthorne's tales, "My Kinsman, Major Molineux" (1832). On his quest for his own kinsman, Pierre encounters a "scarlet-cheeked" woman "horribly lit" by the light of a druggist's window (*P,* 276–77). In the Hawthorne story, which takes place in the 1730s, Robin, a country youth, comes to the city in search of his uncle, who he hopes will help him make his fortune. He is welcomed only by a woman in a scarlet petticoat who tempts him to consent to something he does not readily understand and who therefore underscores the irony of his insistence that he has "the name of being a shrewd youth."[45] At the end of the story, Robin again sees the prostitute in the macabre parade that features his Royalist uncle, tarred and feathered. Caught up in the contagion of revolutionary fervor, Robin finds himself laughing uncontrollably, seduced after all into consenting to something he does not quite understand.

Hawthorne's story is a fable of collectivism, a story about how a group story gets written and incorporates individuals into the plot. Robin is introduced into the plot with an ambiguous construction of subjectivity that the story will thematize: "While he stood on the landing place, searching in either pocket for the means of fulfilling his agreement, the ferryman lifted a lantern, by the aid of which, and the newly risen moon, he took a very accurate survey of the stranger's figure" (MK, 68). The second "he" could be either Robin or the ferryman, who seem to create each other as Robin alights in the eerie dreamscape of a kind of under-world. This mutual creation—or subjection—materially plays out Robin's desire to be positioned, by Major Molineux, within the social world of pre-Revolutionary America. But it also foreshadows Robin's and Molineux's mutual re-cognizing.

The moment of that recognition is painful for both. The hideous pag-eant pauses for a moment while Robin and his kinsman come face to face: "the bitterest pang of all was when his eyes met those of Robin; for he evidently knew him on the instant, as the youth stood witnessing the foul disgrace of a head grown gray in honor" (MK, 85). The narrator again leaves room for a hint of subjective confusion—which *he* knew which *him* on the instant?—in a mirroring that suggests Robin's displacement of Major Molineux as the parade's principal. Robin disappears into a crowd that reconstitutes his subjectivity through "a bewildering excitement . . . [that] seize[s] upon his mind," and inducts him into a revolutionary con-sensus (MK, 85). Collective identity here entails a loss; Robin and his kinsman, like Pierre and Glen, recognize each other into mutual disap-pearance, each variously the crowd's victim. Robin is indeed positioned by his kinsman, whose "spectre" haunts him precisely through the anal-ogy between them (MK, 85).

Despite Pierre's apparent isolation, his encounter with Glen initiates him into a similar revolutionary company. Pierre is "isolated" only "for an instant" before he "fasten[s] his glance upon his . . . apparently unmoved cousin" and refracts Glen's rejection into a blot on the Glendinning name (P, 279). Wishing to "let out all [his cousin's] Glendinning blood," Pierre stresses his own more "legitimate" claim to the name of his father and recasts his challenge in that name and the heroic American tradition it signifies (P, 279). Despite his earlier declaration that "cast-off Pierre hath no paternity," Pierre paradoxically rebels from the values associated with his father's name in the name of the Glendinnings (P, 235).

Glen still mirrors Pierre, but Pierre has ostensibly refused his paternity and has thereby ceased to be Pierre. In this scene, he confronts the conse-quences of his act, but finally refuses to recognize the conventionality of all identity. The young initiate—Pierre, Robin—chooses the group, mean-ingful rather than incomprehensible experience. But the group does not choose Pierre. He cannot make himself known against Glen's accusations of "imposture" and "insanity" because he has no frame of reference—and no audience—for his story (*P*, 279). Glen has the law now. Pierre will attempt to write about the law, but in the end he will be overwritten by the desire to comprehend and to be comprehended. It is therefore fitting that the arrival of the would-be author in New York City should constitute Melville's prelude to the revisioning of authorship in the two chapters about that subject. Neither an interruption nor an afterthought, those chapters form part of the logical progression of Melville's analysis of authorship and identity.

Melville calls attention to the importance of authorship as a theme in *Pierre* with an evident disruption of the plot. "Young America in Literature," the first of the two chapters, begins with the narrator's declaration of authorial independence: "Among the various conflicting modes of writing history, there would seem to be two grand practical distinctions, under which all the rest must subordinately range. By the one mode, all contemporaneous circumstances, facts, and events must be set down contemporaneously; by the other, they are only to be set down as the general stream of the narrative shall dictate; for matters which are kindred in time, may be very irrelative in themselves. I elect neither of these; I am careless of either; both are well enough in their way; I write precisely as I please" (*P*, 286). This unexpected discussion of historiographical sense-making interrupts the narrative in progress, the narrative of *Pierre*. The self-reflexiveness of the passage signals a competing narrative or project. Prefacing a discussion of the early authorial successes of Pierre, the passage asks the reader to attend especially to the presuppositions and limitations of authorship. What seems at first glance a declaration of authorial independence ("I write precisely as I please") may be equally construed as a meditation on the inevitability of narrativization as a reflection of an author's need for comprehension and an inevitably predetermined point of view—or, as we shall see, what William James calls *preperception*. It anticipates the narrator's subsequent claim that "each man reads his own peculiar lesson according to his own peculiar mind and mood," and it anticipates many of the criticisms of *Pierre* (*P*, 397). Melville is indeed not telling the story that readers expect to read. And, finally, it presages the Duyckincks' objection that Melville "evidently has not constructed [his story] according to the established principles of the only theory accepted by us until assured of a better, of one more true and natural than truth and nature themselves, which are the germinal principles of all true art" (*LW*, 118). If this is, as Perry Miller suggests, a "private letter" to Evert Duyckinck, then all of *Pierre* emerges as such a letter, the privacy of which is at least in question.[46]

An earlier authorial success made Pierre feel independent, but the illusoriness of that feeling is evident in Melville's frank and bitter critique of the critics and the darling they create. Duyckinck is an implied, but far from the sole, model for the critics and editors who praise the "Perfect Taste" of Pierre's ridiculously trite sketches. The scion of Saddle Meadows is, they claim, "'unquestionably a highly respectable youth' . . . 'blameless in morals, harmless throughout'" (*P*, 287). As such, Pierre comfortably "possesse[s] the poetic nature . . . [and] possesse[s] every whit of the imaginative wealth which he so admired" (*P*, 286); as such, that is, "possession" is conferred on Pierre. He is, after all, perfectly comprehensible, as "among the beautiful imaginings of the second and third degree of poets, he freely and comprehendingly ranged." In this dark parody, Melville indicts the editorial establishment's "dynasty of taste," a scandal, as I have noted, that Fanny Fern's *Ruth Hall* would similarly expose to public scrutiny (*P*, 288).

Pierre becomes the prototype of the "proud man [who] likes to feel himself in himself, and not by reflection in others" (*P*, 304). The clink of coins earned, or so he believes, by his own labor makes him "disdainfully" eye "the sumptuousness of his hereditary halls—the hangings, and the pictures, and the bragging historic armorials and the banners of the Glendinning renown" (*P*, 304). The promise of financial self-reliance gives Pierre a deceptive sense of self-possession. He believes that the success of his early authorial ventures ensures that "if need should come, he would not be forced to turn resurrectionist, and dig up his grandfather's Indian-chief grave for the ancestral sword and shield, ignominiously to pawn them for a living! He could live on himself" (*P*, 304). But, as we have seen, he is naively unaware of the connection between his ancestral legacy and his self-possession, of how much "Pierre" exists only "by reflection in others," and equally unaware of how, conversely, his fame derives from his "successfully"—and "harmlessly"—reflecting others, mirroring a world in perfect accord with the tenets of literary Young America. Pierre's "independence" is thus contingent upon his perfectly representative status—and, in all senses, the name of his father. Believing himself free from his past—from "the banners of the Glendinning renown," from "the ancestral sword and shield"—Pierre fails to recognize his dependency on its terms.

Melville explains that dependency through a metaphor that broadens into a cultural insight. The narrator intrudes on Pierre's fantasies of self-possession with a discussion that feminizes and enslaves the soul of the young American author:

> The mechanic, the day-laborer, has but one way to live; his body must provide for his body. But not only could Pierre in some sort, do that; he could do the other; and letting his body stay lazily at home, send off his soul to labor, and his soul would come faithfully back and pay his body her wages. So, some unprofessional gentlemen of the aristocratic South, who happen to own slaves, give those slaves liberty to go and seek work, and every night return with their wages, which constitute those idle gentlemen's income. Both ambidexter and quadruple-armed is that man, who in a day-laborer's body, possesses a day-laboring soul. Yet let not such an one be over-confident. Our God is a jealous God; He wills not that any man should permanently possess the least shadow of His own self-sufficient attributes. Yoke the body to the soul, and put both to the plough, and the one or the other must in the end assuredly drop in the furrow. (*P*, 304–5)

Whereas Young America's metaphors of enslavement obscure the material conditions of slavery, Melville uses those metaphors to explain them. He insists on a continuity between the conception of personhood characteristic of the liberal ideology of northern capitalism and the logic that justified the peculiar institution. When Pierre must write to support himself, his soul becomes apparent as a *possession*. The soul is gendered female (*her* wages) and enslaved to illustrate "her" possession by the (white male) body.

Mid-century advocates of slavery frequently complicated the moral indignation of northern opponents by claiming that the wage-laborer in the North was no freer—and in fact was typically less comfortably provided for—than the slave in the South.[47] Without sanctioning the proslavery argument, Melville demonstrates the pervasiveness of the assumptions that enable the peculiar institution in American liberalism. Being contracted out makes Frederick Douglass muse that being *owned* means being forbidden to participate in the free selfhood emblematized by the market. But the various constraints on his "freer" authorship complicate the claims of that ideology. Even the free white author presumed in Melville's metaphor is at once aristocratic slaveowner and day-laboring slave. At bottom, a cultural identity premised on an ideology of free selfhood is paradoxical. The "destiny" that makes "the continent" a collective possession confers property rights only on individual members of that collective—that is, on a *person* only insofar as that person is incorporated in, and literally embodied by, that collective. Pierre's identity not only affords him the right to own, it is itself a possession, and it is alienable. The slave metaphor calls into question how potentially "free" and assured selfhood ever is, even for those embodied therein.

Through the terms in which he depicts Pierre's authorship, Melville also examines the relationship between personhood and power. Pierre's reconceived authorship grows out of—and emblematizes—his renunciation of his paternal legacy, the terms of propertied white male personhood through which he defines himself. By feminizing and enslaving Pierre's "soul" (his would-be authorial self), Melville explains both how personhood is constituted and what is left out of that constitution. Feminization and enslavement serve as figurative cultural markers of dispossession; conversely, enslaved men and women, free women, and day-laborers are, in different ways, excluded from the material conditions and denied the metaphysical attributes through which full personhood is constituted in the North as well as in the South. Their exclusion from personhood tautologically justifies the material conditions to which they are subjected. But since Melville's "jealous God" makes self-sufficiency an impermanent "possession," a familiar question implicitly resurfaces: what keeps a government from making white men slaves?

In Pierre, the relationship between authorship and the market dramatizes the implications of an ideology of American liberalism that defines the self as free because self-owned. "Dollars damn me," Melville had written. And for Pierre, "domestic matters—rent and bread—had come to such a pass . . . that whether or no, the first page must go to the printer; and thus was added still another tribulation; because the printed pages now dictated to the following manuscript. . . . Therefore, was his book already limited, bound over, and committed to imperfection, even before it had come to any confirmed form or conclusion at all" (*P*, 392). The market could not promise "independence" to Pierre any more than a liberal ideology ensured independence from the slave system for Melville's father-in-law, Massachusetts Chief Justice Lemuel Shaw, whose support for the

1850 Fugitive Slave Law dismayed the author.[48] More pressing concerns, suggests Melville's metaphor, enslave the soul.

Pierre lacks the language in which to tell his story, and he lacks a readership for it. But mostly, he lacks an appropriate analysis of it. He blames his failure on the editorial establishment rather than the conventional conceptions of authorship and personhood that he shares with them. It is true that Pierre's need to pay the rent commits him to a rushed—and flawed—book, and that his bodily needs actually intrude on his "soul," as the metaphor had predicted. That intrusion finds expression in ludicrous incursions into the book itself. Forced to support himself, Isabel, Delly, and Lucy, who subsequently joins them in New York, Pierre is forced into the position for which he haughtily longs following his early authorial success. But, hungry, celibate, and unemployed, Pierre is haunted by images of food, the body, and employment that resurface in his work: "Tell me not, thou inconceivable coxcomb of a Goethe, that the universe can not spare thee and thy immortality, so long as—*like a hired waiter*—thou makes thyself 'generally useful.' Already the universe gets on without thee, and could still spare a million more of the *same identical kidney*. . . . Lo! I hold thee in this hand, and thou art crushed in it like an egg from which the meat hath been sucked" (*P,* 352–53; emphasis added). But Pierre misses the implications that his rejection of his paternal inheritance—including his familial identity—has on his ability to tell his story. The fool in *King Lear* (a work Melville knew well) uses the image of an egg with the meat sucked out to explain to a deluded Lear what his kingdom is worth once he has divided it between his thankless daughters. Likewise the empty egg in *Pierre* images the "nothing-substance" from which Virtue and Vice are cast as shadows. But Pierre is as unable to translate as he is to tolerate his profound vision. Textual disturbances that might have led to insight into the discrepancy between his experiences and their meaning are instead incorporated unwittingly into his book as accurate but pointless evidence of his dispossession.

The narrator explicitly offers authorship as a metaphor to explain Pierre's failed literary work in relation to his ontological struggle (and his day-laboring soul):

> that which now absorbs the time and the life of Pierre, is not the book, but the
> primitive elementalizing of the strange stuff, which in the act of attempting
> that book, has upheaved and upgushed in his soul. Two books are being writ;

of which the world shall only see one, and that the bungled one. The larger book, and the infinitely better, is for Pierre's own private shelf.That it is, whose unfathomable cravings drink his blood; the other only demands his ink. But circumstances have so decreed, that the one can not be composed on the paper, but only as the other is writ down in his soul. (*P,* 355)

Successful authorship becomes an analogue for insight. And Pierre's two books correspond to the two narratives in *Pierre:* the story of failed authorship, and the insight into the meaning of that failure, a critique of the cultural narrative that circumscribes Pierre's authorship and that has other, more broadly social, consequences. Pierre alternately drowns in and has his blood sucked by his insights; he is, Gothic-style, destroyed by what he himself produces. Unwittingly, he confronts his own possession and the internalized script that marks it, but he cannot finally endure the consequences of his discovery. In writing, in other words, Pierre, no less than Young Goodman Brown or William Wilson, confronts a cultural narrative that destroys him precisely because he is not aware of confronting it.

The resemblance, especially to William Wilson, is striking. Pierre lashes out against the emblem of his dispossession, Glendinning Stanly, who, after inheriting Pierre's material legacy, returns to New York to seek its last two vestiges: Lucy Tartan, and Pierre's reputation—his good name. Amidst echoes of "William Wilson," Pierre stabs the image who mirrors— and threatens to make public—his worst fears about himself. Indirectly, he kills himself. The troubling suspicion is thereby raised that, like his literary forefather, Pierre strikes out at a reflection of his own cultural anxiety.

Like a good Young American, Pierre sacrifices himself and his book to his father's good name and, ultimately, proves himself a worthy—if dead— heir to the fathers' heroic legacy. But even the most insightful author cannot fully escape cultural dictates. For the narrator of *Pierre,* Nature is refracted through rather than reflected in the poet's gaze: "Say what some poets will, Nature is not so much her own ever-sweet interpreter, as the mere supplier of that cunning alphabet, whereby selecting and combining as he pleases, each man reads his own peculiar lesson according to his own peculiar mind and mood" (*P,* 397).[49] "Reading" here marks a repressed authorship, and the evident individualism (one could almost call it a potential "self-reliance") of this passage is undercut by "cunning alphabet." Among the many connotations of "cunning," a sense of canniness bordering on deceit seems here to suggest a prior meaning that interacts with the "peculiarity" of the perceiver. And that prior meaning seems to be what makes experience comprehensible as a shared system of signs. The narrator gives as an example of this process the christening of "The Mount of the Titans" by a "moody disappointed bard": "from the spell of [that] name the mountain never afterward escaped; for now, gazing upon it by the light of those suggestive syllables, no poetical observer could resist the apparent felicity of the title" (P, 397). The "cunning alphabet" magically constricts the range of meanings, thereby making experience comprehensible. The reading is subject to change; indeed, the "moody bard" changed the name of the mountain from "The Delectable Mountain," a name "bestowed by an old Baptist farmer, an hereditary admirer of Bunyan and his most marvelous book" (P, 397). But those changes are restricted by a cultural language—exemplified here by Bunyan's book—and they alter nature accordingly.

The moody bard offers a solipsistic counterpoint to the Young American literary nationalists. What he does for "The Mount of the Titans" they sought to do for the nation. But Pierre embodies the fate of the author who takes their precepts too literally. At points, his narrative encounters and submits to their prewritten script, and he cannot tell his own story. Elsewhere, he recapitulates the bleak underside of their methods, and again his story cannot be told. In either case, he succumbs to a destiny that he himself unleashes, believing it all the while to be manifest. But Melville's critique reaches past Young America and into the factors of which its members took insufficient account. The man who complained, "Dollars damn me" knew all too well the cost of the intrinsically paradoxical nature of his profession. The market both created and constrained him; the professional author was indeed the creature of the market. Yet so was the dilettante. When the story a young Pierre wants to tell coincides with the story his audience wants to hear, he is equally the market's creature.

Melville's meditation on authorship forced him, as he said of Emerson, to go down stairs five miles or more. "What I feel most moved to write, that is banned," he lamented. Yet perhaps the passive construction of the second clause has obscured the passivity of the first. Like the rebellious Pierre, Melville *feels moved* to write against the grain, but, as he shows in Pierre, we are *moved* by the same forces we think we oppose. What he found in his own five mile dive was not the bottom, but the plummet. The final hash, the botched book itself, could best tell the story of conflicting stories—and thereby tell the story of how a story is shaped by internal and external demands. His lament prefaces my discussion of a companion "thought-diver," Harriet Wilson, whom Melville never knew but who offers a similar analysis of the shaping of her story in *Our Nig*.

The Stranger in the House

Melville found his story difficult to tell when it ran against the expectations of his audience. Harriet Wilson's very existence ran counter to the expectations of an antebellum United States audience, for whom an African-American woman writer was a curiosity. Nor did they expect, as she knew, a "free" black woman in the North to be enslaved. Unlike Pierre, Wilson's protagonist, Frado, is not explicitly an author, and authorship does not seem to be Wilson's primary concern. Yet, as an apparently appended preface makes clear, political and economic concerns limit the story that Wilson can tell about Frado. Reluctant to "palliate slavery at the South," Wilson hopes to avoid "disclosures of its appurtenances North."[50] But her story of how a child has internalized a cultural definition of selfhood and of how that selfhood marks the child a mulatta—marks her, that is, by race and gender—cannot avoid such disclosures. The constraints on her story become a part of her story: in what cannot explicitly be told about Frado lies another story about cultural identity in the United States. Unlike Melville, Wilson does not write with the Young American literary nationalists in mind, but her analysis of authorship and identity in the United States addresses their chief concerns.

Evidence of the untold story emerges in discrepancies such as the intrusion of a first-person subject, an "I," in a third-person narration. It is a story told through indirection, the story of a subjectivity intrusive because unexpressed. Henry Louis Gates, Jr., reads these intrusions as "first-person lapses," traces "of an inexperienced author struggling with or *against* the received conventions of her form."[51] But such lapses may equally chronicle the process of subjection in which lived experiences are comprehended, or narrativized, according to cultural prescriptions. From Frado's story comes a tale of illegitimacy and miscegenated unions, of challenges such as that embodied by Melville's Isabel Banford to the stability of identity and inheritance represented by the patronym. But to contain the threat, those challenges must be reinscribed within a cultural narrative that positions Frado herself. That reinscription is the untold story recounted through the rhetorical disjunctions of *Our Nig*.

Confusion and subterfuge begin with the preface to *Our Nig*, in which the use of the first-person pronoun turns Frado, post facto, into the author of her incompletely told story. A third-person "writer confesses her inability to minister to the refined and cultivated, the pleasure supplied by abler pens," but explains that, "deserted by kindred, disabled by failing health, I am forced to some experiment which shall aid me in maintaining myself and child without extinguishing this feeble life" (*ON*, 3). Like Fanny Fern's Ruth Hall and many of her literary sisters, she writes to support herself and her child, to participate in the literary market. Financial exigency actually pushes the speaking subject, "I," through literary conventions, such as the apologia, that confine "the writer" to a third-person characterization. The market appears almost to produce a speaking subject, here literally an author, in accordance with a presumably free selfhood suggested by the earning potential of this American subject. Copyright laws and the northern black subject's putative self-ownership ensure that this text may yield a profit, although it is unclear for whom.[52] The preface suggestively articulates uneasiness at the writer's dependence on the patronage of an audience, a dependence further complicated by political considerations: "I would not from these [economic] motives even palliate slavery at the South, by disclosures of its appurtenances North. My mistress was wholly imbued with Southern principles. I do not pretend to divulge every transaction in my own life, which the unprejudiced would declare unfavorable in comparison with treatment of legal bondmen; I have purposely omitted what would most provoke shame in our good anti-slavery friends at home" (*ON*, 3). In telling what she has omitted, however, the narrator in effect hints at the story that she claims to be withholding. Evidence of an untold story begins to emerge.

Gates, David Ames Curtis, and, more recently, Barbara A. White have convincingly established Wilson's efforts to protect herself and her young son from the hideous abuses of the poor farm.[53] Nonetheless, the financial exigency offered as the exclusive motivation for her authorship is at least complicated by her sense of her intended audience. "I sincerely appeal to my colored brethren universally for patronage," she writes, "hoping they will not condemn this attempt of their sister to be erudite, but rally around me a faithful band of supporters and defenders" (*ON*, 3). This is a book for "colored brethren universally," a collectivity with, hypothetically, the economic strength and self-sufficiency to bypass white patronage. *Our Nig* may constitute a plea for this hypothetical audience. But the plea also challenges the putative profit motive of the work, just as the confession of omission undermines a politically-motivated silence.[54] The "common penury" of Wilson's "colored brethren" has inspired another contemporary reader of *Our Nig* to look beyond the transparency of this claim. For Claudia Tate, "the novel, its preface, and appendix cloak the allegory of desired authorship, structured as the story of frustrated motherhood."[55] This claim does not mitigate the autobiographical validity of Wilson's economic need or her genuine maternal anguish. But whatever her motives for writing, Wilson ultimately produced a narrative that bears witness to the limitations on her story and on her analysis.

The writer even expresses reservations about trying to tell her story. She is concerned, first of all, that it will contribute to the South's critique of northern racism and figurative "slavery," thereby mitigating the perniciousness of the peculiar institution. She even allows that concern to shape her narration. But the market, too, can shape a story. Economic need threatens to turn the narrator into the double of Samuel, the protagonist's eventual husband, one of a company of "professed fugitives from slavery, who recounted their personal experience in homely phrase and awakened the indignation of non-slave holders against brother Pro" (*ON*, 126). Despite the obvious political differences, her own hybrid text, part sentimental narrative and part slave narrative, might also exploit fashions and profit from suffering itself.[56] Yet Samuel presents another problem as well. Insofar as he awakens indignation, Samuel does serve the antislavery cause, but he also embodies the commodification of the black subject within a racist discourse that prescribes the experiences and accounts of the fugitive slave. Moreover, even while lecturing, Samuel "had little spare money" (*ON*, 127); not surprisingly, this black subject does not even profit from his commodification.

In the end, Wilson analyzes the profit motive. The young, white Ruth Hall expressed the longings of a muted reading public. The tale of *Our Nig*'s narrator, by contrast, strikes too deeply at the wellspring of cultural values in her analysis of the terms of cultural identity to call forth such an avid readership, and Wilson knows it. Instead, she undercuts her own professed profit motive and frees the adjective "southern" from its geographic referent, as she risks provoking, and alienating, her potentially most *profitable* market: white northerners. Her disclosures do not "palliate slavery at the South"; rather, they indict a Union that is predicated on protecting the right to possess human chattel and a literary market that confirms as it mirrors that premise.

Her critique of the cultural narrative that positions Frado, in this case the national narrative of the Union such as Lincoln advocated, begins with Frado's mother, Mag, a name suggestively close to "Nig," the name Frado is given by the Bellmonts. The unmarried, pregnant white woman finds herself friendless until Jim, a black man, promises to care for her. She marries him, but he dies a few years after their marriage, leaving her with two mulatta daughters whom she cannot support. Mag and her new consort deposit Frado, the more rambunctious of the daughters, in the house of a white family, the Bellmonts, where she is illegally indentured and treated as a slave. It is the Bellmonts who name her anxiously into her existence in their house not quite divided. In this synthesis of slave and sentimental narrative forms, which emphasizes similarities between the white Mag and her mulatta daughter Frado, Wilson shows how the defining terms of a cultural narrative commodify the black female subject.

Frado's history begins with her mother's exclusion from her white community. Becoming a mother without being a wife (or widow), Mag commits a particularly egregious crime in sentimental literature—the crime against the name of the father. Mag's own lack of home and family makes her more susceptible to her feelings: "As she merged into womanhood, unprotected, uncherished, uncared for, there fell on her ear the music of love, awakening an intensity of emotion long dormant" (*ON*, 5). While this depiction does not quite deviate from sentimental convention, the emphasis is unusual. Mag's seduction and desertion are completed by the end of the first paragraph, which stresses her loneliness even more than her lack of guidance. Moreover, the narrative is concerned less with the fate she earns than with the place to which the culture consigns her. Divorced from the context of family, she challenges its terms. Yet that challenge is motivated by her longing for the connection provided by the family. The threat she represents appears to inhere at least as much in the intensity of her emotion as in her actions, and she is given no opportunity for redemption. No one teaches her to channel her passions into the reproduction (literal and figurative) of the gendered identities—the inheritance—configured in relation to the name of the father. Her "offspring" marks the tenuousness of paternity in the absence of strict social guidelines, even though the baby dies at birth. A mother who is not a wife complicates the principle of inheritance governed by the patronym. As a result, Mag finds that "the great bond of *union* to her former companions *was severed*" (*ON*, 6; emphasis added). Emblematically, that severance marks not so much her exclusion from the Union, but her inclusion *as an outcast.*

From within the terms of a cultural narrative, Mag becomes *unnatural;* the text carefully establishes her outcast status as precipitating rather than stemming from the disruption of "natural" maternal bonds. Her reaction to the death of her illegitimate infant recalls that of many enslaved mothers. " 'God be thanked,' ejaculated Mag, as she saw its breathing cease; 'no one can taunt her with my ruin' " (*ON*, 6). Similarly, Harriet Jacobs, in *Incidents in the Life of a Slave Girl,* watching lovingly over her child, nonetheless "sometimes . . . wished that he might die in infancy." She remarks, "death is better than slavery. It was a sad thought that I had no name to give my child."[57] Without such a name, a child in effect inherits dispossession and is named into namelessness. Significantly, Mag genders the child through the pronoun "her," while the narrator denies her personhood with the neutering "its." Identity results from recognition and naming.

Wilson uses Mag's unself-consciousness to explain how identity is gendered—and engendered. Mag inadvertently accedes to her new identity because she has internalized the assumptions of her community. In other words, because of her initial status as insider, she accepts her new status as outcast without question. Conspicuously, she forfeits what is perhaps the most important female currency in the sentimental narrative: her virtue. Jacobs also refers continually to her reluctance to tell her tale because of the loss of virtue—her illicit relation with a white man who fathers her two children out of wedlock—at its center.[58] At several key moments in the story she is nearly silenced by her reluctance to speak of her "indiscretion." Yet she is at the same time aware of the processes by which the enslaved woman is dehumanized through an exclusion from a conventional gendered identity. Claimed early from a loving family as the property of an arbitrary master, she is sensitive to the contradictions of the master's culture and to the arbitrariness of the terms of her exclusion. As an enslaved woman, she embodies those contradictions. Jacobs observes, for example, that in a culture that defines womanhood through the principle of virtue, it "is deemed a crime in [the enslaved woman] to wish to be virtuous" (HJ, 62). Legally prevented by her master from marrying the man she loves, a freeborn black carpenter, she defies her master by bearing the children of another white man. Whereas Mag understands her motherhood as the result of a criminal act, Jacobs turns her own motherhood into an act of rebellion both by defying her master and by insistently predicating her identity on her motherhood rather than her virtue. Unlike Mag, Jacobs does not fully accept the cultural insistence on virtuous (i.e. legal) motherhood as one of the cornerstones of female identity (the other being virtuous spinsterhood) but instead offers a critique of the slaveholding South precisely on the grounds that it intrinsically withholds virtue from some mothers.

Mag's paternally dispossessed child differs from the children of Harriet Jacobs because the latter are the clearly marked property of *a*, if not *their*, white father. As illegitimate children, Mag's white and Jacobs's nonwhite children emblematize both the cultural transgression that has transpired and the possibility of unwitting incest, the crossing of the most primal cultural boundary. But the property status of children of enslaved mothers and the laws against miscegenation ostensibly protected the reproduction of the white family from the threat Mag's child represents. An enslaved mother reproduced property, while a free white mother produced citizens.[59] Mag's illegitimate child is too ambiguous. No rebel, Mag accepts her community's censure of her.

"You's down low enough," Jim tells her in one of literature's least romantic marriage proposals, "I don't see but I've got to take care of ye. 'Sposin' we marry" (*ON*, 12). Jim's language attests to the extent to which both he and Mag have internalized, have come to believe in, the appropriateness of their status. "I's black outside, I know," notes Jim, "but I's got a white heart inside. Which you rather have, a black heart in a white skin, or a white heart in a black one?" (*ON*, 12). While he recognizes that color is only skin deep, Jim does not question the symbolic system that gives color meaning. He is attracted to Mag's whiteness, to "the pleasing contrast between her fair face and his own dark skin; the smooth, straight hair . . . on her now wrinkled but once fair brow" (*ON*, 11). The narrator assumes the reader's acquiescence in Jim's standard of "natural" beauty, derived, like decorum, from internalized cultural values, and she assumes the reader's concurrence in the community's attitude toward Mag and Jim's marriage: "You can philosophize, gentle reader, upon the impropriety of such unions, and preach dozens of sermons on the evils of amalgamation.

Want is a more powerful philosopher and preacher. Poor Mag. She has sundered another bond which held her to her fellows. She has descended another step down the ladder of infamy" (*ON*, 13). Jim's response makes it hard to determine whether or not the "gentle reader" includes the Preface's anticipated "colored brethren," but it surely presumes white readers, who would have found miscegenation between a white woman and a black man especially disturbing. The narrator uses Mag's desperation to demonstrate the superior status accorded an impoverished white woman outcast over a free black man. But Mag's break with her community rather than her marriage itself evokes the narrator's "Poor Mag," and "infamy" registers an ironic distance from the censure of the community.

As white masters frequently prevented the marriages of enslaved women, such as Jacobs or Frederick Douglass's Aunt Hester, Mag's marriage is, practically speaking, annulled by her white northern community. The language of the text stresses the social consequences of her marriage. In the three paragraphs describing their marriage and Jim's death, Wilson uses the word "union" twice: Jim "was determined [Mag] should not regret her union to him" (*ON*, 14), and "her union with a black—was the climax of repulsion," causing her to be "expelled from companionship with white people" (*ON*, 15, 16). Mag's amalgamation is an *alternative* union, one that challenges the internal boundaries of the Union. Marriage between a white woman and a black man, which legitimizes Mag and Jim's children—and which, therefore, necessitates creating a legal position (and name) for them—is even more challenging than Mag's extralegal behavior. Although neither Mag nor Jim intends defiance, their children embody the challenge; hence the laws that sought to exclude Mag's children, like Jacobs's, from the name of their father.

Their daughter Frado's fate throughout *Our Nig* evinces the anxious efforts of her culture to (re)position her. Significantly, Mag's first reference to her and Jim's two children concerns their fate following his death. She *snarls* a response when Jim's successor suggests that they give away the children because of economic constraints: " 'Who'll take the black devils?' " Blackening her daughters, she expresses her own invisibility as the *white* mother of a *black* man's children, and she disclaims her social as readily as her biological relation to those children. Her understanding of her dilemma echoes a prevalent argument that was used to oppose abolition or to advocate colonization: the economic dependency of free, especially freed, blacks. Frado is accordingly all but sold into slavery. So thoroughly does Frado internalize her indentured status that it is almost impossible to remember, during the course of the narrative, that she is legally free. She is left in the care of the Bellmont family, despite Mag's initial protest that Mrs. Bellmont "is a right she-devil!" (ON, 17). The life to which Frado is subsequently subjected follows a conventional senti- mental plot in which an abandoned girl suffers abuse at the hands espe- cially of the wicked female members of a surrogate family until the happy ending.[60] But the sentimental narrative becomes a slave narrative when the mulatta subject enters "the two-story white house, north" of the Bell- mont family. The mulatta product of miscegenation cannot marry into the white American family. Frado's introduction reveals the tensions of a house almost divided and the strategies used to cover them up.

The Bellmonts agree to "keep" Frado only after Jack Bellmont, the son who actively befriends her, renames and thus repositions her:

> "She's real handsome and bright, and *not very black, either*" [emphasis added].
>
> "Yes," rejoined Mary; "that's just like you, Jack. She'll be of no use at all these three years, right under foot all the time."
>
> "Poh! Miss Mary; if she should stay, it wouldn't be two days before you would be telling the girls about *our* nig, *our* nig!" retorted Jack.
>
> "I don't want a nigger 'round *me*, do you, mother?" asked Mary.
>
> "I don't mind the nigger in the child. I should like a dozen better than one," replied her mother. (ON, 25–26)

Frado would be satisfactory to the Bellmonts as a white child or as a slave. Mrs. Bellmont, "imbued with *southern* principles," in particular wants a slave—and an unambiguously black one, as her subsequent insistence on Frado's exposure to the sun makes clear. Jack articulates precisely the anxieties Frado produces when he measures her in terms of her simili- tude to white culture: "not very black." But he immediately renames her into an identity that establishes her "blackness" and her lack of self- possession. "*Our* nig" emphasizes the family's possession of Frado, at worst as a slave, at best as a pet, which the more than nominal affinities between "Frado" and the family dog, "Fido," underscore.

Although it is only Mrs. Bellmont and Mary who physically abuse Frado, and although she is defended by Mr. Bellmont, two of his sons, and his sister, the narrative iconographically implicates Frado's supposed benefactors in her enslavement as well. Frado, accompanied by the family dog, tries once to run away. When Fido returns, Jack, James, and Mr. Bellmont, motivated by compassion, trick him into betraying her hiding place: "'Fido! Fido! Frado wants some supper. Come!' Jack started, the dog followed, and soon capered on before, far, far into the fields, over walls and through fences, into a piece of swampy land. Jack followed close, and soon appeared . . . coaxing and forcing Frado along with him" (*ON*, 49–50). Whatever their motivation, three white men and a dog cannot hunt a young black girl in a swamp without unmistakable resonances—particularly, in the North, following the passage of the Fugitive Slave Act, which, its critics contended, nationalized slavery. "A frail child, driven from shelter by the cruelty of his mother, was an object of interest to James" (*ON*, 50). As such an object, Frado evokes the compassion of the men. But despite their promises, the Bellmont children never take her to live with their families when they leave home. In fact, the Bellmont family domesticates Frado into a position that explicitly corresponds to the domesticated slaves whom southerners welcomed into their families as evidence of their "benevolent" institutions.[61] As "our nig," she is a possessed "object of interest." Frado's domestication reinscribes the relationship of a mulatta child of a white mother to the American family. Her exchange value is thus double: as a worker and as "our nig," in which the mulatta implicitly becomes "black," she holds the house together.

In the reputedly kind and gentle Mr. Bellmont, Wilson offers a thinly disguised critique of a logic reminiscent of Lincoln's, a critique that indicts northern accommodationists. The Bellmonts' "two story white house, north," as the subtitle describes it, is indeed a house divided. But neither "story" really wants to liberate Frado. Mr. Bellmont, who apparently inclines toward nurturing, "was a kind, humane man, who would not grudge hospitality to the poorest wanderer, nor fail to sympathize with any sufferer, however humble. The child's desertion by her mother appealed to his sympathy, and he felt inclined to succor her" (*ON*, 24). But when pressed by his sister Abby, Frado's strongest female ally, to explain why he tolerates his wife's and daughter's abuse of Frado, he refuses responsibility[62]:

"How am I to help it? Women rule the earth, and all in it."

"I think I should rule my own house, John,"—

"And live in hell meantime," added Mr. Bellmont. (*ON*, 44)

Bellmont ascribes his inaction to his desire to preserve the peace in his "union." He is himself, he claims, a victim of women's putative rule. But a previous incident has already thoroughly obviated that claim. When Mr. Bellmont had championed Frado's education, deciding, over the vociferous objections of his wife and daughter, to send her to school, his authority had been unquestionable: "He was a man who seldom decided controversies at home. The word once spoken admitted of no appeal; so not withstanding Mary's objection that she would have to attend the same school she did, the word became law" (*ON*, 30–31). Later, his dying son will send his father to summon Frado, thus circumventing Mrs. Bellmont's prohibition, because Mr. Bellmont "was a messenger . . . who could not be denied" (*ON*, 83). With the power to convert word into law, Mr. Bellmont could surely authorize a more humane treatment of Frado. He chooses not to and takes refuge in the language of obedience, a language that follows the logic of Lincolnian rhetoric. So well did Wilson capture the Lincolnian posture that *Our Nig* seems almost prophetic, the mark of good analysis. The humble posture of the sixteenth president, as in the First Inaugural Address, could not obscure the widespread disregard for and reshaping of the law for which he was renowned.

Like Pierre, Frado is possessed, internalizing a prescripted identity through which the Bellmont family breaks the mischievous child in spirit as well as body. Her one gesture toward active resistance is itself authored by Mr. Bellmont, who, chastened by the death of James, counsels her to try to avoid undeserved beatings if she could do so without being "saucy and disrespectful" and only "when she was sure she did not deserve a whipping." He is concerned that she is " 'looking sick,' " and that she " 'cannot endure beating as [she] once could' " (*ON*, 104–5). Frado soon finds

> an opportunity . . . of profiting by his advice. She was sent for wood, and not returning as soon as Mrs. B. calculated, she followed her, and snatching from the pile a stick, raised it over her.
>
> "Stop!" shouted Frado, "strike me, and I'll never work a mite more for you;" and throwing down what she had gathered, stood like one who feels the stirring of free and independent thoughts. (*ON*, 104–5)

Frado's temporary victory consists largely of reversing roles. The hint of identification or even subjective confusion in her use of pronouns, "she followed her," is followed up when Mrs. Bellmont carries Frado's bundle into the house. But it remains "Frado's bundle." As long as the system exists, Frado will continue to be enslaved by it. The simile ("like") undercuts the claim to "free and independent thoughts," the rhetoric in which Frado manifests her belief in her own self and in self-ownership. Her momentary triumph nevertheless leaves her still in the Bellmont house, an immobilization that stems from her internalization of the Bellmont's narrative.[63]

From Mrs. Bellmont, she derives a sense of unworthiness based in inaccurate physical self-perception, what W. E. B. Du Bois calls "double-consciousness": "She determined to flee. But where? Who would take her? Mrs. B. had always represented her ugly. Perhaps every one thought so. Then no one would take her. She was black, no one would love her. She might have to return, and then she would be more in her mistress' power than ever" (ON, 108). A slave might be reluctant to risk the consequences of a failed escape attempt, but Frado is legally free to go. Her enslavement is figurative, the result of her internalization of the Bellmonts' representations of her. She subscribes to a commodification based on physical appearance, the reliance of the sentimental heroine on her beauty, but sees herself "through the eyes of others," according to their standards of evaluation.[64] As a result, she believes herself to be ugly and unlovable, having no recognizable place in the world. The pious Aunt Abby further undermines her: "She resolved to speak to Aunt Abby. *She* mapped the dangers of her course, her liability to fail in finding so good friends as John [Mr. Bellmont] and herself" (ON, 108). Aunt Abby's counsel hauntingly echoes the cultural narrative of Mag's fall and thus reinforces the narrative of Frado's "benevolent" enslavement. Her "benefactors," in other words, conspire to keep her in her place—and have perhaps more power than her enemies to do so. Although the two "shes" distinctly refer to different people—Frado and Aunt Abby—the pronominal resonance suggests Frado's susceptibility to her benefactors' perspective. In the logic of the sentence, Aunt Abby displaces Frado, who sees the world through her interlocutor's eyes.

Aunt Abby and James in particular labor to instill in Frado a morality, in the form of Christian values, that keeps her firmly in her assigned place. The efficacy of this strategy is evident in Frado's decision not to employ a familiar slave practice of "administering poison to her mistress to rid herself and the house of so detestable a plague" (ON, 108); she is "restrained by an overruling Providence; and finally decide[s] to stay contentedly through her period of service" (ON, 109). In her very conceptualization of the crime, Frado manifests the logic of her decision not to commit it. She plans to poison her mistress to rid not only herself but *the house* of her. In her mind, Frado has become indeed a part of the Bellmont family. The Providence that she is taught to believe *rules over* this world *overrules* Frado, and this rhetorical inversion indicates her self-negation. The legal and moral diction (overrules) replaces religious diction (rules over) to show a Frado who is "overruled" into an obedience to the letter of that law because she has internalized a culturally-derived morality. She will not only remain in the house, but she will *stay contentedly* therein, blaming the mistress exclusively for her mistreatment so as to exonerate "the house." She cooperates with the Bellmonts who, like Lincolnian nationalists, have to find a place for the black subject in their "American family" that neither implies the possibility of miscegenation, nor raises the specter of balkanization (or confederacy). Through this process the word indeed becomes law, and Frado obeys it. Storytelling is an activity, and Frado overrules her own actions, just as she overrules her version of events, the story she tries to tell. Her account of her experience in the Bellmont house conforms to the position she accepts within that house.

By making authorship an important part of her analysis, Wilson explains the difficulty for an African-American woman of telling a story that does not confirm her position in the national narrative. *Our Nig* has been read as, and certainly appears to be, an autobiography. The narrator herself suggests, in the preface and in the letters that conclude the manuscript, that she *is* Frado, and both end up needing to support a child. Indeed, as the impressive archeology of Curtis, Gates, and White demonstrates, there are undeniable similarities between Frado and Wilson. Nonetheless, the conclusion that the "I" of the preface is strictly autobiographical or that Wilson did no more than borrow from her life in creating Frado requires an imaginative leap. Once taken, such a leap obscures the gap between Wilson and Frado (and Wilson and "Our Nig") through which Wilson re-presents the authorizing conventions within which "Our Nig" writes. The authorial signature, in other words, is part of Wilson's story:

Our Nig;

or,

Sketches from the Life of a Free Black
In a Two-Story White House, North
Showing That Slavery's Shadows Fall Even There
By "Our Nig"

The quotation marks alert the reader to an authorial persona. "Our Nig" is to Wilson what the Frederick Douglass of the title *Narrative of the Life of Frederick Douglass, an American Slave* is to Frederick Douglass the author: as the character Frederick Douglass tells the story of how Frederick Bailey becomes Frederick Douglass, "Our Nig" tells the story of how Frado becomes Our Nig and what happens when she tries to tell her story. From the discrepancies between Wilson and "Our Nig" emerges the story of an author's struggle with the prescriptive conventions of form and plot. As White also observes, "Wilson clearly wanted to tell a more complex story than the political agendas or literary forms of her day could contain" (BW, 38).

Undoubtedly, the authorial signature marks a transformation. Gates notes an ironic reversal of "the power relation implicit in renaming-rituals. . . . Transformed into an *object* of abuse and scorn by her enemies, the 'object,' the heroine of *Our Nig*, reverses this relationship by *renaming herself* not Our Nig but 'Our Nig,' thereby transforming herself into a *subject*" (*ON*, li). That subject, he explains, "writes her own thinly veiled fictional account of her life in which *she* transforms her tormentors into objects, the stock, stereotypical objects of the sentimental novel" (*ON*, li). Yet the transformation mapped by Gates is smoother than the disruptions within the text suggest. I return here to what Gates calls the "first-person lapses" that appear in the first three chapter headings, "Mag Smith, My Mother," "My Father's Death," and "A New Home for Me." As Frado is moved simultaneously toward her "enslavement," the first-person subject dissolves into third-person narration. I have already suggested that these intrusions trace a process of subjection, yielding evidence not necessarily, as Gates contends, "of an inexperienced author struggling with or *against* the received conventions of her form" (*ON*, xxxvii), but rather of a highly crafted narrative that *re-presents* that struggle. These chapters chronicle self-dissolution, as Mag is systematically banished from "the bond of union" with her community, and as Frado is named into her new identity. The discrepancy between the first-person chapter headings and the third-person narration marks the representation of a self as an other—or the recognition of the alterity of the self. This rhetoric, in other words, drama-tizes the positioning of the subject. Quotation marks around the authorial signature show "Our Nig" being spoken into existence. The heroine is obviously a subject, but I do not see, as Gates does, a move from object to subject. I see instead the conspicuous representation of a *subject* opposed not so much to an object as to the idea of a "free" self.

In this sense, *Frado* does not objectify her tormentors, or, for that matter, her friends, who are even more responsible for naming her into her position within the culture. Rather, Wilson offers an analysis of the processes of subjection that extends, by implication, to the entire House of Bellmont (and beyond). *Wilson* rather than "Our Nig" trumps those who rename Frado. The difference is subtle, but central to my reading of the text. The quotation marks that enclose the authorial "Our Nig" depict the cultural positioning of the "author." "Our Nig" the author has exchange value as a curiosity, an *"object* of interest" like her character—an exchange value that "H. E. Wilson" cannot rival—but only if she is properly positioned and delivers the appropriate goods. An "autobiographical" account of a "slave" narrative, with strong characteristics of a sentimental narrative as well, may be marketable in the late 1850s. But Frado is *literally* neither a slave, nor a sentimental heroine, and this narrative is not finally just an autobiography. It is instead a *narrative about* autobiography, *about* what writing for a particular market does to this African-American woman in pre–Civil War New England—and, more generally, *about* cultural identity. The "I" in the Preface is, finally, a split subject; "Our Nig" writes an autobiography, whereas H. E. Wilson writes a sociopolitical allegory for "colored brethren universally." But the allegory, which shows how the market and the cultural conventions it at once expresses and reinforces, only works through the contrast between the author and the character or narrator that makes the split visible.

Our Nig ends with an ominous last sentence that signals a change of tone and an alternative plot. The narrative chronicles the process by which Frado becomes "Our Nig"—her commodification within the Bellmonts' and the nation's analogous domestic plots. The penultimate paragraph ends by requesting the "sympathy and aid" of the reader (*ON*, 130), and the appended letters attest to the autobiographical status of the narrative. But the last sentence evokes a surprisingly disjunctive Biblical narrative: "Frado has passed from [the surviving Bellmonts'] memories, as Joseph from the butler's, but she will never cease to track them till beyond mortal vision" (*ON*, 131). The survivors mentioned are few—only the invalid daughter, Jane (ironically), and her husband, and James's wife and child. But they were among those who befriended her, accounting, perhaps, for Frado's unrequited attachment to them. After all, who else does she have?

Yet the reference to *tracking*, especially in the context of a narrative of enslavement, is at the very least discomfiting. In Genesis, the imprisoned Joseph interprets the dream of a fellow inmate, the butler, prophesying his release. He asks only that the butler, on his release, tell the Pharaoh of him, but the butler forgets. Analogously, Jack, Jane, and their families go west, leaving Frado in the house where "there seemed no one capable of enduring the oppressions . . . but her" (*ON*, 109). Joseph is released from prison two years later, when the Pharaoh has a dream that reminds the butler of his promise; Frado, however, can hold no such hope, since her benefactors have all died. She is forgotten, left alone in the house to be its historian. *She* gets the final word. In an eerie echo of the language of slavery, *she* will track *them* into enslavement to *her* plot. But, as we have seen, she does not tell a sufficiently analytic story of the House of Bellmont. She must tell *her* story, not *theirs*.

Joseph's extended story of enslavement and exodus explains the ominousness of Wilson's own retelling of Frado's story. Joseph's accurate reading of the Pharaoh's dream makes Egypt flourish during a time of drought and famine. Joseph, a Jew, becomes a powerful figure and eventually saves the lives of his family, including the brothers who sold him into slavery. He is forgotten a second time ("there arose up a new king over Egypt, which knew not Joseph" (Exodus 1:8), and the enslavement of the Jews results from this forgetting. Yet the new Pharaoh is also severely punished for that enslavement with a series of plagues, and, in the end, it is Joseph's story that gets told. The chapter begins with the epigram from Ecclesiastes, "Nothing new under the sun" (*ON*, 126), a phrase that suggests prescriptedness.[65] The story of oppression and enslavement is indeed an old one, and it includes the unwillingness of the oppressor to profit from the lessons—the stories—of the past. Yet the lessons are taught and retaught through the ages. While the text demonstrates an internalization of cultural values that prescribes the story *Frado* may tell, Wilson analyzes those dynamics. And it is *she* who writes the history of the divided house; *she* writes—or analyzes and rewrites—the American narrative.

"Our Nig," however, haunts the house more in what she embodies than in what she writes, and it is her story that constitutes Wilson's American narrative. The family has repressed her, but she will return as the uncanny emblem of what they have forgotten. She shows, for example, how the mulatta is figuratively "blackened," just as Mrs. Bellmont literally sends her into the sun to black out evidence of her kinship relations with the white American family. *Our Nig* similarly indicts "professed abolitionists, who didn't want slaves at the South, nor niggers in their own houses, North. Faugh! to lodge one; to eat with one; to admit one through the front door; to sit next one; awful!" (*ON*, 129). The sentiments of those professed abolitionists assign the African-American subject a circumscribed place comprehended by, but not integrated into, We the People, a place that allows enslavement. Thus Wilson exposes the fictionality of the northern national narrative in which slavery is "un-American," and "Our Nig" waits to be remembered and (prophetically) avenged. Perhaps she tells her story primarily to her colored brethren after all.

The histories of both *Pierre* and *Our Nig* attest to the risks of their projects. As both texts maintain, even those who stand to benefit from revisions of culturally-sanctioned historical narratives are reluctant to endure the challenge to conceptions of personhood that such revisions entail. The extent to which *Pierre* has traditionally been confounded by and confused with Pierre's failed narrative must accordingly call the viability of Melville's project into question. Many of his contemporary readers and reviewers advocated that the author of *Pierre* be institutionalized rather than canonized; the Duyckincks attributed the "literary mistakes" of *Pierre* ("its conception and execution") to European influences: "The passion which he sought to evolve . . . was in the worst school of the mixed French and German melodramatic" (*CAL*, 2:674). And obscurity greeted *Our Nig* for more than a century. Yet not surprisingly, both works have resurfaced at a time when the national subject—its inclusions and exclusions—has come again to the forefront of critical consciousness. The Pharaoh's most recent nightmares, it seems, have summoned lost and forgotten works, part of the reconstitution of literary history in the United States. Together, *Pierre* and *Our Nig* mark a chapter of that history, and they forecast a theory of double-consciousness.

3

......

"The Strange Meaning of Being Black"

The Souls of Black Folk and

the Narrative of History

At the end of his 1935 *Black Reconstruction,* in a chapter entitled "The Propaganda of History," W. E. B. Du Bois analyzes the production of American historical narratives and their role in healing political rifts and helping the United States emerge from the Civil War as a united nation. Chagrined that "the real frontal attack on Reconstruction, as interpreted by the leaders of national thought in 1870 and for some time thereafter, came from the universities and particularly from Columbia and Johns Hopkins," his thoughts must have returned to Harvard's History 13, to the appeals for objectivity in the study of history made by his professor, and later his dissertation advisor, historian Albert Bushnell Hart.[1] Du Bois lamented that "in a day when the human mind aspired to a science of human action, a history and psychology of the mighty effort of the mightiest century, we fell under the leadership of those who would compromise with truth in the past in order to make peace in the present and guide policy in the future" (PH, 727). As was so often the case in antebellum debates, the interests of the African Americans after the war were subordinated as well to the construction of a unifying national narrative. The Civil War Amendments addressed constitutional uncertainties by abolishing slavery, nationalizing citizenship, and establishing universal male suffrage.[2] African Americans were now legally national subjects, but most narratives of the reconstructed nation, as Du Bois's analysis makes clear, still did not tell a story of their equality and full personhood.

The proliferation of histories of the United States in the late nineteenth and early twentieth century attest to the extent to which historians assumed the task of narrating the nation.[3] For Du Bois, the "frontal attack on Reconstruction," the rewriting of this period of United States history, began with professor of political science and constitutional law John W. Burgess and professor of history and political philosophy William A. Dunning, both of Columbia University (PH, 1035). In the preface to his 1902 *Reconstruction and the Constitution, 1866–1876*, Burgess called for "the re-establishment of a real national brotherhood between the North and the South" which, he argued, could only be accomplished with a mutual acknowledgment of wrongdoing: the South for secession, and the North for reconstruction.[4] Burgess believed the white North was well prepared for his thesis. Increased migration of African Americans to the North during this period added to northern white anxieties about heterogeneity. This migration joined the so-called "new immigration" from southern and eastern Europe already perceived by many in the North as a challenge to American absorptiveness. In addition, the imperialistic incorporation of territories inhabited by nonwhites into the United States raised concern about the place of a large unassimilated and, many argued, unassimilable population. Burgess remarked that United States imperialism, "under the direction of the Republican party, the great Northern party," was teaching the North lessons already learned by the South, "that there are vast differences in political capacity between the races, and that it is the white man's mission, his duty and his right, to hold the reins of power in his own hands for the civilization of the world and the welfare of mankind" (*RC*, viii–ix).

Five years later, in *Reconstruction: Political and Economic, 1865–1877*, a volume of *The American Nation*, a series edited by Hart, Dunning explained the white southern response to reconstruction in terms made familiar in the North by the "race suicide" arguments of proponents of the restriction of immigration: "What animated the whites was pride in their race as such and a dread, partly instinctive, partly rational, lest their institutions, traditions, and ideals were to be appropriated or submerged."[5] And he described the "relief of the general public" following the election of Rutherford B. Hayes, and the "bargain" that gave Republicans control of the national government and southern whites the directive to "rule the Negroes" (*RPE*, 340–41). Evidently, the "general public" did not include descendants of Africans, who, Dunning noted, "had no pride of race and no aspiration or ideals save to be like the whites" (*RPE*, 213).

In 1903, as the nation so clearly turned from (and on) its early reconstructive policies, *The Souls of Black Folk* worked formally toward a critique of the construction of the new historical narratives. Du Bois was not alone in his alarm. A September 1890 *Atlantic Monthly* piece entitled "The Perils of Historical Narrative" had warned that the demands of narrative—of storytelling in general—corrupted the presentation of facts thought to constitute history.[6] In many ways, the project that resulted in *The Souls of Black Folk* shared the concerns that motivated central historical and sociological inquiries of this period, inquiries that centered on what Peter Novick calls "the objectivity question."[7] But the work of this American sociologist, historian, and fiction writer of Afro-Caribbean descent went further than most of these projects in analyzing the political importance of formal strategies of representation.

The Souls of Black Folk posits a connection between creating a narrative and struggling with the terms of a cultural identity, a connection that turns aesthetic creation into a political gesture. Already the trained social scientist was beginning to explore the union of art and propaganda, which he believed to be inevitable and which he made the subject of important inquiry during his editorship of *Crisis* magazine.[8] Neither a collection of essays, nor a traditional narrative, *The Souls of Black Folk* challenges the formal boundaries of genres and disciplines; it presents a fractured narrative, an experiment that stresses different ways of looking at the representation of black America(ns). The work makes scant claim to "objectivity"; it is, rather, *about* objectivity, and its generic hybridity depicts the struggle, against preconceptions as well as expedient sociohistorical narratives, to re-present a history of the United States that acknowledges and depicts the centrality of African Americans to that story. *The Souls of Black Folk* demonstrates how restoring descendants of Africans to their central place in United States history necessarily entails interrogating the writing of the American story—and questioning the disciplinary boundaries of history.

Historians like Burgess and Dunning wrote that story in accordance with the racist segregationist policies of Jim Crow laws, which logically extended a developmental narrative of black progress in which Africans had never successfully created a civilization. In *The Souls of Black Folk*, Du Bois responded not only with a counternarrative but also with an analysis of the comprehension and comprehensiveness that make a cultural narrative at once so appealing and so prescriptive. Chapters that can be read as essays in that work convey the sense of a continuing story that changes as it unfolds—and as it is reread; they offer an implied narrative that at the same time calls into question the progressive and developmental principles of narrativity that govern the historical narratives. It was for such a project that Du Bois eventually answered the appeal of A. C. McClurg and Company in the first years of the twentieth century that he bring out a collection of his essays. The young social scientist had at first "demurred," he recalled from the perspective of 1940, "because books of essays almost always fall so flat."[9]

Du Bois dramatizes his fear of being unable to tell his story effectively in the fate of John Jones, protagonist of the penultimate chapter and only fictional story of the collection, "Of the Coming of John." The story, which had not appeared elsewhere, offers a thematic commentary for the volume. John is not a writer like Melville's Pierre, nor even the author of his own story like Wilson's "Our Nig," and his struggle with cultural prescriptions is less evidently a struggle for authorship. But John is as effectively silenced as either when he attempts to make visible the dynamics of oppression—in particular, the creation of invariably oppressed black subjects. John strives to tell his story against profoundly internalized prescriptions within himself and within others.

At the beginning of this story, the black scholars of the fictional Wells Institute "seem in the sinister light to flit before the city like dim warning ghosts."[10] The story ends as John Jones awaits a lynch mob in his hometown of Altamaha, Georgia. John's immediate crime is the murder of a boyhood friend, the white John Henderson, whom he has caught sexually assaulting his sister. But, as the story makes clear, the crimes are set in motion by Altamaha's reluctance to move into the twentieth century, a move nevertheless precipitated by the return of both Johns after many years away at school. The spectral opening of the story calls attention to the uncanniness of the educated black subject. The crimes perpetrated against and committed by John Jones have their source in the cultural threat that he embodies.

John Jones is but one among the black subjects throughout *The Souls of Black Folk* who collectively loom, as one chapter puts it, as a "dark human cloud that clung like remorse" to remind a guilty nation not only of its ongoing crimes, but also of the dissolution that seems the inevitable fate of empires (*S*, 375). The "dim warning ghosts" mark the return of what the "new American race," heralded as the embodiment of the nation's absorptive powers, could neither assimilate nor successfully suppress, as well as the return of the repressed cultural threats around which Du Bois constructs at once his story and history. Details within "Of the Coming of John," such as a resolution of John's that echoes a diary entry from a twenty-five-year-old Du Bois, suggestively establish John as the Du Bois who, under other circumstances, might have been. This is not to say that John is autobiographical; rather, he is, in some sense, typical, a dramatic characterization of the potential fate of anyone who would challenge the status quo.

Du Bois calls this story "a tale twice told but seldom written" (*S*, 359). A twice-told tale refers colloquially to its familiarity, as in folk wisdom, or even to its tediousness, and Du Bois does suggest that John's failure to communicate a story of racial oppression effectively may be a familiar—or predictable—story to others who have sought to do so. But it may be less familiar (and harder to tell) to a broader audience. The story of John's fate may be folk wisdom, but it is "seldom written." In writing it, Du Bois tells two tales: a story about John's failure to communicate and an analysis of a storyteller's struggle. John's unsuccessful efforts to make his community aware of racial inequities attests to the difficulty of telling—or writing— about racial oppression against a prevailing narrative of racial inequality and the temptations of comprehension offered by that narrative. Through John's difficulty, Du Bois represents and analyzes his own struggle with the conventions of an authorizing narrative, a struggle that recasts *The Souls of Black Folk* as itself a twice-told tale—a history and an account of writing that story. *The Souls of Black Folk* responds to the need for stories about and from the souls of black folk, and those stories necessarily occasion the narrative of a very different nation.

"Dim Warning Ghosts"

The narrative Du Bois constructs formally expresses the indirection and critical perspective of "double-consciousness," the "sense of always look- ing at one's self through the eyes of others, of measuring one's soul by the tape of a world that looks on in amused contempt and pity" (*S*, 364). Although this line from the first chapter of *The Souls of Black Folk* may be the most cited line in the text, readers frequently miss the challenge implicit in the *sense* of looking through others' eyes. Du Bois describes not only the pain of measuring oneself by a contemptuous and pitying world, but also the empowerment that comes with knowing one is doing so. Du Bois's double-consciousness refers to the consciousness of an other- wise internalized process and pain—to the consciousness, in effect, of two selves. His two consciousnesses explore the implications of self-consciousness as a social phenomenon. His analysis extends the sociological and psychological theories that held that any "self" knows itself at least partly as the object of perception, in relation to—through the eyes of—others. According to prominent sociologist Franklin Giddings, for example, "organized society" shaped the "self" by "approvals and disapprovals" through which it "selects and perpetuates the adequate."[11] Du Bois's insight into the cultural preoccupation with self-consciousness—and with the oppressive possibilities of that preoccupation—grew out of the conflicts entailed in being an American descended from Africans.

Du Bois had sources for the concept of double-consciousness in American transcendentalism and in nineteenth-century medicine.[12] His transformation of those sources offers a clear sense of his own project. In a medical context, "double consciousness" describes the pathological condition whereby two distinct personalities having no knowledge of each other "coexist" in the same body. Notwithstanding the personal anguish entailed in this double-consciousness, the phenomenon generated metaphysical speculation on the nature of the self. This condition greatly interested Gertrude Stein (like Du Bois, a student of Harvard professor William James), and, in laboratory work conducted in 1896, the year before Du Bois first published his discussion of double-consciousness, she sought to disprove the theory of separate personalities.[13] Both she and Du Bois were interested in the eerie *sense* of housing a stranger to which an awareness of a personality not experienced as the "self" gives rise. Here again is the embodiment of the uncanny: the strange familiarity of the self in and as an other. The *feeling* of two-ness, the consciousness of a split, interested Du Bois, marking, for him, the strategies of an oppressive and exclusionary social order rather than a pathological state. The disruptions in the narrative of identity of medical subjects suffering from double-consciousness become, in Du Bois's formulation, the discontinued narrative of identity imposed on black Americans.

For Emerson, too, "double consciousness" led to an inquiry into the "I." In "The Transcendentalist" (1843), he uses the term to describe the uncomfortable tension between "the two lives, of the understanding and of the soul," which remain irreconcilable.[14] That tension is ultimately productive, however, leading to questions—"What is my faith? What am I?" (T, 206)—and eventually blossoming into an advantage born of insight. A later essay, "Fate," offers a circus equestrian jumping nimbly between horses, the metaphoric "horses of his private and his public nature," as the figure of double consciousness.[15] The equestrian can cheat misfortune by jumping onto the horse of his public nature—in other words, by identifying with the larger world through whose eyes his or her suffering is inconsequential, if not beneficial. Such is the solution Emerson proposes "when a man is the victim of his fate," be that victimhood a result of "sciatica in his loins" or of his being "ground to powder by the vice of his race" (F, 966–67).

That vice, a word that in the nineteenth century could equally mean "vise," was far more pressing—and less ambiguous—for Du Bois than for Emerson. And the solution was hardly satisfactory. Yet to see himself through the eyes of that larger world—deliberately and defiantly—was precisely what Du Bois set out to do. And amused contempt and pity were not all that he saw. In the *sense* of looking through others' eyes he called attention to a rift between experience and evaluation, a rift exploited to mark a black subject's distance from a normative white self. Yet the construction not only of African-American personhood but of all American personhood became visible through the workings of Du Bois's double-consciousness. Such is the "gift" of "second-sight," he argued, accorded to and waiting to be claimed by the descendants of Africans "in this American world" (S, 364).

"Of the Coming of John" recounts the coming to such a consciousness and the danger it represents for all concerned. At its base is the profound alienation, the epiphanic self-estrangement John Jones experiences while awaiting his own lynching. Thinking back to his school days, he "wondered how Brown had turned out, and Carey? And Jones—Jones? Why, he was Jones, and he wondered what they would all say when they knew" (S, 535). Jones's nearly disclaimed patronym, the pause between Joneses, explains his threat to his community: John challenges an inherited notion of self that constitutes his subjectivity. His education, which stands between the Jones of his memory and the man awaiting lynching, has effected a dramatic change, cutting him off from his legacy, from the way he is constituted within his community. In trying to articulate this change, John challenges the beliefs and assumptions that make the world comprehensible to the inhabitants of Altamaha.

The opening chapter of *The Souls of Black Folk*, "Of Our Spiritual Strivings," heralds John in "the would-be black savant . . . confronted by the paradox that the knowledge his people needed was a twice-told tale to his white neighbors, while the knowledge which would teach the white world was Greek to his own flesh and blood" (S, 365–66). John literally learns Greek, and his Greek lessons prompt his contemplation of cultural signification: "he pondered long over every new Greek word and wondered why this meant that and why it couldn't mean something else, and how it must have felt to think all things in Greek" (S, 524). The arbitrary relationship between words and meaning that John learns yields him access to a corresponding social gap: "He grew slowly to feel almost for the first time the Veil that lay between him and the white world; he first noticed now the oppression that had not seemed oppression before, differences that erstwhile seemed natural, restraints and slights that in his boyhood days had gone unnoticed or been greeted with a laugh" (S, 525). The discovery marks John's metamorphosis into a more active reader; he can now historicize a cultural conception of nature and thereby name oppression. In this way, John is educated into his double-consciousness. But when John tries to talk about that oppression, and about the discrepancy between experience and evaluation that allows it, he meets with the resistance of both communities, black and white Altamaha. Ironically, they are similarly motivated to silence him. John embodies a double threat to the community: he counsels a literal disruption of the cultural status quo, and he embodies, and thus makes visible, the false terms by which the subject is constructed. John comes back unnatural, a monstrous challenge to their vision of nature itself.

The threat that John poses to Altamaha is clearly articulated in the apoplectic response of Judge Henderson, white John's father and black John's former employer, to the returning scholar's request to start a Negro school. Rails the Judge, "when [your people] want to reverse nature, and rule white men, and marry white women, and sit in my parlor, then, by God! we'll hold them under if we have to lynch every Nigger in the land" (S, 531). John threatens to "reverse nature," which is to say (as Judge Henderson cannot), to expose nature as culture. The Judge's "nature" ensures white dominance and the sanctity of the white home; it brooks no opposition and is therefore beyond the possibility of reform. The Judge makes clear that his order—what makes his world comprehensible—rests on a carefully defined and rigorously naturalized racial and gender hierarchy. His evident anxiety stems both from the incomprehensibility that John threatens to introduce and from the challenge John poses to his patriarchal inheritance. Judge Henderson imagines those threats coming from black *men* (there are no black women explicitly in his vision). The Judge cannot conceive of a system that precludes dominance and oppression—to him, the order of things. A similar binarism characterizes the justification offered by Frederick Douglass's Mr. Gore for the brutal shooting of a slave: "He argued that if one slave refused to be corrected, and escaped with his life, the other slaves would soon copy the example; the result of which would be, the freedom of the slaves, and the enslavement of the whites."[16]

Where both speakers evince a fear of displacement, Judge Henderson's domestic language particularly expresses his fear of being displaced as a *patriarch,* as the figure of the law. Clearly, John's analysis challenges the Judge's patriarchal prerogative—the terms through which he ensures his ownership of white women and of his home. As the absence of John Jones's father seems to attest, there can be only one patriarch in Altamaha. The unquestioned proprietorship that the Judge wants to safeguard extends to what he leaves unmentioned. His son assumes sexual entitlement to John Jones's sister, for example, precisely because she is excluded from the terms of (white) womanhood, from the potential to be a white man's wife. John Jones's analysis challenges the definition and distribution of the terms of personhood that correspond to the needs and specifications of the empowered white man.

Altamaha can also see only one John at a time, as the title avows and the narrator confirms: "It was singular that few thought of two Johns,—for the black folk thought of one John, and he was black; and the white folk thought of another John, and he was white. And neither world thought the other world's thought, save with a vague unrest" (*S,* 523). Altamaha, in other words, lives according to the doctrine of separate but equal, which advocates two mutually exclusive social worlds, each with its own John. But the reader of *The Souls of Black Folk* who arrives at this story will already have lived through the discrediting of that doctrine in the earlier chapters. Both worlds are in fact compelled to think if not the white world's thoughts, then at least thoughts that uphold the dominance of the white world. But the white world is as bound to those thoughts as the black world. And it is the black subject who is "gifted with second-sight in this American world" (*S,* 364). John's education, which forces him to confront a "vague unrest," teaches him that the thoughts of both worlds are constructed by an inherited system of obscured origins. That system, moreover, defines "nature" and constructs differences according to that definition. John's obvious oppression under that system motivates him to endure the (more than) vague unrest.

John compels both worlds not only to see two Johns but to see that they have not been seeing two Johns; he pushes them toward a double-consciousness that exposes the singularity of separate but equal.[17] The anxiety of the white community comes through the gossip of the white postmaster who reports that John is "'givin' talks on the French Revolution, equality, and suchlike'" (S, 532). John's version of history disturbs the equilibrium of Altamaha by contesting the accepted version and forcing both black and white Altamaha to sense that they have been seeing the world through the eyes of an other. When, that is, he insists on contesting the legacy of exclusionary binarism, a contest emblematized by two Johns, he shows the Veil (Du Bois's principal metaphor for racial separation) to be as well a mirror in which the black subject embodies the ever present possibility not so much of the displacement of the white subject but of the disappearance of all subjects as they are known to themselves.

The Veil becomes a mirror when the two Johns confront each other in a theater in New York City where John Jones has unconsciously followed a white couple into a performance of *Lohengrin*. The white northern woman teases her white southern escort by counseling him not to "lynch the colored gentleman simply because he's in your way," to which the escort protests that black-white relations in the South have been misrepresented. As evidence of the warmth between the races, he recalls that his "'closest playfellow in boyhood was a little Negro named after [him], and surely no two,—'" but he is interrupted when he discovers John sitting beside him (S, 526). The childhood playmates fail to recognize each other until the usher, at the behest of John Henderson, asks John Jones to leave the theater. The moment of recognition shows each John who he has become to the other John, shows him the distance he has traversed from his childhood; each John, in other words, confronts himself in the eyes of the other.

John Henderson freezes, while John Jones resolves upon a heroic course of action. The latter acknowledges his own inability to escape his fate and decides to return home to his "manifest destiny," a phrase that suggests that John envisions his disruptive role as endemically American and progressive, and that he maintains the right to claim racial uplift as a heroic American ideal (S, 528). Another heroic script explains what is at stake: " 'I will go into the King,' " he vows, " 'which is not according to the law; and if I perish, I perish' " (S, 528). The citation, which is from the Book of Esther, alludes to Queen Esther's decision to unveil herself to King Ahasuerus as a Jew in order to save her people from the plotting of the king's evil minister, Haman. The quotation appears elsewhere, in Du Bois's "Program for the Celebration of My Twenty-Fifth Birthday," a statement written while he was studying in Germany. He invokes it when he resolves to do race work, to "make a name" for himself in order to "raise [his] race."[18] The biblical quotation is significant as much for its wording as for the heroic idea. Esther's actions are "not according to the law," a phrase that underscores the impact of the challenge upon which the twenty-five-year-old Du Bois and, a decade later, John Jones resolve. Any challenge to the (obscured) construction of subjectivity, and of nature, calls into question the system of genealogy and inheritance that is figured in and as "the law." To call that system into question is to risk perishing, a risk that suggests not only his possible fate at the hands of a hostile audience, but also the subject's more figurative "perishing" as a recognizable (and self-recognized) subject. When John challenges oppression, he also challenges the dominant narrative that constitutes social existence in Altamaha. The challenge of the Veil lies in its potential to reveal white and black American subjects as mutual reflections of an abstraction.

Du Bois had numerous literary and historical prototypes for the Veil, yet among them, none better captures and analyzes the cultural anxiety emblematized by the Veil than one of Nathaniel Hawthorne's *Twice Told Tales*, "The Minister's Black Veil." When he labels "Of the Coming of John" a "tale twice told," he might even intend a veiled allusion to Hawthorne—as well as an allusion to the Veil. In Hawthorne's story, the gentle Reverend Hooper, who anticipates John Jones, appears for a Sunday sermon with his face covered by a black crape veil. The veil, which he tells his fiancée is "a type and a symbol" of the face a human being shows to the world, transforms him, in his parishioners' eyes, " 'into something awful' . . . 'and makes him ghostlike from head to foot.' "[19] Hooper intends the veil to remind himself and his parishioners of the "secret sin, and those sad mysteries which we hide from our nearest and dearest, and would conceal from our own consciousness, even forgetting that the Omniscient can detect them" (MBV, 373).

Reverend Hooper's discourse of sin particularizes the veil as a symbol for his Puritan community. But the broader significance of the veil inheres in its demonstrating the importance of an ongoing process of recognition to one's experience of self. The veil, as J. Hillis Miller observes, "interrupts the universal process necessary to all human society—community life, family life, and face to face 'interpersonal' relations—whereby each of us interprets the countenances of those around us as signs of those persons' selfhoods."[20] An anxious rather than complacent sense of self is the legacy of the veil, and, as Miller also notes, it profoundly troubles the act of mirroring. The mirrored veil disrupts the minister's toast at a wedding: "catching a glimpse of his figure in the looking-glass, the black veil involved his own spirit in the horror with which it overwhelmed all others" (MBV, 376). The grammar of the sentence, in which "the black veil" displaces the expected third-person subject ("he"), emblematically gestures toward the veiled minister's presence as a disturbing disappearance, a dim warning ghost. The veil acts as a mirror that reflexively mirrors mirroring—demonstrating how mirrors may construct what they putatively reflect. John Jones finds his early twentieth century audience no more prepared to challenge the narratives of their identities than Reverend Hooper's Puritan congregation are to challenge theirs.

The blackness of the minister's veil weighs increasingly on the congregation, imparting a blackness—a solemnity and a monstrosity—to the minister himself. In an earlier historical prototype for the Veil, Thomas Jefferson's "immoveable veil of black which covers all the emotions of the other race," blackness is itself a veil and marks the members of "the other race" intrinsically as outcasts from white America. Yet Jefferson's veil is also a mirror, reflecting the white guilt that it is meant to absolve. Jefferson alludes to the veil in Query 14 of *Notes on the State of Virginia* in which he explains the proposed alterations of English common law, including an act to emancipate slaves born after the passage of the act. Emancipation, he explains, would require a plan for colonization, since irreconcilable animosities—"deep rooted prejudices entertained by the whites; ten thousand recollections, by the blacks, of the injuries they have sustained"— would ensure "the extermination of the one or the other race" (NSV, 264). The veil represents Jefferson's effort to add "physical and moral" to "political" objections to coexistence, to explain the greater beauty of the white race, "the fine mixtures of red and white" as opposed to "that eternal monotony" of the "immoveable veil of black" (NSV, 264). The veil is monotonous because it masks emotions, but surely monotony is not the gravest of Jefferson's concerns in this passage. The veil of blackness facilitates a dissembling beneath which lurk the "ten thousand recollections" because of which he has just advocated colonization (*NSV,* 264).[21] The "natural" differences through which Jefferson justifies colonization in fact betray the expected retribution for enslavement, an expression (however unwitting) of white guilt.

Another anxiety surfaces in this passage as well when Jefferson summons, as proof of white aesthetic superiority, the conventional white belief in "their [blacks] own judgement in favour of the whites, declared by their preference of them, as uniformly as is the preference of the Oranootan for the black women over those of his own species" (*NSV,* 265). Africans are generically male in this passage, unless gendered female as the object of bestial desire. By association, sexual desire bestializes black men and women even as it ostensibly demonstrates black acknowledgment of white aesthetic superiority. Beneath the monotonous veil is also lust, black male lust for white females, a threat to white womanhood—and thereby to the white patriarchal prerogative that Judge Henderson also safeguards. Significantly, this fantasy considers neither the implications of the much more evident white male lust for black females, nor the products of such unions in the light-skinned descendants of Africans with their "fine mixtures of red and white." In the veil, white America sees reflected an (unrecognized) image of its own guilt and anxieties.[22]

For Du Bois the Veil is imposed by a white world, as John Jones discovers. But the fate of Hawthorne's minister attests to the difficulty of explaining the veil. John Jones is equally unsuccessful when he returns to Altamaha. His exclusive attention to his tale, and insufficient attention to its telling, undermines his ability to communicate to any audience, black or white. John apparently does not apply what he has learned—the arbitrariness of cultural signification—nor does he seem troubled by how that signification might affect his tale telling. Instead, he launches into the need for "new ideas" and the importance of "the rise of charity and popular education, and particularly of the spread of wealth and work." Asking "what part the Negroes of this land would take in the striving of the new century," he sketches "the new Industrial School that might rise among these pines" and speaks "in detail of the charitable and philanthropic work that might be organized, of money that might be saved for banks and business." His talk concludes with the only direct discourse of the passage, in which he shows an insensitivity to his religious audience of which Du Bois himself had at times been guilty[23]: "To-day . . . the world cares little whether a man be Baptist or Methodist, or indeed a churchman at all, so long as he is good and true. What difference does it make whether a man be baptized in river or wash-bowl, or not at all? Let's leave all that littleness, and look higher" (S, 529–30). John asks his audience to aspire to a vision of advancement for which he gives them no context. While readers of *The Souls of Black Folk* typically place the emphasis in this story on the community's inability to understand, the language of the story forcefully calls at least equal attention to John's inability to communicate.

John's formulation of his task predicts his failure. He casts his heroism in the language of "manifest destiny" and in the image of a biblical heroine, but he is unable to transfer—or even transpose—his heroic scripts onto Altamaha. The problem inheres less in what he proposes than in his apparent submission to pre-texts. In fact, in his most heroic moments John reaches for heroic scripts (Esther, *Lohengrin*) that do not help him formulate his analysis and that may even obscure his insights. Significantly, "manifest destiny" implies a twice-told tale: "destiny" is foreordained; "manifest" is the telling of what has already been decreed (foretold). John does not seem to understand that it is the manifestation (the telling) that *creates* destiny and therefore the telling that must first be addressed.

His other narrative is equally revealing. Whereas Esther appeals to a receptive audience, a loving and beloved "King," John Jones has no such counterpart. The discrepancy should make clear to him the difficulty of his task, but John, who "spoke an unknown tongue," is an ineffective translator, unable to communicate his discovery to any audience, white or black, unable to fashion his critique into an effective counternarrative (S, 530). John succeeds only, like Pierre or William Wilson, in destroying himself as he destroys John Henderson, his mirror image, although he is tragically undeceived about the extent if not the cause of his failure. John recognizes that he has attempted to communicate a message for which his community is not ready and for which he had insufficiently prepared them. His self-destruction can only express—it cannot change—the not always repressed violence of the system that oppresses and eventually will destroy him. He is unable, in the end, to turn the double-consciousness of his self-estrangement into an aesthetic principle through which to shape a counternarrative. *Lohengrin* returns at the end of the story as John turns the lynch mob into an opera: the heroine breaks faith with her lover by demanding to know his identity, and (conversely) the town cannot accommodate its estranged dark son when he questions the terms of his own identity.[24] The words of the white northern woman come prophetically back on the strains of the music as John Jones is indeed lynched for having been in John Henderson's way.[25]

John Jones is unable to rewrite the tragic ending precisely because he too willingly submits to prewritten scripts. Where John reiterates the declaration of heroism of a twenty-five-year-old Du Bois, an older and more experienced writer explains the governing aesthetic, and the narrative struggle, of *The Souls of Black Folk* in this penultimate chapter. Those who would tell such stories as John wishes to tell come as strangers—rather than heroes—to their own communities and even to themselves. Du Bois makes the experiences of estrangement the central experience of *The Souls of Black Folk,* and that experience simultaneously represents the limits and provides the terms of his analysis. The first chapter begins with what Michael Cooke calls "the stock scene of racial discovery," occasioned by a children's game, an exchange of greeting cards, in a Massachusetts schoolyard during which "one girl, a tall newcomer" refuses to exchange greeting cards with the narrator (*S*, 364).[26] Du Bois presents the moment in the language of a conversion: "Then it *dawned upon me with a certain suddenness* that I was different from the others; or like, mayhap, in heart and life and longing, but shut out from their world by a vast veil" (*S*, 364; emphasis added). With the exchange of greeting cards the children recognize each other and reaffirm each other's experience of self. With his exclusion from that exchange Du Bois must confront his alienation in a white world.

The recognition figured by the greeting cards becomes, for Du Bois, a re-cognizing similar to the dramatic moment of racial discovery in James Weldon Johnson's *Autobiography of an Ex-Coloured Man,* when the narrator, informed of his African ancestry, runs to a mirror, emblem of a mirroring cultural gaze, to watch first his mother and then, by implication, himself blacken. The ex-colored man blackens again, still more dramatically, when he confesses to his beloved that he is "passing" and "under the strange light in her eyes . . . felt that [he] was growing black and thick-featured and crimp-haired."[27] Like the ex-colored man, Du Bois, whose exclusion comes from a white girl, finds himself excluded from a sexual economy, positioned by a gender and sexuality that are inextricable from the race that descends with the Veil. The protagonist in such scenes enters into the terms of a (re)constituted identity, and the challenge of these moments of estrangement lies in their potential to expose all identity as an endless unfolding of such moments (typically less conscious) of cultural reconstitutings.

With the descent of the Veil, the narrator becomes aware of "a world which yields him [the Negro] no true self-consciousness, but only lets him see himself through the revelation of the other world" (S, 364). Du Bois does call straightforwardly for a cultural representation that does not measure black experience according to a white paradigm, but such a representation must be built upon a critique of conventional representational strategies, and he grounds his critique in a revisioning of the concept of "true self-consciousness." "Self-consciousness" was a pervasive term at the turn of the century, when politicians and academics alike stressed the importance of a *national* self-consciousness, perpetuated through such disciplines as history and sociology, to the continuing development of an American identity. In that context, "self-consciousness" increasingly measured the successful education of "people into homogeneity of social desires" in the interest of national "unity and strength."[28] National self-consciousness referred to consciousness of an American identity, but that identity—as the language suggests—at once entailed and reinforced consciousness of a national self. Personally and nationally, the term named a comfortable and continuous correspondence between perception and experience that simultaneously created and witnessed American character. But the African American, as Du Bois notes, is excluded from that self-consciousness and experiences a discrepancy between the consciousness of a black self and of an American self. From that discrepancy, Du Bois generates an analysis in which consciousness reproduces a particular (homogenized) self, a self that experiences *difference* as *inferiority*. In Du Bois's reformulation, the comfortable correspondence, the wholeness, creates rather than defines the self.

The "two-ness" Du Bois describes must be understood against the oneness of this comfortable correspondence. Hence the pain of discovery as the African American "feels his two-ness": "an American, a Negro; two souls, two thoughts, two unreconciled strivings; two warring ideals in one dark body, whose dogged strength alone keeps it from being torn asunder. The history of the American Negro is the history of this strife,—this longing to attain self-conscious manhood, to merge his double self into a better and truer self" (S, 364–65). "In this merging," Du Bois insists, "he wishes neither of the older selves to be lost." He would neither "Africanize America" nor "bleach his Negro soul in a flood of white Americanism" (*S*, 365).

The difficulty of imagining a merging that does not result in the disappearance of the African American is evident in apparent contradictions in Du Bois's work and in the extent to which he has been misunderstood. That difficulty was compounded by the coincidence of his analysis with his advocacy of programs of social uplift. For Du Bois, analysis and politics were inseparable but, as John Jones illustrated, not always compatible. In "Of Our Spiritual Strivings," the narrator advocates expanding the idea of America, and what he ostensibly longs for—"the ideal of fostering and developing the traits and talents of the Negro, not in opposition to or contempt for other races, but rather in large conformity to the greater ideals of the American Republic" (*S*, 370)—seems fundamentally in accordance with the language of the jeremiad, a language amplified by Du Bois's insistence that "there are to-day no truer exponents of the pure human spirit of the Declaration of Independence than the American Negroes; there is no true American music but the wild sweet melodies of the Negro slave; the American fairy tales and folk-lore are Indian and African; and, all in all, we black men seem the sole oasis of simple faith and reverence in a dusty desert of dollars and smartness" (*S*, 370). Yet Du Bois uses this language to underscore a gap between "white" and "American" that at least complicates the putative celebration of, and longing for, "self-conscious manhood." If it is "possible for a man to be both a Negro and an American," if, that is, "white" and "American" are not synonymous, then white Americans ought to have as much of a dual identity as black Americans (*S*, 365). However, a dominant white culture that controls the means of cultural dissemination can certainly perpetuate the fiction of cohesion, as well as the reality of black social exclusion, as Judge Henderson clumsily, even parodically, but nonetheless successfully demonstrates. Hence, the *sense* of being looked at offers the possibility of a privileged insight into the strategies of cultural narratives: "the Negro is a sort of seventh son, born with a veil, and *gifted* with second-sight *in this American world*" (*S*, 364; emphasis added). It is thus that the Veil becomes a mirror, and the African American becomes "the swarthy spectre . . . at the Nation's feast" (*S*, 366).

Du Bois never actually claims the longing for the "self-conscious manhood" that excludes not only black America but half of white America as well.[29] Rather, he understands that longing as "the history of the American Negro," the story of a narrative that equates "self-conscious manhood" with whiteness and full personhood and forces African Americans to struggle for separate causes with "half a heart in either cause" (S, 365). A "better and truer self" is hard to experience but easy to wish for when one is working "for a poverty-stricken horde" and against "white contempt" (S, 365). That longing causes the specters to come to the nation's feast as incomplete selves, but they are haunting presences with untold stories pressing to be heard. Du Bois adds to that pressure by analyzing the longing and the narrative that generates it.

His jeremiad departs from the traditional strategy that invokes, even (and perhaps especially) at its most progressive and prophetic, a covenant on which cultural cohesion rests and from which contemporary society threatens to depart. When he summons "the greater ideals of the American Republic," when he invokes the Declaration of Independence, as he does more than once in *The Souls of Black Folk*, Du Bois underscores what others gloss over: that to (re)place African Americans at the center of United States history is to call into question the meaning and writing of that history.

From the outset, "The Forethought" announces the subtle difference of *The Souls of Black Folk* from histories by black as well as white Americans of the late nineteenth century. As August Meier observes, African-American historians in the decades following emancipation stressed "race pride and solidarity in the study of Negro history."[30] William T. Alexander, for example, presents his *History of the Colored Race in America* "to the Colored Race in America . . . with an earnest desire that it will be the means of acquainting them to a fuller extent with the history of their race and their civil and political liberties."[31] And Edward A. Johnson dedicates his *School History of the Negro Race in America* "to the many thousand colored teachers in our country" because "the children of the race ought to study some work that would give them a little information on the many brave deeds and noble characters of their own race."[32] These works all express the need to tell an untold story. Du Bois is especially concerned with the difficulty of telling that story, with the conventions that interfere with its telling. In his own story, he hopes to "show the strange meaning of being black here at the dawning of the Twentieth Century" (S, 359). His pronouns declare that he writes largely for an audience unfamiliar with "the spiritual world in which ten thousand thousand Americans live and strive," for a white world that must be convinced of the importance of his project: "This meaning is not without interest to *you*, Gentle Reader; for the problem of the Twentieth Century is the problem of the color-line" (*S*, 359). African Americans are "them," and he claims that *The Souls of Black Folk* will raise the Veil "that *you* may view faintly its deeper recesses,—the meaning of its religion, the passion of its human sorrow, and the struggle of its greater souls" (*S*, 359; emphasis added).

Du Bois reserves the first-person pronoun for the ultimate unveiling of "The Forethought": "And, finally, need I add that I who speak here am bone of the bone and flesh of the flesh of them that live within the Veil?" (*S*, 360). For Arnold Rampersad, that declaration boldly marks Du Bois's departure from the standards of "scholarly 'objectivity,' " learned from Albert Bushnell Hart, that characterized *The Philadelphia Negro* (1899), a sociological study commissioned by the University of Pennsylvania. That declaration crystallizes Du Bois's critique of the historical style in which he was trained, proclaiming the bias that the historian is supposed to forswear. His affiliation with "them" clarifies as it changes his relation to "you," the "Gentle Reader" to whom "the strange meaning of being black here in the dawning of the Twentieth Century" is of interest since "the problem of the Twentieth Century is the problem of the color-line" (*S*, 359). Neither is objective, and their common interest in the color-line begins to convert the "them" and the "you" into an "us." The white reader of *The Souls of Black Folk* who is unable to merge comfortably into an "us" experiences a kind of double-consciousness: the unveiling of the Veil forces the white reader to see white America through the eyes of an other. Du Bois thus captures the experience of double-consciousness not simply as a black writer, but as a black writer who is willing to forgo the authority of a sanctioned social scientific form, a form that, as *The Souls of Black Folk* makes clear, will not allow him to tell his story: the "sociologists [who] gleefully count his bastards and his prostitutes" are deaf to "the striving in the souls of black folk" (*S*, 368, 371).

This is not to say that *The Souls of Black Folk* was a book written exclusively for a white audience; on the contrary, Du Bois acknowledges the need to negotiate "the paradox that the knowledge his people needed was a twice-told tale to his white neighbors, while the knowledge which would teach the white world was Greek to his own flesh and blood" (*S*, 365–66). But twice-told tales are obviously worth telling, and John Jones surely profits from his Greek lessons, assuring his sister that he prefers the obvious unhappiness of his more informed state to the more unconscious misery of his ignorant youth. Du Bois also responds, in *The Souls of Black Folk*, to the accommodationist vision of Booker T. Washington whom he criticizes, in "Of Mr. Booker T. Washington and Others," for having "so thoroughly" learned "the speech and thought of triumphant commercialism, and the ideals of material prosperity, that the picture of a lone black boy poring over a French grammar amid the weeds and dirt of a neglected home soon seemed to him the acme of absurdities" (*S*, 393). As Rampersad notes, Du Bois revises the anticipated journey adapted from the slave narrative by Washington in his 1901 autobiographical *Up From Slavery*, a journey that charts the making of an American out of a chattel.[33] *The Souls of Black Folk* de-forms the narrative of that journey to expose the dominant (and exclusionary) plot of Americanization as something against which African Americans have had to strive for self-representation. Beginning with his own self-estrangement, Du Bois offers *The Souls of Black Folk* not to end but to depict "the striving in the souls of black folk." By the end of *The Souls of Black Folk*, Du Bois will have evolved a "we" that brings both "them" and "you" to a new understanding not of "Negro history," but of "American history." And, as the textual construction of the work demonstrates, a recentered history offers insight into the making of Americans.

Clearly, Du Bois intended *The Souls of Black Folk* to reach beyond the audiences of his previous booklength studies, *The Suppression of the African Slave Trade to the United States of America, 1638–1870* (Du Bois's doctoral thesis, which was published as the first volume of the Harvard Historical Studies series) and *The Philadelphia Negro*. Although respected historical and sociological work, neither study had sufficiently compelled white America to confront its own image in the mirroring gaze that Du Bois had exposed. An *Atlantic Monthly* review of the published dissertation registers disappointment at the author's "lack of appreciation of the subject in its historical proportions."[34] The reviewer wants more context and a more developed narrative from Du Bois, remarking that the young scholar has "failed in a satisfactory answer to the historical problem involved in his thesis by trying to isolate it too completely, not only from the institution of slavery and the inter-state slave trade, but from those considerations of the development of ethics which lie at the basis of all final political action" (562). Treating the historical work of novelist and historian Edward Eggleston as well, the reviewer suggests both that "working in fiction might give vitality to the historian's labor" and that the enthusiastic activity in evidence in history projects might satisfy "those who are disposed to regret the barrenness of current American literature in certain directions, particularly in the field of poetic and imaginative production" (568, 559). Du Bois responded to the call for a vital American literature with *The Souls of Black Folk*, double-consciousness recast as a twice-told tale.

Recurrent allusions and cross references among the chapters construct an incremental rather than a progressive narrative and call attention to an author's constructing, to an *authorship* stemming unabashedly from biases and in the service of a point of view. The author vows *"to tell again* in many ways, with *loving emphasis* and *deeper detail,"* a more than twice-told tale; he writes against the seamless narrative explicitly advocated in the service of efficient "Americanization," as, in a particularly remarkable example, a pedagogical handbook from the 1920s counsels that the immigrant student can best be made to feel like "an American in the making" when American history is presented "in narrative form. The method should be oral. Details are to be avoided."[35] As early as 1903, by contrast, *The Souls of Black Folk* interrogated the connection between such narratives and a socialization that had left African Americans with a "painful self-consciousness." And Du Bois's authorship accordingly emerges in constant engagement with the expectations that those narratives shaped.

Visionary History and a Tale Twice Told

The first chapter of *The Souls of Black Folk*, "Of Our Spiritual Strivings," originally appeared as "The Striving of the Negro People" in the July 1897 *Atlantic Monthly*, marking what David Levering Lewis calls "Du Bois's national debut" (DLL, 98). In the lead article of that same issue, "The Making of the Nation," Princeton professor of jurisprudence and political economy (and southern gentleman) Woodrow Wilson presented an analysis of the United States that he would elaborate in his five-volume *A History of the American People.* One of the most celebrated intellectuals in the nation, Wilson advocated a visionary role for the historian and channeled the most pressing concerns about heterogeneity and sectionalism into a potent vision of a nation poised to dominate a century. Calling for a new generation to turn its attention to the project of realizing the nation,

Wilson asks, "Are we even now, in fact, a nation?" to which he quickly responds, "We still wait for its [the nation's] economic and spiritual union."[36] It is not surprising that Wilson should write forcefully on this subject, since national upkeep had devolved particularly, although by no means exclusively, upon academic historians and social scientists during this period.

Wilson was 'more than prepared to assume that role; he was eager. The previous autumn, he had commemorated the 150th anniversary of his alma mater, the College of New Jersey, and had helped to transform it into Princeton University with an address entitled "Princeton in the Nation's Service." In it he celebrates education as a national—and nationalist—endeavor and speaks of the danger that the American people might "lose our identity." For Wilson, the nation faced danger as much from isolation and ignorance as from undue influence. The United States, he cautioned, ran a perpetual "risk of newness" that stemmed from an insufficient understanding of how the new nation had built on the foundation of an old world, designing institutions that preserved and implemented its ideals. "The College should serve the state as its organ of recollection," he proclaims; education should elucidate the historical narrative in which change becomes progress only when it "draws its springs gently out of the old fountains of strength, builds upon old tissue, covets the old airs that have blown upon it time out of mind in the past."[37] When, in 1912, Du Bois endorsed the Democrat Woodrow Wilson for president of the United States, he did it as a pragmatic measure. Wilson seemed more sympathetic than his Republican and Progressive opponents—William Howard Taft and Theodore Roosevelt, respectively—to issues of concern to African Americans, and he had a real chance to win. Intellectually, however, Wilson typified exactly the kind of visionary that inspired Du Bois to be revisionary. Whereas Wilson built his vision of American identity on what he hoped would be the stable foundation of the language of kinship, Du Bois constructed his revisionary paradigm on what he knew to be the unsteady classificatory system of race.

Prolific and dynamic, Wilson was the most powerful and well-known but not the only leading scholar of the social sciences to call for visionary narratives of United States history and for a reassertion, in light of immigration and migration, of a coherent American identity. These scholars advocated histories that would tell a national story as a continuous evolution, an unfolding reminiscent of Manifest Destiny, to answer an agenda that in many ways resembled that of the mid-century literary nationalists. The summons came from and for the universities to contribute the most important voices and serve as the training ground for a renewed and palpable nationalism. In the rhetoric of these calls to service, both Wilson and Du Bois found their subjects.

University of Chicago professor Emil G. Hirsch sounded the call in the lead article of the second issue of the *American Journal of Sociology,* founded by Hirsch's prominent colleague, sociologist Albion W. Small. Appearing in September 1895, the year in which Du Bois, then a young teacher at Wilberforce University in Ohio, became the first African American to receive a Harvard Ph.D., Hirsch's piece manifests an exuberantly self-conscious nationalism located in the development of the American university. He observes that "the last decade of our century augurs so well for our nation because it proclaims the independence of the American university, as confidently as did the fourth quarter of the eighteenth compel recognition of the political autonomy of the republic by the nations of the earth."[38] This late-nineteenth-century social scientist could almost be writing for the *Democratic Review* when he contends that "the American has no more urgent circumstance to weigh and to remember than that he is neither in Germany nor in England—but in America" (EH, 115). Writing at a time when most serious scholars had pursued at least some part of their academic training in either Germany or England, Hirsch seems more to plead than to celebrate. Hailing both the university professor and the university student as "the Columbus of unknown seas, the Livingstone of unvisited continents," he urges "the American scholar" to acknowledge that the "nation has claims upon him. She is his mother and into her household he is expected to introduce his bride, his science" (EH, 121, 126). Like Pierre Glendinning, the scholar is expected to be at once heroic and dutiful, daring explorer and obedient son and husband. Recasting the language of exploration and conquest in the language of domesticity, Hirsch urges the American scholar to develop an indigenous course of study. Hirsch's program, like Young American literary nationalism, envisions a university that simultaneously creates and reflects the nation.

Slavery as a metaphor recurs in Hirsch's essay to represent a university too dependent on European models. He sees a "final triumph" in "the emancipation of the American university from slavery to [the pedagogical] prejudice" that the professor's role was "transmission of knowledge" (EH,

117, 116). A more interactive and independent scholar is thus liberated from a fate that Hirsch expresses through a figure used as well by Du Bois and Booker T. Washington, among others: that of having been "condemned so long to act the part of the hewers of wood and the drawers of water" (EH, 121). Such allusions to slavery implicitly identify the university with the project of reconstructing the nation—putting slavery in the past—but they also remind the reader of the fate of the unliberated subject. Enslavement to European models, as opposed to participation in an American liberty promised by the American university, can result in the loss of identity threatened by Wilson in his Princeton oration one year later—a loss dramatized by Hirsch's figure as an exclusion from personhood. Yet that loss was equally the result of a too vigorous declaration of independence from an important past. Wilson and his cohorts actually stressed America's European (especially English) ancestry and viewed the United States as the fulfillment of the best English principles, which flourished in the New World, unhampered by England's "insular conservatism," as Harvard literary historian Barrett Wendell called it.[39]

Liberty and democracy needed their guardians, and the university was to train scholars suited to that role. Hirsch's allusion to slavery evokes the precariousness of both the foundations of the reconstructed cultural identity and the nation it expressed. Although the United States had survived sectional war and emerged intact as a nation, the previously unthinkable had happened and, as every survivor would know, could happen again. For Hirsch, study in and of the United States would ensure a coherent nationalism that would avoid sectionalism and its dangers. Du Bois's Ph.D. notwithstanding, the descendants of Africans invoked by Hirsch's metaphors of freedom and uplift were themselves included only problematically, as we have seen, in the national self-consciousness for which he calls.

Amidst the summons to national self-consciousness rose the modern university and the nascent disciplines of the social sciences, the study of peoples and peoplehood. Never before nor since have educators in the United States so conspicuously and enthusiastically entered into the project of nation-building. Education was not only the cornerstone for Americanization initiatives, it was also increasingly identified with opportunities for rejuvenation and mobility for native-born white Americans as well. In an anthology compiled by prominent educator, psychologist, and William James student G. Stanley Hall, "university workers in political science and history" were summoned to articulate a cultural identity and national destiny.[40] As one of the historians in Hall's anthology explained, the task of the historian was to discover and express a national culture:

> we are, as a people, now engaged in a confused struggle with the problem of our own national self-consciousness. We want to know what is the spirit that is in us as a nation. We must know this, in order to be properly master of ourselves and of our destiny. We must know this, in order to know our place in universal history, in order to appreciate the special task that falls to us in the solution of that universal problem of the full realization of man, of humanity "standing complete and wanting nothing," at which, whether blindly or consciously, all nations and peoples are at work, and their work upon which constitutes the living and essential substance of history. Our politicians need this, that they may become statesmen. And both statesmen and people need this, the former, in order that their labor may be truly constructive and enduring; and the latter, in order that they may willingly cooperate in the pursuit and realization of true political ideals.[41]

A "national self-consciousness," belief in the nation as a coherent entity, posits the collective subject, the "we" whose self-consciousness in turn confirms that nation. Nationalism, in this formulation, entails the discovery rather than the creation of a narrative—the "universal history" in which United States nationals already have, but must still learn, their "place in universal history." It nonetheless falls to the historian to articulate or conspire with the spirit that is already in "us." With the clear delineation of the state, politicians become statesmen and people become a people.

With that end in mind, both Wilson and Du Bois presented their analyses of the national narrative—of the meaning of the "full realization of man" and the constitution of "the people"—to the readers of the *Atlantic Monthly.* Already evident in both "The Making of the Nation" and "The Striving of the Negro People" was the sense that rhetoric must be harnessed and carefully deployed, that the man of ideas should also be an accomplished man of letters and a public spokesperson. Wilson would move from the presidency of Princeton to politics, eventually to the Oval Office, and Du Bois too would find university walls too confining for his life's work.

"The Making of the Nation" reads as a cross between a historical analysis and a campaign speech, in keeping with the role of statesman historian that Wilson advocated. According to the future president, "the whole process of statesmanship consists in bringing facts to light, and shaping law to suit, or, if need be, mould them" (MN, 10). The statesman is thus none other than the visionary historian, and, conversely, the visionary historian is a statesman. Wilson, the statesman historian *par excellence,* speaks both as the current historian and the future statesman when he remarks, "Everybody knows the familiar story: it has new significance from day to day only as it illustrates the invariable process of nation-making which has gone on from generation to generation, from the first until now" (MN, 8). The visionary historian writes a narrative that re-codes the story to create coherence—"one continuous story"—through a unity that minimizes difference and is formed and plotted with regard to the political expediencies of the present.

Although "The Making of the Nation," a piece written for publication rather than oration, is less rhetorically electric than Lincoln's speeches, the works of Wilson and Lincoln share a strategic deployment of anxiety. In the historical narrative that at once responds to and rearticulates the call for an American history, Wilson summons just enough anxiety to reinvigorate an investment in the fate of the nation among the populace, but not enough to constitute a serious challenge to the nation. As Lincoln had fashioned a heroic task for the post-heroic generation out of the need to preserve the Union, so Wilson offers his own generation the task of completing the work of their grandfathers. Geoeconomic differences among sections, he argues, have always complicated national integrity: "We have left the matter of boundaries to surveyors rather than states-men . . . have by no means managed to construct economic units in the making of States . . . and have left the making of uniform rules to the sagacity and practical habit of neighbors ill at ease with one another" (MN, 2). Movements such as Populism arise, he remarks, as a reminder of sectionalism. Hence, the "temporary danger" that the absence of a "common mind" will lead to a sectional conflict that will, in turn, point up "that there is not even yet any common standard, either of opinion or of policy, underlying our national life" (MN, 3). Thus he sounds the alarm for many of those dangers that led to civil war. "The Making of the Nation" alter-nates between a warning that the contemporary nation is insufficiently attentive to the goals that will ensure unity and a faith in the political mission of the nation—in a unity that will prevail and allow the nation to spread the democratic Word. In the rhythm of the passage, the "temporary danger" builds to a crescendo and vibrates with the challenge posed to nationalism: "The nation is to-day one thing in Kansas, and quite another in Massachusetts" (MN, 3). It is then cut off by a simple, straightforward reassertion of Wilson's fundamental faith in the nation: "There is no longer any danger of a civil war" (MN, 3). Wilson repeats this rhythm throughout the essay to articulate a real and present danger of sectional conflict, which, however, will invariably resolve itself.

The nationalist efforts of the people in view of the threat of sectionalism can promote the quicker growth of the nation, but ultimately nationalism cannot be stopped. Sections, for Wilson, mark different stages of development rather than intractable points of view. Wilson celebrates "currents of national life" that "run from sea to sea," which, having "long been gathering force, . . . cannot now be withstood," an irresistible flood of nationalism (MN, 3).[42] His veritable riptide rushes in with all the force of a manifest destiny, an irresistible expanding to which he paradoxically attributes the intrinsic problems of the political entity and their equally intrinsic solutions. The states were brought together by what he calls "the inevitable continental outlook of affairs . . . if nothing more, the sheer necessity to grow and touch their neighbors at close quarters" (MN, 6). Wilson finds the "vacant continent" vexing, an allure irresistibly tempting toward expansion. Beginning with the Louisiana Purchase, that allure "opened the continent to the planting of States," which could not but result in nationalization (MN, 9). The closing of the western frontier that Frederick Jackson Turner had already begun to announce in 1893 left the dissatisfied within the nation "without outlet" or "easy escape," but the resulting compression represents a fusion rather than an explosion (MN, 3).[43] Confrontation and homogeneity were equally unavoidable in his vision: "As the country grows it will inevitably grow homogeneous. Population will not henceforth spread, but compact; for there is no new land between the seas where the 'West' can find another lodgement. The conditions which prevail in the ever widening 'East' will sooner or later cover the continent, and we shall at last be one people" (MN, 4). Wilson heralds the interdependence that, as Thomas Haskell has convincingly argued, characterized late nineteenth-century United States culture.[44] And that interdependence completed the symbolizing of both geosocial region and geological terrain performed by the rhetorical strategies of Manifest Destiny. Wilson eagerly anticipates the progressive development that, no less than Emerson's gardens, will move the terrain toward indistinction, conquering it, in effect, in the name of "one people." Like Manifest Destiny, this process "cannot be stayed" (MN, 4).

Also in keeping with the strategies of Manifest Destiny, the statesman historian promotes nationalism by telling the national story. The resolution of sectional conflict—the inevitable growth into homogeneity—is the subject of the "one continuous story" of national development that Wilson advocates. He makes considerable use of what, referring to Abraham Lincoln, I have previously called the logic of history, although he more explicitly and consistently advocates the writer's activist (and heroic) role than either Lincoln or the proponents of Manifest Destiny. Wilson urges that "we . . . constantly recall our reassuring past. . . . It is only by thus attempting, and attempting again and again, some sufficient analysis of our past experiences that we can form any adequate image of our life as a nation, or acquire any intelligent purpose to guide us amidst the rushing movement of affairs. It is no doubt in part by reviewing our lives that we shape and determine them" (MN, 4). The meaning of the past, like the nation itself, is dormant; the statesman historian performs the analysis that brings forth not facts "but consciousness and comprehension of the facts" (MN, 10). For Wilson, the nation inheres in that consciousness and comprehension; it is known through its own narrative. In a telling juxtaposition, Wilson follows his analysis of "the strain" created by the disappearance of the frontier, an image that hints at imminent explosion, with the observation that "the history of the United States has been one continuous story of rapid, stupendous growth, and all its great questions have been questions of growth" (MN, 9). The straining indeed bursts forth, but only into a positive image of growth, a transformation underwritten by "one continuous story." Hence the fusion in place of an explosion. While the story can only be continuous if territorial expansion is redefined as socioeconomic development, the task of redefinition falls to the continuous story, evidently the direct heir of Manifest Destiny.

In the American story that Wilson tells in "The Making of the Nation," the colonies had always been united by "common interests" and threats, but unity was impossible while they were unaware of what they shared (MN, 5). It fell to the leaders of the fledgling nation not only to turn separate colonies into united states, but to bring those states "to a new common consciousness and at last to a real union" (MN, 6). The nation, in other words, required a perceived unity, an identity that could manifest its destiny. The statesman historian continues that task, and Wilson, a southerner, returns for an example of such leadership to "the great Lincoln . . . who seemed to embody, with a touch of genius, the very character of the race itself," as Lincoln himself had turned to the southern Jefferson (MN, 12). Wilson gives that embodiment fuller expression at the end of the essay when he proclaims his unquestionable belief in "a guardian destiny! No other race could have accomplished so much with such a system; no other race would have dared risk such an experiment" (MN, 14). Clearly, he means the American race, but who is included in that race? What is the "one people" created by—or expressed in—Wilson's narrative? What must be excluded to complete the "unfinished, unharmonized" nation? (MN, 8).

Wilson's "American race" describes an amalgamated nation. In 1901 he would pen a preface to a historical encyclopedia acknowledging "the bewilderment . . . of the statesmen and of the historian" in view of the influx of races into the United States: "Men out of every European race, men out of Asia, men out of Africa have crowded in" to make "a new race" to which he attributes "the present separateness and distinctive character of the United States among nations." But Wilson marvels that "our institutions and our life as a people" remain untouched. Instead, those who have come in "have merged their individuality in a national character already formed; have been dominated, changed, absorbed."[45] The power and absorptiveness of the ideas embodied in the institutions and social life of the United States make common blood unnecessary.

Yet, in "The Making of the Nation," the troubling implications of that absorptiveness are obscured by Wilson's language, by his use of "kinship" to describe national ties; the colonies' "kinship in life and interests and institutions" was brought to consciousness first by the Indian and the French threats on their borders and then by England, which, by "making them wince under common wrongs . . . drove them into immediate sympathy and combination, unwittingly founding a nation by suggestion" (MN, 5). External violence turns the colonies into a defensive entity, but Wilson does not address the internal violence implicit in their becoming an independent and unified political entity. Instead, kinship precedes the nation in a formulation that ambiguously draws on and transcends a blood discourse. Wilson's strategic use of kinship has an important source in the theories of mid-nineteenth-century British liberal Walter Bagehot, whom Wilson heartily eulogized in speeches and essays in the 1890s. In a section of his *Physics and Politics* entitled "Nation-Making," Bagehot notes the importance of a "cohesive 'family' . . . for a campaigning nation." By contrast, "loosely bound family groups . . . where the father is more or less uncertain, where descent is not traced through him, where, that is, property does not come from him" mean "an ill-knit nation," and such a "nation which did not recognize paternity as a legal relation would be conquered like a mob by any other nation which had a vestige or a beginning of the *patria potestas*."[46] The nation, according to Bagehot, holds together in the name of the father, a shared symbolism, including carefully articulated gender relations, that Wilson figures in his use of kinship.

Wilson's "kinship" is thus not ostensibly racial but a result of "the slow providence which binds generations together by a common training" (SAH, 184). He believes in a national *character* before which he downplays "physical heredity and . . . the persistence of race characteristics" (SAH, 183), but he can do so only because the English-Americanness he imagines has such remarkable powers of absorptiveness: everyone seems willing to tell—and be told—the same story. Accordingly, an American identity did not, for Wilson, begin "when the federal Constitution was adopted" (MN, 3). He does not concur with those who would hold "that the strong sentences of the law sufficed to transform us from a league of States into a people single and inseparable" (MN, 3). Instead, Wilson argues for one continuous story of a growing awareness of a kinship that generated the constituting of the nation, a self-consciousness that breathes new life into the strong sentences of positive law.

For Wilson, the articulation of that preexisting kinship turns a geopolitical entity into a nation. His model works implicitly through what one of the first sociologists in the United States, Franklin Giddings, calls "a reciprocal consciousness of kind," a mutual recognition that "another person is like one's self."[47] Giddings describes how "the reciprocal consciousness of kind, acting upon common possessions, interests, and ideas, converts their images, symbols, and names into social emblems and shibboleths" (FG, 123). An individual's consciousness that symbols evoke common responses in him or herself and others generates "emblems and shibboleths" that, circularly, figure a group identity. Such an identity was variously named by turn-of-the-century sociologists; William Graham Sumner called it "folkways," for example, while Giddings preferred "the social mind," but most agreed on the formation of an incontestable cultural character shaped by repeated exposure to what Giddings calls "inherited usage, custom, or discipline" (FG, 125).[48] Yet, despite that shaping, the kind precedes the consciousness: Giddings posits a likeness—a kinship—of which the members of the group become aware. That awareness does not *create* the group; rather, the group coheres around a postulated germ of similitude. Englishness (or English-Americanness) was that similitude for Wilson, as it was for Barrett Wendell, with whom Du Bois studied writing at Harvard. For Wendell, a common language, such as that which has "compelled America, almost unawares, to share [ideals] with England," is a force "more potent in binding men together than any physical tie" (*LHA*, 521, 523). Yet for both Wendell and Wilson, the metaphor of kinship at once exemplifies and promotes physical (and biological) dimensions gradually assumed by what Wilson calls "the spiritual forces of which institutions themselves are the offspring and creation" (SAH, 184).

For policymakers, historians, and social scientists at the end of the nineteenth century, internal threats to a coherent cultural identity typically outweighed external ones; the "new American race" accordingly stressed a connection to rather than a break from Western Europe, mainly England, as in Wilson's formulation, and Germany.[49] John W. Burgess asserted America's Teutonic heritage to explain American institutions and to justify American imperialism as expressions of racial identity. And Wilson's kinship allowed for the claim, in his 1896 eulogy for Bagehot, that "in studying Walter Bagehot, the literary politician, we come to a man of our own country and nationality."[50] Assumptions of a Teutonic and especially Anglo-Saxon heritage could even facilitate postwar healing by demonstrating that unity with past enemies was not only possible, but that kinship ties, which could not be severed, made such reunion inevitable. Yet those assumptions could only exacerbate racial tensions.[51] While Wilson presumes the power of absorptiveness, he does not consider the fate of those groups absorbed by Englishness but unable (or unwilling) to claim kinship with the English. He assures the reader of "The Making of the Nation" that "even the race problem of the South will no doubt work itself out in the slowness of time," as memories of war grow dimmer and as "blacks and whites" gain "an easier view of the division of labor and of social function to be arranged between them" (MN, 10). Of what that division will be, however, he offers no prediction. Evidently, the "one people" cannot be quite the homogeneous group that Wilson foresees.

Heterogeneity complicated not only claims of kinship through which a latent cultural identity was posited, but also, many argued, compromised democracy itself. Anxious responses to heterogeneity among those less professedly sanguine than Wilson about English-American absorptiveness found expression in the perceived threat to the body politic and in more personal threats to the bodies of the polis (miscegenation). Sociologists such as Giddings describe "a passion for homogeneity of type" according to which the social mind molds constituent elements and excludes or otherwise "eliminat[es] irreconcilable differences" (FG, 289). Homogeneity ultimately allows for liberty, but heterogeneity "not only . . . necessitate[s] coercive [rather than liberal] forms of organization . . . but also such like-mindedness as there is . . . creates coercive rather than liberal types of organization" (FG, 221). This perceived correlation between heterogeneity and coerciveness justifies much of the opposition to immigration and migration during this period. White oppression is herein attributed to heterogeneity and specifically to groups not perceived as "like-minded."

In an 1893 *Atlantic Monthly* essay entitled "European Peasants as Immigrants," for example, Harvard scientist N. S. Shaler warns of the consequences of unrestricted immigration on United States social institutions by considering the putative consequences of having imported Africans—"an essentially alien folk"—for slavery.[52] N. S. Shaler is the same Nathaniel Shaler who, Du Bois recalls in *Dusk of Dawn,* "invited a Southerner, who objected to sitting beside me, out of his class" (*DD*, 581). Shaler nevertheless adheres to the prevalent sociobiological discourse of race when he cautions that "where the black population becomes dominant, only the semblance of a democracy can survive; the body of the people will, as in Hayti, shape their society and their government to fit their inherited qualities" (NS, 647). The most profound threat posed by black Americans, according to Shaler, lies in what they force white America to become. The only alternative that he can imagine to the demon of "Hayti" is a more totalitarian (obviously coercive) government: "What a wretched shadow of our ideal state this authority will be! In place of an association of true freemen, all by divine right equal heritors in the duties and privileges of the citizen, we shall have the most vicious and persistent form of despotism, a race oligarchy" (NS, 647). Opposed to the oppression of the descendants of Africans, Shaler nonetheless cannot imagine the association of black and white "freemen" hopefully legislated by the Civil War Amendments.

Shaler's allusion to "the body of the people" suggestively depicts the black American's threat to the integrity of the white American body as well as to the social body politic. It thus underscores tensions inherent in such paradigms as Wilson's use of kinship. The rise and popularity of the science of eugenics in conjunction with discussions of the "new American race" in the early twentieth century attest to the prevalence of these concerns. The reproduction of a particular America as ensured by the protection of the American gene pool constituted the debt owed by contemporary society to the future. "Shall the future American be an Anglo-Saxon or a Mulatto?" runs epigrammatically through *The Leopard's Spots: A Romance of the White Man's Burden* (1902), the first novel of a trilogy by white supremacist and novelist Thomas Dixon, which, with his second volume, *The Clansman*, inspired D. W. Griffith's popular *Birth of a Nation*.[53]

Many turn-of-the-century narratives of the nation explicitly cast the challenge posed by heterogeneity to the integrity of America as a challenge to the existence of Americans. Memories of the Civil War invested immigrant ghettos and other pockets of racially or ethnically similar groups with a potentially treacherous national divisiveness. Theodore Roosevelt, for example, conjoins threats of regionalism and sectionalism with the challenge of "alien elements, unassimilated, and with interests separate from ours . . . [as] mere obstructions to the current of our national life" in an 1894 issue of the *Forum*.[54] Educator and philosopher John Dewey similarly warns in a 1902 speech: "unless we Americanize them they will foreignize us."[55] The core of that threat surfaces in Roosevelt's repeated reminders, in "True Americanism," that "the man who does not become Americanized nevertheless fails to remain a European, and becomes nothing at all" (TA, 26). Roosevelt could not have been more explicit than in this direct statement of the ontological challenge: to cease to be a clearly defined national subject is to become "nothing at all." Yet not every group could assimilate. Shaler expresses a widely-held belief when he maintains that *inherited* qualities made some groups, such as descendants of Africans, intrinsically incompatible with American ideals. Roosevelt very typically alludes to European immigrants, and he equally advocates "keep[ing] out races which do not assimilate readily with our own" (TA, 27) and will therefore inevitably, in Dewey's words, "foreignize us." But allegedly unassimilable races were already part of America and of American history, and their untold stories troubled the national narrative.

The idea of assimilation as mutual change, offered by some progressives who favored immigration, was scarcely ventured by white Americans with regard to black American culture at the turn of the century. Instead, what white America called "the Negro problem" moved to the legislatures and the courts, to the Jim Crow policies that led to the Supreme Court's "separate but equal" decision in *Plessy v. Ferguson* (1896), which addressed the constitutionality of segregation. The case entailed the allegation of Homer Plessy, a man claiming one-eighth African descent, that the 1890 Louisiana state legislation that provided "equal but separate accommodations for the white and colored races" violated his guarantee, under the Thirteenth and Fourteenth amendments respectively, of protection from servitude and of the rights and privileges of a nondiscriminatory national citizenship.[56] *Plessy* legislated racial classification, legally articulating and perpetuating the permanent alien status that Shaler's essay explicitly assigned to descendants of Africans. The *Plessy* decision upheld legislation that signaled that American citizenship had been again redefined in accordance with ideas about the "new American race." In so doing, argued dissenting Justice John Marshall Harlan, the Court agreed to uphold legislation "inconsistent not only with that equality of rights which pertains to citizenship, National and State, but with *the personal liberty enjoyed by every one within the United States.*"[57]

For Harlan, the decision posed a threat to the Union analogous to the threat Lincoln had seen in slavery: "If this statute of Louisiana is consistent with the personal liberty of citizens, why may not the State require the separation in railroad coaches of native and naturalized citizens of the United States, or of Protestants and Roman Catholics" (*PF*, 558). Evidently, although the Court upheld it, the doctrine of separate but equal raised too many questions sufficiently to address "the Negro problem." Alternatives, only occasionally proposed by white theorists, sought the *physical* absorption of black by white culture. The founder of American anthropology, Columbia University professor Franz Boas, for a notable example, maintained in 1909 that "the question before us is that of whether it is better for us to keep an industrial and socially inferior large black population or whether we should fare better by encouraging the gradual process of lightening up this large body of people by the influx of white blood."[58]

Du Bois knew that an equal place for African Americans in the nation, equal access to the rights and privileges of personhood, required a different story of the past. To be most effective and convincing, Du Bois's alternative story had not only to refute current stories but to analyze prevailing assumptions about the form of those stories as well as their content and language. He adopted the role of visionary historian that Wilson advocated, but with a markedly different outcome in form as well as content. Whereas for Wilson history entails "attempting, and attempting again and again, some sufficient analysis of our past experiences," such an attempt on Du Bois's part would begin with the analysis of a very different "our."[59] When, that is, the "our" refers to black rather than white Americans, the analysis decenters the narrative and re-presents the plot. The history of African Americans in the United States could not, for him, be told as "one continuous story"; rather, it was a story that, having been repeatedly suppressed and repressed, must struggle against Wilson's continuous story. In the more than twice-told tale of his repeated attempts, Du Bois makes his struggle increasingly apparent. He decries what Wilson celebrates: in Wilson's words, a "past . . . [that] has made us a nation, despite a variety of life that threatened to keep us at odds amongst ourselves [and that] has shown us the processes by which differences have been obliterated and antagonisms softened" (MN, 4). The "self-consciousness" that Wilson sees as nation-building is the "self-consciousness" from which Du Bois, as an African American, has been excluded. Du Bois can only emerge from the obliteration of differences that Wilson applauds with a double consciousness. *The Souls of Black Folk* shows what has been lost or repressed in the "our" of Wilson's "our past experiences"—or, for that matter, Wendell's "our ancestral English language" (*LHA*, 10)—and retells the story of exclusion as the history of subjectivity in the United States. If Wilson calls for visionary histories, Du Bois answers with a *re*visionary history, a narrative that calls the terms of that visionary narrative into question.

Primarily, Du Bois complicated the homogeneity sought by the "one continuous story" when he explored the construction of racial and cultural identities within that story. The logic of his revisions begins to emerge in the change of titles when the *Atlantic Monthly* essay "Strivings of the Negro People" becomes "Of Our Spiritual Strivings," the first chapter of *The Souls of Black Folk*. The "our" of the title insists again that Du Bois is, as the "Forethought" declares, "bone of the bone and flesh of the flesh of them that live within the Veil" (*S*, 360), but the description of "two-ness" with which the chapter begins makes apparent the instability of the "our" as well. Throughout *The Souls of Black Folk,* Du Bois uses pronouns ambiguously, speaking from within "we"'s that variously figure white and black America. A similar strategy characterizes his 1897 address to the American Negro Academy, "The Conservation of Races," as Du Bois summons a *"we,* who have been reared and trained under the individualistic philosophy of the Declaration of Independence and the laisser-faire philosophy of Adam Smith" and who "are apt to think in *our American* impatience, that while it may have been true in the past that closed race groups made history, that here in conglomerate America *nous avons changé tout çela."*[60] Here "we" and "our" ("nous") encompass but also distinguish between black and white America, an expression of "twoness" that also moves significantly toward envisioning the construction of whiteness and blackness and, by extension, of personhood in the United States.

Du Bois foregrounds the racial emphasis that Wilson obscures. The argument of "The Conservation of Races" turns on Du Bois's assertion that the scientifically vague concept of "race" is "clearly defined to the eye of the Historian and Sociologist" and that therefore "the history of the world is the history, not of individuals, but of groups, not of nations, but of races" and race, conversely, is "the central thought of all history" (COR, 817). As Anthony Appiah argues, Du Bois's conceptualization of race often threatens to subvert his own postulation of its sociohistorical genesis. Appiah acknowledges Du Bois's effort to define a sociohistorical basis for a group identity in shared experience but argues that shared experience already presumes the group. In the end, he claims, Du Bois could not escape the nineteenth-century biological definitions of race that he disavowed, nor did he fundamentally want to escape them since belief in a biological concept of race would allow him to claim Africa as the homeland for which he longed. Yet while Appiah reads Du Bois's claim that the history of the world is the history of races as an assertion, I read it as a description of history: with its ongoing stories about race, "history" has indeed shaped racial identity, forming groups that *in retrospect* can be shaped (and reinforced) by common experiences.[61] In my reading, Du Bois continues to struggle with the powerful nineteenth-century narratives that dominated the turn-of-the-century discourse of race. Du Bois's *acknowledged* uncertainty is an important part of his strategy.

The argument advanced in "The Conservation of Races" demonstrates a powerful relation between history and social truth. Du Bois attributes "the cohesiveness and continuity" of racial groups to "spiritual, psychical, differences. . . . The forces that bind together the Teuton nations are," he argues, "first, their race identity and common blood; secondly, and more important, a common history, common laws and religion, similar habits of thought and a conscious striving together for certain ideals of life" (COR, 818). The story of that conscious striving is the visionary history for which Wilson pointedly calls, and, like Wilson, Du Bois is unwilling to relinquish physiological differences entirely, yet he complicates them with an analysis of the power of ideas and the institutions that reflect and implement them. But the two leaders make very different use of that ambiguity. Du Bois analyzes and challenges the language of kinship that Wilson adopts in place of "common blood."

By 1940 Du Bois would extend the logic of his insights to assert with conviction only the scientific uncertainty of the meaning of racial and cultural heritage. Pondering his intuitive connection to Africa in *Dusk of Dawn*, he explains, "the mark of that heritage is upon me in color and hair. These are obvious things, but of little meaning in themselves; only important as they stand for real and more subtle differences from other men. Whether they do or not I do not know nor does science know today" (*DD*, 639). He recalls the changes in the conceptualization of race since he wrote "The Conservation of Races" but reaffirms "the first article of a proposed racial creed . . . 'that the Negro people as a race have a contribution to make to civilization and humanity which no other race can make'" (*DD*, 639). Du Bois, locating the group identity of his African ancestors in "a common history . . . a common disaster and . . . one long memory," insists that "the real essence of this kinship is its social heritage of slavery; the discrimination and insult; and this heritage binds together not simply the children of Africa, but extends through yellow Asia and into the Soul Seas." Here is the "unity that draws [Du Bois] to Africa" (*DD*, 640), but a unity that has been imposed by white oppression could presumably end were the end of discrimination, insult, and their aftermath to make them unnecessary. Never would the heritage of slavery completely vanish, but centuries of achievement free from its effects could certainly lessen the ties that bind.

In the meantime, racial narratives have both purposes and limitations. For Appiah, Du Bois's historical narrative, his assertion of a common history, "seduces us into error" in its inability to resist "the appeal of the earlier conception of race." But in insisting that Du Bois merely buries "the biological conception [of race] below the surface" of his sociohistorical reconceptualization, Appiah deemphasizes the importance of the uncertainty of which Du Bois makes very deliberate use (AA, 34). From this uncertainty follows the constructedness of all sociohistoric narratives, including Du Bois's own. Launching subsequently into the gorgeous account of his first glimpse of Africa, he generates one among the myriad narratives of identity that he, or anyone, might construct.[62] It is the cultural—and even personal—function of such narratives that most interests him. Du Bois challenges the language and metaphors of a kinship system—explicitly in *Dusk of Dawn* but also conceptually in "The Conservation of Races" and "Of Our Spiritual Strivings"—as they are configured in sociohistorical narratives of nationalism. In the language of kinship, he locates the source of the impulse to scientize (and sometimes mythologize) race, an exclusionary as well as an inclusionary impulse.

From the perspective gained by his analysis, Du Bois called attention to the assumptions and procedures—the symbols and the language—that informed the construction of group identity in the reconstructed United States. In his 1901 *Atlantic Monthly* essay, "The Freedmen's Bureau" (which became the second chapter of *The Souls of Black Folk*), Du Bois sought to retell the story of Reconstruction, "the period of history from 1861 to 1872," he explained in the revised version, "so far as it relates to the American Negro" (S, 372). The failure of Reconstruction as Du Bois assesses it in this essay, resulted from the Reconstruction government's insufficient understanding and analysis of the task of transforming a social order, from an inadequate commitment of resources and a view of "Negro suffrage as a final answer to all present perplexities."[63]

Du Bois's own analysis extends to the ideological concerns that undermined Reconstruction, concerns that emerge in the essay as competing narratives of cultural identity. He represents one narrative through the figure of Lincoln, whom Wilson described as embodying "the very character of the race itself." Du Bois's description of Lincoln as "the long-headed man, with care-chiselled face, who sat in the White House" foregrounds the process of symbol making, the conversion of a human being into a national icon such as Wilson performs (*FB*, 356).[64] The description amplifies the statuelike features of a man who had been monumentalized in many media to become a social emblem almost (and maybe even) before his death. In a transaction Du Bois may have known of, Augustus Saint-Gaudens received a $100,000 commission for a statue of a seated Abraham

Lincoln on October 20, 1897. Saint-Gaudens's Standing Lincoln already presided over Lincoln Park in Chicago, but it was his seated Lincoln that would become the model for Daniel Chester French's figure in the Lincoln Memorial in Washington. "The Freedmen's Bureau" replaces Lincoln as national emblem with representations of an alternative narrative:

> two figures ever stand to typify that day to coming men: the one a gray-haired gentleman, whose fathers had quit themselves like men, whose sons lay in nameless graves; who bowed to the evil of slavery because its abolition boded untold ill to all; who stood at last, in the evening of life, a blighted, ruined form with hate in his eyes. And the other, a form hovering dark and mother-like, her awful face black with the mists of centuries, had aforetime bent in love over the white master's cradle, rocked his sons and daughters to sleep, and closed in death the sunken eyes of his wife to the world; ay, too, had laid herself low to his lust and borne a tawny man child to the world, only to see her dark boy's limbs scattered to the winds by midnight marauders riding after Damned Niggers. (FB, 360)

Du Bois's narrative replaces the white fear of black men's lust for white women with the more historically accurate depiction of the white slave-holding man's rape of enslaved women. In fact, as Du Bois notes earlier in the essay, black men had been "emasculated by a peculiarly complete system of slavery" (FB, 357).

Here is the alternative kinship narrative that complicates the reconstitution of a coherent group identity. These figures' legacy of hatred—"hating they went to their long home, and hating their children's children live to-day" (FB, 360)—erects barriers to reconstructing the nation. When he revised the essay for *The Souls of Black Folk*, Du Bois resolved the grammatical ambiguity of the second "hating" with two carefully placed commas around the word ("and, hating, their"). As it reads here, however, the two figures, ghostlike, live to hate "their children's children . . . to-day"; they remain haunting presences betokening the ongoing threat of violence perpetrated rather than resolved by Wilson's one continuous story. Above all, their emblematic significance rests in their status as parents and in their complication of every family metaphor as they draw attention to the question of heterogeneity in the reconstructing nation. The kinship system in the United States is, by any standards, at best a complicated legacy. Yet its centrality to narratives of the nation explains the importance of race to Du Bois's revisionary narrative.

The race-pride with which the black community, including Du Bois, responded must be seen less as an acceptance of the scientific or legal definitions of race perpetuated by a dominant white establishment than as a response to the effacement of black achievement by that establishment. Claims such as Dunning's, that "the negro had no pride of race and no aspiration or ideals save to be like the whites" (*RPE*, 213), demanded an answer. Paradoxically, of course, asserting black achievement could scarcely avoid reaffirming those racial categorizations. The author of a 1901 *American Journal of Sociology* essay entitled "The Race Problem: As Discussed by Negro Women," recounts an anecdote with an analysis reminiscent of that offered by Du Bois in the depiction of the stock scene of racial discovery in his 1897 "The Striving of the Negro People": "The attention of a friend of mine was once called to a singularly bright and attractive little colored boy. He sighed, and said: 'Yes, the boy will continue to be clever until he finds out that he is black.' The leaders of the race wish to develop such a spirit in their people that such boys will do all the better after they *find out that they are black.*"[65] Blackness is a *discovery,* a cultural positioning, and the women in the essay suggest not that the positioning be scientifically justified, but that it be embraced—culturally, not racially. Blackness here becomes a motivating factor, but all too readily it also becomes like an essence—and always in relation to a normative whiteness that not only defines it and is defined by it, but also sets forth the terms by which black achievement is measured. Efforts to demonstrate the invalidity of scientific racial classification could take a practical or theoretical form. Du Bois himself oscillated between, on the one hand, insisting on a black achievement that practically disproved assertions of inferiority, and, on the other hand, elucidating (theoretically) the cultural narrative in which scientific racial classification was inscribed. Sometimes, as Appiah suggests, those strategies were antithetical.

Yet Du Bois does manage to bring these strategies together effectively when he works to fashion an aesthetic innovation capable of expressing the cultural positioning of African Americans. Blackness remains a cultural rather than biological identity—one that allows for a certain critical distance. A different cultural experience, moreover, translates into unique forms of expression. Such is the premise that motivates "The Conservation of Races." In it, Du Bois advocates Pan-Negroism, a cultural program built on a common cultural experience across national boundaries. In a passage that seems to argue for a racial identity, Du Bois actually offers cultural identities—or identifications ("an American, a Negro")—in place of rather than according to the transcendental assumptions of a Volksgeist. "For the development of Negro genius," he declares,

> of Negro literature and art, of Negro spirit, only Negroes bound and welded together, Negroes inspired by one vast ideal, can work out in its fullness the great message we have for humanity. We cannot reverse history; we are subject to the same natural laws as other races, and if the Negro is ever to be a factor in the world's history—if among the gaily-colored banners that deck the broad ramparts of civilization is to hang one uncompromising black, then it must be placed there by black hands, fashioned by black heads and hallowed by the travail of 200,000,000 black hearts beating in one glad song of jubilee. (COR, 820)

In a vision that militates against "absorption by white Americans," Du Bois underscores the terms of that absorption (COR, 820). It is *history* to which he wishes to add a black presence, and it is *natural laws* that "subject" him to a racial identity. But what, to Du Bois, are history and natural laws? They are the result, he explains more than forty years later in *Dusk of Dawn*, of "age-long complexes sunk now largely to unconscious habit and irrational urge, which demanded on our [African Americans'] part not only the patience to wait, but the power to entrench ourselves for a long siege against the strongholds of color caste" (*DD*, 771).

A black aesthetic offers not only such entrenchment but also the means potentially of breaking habits. Where Appiah reads "pathos" in "the gap between [Du Bois's] unconfident certainty that Africa is 'of course' his fatherland and the concession that it is not the land of his father or his father's father" (AA, 34), I read a critique of the putatively natural laws that, in the name of the "father," speak a geopolitical entity into existence as a "fatherland." The law, Du Bois suggests, articulates his connection to Africa, which he embraces accordingly—and defiantly.[66] What he most poignantly expresses here is the excluded African American's pressing social and political *desire*, in the contemporary world, for a homeland. The 1897 plea for the development of Negro genius anticipates that more developed expression, as does the *black folk* of the title *The Souls of Black Folk*. Surely that title evinces a debt to the Germanic concept of the Volk, and it more than hints at what Rampersad has identified as "Du Bois's shift toward what one might call cultural nationalism in the black" (*SLI*,

119). Yet, as Rampersad also observes, the "folk" of the title is ambiguous, complicated by the plural "souls." For Rampersad, "souls" refers to the "two-ness" in "Of Our Spiritual Strivings" (*SLI*, 117). There is also a potentially oppositional interplay between the plural subject "souls" and the singular (although collective) subject "folk."

Moving among pronouns in *The Souls of Black Folk*, Du Bois alternately identifies with and distances himself from other black subjects. In "Of the Meaning of Progress," a chapter of *The Souls of Black Folk*, Du Bois, recounting his experiences as a summer school teacher in rural Tennessee, offers an especially clear description of the "black folk": "I have called my tiny community a world, and so its isolation made it; and yet there was among us but a half-awakened common consciousness, sprung from common joy and grief, at burial, birth, or wedding; from a common hardship in poverty, poor land, and low wages; and, above all, from the sight of the Veil that hung between us and Opportunity" (*S*, 410). The common consciousness springs not from racial kinship but from common experiences, especially of oppression, premised on assumptions of that kinship. But each generation responds differently to the world. The Veil is not enough to contain these differences, and blackness changes meaning across generational lines. Each generation is organized with respect to its experience of slavery, which in turn defines its cohort's experience of blackness. The common bond created by the Veil is, finally, tenuous. The black folk disperses into the particular experiences of different souls: "All this caused us to think some thoughts together; but these, when ripe for speech, were spoken in various languages" (*S*, 410). Responses to the world range from the "dark fatalism" of those who had lived through slavery to the "listless indifference, or shiftlessness, or reckless bravado" of those who only dimly remembered it and finally to the ambitiousness and daring of those, like John Jones, "whose young appetites had been whetted to an edge by school and story and half-awakened thought" (*S*, 410). Here is no transcendent Volk, but folk, a community of striving souls. African-American culture exists for Du Bois in the poetry of creative responses to oppression, in the variety and range of individual responses, from dark fatalism to indifference or recklessness to hopeful defiance, that comprise a collective spirit that does not bow but sings.

Legally and rhetorically, "the Negro problem" is created by the mirroring gaze of white America, ironically, suggests Du Bois, in its own image. Du Bois offers Pan-Negroism, racial unity in the service of revisions and revisionary history, as an alternative to the "absorption by the white Americans" tantamount to "self-obliteration" (COR, 820–21). Even in the somewhat contradictory ideas about race that he expresses in "The Conservation of Races," he conspicuously and creatively transforms as he embraces a racial identity that he has been assigned by the watchful (and coercive) gaze of Historian and Sociologist. In that essay, he delineates "eight distinctly differentiated races, *in the sense in which History tells us the word must be used*" (COR, 817; emphasis added). Rhetoric and history dictate categories that need not be essentialist to be compelling—even inescapable. With the plaintive observation that "our own haven of refuge is ourselves," Du Bois justifies the need for the American Negro Academy (COR, 822). But the racial identity of the African American in this essay is provisional: "We believe it the duty of the Americans of Negro descent, as a body, to maintain their race identity until this mission of the Negro people is accomplished, and the ideal of human brotherhood has become a practical possibility" (COR, 825). Evidently, this identity is designed to accelerate, however implausibly, the end of race identity through a critique of cultural coerciveness (a critique enabled by the gift of a second-sight) hinted at in the manifesto, and developed, by 1903, into *The Souls of Black Folk*.[67] Du Bois's cultural nationalism militates against biological classification as it offers an alternative—and analytical—narrative of identity.

In "Strivings of the Negro People," and even more completely in *The Souls of Black Folk,* Du Bois unfolds his assessment of "the Negro problem" into an ongoing analysis of the "new American race" and the Veil that is intrinsic to it. In the tall newcomer of that essay who peremptorily refuses his greeting card, he summarizes the position of Shaler and like-minded race theorists, as well as the Supreme Court decision of *Plessy*. The girl who refuses to exchange cards with her black classmate denies the recognition that Franklin Giddings calls the "reciprocal consciousness of kind." She thus refuses what one writer in the *American Journal of Sociology* sees as essential to nation-building: "a potential fellowship—a possibility of growing to see important things from the same viewpoint" that moves "the coercive process of nation-forming" into the "attractive process of nation-perfecting" or, again in Giddings's terms, progresses from coerciveness to liberty.[68] In Du Bois's re-presentation, the tall newcomer (and what she stands for) makes visible an obscured coerciveness at the core of American liberal society and turns the "self-consciousness" by which sociologists mark identity within a group into the "painful self-consciousness" found in "Of the Faith of the Fathers" (originally "The Religion of the Negro" in *The New World*). "The problem of the Twentieth Century is the problem of the color-line," Du Bois maintained, not long after *Plessy* had established color as a legal determination based on a blood discourse (and called by Mark Twain a "fiction of law and custom"[69]).

By 1920, the second-sight that Du Bois describes in the first published essay and the first chapter of *The Souls of Black Folk* had become the more dramatic and ominous "clairvoyance" of "The Souls of White Folk":

> I see in and through them. I view them from unusual points of vantage. Not as a foreigner do I come, for I am native, not foreign, bone of their thought and flesh of their language. Mine is not the knowledge of the traveler or the colonial composite of dear memories, words and wonder. Nor yet is my knowledge that which servants have of masters, or mass of class, or capitalist of artisan. Rather I see these souls undressed and from the back and side. I see the working of their entrails. I know their thoughts and they know that I know. This knowledge makes them now embarrassed, now furious! They deny my right to live and be and call me misbirth! My word is to them mere bitterness and my soul, pessimism. And yet as they preach and strut and shout and threaten, crouching as they clutch at rags of facts and fancies to hide their nakedness, they go twisting, flying by my tired eyes and I see them ever stripped,—ugly, human.[70]

Biology has completely melted into culture in this description, as Du Bois declares himself "bone of their *thought* and flesh of their *language*," and as embodied souls are disemboweled and stripped of their self-tailorings. Still, it is now the white folk of whom he declares himself flesh and bone—the white folk threatened by his existence, as is evident in the concern continually articulated not only in such texts as Thomas Dixon's but also in the race and immigration debates of the period. The real challenge, of course, is to culture expressed, as in the passage from "The Souls of White Folk" quoted above, through a *metaphorical* nature.

Du Bois's scrutiny carries the threat of a kind of cultural anarchy. When he claims, in both "The Conservation of Races" and "Of Our Spiritual Strivings," that the Negro is the true American, Du Bois pushes the

United States, by implication, into an identification with England, the colonizer, that forces black Americans, like the colonies in Wilson's formulation, to see what they have in common: a kinship that is, for Du Bois, at least ambiguously *provisional* and thus reflective of the tenuously constructed (white) American identity. The last chapter of *The Souls of Black Folk* attributes the assumptions of racial discourse to "the arrogance of peoples irreverent toward Time and ignorant of the deeds of men" (*S*, 544). Such assumptions, he stresses, a thousand years earlier "would have made it difficult for the Teuton to prove his right to life," and a thousand years before that "would have scouted the idea of blond races ever leading civilization" (*S*, 544). The categorization of the color line clearly imposes identity in a manner that, in the language of turn-of-the-century sociology, could be called coercive. As Justice Harlan points out in his dissent from the *Plessy* decision, the liberty of *all* citizens is at stake; infractions multiply. Making visible the coerciveness of American identity, black Americans could evoke as much anxiety in their resemblance *to* as in their difference *from* white Americans.

Du Bois's apparent cultural nationalism left a critical legacy of confusion. Where August Meier witnesses Du Bois's "striving and groping toward a cultural nationalism . . . [based on] the notion of innate race differences," for example, John Higham, reading "The Conservation of Races" and "Of Our Spiritual Strivings" as "starkly dualistic," argues for Du Bois's assimilationist vision deriving from the global vision of the "ideal of human brotherhood."[71] The African-American identity that Du Bois advocates is not only, nor even primarily, defensive. The provisionality of *race* does not mean, for Du Bois, the disappearance of African-American *culture;* on the contrary, his ideal of human brotherhood stems from the *conservation* and celebration of an Afro-ethnic culture, the beauty that has grown out of oppression. Transforming race, he also argues for its transformative powers: "as a race we must strive by race organization," he tells his American Negro Academy audience, "by race solidarity, by race unity to the realization of that broader humanity which freely recognizes differences in men, but sternly deprecates inequality in their opportunities of development" (COR, 822). The concept of differences here enriches and liberates: it recognizes that there are as many differences as experiences.

The critical confusion attests to the difficulty of the story Du Bois sought to tell. *The Souls of Black Folk* challenges and revises the habits of thought at once expressed in and shaped by putatively scientific categories. "I could not lull my mind to hypnosis by regarding a phrase like 'consciousness of kind' as a scientific law," recalls the narrator of *Dusk of Dawn* (*DD*, 590). Instead, in *The Souls of Black Folk*, he invites the reader into the world behind the Veil, a world angry and often desperate, but a world in which even amidst the ravages and memories of the ravages of slavery the "haunting echo" of the sorrow songs gives voice to "the most beautiful expression of human experience born this side the seas" (*S*, 536–37). Here is no dearth, but a culture attesting to African, to *human*, achievement. In America, Barrett Wendell had written, "each of us has an inalienable right to strive for excellence" (*LHA*, 530). With *The Souls of Black Folk*, Du Bois challenges the story of that "us" as he claims the right to strive. He offers a story of America told through the striving in the souls of black folk, a tale always in process and endlessly revised.

Historian of the Veil: Reconstructing the Plural Subject in *The Souls of Black Folk*

From the first chapter of *Dusk of Dawn*, "The Plot," Du Bois explains and analyzes the textuality of his life and his world, establishing himself as an example as much as an actor. He intends, he declares, to write about how he and others with him "have had their lives shaped and directed by [the] course of events" (*DD*, 558). "Plot" refers at once to his text and to the course of human events, which, as he frequently observes in *Dusk of Dawn*, is understood through the continuous stories that constitute history. *Dusk of Dawn* describes what *The Souls of Black Folk* enacts: Du Bois's lifelong attempt to tell his story from within and against the dominant history of the white world, beginning with his early New England school days, when he "studied history and politics almost exclusively from the point of view of ancient German freedom, English and New England democracy, and the development of the United States" and sought to "bring criticism from what I knew and saw touching the Negro" (*DD*, 574), only to discover that "race" was "a matter of culture and cultural history" and only the white race had a history (*DD*, 626). Subtitling the book "An Essay Toward an Autobiography of a Race Concept," Du Bois depicts the inscription of his "self" within a restrictive American identity, and his experiences within a prescriptive cultural narrative.

From the perspective of *Dusk of Dawn,* he assesses the achievement and meaning of what had already been a full career (although it was far from over). The concluding paragraph of the middle chapter in *Dusk of Dawn,* "The Concept of Race," describes his efforts to understand and come to terms with "the race concept which has dominated [his] life," a description that exquisitely, if perhaps unintentionally, unfolds the schematization of *The Souls of Black Folk:* "It was . . . first a matter of dawning realization, then of study and science; then a matter of inquiry into the diverse strands of my own family; and finally consideration of my connection, physical and spiritual, with Africa and the Negro race in its homeland. All this led to an attempt to rationalize the racial concept and its place in the modern world" (*DD,* 651). From the "dawning realization" captured in "Of Our Spiritual Strivings," through the early historical and sociological essays, followed by the more or less obviously personal material of the late chapters, and concluding with Du Bois's "connection . . . with Africa" in "The Sorrow Songs," this passage casts the logic of *The Souls of Black Folk* as the discovery of his inscription as a "race concept." In the 1903 work, Du Bois chronicles his inquiry into his own grappling with the prescriptiveness of the cultural narrative by which he finds himself subjected. The complexity of the subject and the intricate formal strategy of the collection troubled Du Bois, who worried "that 'the style and workmanship' of his book did not make its meaning 'altogether clear.' "[72] He chose to be more direct in *Dusk of Dawn.* But *The Souls of Black Folk* demonstrates, at least to the patient reader that he asks for in the "Forethought," how the construction of narratives shapes the experience of self. The challenge of the story he is trying to tell, and the need to tell it through indirection, explain the sociopolitical relevance of his formal innovation in this generically hybrid work.

The movement of *The Souls of Black Folk* from the historical and sociological into the personal parallels the broader cultural logic in which history articulates and disseminates cultural identity. Du Bois's work analyzes the emergence of the personal from history and sociology. The later chapters of *The Souls of Black Folk* complicate rather than exemplify the assertion of an African-American identity and the scientific and cultural narratives in which such an assertion might participate. A contradictory use of pronouns asserts a complex nexus of cultural affiliations. Structurally, the text works as a metaphor for the struggle it investigates: somewhere between a collection of essays and a progressive narrative, *The*

Souls of Black Folk expresses the tension between the pull toward and the resistance to the shaping, directive properties of narrative. Through the ensuing tension, the author emerges struggling, in plain view, with the prescriptions of a narrative of American identity.

As an author, Du Bois had to contend not only with the minds that he describes in "Of the Quest of the Golden Fleece" that are "loth to have [their conclusions] disturbed by facts" (*S*, 457), but also with white appropriation of his texts, with editorial as well as cultural interferences with the story he wished to tell. Robert Stepto notes the importance to Du Bois of the distortions of his June 1901 *World's Work* essay, "The Negro as He Really Is," created by insultingly captioned photographs ("A Pickaninny Cake Walk" beneath a photograph of a group of children, for example) for which he was of course not responsible.[73] When a substantially revised "The Negro as He Really Is" appeared two years later in *The Souls of Black Folk* as "Of the Black Belt" and "Of the Quest of the Golden Fleece," both of which sought to challenge the perspective of "the car-window sociologist," Du Bois certainly, as Stepto suggests, had those representational distortions in mind (*S*, 469). Against such distortions and through language as well as form, Du Bois fashions a narrative of the subjection of the African American into a counterplot that breaks the perceptual habits that constitute expectations.

Du Bois analyzes as he reverses the logical progression of sociological and historical narratives. Such narratives confer personal identity through a comprehensive and comprehensible depiction of a collective identity, and they work to answer the question posed by Albert Bushnell Hart, "what is the meaning of the history of the American nation as a whole?"[74] Du Bois, by contrast, asks the meaning of that question—and its implications for "the strange meaning of being black in the Twentieth Century." He seeks to tell the story obscured by the familiar, the story of strangeness and estrangement. In the "Forethought," he divides *The Souls of Black Folk* into two sections, to which he refers, respectively, as "the world of the white man" and the world "within the Veil" (*S*, 359). The journey of this work is a journey into blackness, which he casts as a journey into double-consciousness, one that offers insight rather than comprehensibility—and that offers insight *into* comprehensibility.

In the last chapter of the first section, "Of the Sons of Master and Men," "the casual observer visiting the South" is almost lulled into a false sense of peace until, as though adjusting to the dark, in a gradually dawning sense of things he had not at first noticed[, s]lowly but surely his eyes begin to catch the shadows of the color-line: here he meets crowds of Negroes and whites; then he is suddenly aware that he cannot discover a single dark face; or again at the close of a day's wandering he may find himself in some strange assembly, where all faces are tinged brown or black, and where he has the vague, uncomfortable feeling of the stranger. He realizes at last that silently, resistlessly, the world about flows by him in two great streams (S, 488)

Woodrow Wilson's unifying "currents of national life" are, with the insight offered by the Veil, the markedly divided "two great streams." Although not quite a double-consciousness, the "dawning realization," recalling the language of the stock scene in the first chapter, brings white observers very close to the perspective of double-consciousness, especially when surrounded by brown and black faces and experiencing themselves as strangers. But most important for Du Bois, in the dawning realization the observers see themselves beginning to see and are thus ready to follow the narrator into the Veil. "Leaving . . . the world of the white man," Du Bois writes in the "Forethought," "I have stepped within the Veil, raising it that you may view faintly its deeper recesses,—the meaning of its religion, the passion of its human sorrow, and the struggle of its greater souls" (S, 359). His intriguing use of the preposition "within" turns a figure of identity into a geographical space, which moves counter to the direction of the cultural plots of Manifest Destiny and its heirs, plots that use a geographic space (the continent, for example) to express an apparently latent identity.

Cultural plots such as those that generated Wilson's kinship narrative turn the sociohistoric into the ontological, common experiences into common roots. By contrast, Du Bois's investigation of the strange meaning of being black discloses the troubling exclusions that disrupt that narrative, the cultural repressed that reenvisions the ontological as the sociohistoric. Existence, in this reformulation, is always conspicuously theorized within culture and history. Du Bois thereby unravels these cultural plots in the name of—and to foreground—a constructed subject, who in turn forms the basis of his analysis of the kinship narrative. His analysis begins with the assertion, in "Of the Dawn of Freedom," the revised version of "The Freedmen's Bureau," "of the emancipated Negro as the ward of the nation" (S, 378). Here is language resonant at once with the "domestic dependents" of the *Cherokee Nation* decision, with Lincoln's Second Inaugural Address, which calls on the nation to care for the widows and orphans of the war dead, and with Frederick Douglass's 1876 Lincoln Park (Washington) oration, in which he calls African Americans the "step-children" of Abraham Lincoln, "children by adoption." The emancipated slave, for Du Bois, is one of those orphans and must therefore be brought into a reconstructed American family. But the terms of this adoption constitute precisely "the Negro Problem."

I have already shown how the "gray-haired gentleman" and the "form hovering dark and mother-like" introduced in "The Freedmen's Bureau" emblematized the problems facing the reconstructing nation. Du Bois amplified those figures' interactions and parental roles in the editorial changes he made in this passage. The changes are subtle but important. In the 1901 *Atlantic Monthly* essay, the motherlike form had "bent in love over the white master's cradle, rocked his sons and daughters to sleep, and closed in death the sunken eyes of his wife to the world," had, in other words, mothered generations. The same figure in the 1903 revisions had "quailed at that white master's command, had bent in love over the cradles of his sons and daughters, and closed in death the sunken eyes of his wife" (*S*, 383). The motherlike form fears her master, and the depiction of that fear makes her subsequent actions more ambiguous than in the earlier version. The juxtaposition of the fear of the master and the love for his children suggests the possibility of rape and complicates the maternal relationship that she has with his children. I do not mean to suggest that, like Roxanna in Mark Twain's *Pudd'nhead Wilson,* she has switched her child for the master's child. Rather, Roxanna's substitution could be read in this context as an analogue for the displaced love of the enslaved mother for the children of her master, a master who was literally in some cases the father of her own children as well. These figures, scarred not only as parents but as parents—literally and metaphorically—of common children, complicate the reconstruction of the nation. Where Woodrow Wilson offers a kinship narrative, Du Bois suggests a kind of family feud growing out of the kind of family created under the slave system. The structural and verbal repetition of the poetic last line suggests the problem: "but, *hating,* they went to their long home, and, hating, their children's children live to-day." The children are perpetuating (lulled, it seems, almost by force of habit) a conflict that they ought to be reconceptualizing, and the figures will "typify that day" not, as in the earlier version, "to coming *men*," but, even more ominously, "to coming *ages*" (*S*,

383; emphasis added). Du Bois brings the threat of violence, exacerbated rather than mitigated by the kinship narrative, into focus through this legacy of hate.

These two figures, and their relationship, also typify the kind of history that Du Bois set out to write in *The Souls of Black Folk*, a history that attends to what has not been written and especially to the return of what the historical and sociological narratives have repressed. That repressed returns as the haunting presence with which the chapter concludes: "I have seen a land right merry with the sun, where children sing, and rolling hills lie like passioned women wanton with harvest. And there in the King's Highway sat and sits a figure veiled and bowed, by which the traveller's footsteps hasten as they go. On the tainted air broods fear. Three centuries' thought has been the raising and unveiling of that bowed human heart, and now behold a century new for the duty and the deed. The problem of the Twentieth Century is the problem of the color-line" (*S*, 391). This chapter considers the discrepancy between the policies of the Freedmen's Bureau—like the "poetic justice" of the plan to redistribute slave-owners' land among the formerly enslaved—and their enactment, "poetry done into solemn prose" (*S*, 379). Missing from the Bureau's policy was an analysis of the real problems of Reconstruction. Du Bois, conversely, turns the prose of history into poetry—the lyricism of his concluding passage—when he performs such an analysis. The figure in the passage is ominous because veiled, the eerie creation of an oppressor that has tried to make that figure invisible and has produced a mysterious, thus fearsome, creature. The figure is not explicitly identified by race or gender—although the Veil in the context of Du Bois's work suggests race— but exudes the ominousness of a being deprived of the full expression of personhood (self-conscious man- or womanhood). Oppression takes many forms along the axes of race, gender, ethnicity, religion, sexuality, class (as Du Bois increasingly sought to argue), and it shapes its own haunting presences. The veiled figure is certainly of the oppressor's making. The twist in the passage that conspicuously turns the veiled figure into a metaphor for the human heart suggests that three centuries of progress— advances in articulating human rights—must now confront racism, and the fate of the veiled figure is the fate of humanity. For Du Bois, the history of *The Souls of Black Folk* was a profoundly moral project, one that enabled "the duty and the deed" of the unveiling, and that project in-

cluded attending to—and analyzing—the uncanniness of the black American for white America, and its implications.

   The chapters in the white world section of *The Souls of Black Folk* trace
the perpetuation of the racial discord and of the economic and psychological slavery that created that uncanniness largely to American imperialism, which perpetuates and develops the racism on which it is built. In
Dusk of Dawn, Du Bois epitomizes "the history of our day . . . in one
word—Empire; the domination of white Europe over black Africa and
yellow Asia, through political power built on the economic control of
labor, income and ideas. The echo of this industrial imperialism in America was the expulsion of black men from American democracy, their
subjection to caste control and wage slavery" (*DD*, 623–24). Imperialism,
he explains in at least one-third of the chapters in *The Souls of Black Folk*,
turns "human beings" into "material resources," removing them from the
access to property and cycles of inheritance and creating an alienated
population emblematic of the limitations as well as the power of white
domination: a figure veiled and bowed (*S*, 428). His effective use of "slavery" in the *Dusk of Dawn* quotation, as well as throughout *The Souls of
Black Folk*, insists on the threatening discord perpetuated by such an
exclusion, and by a system rechanneled but not excised.

   Altamaha's Judge Henderson makes clear the property and domestic
terms in which white Americans might understand the threat of black
Americans: " 'they want to reverse nature, and rule white men, and marry
white women, and sit in my parlor' " (*S*, 531). It is a sentiment echoed
by the White Man, Roger Van Dieman, an allegorical figure in "The
White World" chapter of *Dusk of Dawn:* "It would seem that colored folks
were a threat to the world. They were going to overthrow white folk by
sheer weight of numbers, destroy their homes and marry their daughters"
(*DD*, 671). The terms by which imperialism justifies exploitation—property and inheritance—become the very terms through which white dominance and the white American family are threatened. And since these
"colored folks" are always men in these scenarios—men who want to
marry white women—they constitute a particular and displacing threat to
white paternity and patriarchy. Ironically, this threat assigned to black
men pales before the real challenge to the American family perpetuated
by white men. Walter Bagehot, it will be remembered, predicted imminent dissolution for any nation that sanctioned "loosely bound family

groups . . . where the father is more or less uncertain, where descent is not traced through him, where, that is, property does not come from him"—precisely the family created (or decimated) by the concubinage of slavery and its counterpart under imperialism.

Du Bois's veiled figure joined a host of specters who haunted the imperial nation, perceived threats to the American family. Shortly before the publication of *The Souls of Black Folk*, for example, the Supreme Court case of *Downes v. Bidwell* (1901) registered the cultural anxiety captured by Du Bois. The case turned on the constitutionality of imposing an import duty on Puerto Rico, a territory belonging to the United States, and it thereby established that a territory could be owned and not incorporated— that is, it legislated United States imperialism. The case divided the Court, and the language of both sides returned continually to the fate of the "body politic" and to the question of who was fit for citizenship and how it should be determined when, if ever, "the acquired territory has reached that state where it is proper that it should enter into and form a part of the American family."[75] Overseas expansion raised a familiar paradox; both options—full and equal incorporation of United States territories and United States possession without incorporation—challenged the integrity of the nation. Incorporation threatened to make "all citizenship of the United States . . . precarious and fleeting, subject to be sold at any moment like any other property. That is to say, to protect a newly acquired people in their presumed rights, it [would be] essential to degrade the whole body of American citizenship" (*DB*, 315). Yet, a dissenting justice warned that possession without incorporation created "a disembodied shade, in an intermediate state of ambiguous existence, for an indefinite period" (*DB*, 372). The case resolved, or refused to resolve, in an echo of *Cherokee Nation* and *Dred Scott:* Puerto Ricans were neither citizens of the United States, nor aliens. Thus the emerging imperial nation once again legislated its own ghosts into existence in the name of the (white) American family, and once again these presences were haunted by virtue of their resemblances as forcefully as their differences.

The process through which oppression creates its own demons fascinated Du Bois, who refocused rather than denied the challenge posed by African Americans to the "American family." In the story that he tells in "Of the Dawn of Freedom," nothing speaks more deeply of the meaning of national conflict than the fleeing slaves who formed a "dark human cloud that clung like remorse on the rear of those swift columns, swelling at times to half their size, almost engulfing and choking them." By sheer mass, they overwhelmed attempts to repel them, but "trudged and writhed and surged, until they rolled into Savannah, a starved and naked horde of tens of thousands" (S, 375–76). By "Of the Faith of the Fathers," which inaugurates the Veil section of *The Souls of Black Folk*, the swelling crowd threatens to mobilize, from despair, into a more conscious radicalism, possibly anarchy. The chapter ends ominously, awaiting "the Awakening . . . when the pent-up vigor of ten million souls shall sweep irresistibly toward the Goal, out of the Valley of the Shadow of Death, where all that makes life worth living—Liberty, Justice, and Right—is marked 'For White People Only'" (S, 505). White oppression generates this movement; the tenets and assumptions of imperialism force nonwhite Americans into a deprived and potentially threatening mass.

The Veil section, however, is more concerned with the cultural challenge posed by black America, the challenge of the mirror, than with the social threat of rebellion. This section treats what Du Bois finds largely missing from the earlier pieces, the personal rather than historical or sociological experience of being black in America. Du Bois does not dramatically alter his perspective in these chapters (most of which he had not previously published), but through a slight shift in emphasis, he explores the internalization that makes his own experiences so hard to analyze and recount, the dynamics that doom John Jones.

That shift is noticeable in a comparison of the voice in his autobiographical chapter in the earlier section, "Of the Meaning of Progress," with that in the later chapters of the Veil section. The earlier chapter offers a painfully poignant account of Du Bois's experiences teaching school during consecutive summers in the hills of Tennessee. Yet he remains an outsider in the story; he shares his perspective more with his reader than with the community. He assumes, for instance, that his reader shares his preference for staying with the families whose houses were clean and who gave him enough to eat rather than families such as the Eddingses over whose beds "herds of untamed insects wandered" (S, 409). And he expects his reader to join in his surprise when the white commissioner of schools excludes Du Bois but not his white traveling companion from his supper table, when, that is, "the awful shadow of the Veil" falls (S, 407). His depiction of the community is compassionate, even loving, but also sociological. He is a participant observer whose readers constitute his peers. Even when he wonders about the meaning of "progress" (and his service in its name), he assumes the reader's shared perspective, and when, "sadly musing," he rides "to Nashville in the Jim Crow car," he addresses a reader who shares his dismay (*S,* 414).

A passage added to "Of the Black Belt," one of the chapters revised from "The Negro As He Really Is," registers a different perspective as *The Souls of Black Folk* moves within the Veil. While passing through the section of Georgia that had formerly been the disputed Cherokee territory, the narrator, acting as a tour guide, invites an evidently white male reader to join him in "the Jim Crow Car" (*S,* 440). He assures the reader that "there will be no objection,—already four other white men, and a little white girl with her nurse, are in there. Usually the races are mixed in there; but the white coach is all white. Of course this car is not so good as the other, but it is fairly clean and comfortable. The discomfort lies chiefly in the hearts of those four black men yonder—and in mine" (*S,* 440–41). In this chapter, he speaks unambiguously from within the Veil to a reader that does not share his experience or understand his perspective. He asks that reader not to be a scientist, not just to perceive, but actually to experience life within the Veil, a life organized around exclusion and prohibition. But Du Bois does not allow the white reader to become an insider; instead, he invites that reader into an experience that Du Bois tenders more tentatively in the earlier "Of the Sons of Master and Men," the experience of double-consciousness, of seeing white America through the eyes of black America. He simulates that experience in the storytelling itself. Moving unpredictably between past and present tenses, the narrator alternatively includes the reader on his journey and excludes him from an experience that has already transpired. The reader moves—or is moved—arbitrarily into and out of a shared perspective.

The white reader is made to experience and to analyze double-consciousness in the sequence of the four new chapters with which *The Souls of Black Folk* concludes: "Of the Passing of the First-Born," "Of Alexander Crummell," "Of the Coming of John," and "The Sorrow Songs." These chapters vividly demonstrate how the distortion of the Veil makes Du Bois's experience difficult to comprehend. Yet as that distortion becomes his story, the experience of double-consciousness becomes more comprehensible. Du Bois, moreover, reconceives double-consciousness to include the experience of seeing oneself in an other in addition to seeing oneself through the eyes of (and therefore *as*) an other. The sequence begins with an anatomy of grief within the Veil, since expressions of grief typically elicit human sympathy and thus ought to break down the barriers erected by the antipathies of race within a cultural narrative. In "Of the Passing of the First-Born," Du Bois recounts the story of the loss of his son, his first-born, and he depicts, through conventional expressions of grief, the anguish in the father's plaintive laments: "Is not this my life hard enough, . . . Wast thou so jealous of one little coign of happiness that thou must needs enter there,—thou, O Death?" (*S*, 509). "The world's most piteous thing—a childless mother" intones equally familiar terms of consolation: "He will be happy There; he ever loved beautiful things" (*S*, 508–9). Consolation works by formalizing and thus containing the expression of grief, and its familiar terms should elicit sympathetic (if formulaic) identification. But any sympathy, any bridging of the cultural distance between black and white, is undermined when "pale-faced worrying men and women" react to the funeral procession with only a glance and a word, "Niggers!" (*S*, 509). Du Bois asks white America to endure a painful recognition in this response, to see itself through the troubling gaze of an anguished father's eyes.

The Veil necessarily changes the terms of consolation, and this son's death prompts the father to confront exactly what the ostensibly universal name of the father means within the Veil. The father wonders about the inheritance he will pass on to his son as an American citizen with African ancestors. He shows how significantly his perceptions are colored by the color-line, and how different the experience of "father" is on either side, when he confesses to "an awful gladness" in his heart at his son's death. "Blame me not," he explains, "if I see the world thus *darkly through the Veil*,—and my soul whispers ever to me, saying, 'Not dead, not dead, but escaped; not bond, but free" (*S*, 510; emphasis added). Here the father echoes the slave parent's ambivalence toward her sick children, such as Harriet Jacobs articulates, and even the downtrodden (white) Mag's relief at her child's escape from taunting in *Our Nig*. The reference (underscored) is to the passage in 1 Corinthians in which Paul explains "now we see through a glass, darkly; but then face to face: now I know in part; but then shall I know even as also I am known" (13:12). In 2 Corinthians 3:13–18, Paul uses the image of the Veil to represent the flawed understanding of those who have not yet turned to God. Du Bois's echo establishes the Veil not only as a visual impairment within the world, but also as a metaphor for worldly perception. Once again the Veil interferes with self-knowledge, but this interference applies equally to white and black

America. The color-line is one among many arbitrary distinctions that shade as they shape reality. The son dies ignorant of the color-line, escaping the "bitter meanness" that would have "sicken[ed] his baby heart till it die[d] a living death" and the "taunt" that would have "madden[ed] his happy boyhood" and inaugurated the inevitable stock scene (S, 510). The father calls himself a fool for thinking or wishing that "this little soul should grow choked and deformed within the Veil!" (S, 510). The father, in other words, examines his legacy to his son in terms that make the mother's traditional consolation excruciatingly real: the conventional distortions of grief become the actual distortions of life.

The "passing" of the title at once invokes and inverts the paradigmatic slave narrative of Exodus. Unlike the oldest sons of the Jews, this son passes instead of being passed over. Yet the Veil turns his death into a kind of survival, an almost active (although of course unwitting) protest. The dead son, passing from the material to the spiritual world, comes to embody the future in which the father will "awaken," like the souls at the end of "Of the Faith of the Fathers," into a world "above the Veil" (S, 511). And yet, even this hopeful image is distorted, as the dead son also emblematizes the fate of the body that, blackened by the gaze of white America, passes either out of existence (disappears) or into a deformed subjectivity. The dead son, becoming a tragic symbol of everything from which he escapes, demonstrates the power of the white world, which works by controlling the production of meaningful symbols.

The blackening that descends with the Veil marks an internalization of the evaluative terms of whiteness. Many fictional protagonists who choose to live without the Veil, to "pass" into the white world, express the internalization of those terms as a sense of trespassing. The protagonist of James Weldon Johnson's *Autobiography of an Ex-Coloured Man* (1912), for example, begins his story with a confession of "the great secret of [his] life . . . which for some years [he has] guarded far more carefully than any of [his] earthly possessions." Pausing "to analyse the motives" of his confession, he claims to be "led by the same impulse which forces the unfound-out criminal to take somebody into his confidence, although he knows that the act is likely, even almost certain, to lead to his undoing" (JWJ, 3). Metaphors that manifest his sense of himself as a criminal and his secret as a possession tease out the implications of the 1896 *Plessy v. Ferguson* segregation decision. Whiteness, as Plessy's attorney Albion Tourgée had established in *Plessy*, is part of a "reputation" that constitutes

property: "We shall . . . contend that, in any mixed community, the reputation of belonging to the dominant race, in this instance the white race, is
property, in the same sense that a right of action or of inheritance is
property" (OO, 83). Thus Tourgée explained the terms in which subjects
designated nonwhite were excluded—and perhaps explained some of the
motivations (property, inheritance) for that exclusion—from full and entitled personhood in white America. Although the Supreme Court determined that Homer Plessy was not entitled to that reputation, it did establish that a legally white man could sue anyone who treated him as a black
man on such grounds. The *Plessy* decision insisted that a reputation could
be owned only if it were legally true, and neither Plessy's whiteness, nor
that of the ex-colored man was legally true. Their "passing" would therefore be analogous to, if not synonymous with, stealing something—here, a
reputation for whiteness. The decision, which suggests that a reputation
for whiteness is something owned (hence the ex-colored man's "crime"),
comes full circle to the enabling assumptions of slavery and imperialism
that Du Bois studies.

At the end of Johnson's novel, the ex-colored man explains that he has
given up a career in black music literally in, and for, the name of (the
white) father: "My love for my children makes me glad that I am what I am
and keeps me from desiring to be otherwise." But in the face of "a sacri-
ficed talent," he is unable, in his words, to "repress the thought that, after
all, I have chosen the lesser part, that I have sold my birthright for a mess
of pottage" (JWJ, 211). This irrepressible thought surfaces as the story of
Jacob and Esau, a cultural myth about brothers and inheritance, a *cultural*
insistence that one brother must inherit and the two cannot thereafter
peacefully coexist. He has, that is, chosen the fate of Esau, the oldest son,
over that of Jacob, the chosen one (Genesis 27). Significantly, the ex-
colored man makes the African American the heir to Jacob, progenitor of
a nation, a literal founding father. The iconography of God's chosen people, applied to the Israelites in the Hebrew Bible, was commonly assumed
first by the Puritans in the colonial United States and later, in the nineteenth and early twentieth centuries, by groups typically excluded from
the pale—African Americans, most notably, as well as immigrants. Thus
the ex-colored man expresses his own self-imposed exile through his
relinquishment of an enabling (albeit complicated) cultural trope. Nonetheless, the story of the ex-colored man, who lives the early years of his
life in *actual* ignorance of any African heritage, makes clear that *all*

identity—racial, familial—is fundamentally a legal fiction. His concluding regrets poignantly amplify Du Bois's claim, in "Of the Faith of the
Fathers," that "the price of culture is a Lie" (S, 504).

For Du Bois, the lie is most evident in the deceptions practiced by the
oppressed in order to coexist with the oppressor. But those deceptions in
turn mark deeper distortions and deformities, extending to the oppressor
as well as the oppressed. Such is the insight into the Veil accorded the
mourning father by the loss of his son. And, in response, he wishes himself
to pass on: "If one must have gone, why not I? Why may I not rest me from
this restlessness and sleep from this wide waking?" (S, 510). Wearied from
the struggle, he evidently yearns for rest at any cost. Yet a rhetorical
disjunction belies—or at least complicates—this claim. To make more
grammatical sense, "rest" should be replaced with "wrest": Why may I
not *wrest* me from this restlessness and [wrest] sleep from this wide waking? Beneath the longing for peace is the acknowledgement that he must
continue to struggle, that the "me" he would wrest (or rest) is the creature
of that struggle. Significantly, the substitution of "rest" for "wrest" is
evident only in a written text. The activity of writing—the visible sign of
authorship, which shows the father struggling with the legacy of the Veil—
replaces as it refuses a homeland. The son's legacy is not peace but
struggle, not a revised but a revisionary narrative.

The death of Du Bois's oldest child and only son occasions that struggle
and generates the narrative of *The Souls of Black Folk*. Fatherhood forces
him to confront the meaning of the patronym for African Americans, and
the son's death, in this account, emblematically insists on the symbolic
limitations placed on the development of the black American by a discourse of oppression, limitations that must be transformed into creative
analysis. The insights provided by Burghardt's death might logically send
the father back both to the stock scene of his own racial discovery and to a
contemplation of the "American family" in the reconstructed nation to
establish the terms of the exclusion (or unequal inclusion) of African
Americans and to turn the solemn prose of history into the authorial
struggle with which the father earns and anticipates his rest: "sleep till I
sleep and waken to a baby voice and the ceaseless patter of little feet—
above the Veil" (S, 511).

An implication at the end of the chapter on the son's death becomes the
subject of the following chapter, "Of Alexander Crummell." "The tragedy
of the age," writes Du Bois in that chapter, is "not that men are poor" or

"wicked" or "ignorant, . . . but that men know so little of men" (S, 520). The Veil section of *The Souls of Black Folk* works to chart the habits of perception that shape that knowledge and its corollary, Giddings's "consciousness of kind." In "Of Alexander Crummell," Du Bois writes "the history of a human heart—the tale of a black boy who many long years ago began to struggle with life that he might know the world and know himself" (S, 512). In Crummell's achievements, Du Bois finds a hopeful outcome for the struggle, which led the Episcopal priest, the first rector of Du Bois's grandfather's (necessarily) segregated parish through Europe and Africa and back to the United States, where he founded the American Negro Academy and profoundly influenced Du Bois. The history of this human heart opens into an analogue for the age:

> the nineteenth was the first century of human sympathy,—the age when half wonderingly we began to descry in others that transfigured spark of divinity which we call Myself; when clodhoppers and peasants, and tramps and thieves, and millionaires and—sometimes—Negroes, became throbbing souls whose warm pulsing life touched us so nearly that we half gasped with surprise, crying, "Thou too! Hast Thou seen Sorrow and the dull waters of Hopelessness? Hast Thou known Life?" And then all helplessly we peered into those Other-worlds, and wailed, "O World of Worlds, how shall man make you one?" (S, 514)

In this passage, Du Bois implies an understanding made possible by this history. Human sympathy, seeing self in another, broadens into an understanding of the fluidity of "Myself." Human sympathy makes nations, but it also crosses boundaries; here is consciousness of kind universalized into a Du Boisian ideal of human brotherhood rather than particularized in the service of restrictive cultural prescriptions—the uncanny recast as compassion.

But against that ideal the passage rhetorically counterposes the power of those prescriptions. In the contrastive, or at least divergent, use of "us" and "Negroes," Du Bois depicts the two-ness as a struggle between a master narrative in which "us" is always white and black is always "them" and which excludes "Negroes" and his own experience as a black American. This struggle is evident throughout the Veil section in which the personal strives to be seen in its own terms rather than through those of the politically dominant culture. The grammar of that culture literally compels the narrator's dissociated expression of his own experiences. It is a threatening recognition, since, in the "Other-world" of black America, imperial America confronts not only the alienated aggression it has created, but also the return of its own repressed procedures of alienation—the two-ness that white Americans, riding in the Jim Crow car, may experience as they see themselves through the eyes of their black companions.

Du Bois's narrative of African-American subjectivity is finally not inevitable; instead, the concluding chapters of the Veil sequence present a number of different options. The protagonists—the mourning father, Alexander Crummell, and John Jones—embody ways of responding to the psychosocial dilemmas of the color-line and its constrictive subjectivity, each of which contributes to the analysis of the kinship narrative—and of its grammar—that Du Bois revises in *The Souls of Black Folk*. By the end of *The Souls of Black Folk*, Du Bois has depicted the cultural logic, and the inadequacy, of the third-person pronoun ("we," "us") in the United States. The chapters, unified by their thematic resonances, together constitute a revisionary narrative.

The unified plan for *The Souls of Black Folk* that he outlines in the last chapter, "The Sorrow Songs," offers an aesthetic analogue to a refashioned We the People, a revised symbolic legacy that he hopes to bequeath through the dead son (who shares with his living sister the dedication of *The Souls of Black Folk*). A strain from the sorrow songs heads each chapter of the book, complementing a poetic excerpt, like the partial return of a repressed memory, "a haunting echo of these weird old songs in which the soul of the black slave spoke to men" (*S*, 536).[76] The songs are both, Du Bois explains, the legacy of his grandfather's homesick grandmother, who began a family tradition, and "the articulate message of the slave to the world" (*S*, 538). The sorrow songs are at once African and American, "the singular spiritual heritage of the nation and the greatest gift of the Negro people" (*S*, 537). Significantly, that *singular* heritage is a multiplicity. The music goes through stages in the United States that reflect, for Du Bois, an ideal of cultural existence. Like the chapters of *The Souls of Black Folk*, these stages enrich and develop each other: "The first is African music, the second Afro-American, while the third is a blending of Negro music with the music heard in the fosterland. The result is still distinctively Negro and the method of blending original, but the elements are both Negro and Caucasian. One might go further and find a fourth step in this development, where the songs of white America have been distinctively influenced by the slave songs or have incorporated whole phrases of

Negro melody, as 'Swanee River' and 'Old Black Joe'" (*S*, 540). The formal coexistence of traditional, creolized, and amalgamated cultural expressions marks an ideal of harmonic coexistence. All together, the various permutations of the sorrow songs correspond aesthetically to Du Bois's ideal of a multitude of expressions of difference irreducible to binarisms and difficult, in the end, to categorize. There is some retention and some mixture although even the assimilated music expresses mutuality: both forms change. With that mutuality, and particularly with the fourth step, Du Bois makes radical claims for an indigenous black American culture (Negro) and for the centrality of that culture to *all* American culture. Colors commingle and blend on his canvas like watery paints, distinct and interfused, an image of the reconstructed "we" of his revisionary history.

In the penultimate paragraph of the chapter, and of *The Souls of Black Folk*, Du Bois offers a historical counterpart to his musical vision, which he asserts by challenging the prevailing narrative of history:

> Your country? How came it yours? Before the Pilgrims landed we were here. Here we have brought our three gifts and mingled them with yours: a gift of story and song—soft, stirring melody in an ill-harmonized and unmelodious land; the gift of sweat and brawn to beat back the wilderness, conquer the soil, and lay the foundations of this vast economic empire two hundred years earlier than your weak hands could have done it; the third, a gift of the Spirit. Around us the history of the land has centred for thrice a hundred years; out of the nation's heart we have called all that was best to throttle and subdue all that was worst; fire and blood, prayer and sacrifice, have billowed over this people, and they have found peace only in the altars of the God of Right. Nor has our gift of the spirit been merely passive. Actively we have woven ourselves with the very warp and woof of this nation,—we fought their battles, shared their sorrow, mingled our blood with theirs, and generation after generation have pleaded with a headstrong, careless people to despise not Justice, Mercy, and Truth, lest the nation be smitten with a curse. Our song, our toil, our cheer, and warning have been given to this nation in blood-brotherhood. Are not these gifts worth the giving? Is not this work and striving? Would America have been America without her Negro people? (*S*, 545)

The genius of this passage emerges in its use of the "symbolic geography" and constructed subjectivity of the nation to call for a revised historiography and cultural signification.[77] In this high-blown American rhetoric, Du Bois embraces and revisions the threat of black America as a demonic embodiment of the return of what white America's historical narratives have disavowed: the centrality of an indigenous black population ("her Negro people"). The critique speaks through a narrative traced by the pronouns in this passage, a passage that begins with the direct address of the second person: *Your* country. This is evidently a narrative of possession as well.

The descendants of Africans challenge the claim of possession with the active first-person plural, the "we." The critical moment turns on the recentering of history: "Around us the history of the land has *centred.*" The violence of the rhetoric (*"beat back* the wilderness, *conquer* the soil"), reminiscent of the tropes of Manifest Destiny, is amplified by "throttle and subdue," and at this moment the second person moves into third person, "this people" and "they," ambiguously alluding to white America, black America, or (most likely) both. The trials of a nation's history have potentially forged a peoplehood, a "we." But the first-person plural continues to name only black America, and the subsequent third-person ("their battles") consigns white America unambiguously to the third person. Consistent with the fears of the white nation, fears such as Judge Henderson expresses, white Americans are herein rhetorically replaced by black Americans, the true conspirators with the Spirit. To that "ill-harmonized" nation—like Woodrow Wilson's "unharmonized" land—they offer melody. And the only acts of violence performed by black Americans are those in the service of the nation ("their battles . . . their sorrows"). The threat implied throughout, by contrast, is suggestive and passive, emanating from "the nation's heart" or imposed as "a curse" brought on by the refusal of white Americans to listen to their black compatriots. This is not unlike the jeremiad's story of self-destruction, intoned by Lincoln in the Second Inaugural Address, and passed on from generation to generation in national mythology. But Du Bois color codes the jeremiad; the ritual of affirmation becomes a *strangely* familiar story. It is the threat of becoming, in pronominal parlance, a "they" if "this people" (black Americans) does not join the "we." Reconstitution is even less certain in this vision than reconstruction in Lincoln's, contingent, even more than in Lincoln's, upon expanding the cultural signification of collective subjectivity.

The "we" of this revised history is, of course, both American and black, and it heralds a "we" that reimagines a richly inclusive America, envisioned through the variety and spontaneity of the sorrow songs. The rehistoricized progressive Teutonic narrative comes into visionary conflict with other progressive narratives in which it confronts its own absurdity: the argument that certain races "are of proven inefficiency and not worth the saving" at an earlier time "would have made it difficult for the Teuton to prove his right to life" (*S*, 544). What keeps a history from making white men disappear? "So woefully unorganized is sociological knowledge," Du Bois explains, "that the meaning of progress, the meaning of 'swift' and 'slow' in human doing, and the limits of human perfectability, are veiled, unanswered sphinxes on the shores of science" (*S*, 544–45). Race and, generally, human development have presented mysteries that highlight scientific uncertainty. The meaning of progress becomes the veiled sphinx, the destabilizing question, that explains white America's projection of the Veil onto black America. "Sphinxes" also invoke the aesthetic and technological developments of Africa, which counter the German and American sociological narratives of historical progress with a cyclical model of racial ascendancy. "Meaning" is, by implication, a function of power.

In a speech delivered to the National Association for the Advancement of Colored People more than two decades after the publication of *The Souls of Black Folk*, sociologist Herbert Adolphus Miller complained of the untrustworthiness of history. He lamented the difficulty involved in knowing "whether a historical sequence is causal or chronological" but expressed even more concern over the "perversion of history" by historians writing "decidedly from a nationalistic point of view" and, most of all, over the exclusion "from the whole picture" of "the story of the dominated."[78] Du Bois, who reprinted the speech, "Science, Pseudo-Science and the Race Question," in *Crisis*, had, of course, anticipated and probably influenced Miller's critique in *The Souls of Black Folk* as well as his other work. Yet the real power of *The Souls of Black Folk* comes from his having recognized the inseparability of Miller's distinct concerns. In showing how the effort to tell the story of the dominated necessarily deforms the historical narrative, Du Bois explored the connections among narrative (historical sequence), nationalism, and excluded stories. More than an extensive critique emerged from his inquiry; rather, in those connections, Du Bois sought and developed a new way of writing history, one that could imagine a reconstituted and more inclusive "we." At the same time, Du Bois understood the visionary nature of his project, that the process of analysis required by an inclusive "we" would be ongoing and that there would always be untold stories—that those stories motivated his writing and generated his analysis. For that reason, I have called *The Souls of Black Folk* revisionary rather than revisionist history.

Du Bois concludes *The Souls of Black Folk* with the "After-Thought" in which he expresses the wish that "these crooked marks on a fragile leaf be not indeed / THE END" (*S*, 547). And so they were not. His revisionary inquiries were indeed ongoing, and they took place in a variety of genres and arenas. Yet no later work better captures the author alive to his medium, engaged in a modernist rethinking of the conventions underwriting nineteenth-century narrative. And nowhere is he more keenly sensitive to the formal innovations that grew out of and inspired the endless fashioning and refashioning of the stories of We the People. *The Souls of Black Folk* offers an exuberant aesthetic of uncertainty through which Du Bois turned hindrances into exercises of his inalienable right to strive.

4

A "Losing-Self Sense"

The Making of Americans and

the Anxiety of Identity

The Souls of Black Folk can be read as a fractured narrative; *The Making of Americans* cannot be read in any other way. Whereas Du Bois makes the difficulty he experiences in telling his story an important part of his work, Stein takes the struggle to tell her story to an extreme. Relentless repetitive wordplay disrupts a conventional narrative plot to bear witness to an untold story of the making of Americans. So uncompromising are these disruptions that they not only attest to an untold story, they become the focus of the work, challenging the expectations of the vast majority of Stein's readers today no less than they did in the early decades of the twentieth century. *The Making of Americans* is hard work, difficult enough to make readers wonder whether they wish to continue reading, and why. Many—most, in fact—do not. Nearly one thousand pages of unremitting wordplay leave most readers longing for a story. But that longing is her point. After *The Making of Americans*, the pleasure afforded by comprehensibility may seem a little less innocent, and the plot of a conventional narrative a little more confining. In that discomfort lies Stein's challenge and her legacy.

Stein is typically read in a modernist rather than an American cultural context. Her affiliation with avant-garde art movements in Paris, where she lived her adult life, is a well-known context for her language experiments. Those interested in earlier sources of her stylistic innovation attend to the theories of perception offered by her adored professor William James and the research done in the psychology laboratory of Hugo Münsterberg, where a young Gertrude Stein prepared for medical school.[1] Under James and Münsterberg's direction, she conducted experiments that explored how and why habit diminished attention and influenced what could be seen. James called habit society's "most precious conserving agent."[2] Yet experience did not always conform to or accommodate habit, and, James explained, situations where habits proved insufficient, where there was "hesitation," awakened "explicit thought."[3] In her language experiments, Stein sought to prolong that awakening, to disrupt habits of attention in order to gain insight into the unseen.

Aesthetic and psychological contexts, however, do not fully explain why Stein chose to develop her characteristic style in a work entitled *The Making of Americans.* Exclusive attention to the aesthetic context and stylistic experimentation of the work have obscured her engagement with the cultural issues reflected in the subject of the work.[4] The project grew out of Stein's fictionalized account—and analysis—of the failed marriage of her New York German-Jewish cousin and expanded into a study of culture and character centering on immigrant grandparents and their descendants. Americanization initiatives were well under way in all facets of United States culture, from education to medicine, law to the emerging social sciences, before Stein left for Europe and before she began her magnum opus. And, in her words, "any one is of one's period."[5] Additionally, in the cross-cultural experience of immigrants, Stein could extend her exploration of the disruptions in the habits of attention that had intrigued her as a student of psychology.

Immigrants, for Stein, were selves in transit, between narratives as much as between geopolitical locations. Their status at once manifested and provoked an anxiety of identity that Stein represented as a transition between states of consciousness and that corresponded, in her work, to other experiences involving similar transitions. At the beginning of *The Making of Americans,* the narrator describes the feeling of being old to oneself (the narrative of aging) as "a horrid losing-self sense . . . a horrid feeling, like the hard leaving of our sense when we are forced into sleeping or the coming to it when we are just waking."[6] The "horrid feeling" of these moments grows out of a sense that the self is not coextensive with experience, that the body does not fully represent—or embody—the subject (the "I"): while my body was sleeping, I was somewhere else. The experience is one of alienation rather than transcendence: subjectivity experienced as something other than the body but without the transcendence offered by the concept of the soul. With the drugged, visionary moment between sleeping and wakefulness, Stein theorizes a state of consciousness that explains what is at stake in the making of Americans. To the longing for comprehensibility, for coherence, she traces both the need to accommodate the immigrants within a familiar narrative of cultural identity and the eagerness of many immigrants to be thus accommodated.

In Stein, the frustration caused by endless disruptions forces readers to confront their own longing for the narrative conventions that make a work comprehensible. Asking what we are "refusing when we label a text unreadable," one Stein reader suggests that Stein so thoroughly draws her reader into her work that the reader is threatened with a "loss of identity (fear of failure to differentiate from the mother)."[7] The desire for meaning is, in this formulation, a desire for the distance and boundaries that ensure individuation. In the context supplied by Stein's title, however, the boundaries are marked nationally as well as personally. Character and culture come together not in the fear of merging but in the fear of disappearing into incomprehensibility—into an identification not with a mother (or maternal metaphor) but with an immigrant divested of the cultural narratives, and the familiar terms, that mark personhood. To the *anxiety of identity* that arises from this identification, Stein turns her own and her readers' attention.

Throughout *The Making of Americans*, Stein associates a longing for comprehensibility with a longing for narrative. For her characters, that longing leads to a conformity with internalized cultural expectations that confine them; they find themselves inexplicably unable to make productive choices in their lives. The narrator manifests a similar longing, which compromises her ability to tell a story—and especially to tell the story of the making of Americans. Yet that difficulty is the story of *The Making of Americans;* the disrupted narrative shows what has been repressed and suppressed by that process.

Stein began writing *The Making of Americans* in 1903 but stopped later that year; she did not resume composition until 1906, after she had written the novellas *Q.E.D.* (1903) and *Fernhurst* (1904–1905) and the three character sketches published as *Three Lives* (1906).[8] A letter to her friend Mabel Weeks probably written in 1906 offers some hints that may account for the interruption. She confides:

I am afraid that I can never write the Great American novel. I dn't know how to sell on a margin or to do anything with shorts and longs, so I have to content myself with niggers and servant girls and the foreign population generally. Leo he said there wasn't no art in Lovett's book and then he was bad and wouldn't

tell me that there was in mine so I went to bed very missable but I don't care
there ain't any Tchaikovfsky Pathetique or Omar Kayam or Wagner or Whis-
tler or White Man's Burden or green burlap in mine at least not in the present
ones. Dey is werry simple and werry wulgar and I don't think they will interest
the great American publia.[9]

The "Great American novel" she had planned was her "long book," *The
Making of Americans;* the alternative project described by "niggers and
servant girls and the foreign population generally" refers to the character
studies of a native-born white lower-class woman, a black woman, and an
immigrant woman published as *Three Lives.* That work surfaces in this
letter, descriptively at least, as a disruption of the narrative of *The Making
of Americans.*

Following my formulation for such disruptions, *Three Lives,* in this
letter, should mark the press of an untold story and the expression of an
ill-fitting selfhood. Indirectly, it does both. Stein describes turning from
the Great American Novel she had planned to write upon discovering that
the Great American Novel is both about business and is itself a business
venture prescribed by politics and fashion. In a conscious and defiant
gesture, she rejects the speculation of the market for her observation of the
margins from and about which she writes: instead of selling on a margin,
she offers the margins themselves. The pressing story of those margins is
Three Lives. Hers is a different kind of story, she tells Weeks, a story that
will tell simply all that the abstractions of the socioeconomic system do
not represent. But she is also aware of the lack of audience for her stories.
The margins from which she writes hardly constitute the vision of the
nation that its most powerful potential readers wish to have. And with no
"credit" among the American public—no name on which she can cash
in—Stein doubts that she can earn the "interest" of that public, which her
wordplay casts in Latinate nonsense, "publia."[10]

The American public she describes longs for a self-representation
more compatible with the center of power than with the margins of culture.
The reference to "Lovett's book" in the Weeks letter probably alludes to
the *History of English Literature* by an acquaintance of the Steins, Robert
Morss Lovett, a former student of William James and a favorite classmate
of Du Bois. Lovett's literary history, which might be more in the interest of
the publia's self-representation than Stein's own projects, is antithetical to

everything Stein claims she wants to foreground in her own work.[11] By contrast, Stein's experience working in Baltimore while a medical student at Johns Hopkins University had brought her into contact with another America and with Americans whose stories were poorly served by the official narratives. *Three Lives* determinedly presses the margins on a presumably reluctant audience—not to mention a demonstrably reluctant publishing industry, a possible referent for "publia."

But the ill-fitting selfhood expressed by *Three Lives* was not wholly—or even primarily—political. *Three Lives* supposedly takes the reader into the daily lives and minds of black, lower-class, and immigrant characters. Yet contemporary readers of Stein have seen in these stories evidence of her attempt to project elements of her own forbidden stories—such as her own lesbian love triangle chronicled in her 1903 novella *Q.E.D.*, a story either lost or willfully suppressed until it reemerged in a reference in her 1933 *The Autobiography of Alice B. Toklas*—onto characters whose race, class, or ethnicity made cultural transgressions less threatening to the white middle-class readers presumed to be the largest audience for the Great American Novel.[12]

In the Weeks letter itself, Stein's use of dialect enacts a similar displacement. With her brother Leo's rebuff, she moves into pronunciations that mark a speaker's race, class, or immigrant status, beginning with "missable," which captures her anxiety. She is afraid of being not only miserable but miss-able, negligible, like the margins about which she writes. Clearly she wondered, in spite of her irony, whether she had assumed a lesser portion, and Leo would not reassure her otherwise. His reticence, in particular with reference to Lovett's book, provoked an uncertainty that she could not quite dismiss.

The letter reenacts a disturbance in the process of writing *The Making of Americans* created by Stein's need to come to terms with her own sense of exclusion. The undifferentiated populations, dialect, and racist language strikingly illustrate Toni Morrison's claim that "the fabrication of an Africanist persona is reflexive; an extraordinary meditation on the self; a powerful exploration of the fears and desires that reside in the writerly conscious. It is an astonishing revelation of longing, of terror, of perplexity, of shame, of magnanimity."[13] Stein's letter is just such a revelation, although lower-class and foreign characters join Africanist personae. Her racism and classism are evident, as many readers have observed, in her use of these characters to express her own feelings of estrangement.[14] With her substitution of "niggers and servant girls and the foreign population generally" for her sense of her own marginality, she actually stresses her differences from more than her similarity to those populations, in effect re-placing herself more centrally within a (normalized) white middle-class narrative by those differences. Yet, as the letter suggests, *Three Lives* marked her inability to write the Great American novel. As oppressed groups trouble official stories, Stein's depiction of margins signals her unease with the "middle-class narrative" she claims to be writing in *The Making of Americans.*

Three Lives, and perhaps the Weeks letter, were productive disruptions for *The Making of Americans.* Although there is no indication that she acknowledged her racism or classism, she returned to her original project with a more determined focus on depictions of her own estrangement and her difficulty telling the story she wanted to tell. In *The Making of Americans,* she writes self-consciously from within her limitations. She was indeed a white, middle-class woman of her times, but she was also engaged in an important struggle with herself. *The Making of Americans* grapples with the writer's sense of her complicity in the irresistible pull of the cultural narrative, and the limitations of *Three Lives* and of the sentiments expressed in the Weeks letter are an intrinsic part of that story. *The Making of Americans* demonstrates—and, I shall argue, was intended to demonstrate—that no one can tolerate the kind of incomprehensibility necessary for an ongoing disruption of habits of attention—or of the cultural narrative that reinforces them.

Stein risked ugliness and ridicule to explore what those habits made it nearly impossible to see. In "The Making of Americans," according to the character Alice B. Toklas, Stein "was struggling with her sentences, those long sentences that had to be so exactly carried out."[15] This reference to Stein's precision answers charges of arbitrariness and automatism so frequently leveled against her as it calls attention to her authorship. That authorship entails struggling with *sentences,* with the compulsory regulations of conventional grammatical units and the culture they reflect. Stein shows how disruptions of those conventions precipitate an incomprehensibility symbolically tantamount to nonexistence, a "horrid losing-self sense." The fear of self-loss corresponds, in this work, to the fear of not being comprehended or comprehensible: the estrangement of a terrain that is more than alien, that simply makes no sense. *The*

Making of Americans charts that terrain, asking readers to look deeply into the terror of displacement and to understand that terror as intrinsic to a conception of selfhood rendered almost unquestionable by the fear of incomprehensibility.

"Something Not Ourselves": Cultural Anxiety and the Immigrant Narrative

Immigrant narrators who depict themselves as Americans, who spell out their changes of being—or conversions—into Americans, assure an anxious native-born population that they intend not to disrupt but to assume an American identity. Their narratives function like turn-of-the-century historical narratives: they bear witness to an American identity, and they specify the terms of that identity. They tell the story, in the words of Danish immigrant and progressive journalist Jacob Riis, of "the making of an American."[16] Experiences incompatible with that narrative are forgotten, recast, or suppressed in the process. But when they reemerge through contradictions, rhetorical disjunctions, and even expressions of discomfort, they mark the impossibility of a fully successful conversion. In *The Making of Americans* Stein calls attention to those contradictions and disruptions to analyze the anxiety experienced and generated by immigrants at the turn of the century and thereby tell the story of the making of Americans.

Stein was not alone in her interest. Americanization was an important topic and heavily legislated process of the period. The anxiety evoked specifically by the immigrant's unsuccessful, or incomplete, conversion was explored in particular depth by Horace Kallen, a former student of William James, in an essay in which he issued the doctrine that he would later call "cultural pluralism." Offered in consecutive numbers of the *Nation* in February 1915, Kallen's "Democracy Versus the Melting-Pot: A Study of American Nationality" responds to *The Old World in the New,* a work in which the prominent sociologist Edward Alsworth Ross decries the impact of the immigrant on American culture and calls for the restriction of immigration. For Kallen, the homogeneity advocated by Ross is not only antithetical to the spirit of America, but it is the result of an unfortunate yet widely held misperception of American identity. He recognizes the "ethnic dissimilarity" that so troubled observers such as Ross as "one of the inevitable consequences of the democratic principle on which our theory of government is based."[17] Kallen does not argue with the diversity that troubled Ross and his cohort; he agrees that the new immigration had indeed rendered impossible "that inward unanimity of action and outlook which make a national life" (DMP, 219). And he acknowledges that the principles of the American nation had "worked together with economic greed and ethnic snobbishness" to bring about the conversion not of the immigrants but of "the early American nation," which, consistent with the concerns of restrictionists like Ross, is "in the process of becoming a true federal state" (DMP, 219). The "great republic" described by Kallen consists of precisely the "federation or commonwealth of nationalities" feared not only by Ross but by more willing assimilationists such as Theodore Roosevelt or Woodrow Wilson (DMP, 219).

The anxiety generated by the presence of immigrants is expressed with particular force in a comparison offered in a private correspondence between Kallen and his former Harvard English professor, Barrett Wendell.[18] The author of *A Literary History of America* (and the first professor to introduce "American literature" into the Harvard curriculum) is identified by Kallen in "Democracy Versus the Melting-Pot" only as "a great American man of letters, who has better than any one I know interpreted the American spirit to the world" (DMP, 194). "We are submerged," writes Wendell, "beneath a conquest so complete that the very name of us means something not ourselves. . . . I feel as I should think an Indian might feel, in the face of ourselves that were" (DMP, 194). The distance between "the very name of us" and "ourselves" marks a discomfiting disjunction in the narrative of identity: an ill-fitting selfhood. Indians emblematize the anxiety Wendell feels when he confronts the migrants and immigrants. Although immigrants were frequently blamed for the high crime rates in the populous areas in which they lived, Wendell is less concerned with actual violence imported by the refugees and fortune-seekers who were making their way to the New World than with the cultural violation they embodied. By comparison, he becomes an Indian; certainly, the very name "Indians" means something not themselves. In a disturbing analogy, Wendell summons the destruction of a culture to mark the destruction not just of another culture, but of the very culture ("American") responsible for the original destruction.

The analogy is even more complicated. His comparison itself forces him to acknowledge an important distinction. Face to face with the Indian,

Wendell must confront his own descent from immigrants. Uncannily, Kallen's "'hyphenated' American" demonstrates that "a hyphen attaches, in things of the spirit, also to the 'pure' English American" (DMP, 217). The conquest feared by Wendell follows from the logic displayed by Roosevelt when he cautions that hyphenated Americans—in this case, white Americans—risk becoming "nothing at all." What is really at stake for both Wendell and Roosevelt is their recognizability, guaranteed by the control of their ethnic and economic cohort over the means of cultural production and dissemination—that is, over the production and dissemination of their official narrative of identity. Adopting a rhetorical strategy as apocalyptic as Wendell's and Roosevelt's, the German-Jewish immigrant Kallen contends that people "cannot change their grandfathers" and insists that "Jews or Poles or Anglo-Saxons, in order to cease being Jews or Poles or Anglo-Saxons, would have to cease to be" (DMP, 220). Nothing less than social existence is at stake in these debates.

Those who feared "race suicide" understood and represented the threat as a challenge, literal and metaphorical, to the American family. The prominent statistician who supervised and renovated the censuses in 1870 and 1880, Massachusetts Institute of Technology President Francis Amasa Walker, used the information gathered in the census to explain how liberal immigration policies would destroy the American family as an outcome of immigration. In "Immigration and Degradation," an essay that appeared in the August 1891 issue of the *Forum,* Walker statistically demonstrated a decrease in the indigenous (white) birth rate that he traced to immigration. A lowered standard of living brought about by a surplus of labor and the immigrants' putative willingness to work for substandard wages had resulted, claims Walker, in the trend among native-born white Americans to marry later and to have fewer children. More than a decade later, political economist John R. Commons, in his 1904 piece, "Racial Composition of the American People: Amalgamation and Assimilation," drew on Walker's work to insist that the "question of the 'race suicide' of the American or colonial stock should be regarded as the most fundamental of our social problems, or rather as the most fundamental consequence of our social and industrial institutions."[19] Commons seconds the warning of Theodore Roosevelt that "if the men of the nation are not anxious . . . to be fathers of families, and if the women do not recognize that the greatest thing for any woman is to be a good wife and mother, . . . that nation has cause to be alarmed about its future" (218).[20] "Race suicide" evidently resulted from a challenge to the reproduction of established gender roles as well as to the reproduction of children. And the crisis facing the *literal* "American" (traditional white middle-class) family threatened the nation, the metaphoric "American family," with potential extinction, with becoming "nothing at all."

It is therefore not surprising that assimilation efforts used the traditional American family as both metaphor and medium to Americanize immigrants. The "Character Factory" described by journalist Day Allen Willey for his 1909 *Putnam's Monthly and the Reader* audience, for example, made gendered family relations the basis for the conversion of immigrants into Americans. In "Americans in the Making: New England's Method of Assimilating the Alien," Willey articulates the domestic principle of what are essentially four-year colleges:

> the hundred and odd members of the student body are also members of one family. During the four years they become part of a household which as far as possible is patterned after the typical New England home. They become accustomed to opening the day with religious exercises. The young women assist in the preparation of the meals and the care of the buildings, and thus are taught the vocation of the American housewife, while the male students engage in gardening and do other work about the premises, by which they partly pay for their living expenses.[21]

Carefully delineated gender roles mitigate "the peril which threatens [the Yankee's] home" introduced by "the number of foreigners yearly settling on Puritan soil" by training "young men and young women . . . to become apostles of Americanism among those of their own blood" (457, 462). Students become Americans by simulating or replicating rather than marrying into the American family, and they become missionaries, returning to their ethnic ("blood") communities to domesticate them by reproducing the gendered family structure preserved and transmitted in the Character Factories.

So important was the family paradigm to Jacob Riis that he advocated a modification of the Chinese Exclusion Act of 1880 in his 1890 journalistic study of urban immigrant neighborhoods, *How the Other Half Lives*. Riis ends "Chinatown," probably the least sympathetic section of his work, with an alternative to banishing the Chinese, whom he calls "in no sense a desirable element of the population": "I would have the door opened wider—for his wife; make it a condition of his coming or staying that he bring his wife with him. Then, at least, he might not be what he now is and remains, a homeless stranger among us."[22] Although Riis does not advocate miscegenation, he makes the increasingly common suggestion that a family would lead to a *home*, an investment—literally and figuratively—in the nation, which would motivate the alien's Americanization.

The family, which legally defines both genealogical and property relations, shapes identity in relation to inheritance. It is the earliest and most immediate socializing force, and its paradigm of self-abridgment is the handmaiden of culture. The "family plot" is the child's first narrative, which each family member simultaneously enters into and transforms (re-members). The re-membering is at the same time a remembering shaped by a prescribed narrative of identity. The past, although appropriated by the present, always leaves a trace by which each member is comprehended—a kind of narrative family resemblance. To deviate too much from the family plot is to risk disrupting the narrative of identity. Hence, the story that constitutes the child's remembering is a carefully circumscribed account. It prepares the child for an official story of which it is also the earliest manifestation.

Restrictionists and assimilationists alike anxiously sought to safeguard the American family. But if immigrants appeared to pose a threat to the family, so much more did they embody the challenge at the heart of the anxiety. It was, after all, immigrants rather than native-born white Americans who were asked to exchange one family structure for another and one narrative of identity for a radically different one. Studies abounded, at the turn of the century, decrying the disintegration of the immigrant family as the children were Americanized into rejecting their Old World parents. In 1902, for example, philosopher and educator John Dewey called attention to the too rapid "de-nationalization" of immigrant children: "They lose the positive and conservative value of their own native traditions, their own native music, art, and literature. They do not get complete initiation into the customs of their new country, and so are frequently left floating and unstable between the two. They even learn to despise the dress, bearing, habits, language, and beliefs of their parents—many of which have more substance and worth than the superficial putting on of the newly adopted habits."[23] While Russian-Jewish immigrant Mary Antin, author of *The Promised Land*, describes her father's leading role in the family's Americanization, for example, she also describes his increasing inability to provide for his growing family in the United States. Antin protests, perhaps too strongly, that she is not "disowning my father and mother of the flesh," yet she asserts forcefully that she "soon chose [her] own books, and built [her] a world of [her] own."[24] Freud's concept of the "family romance," in which the child rejects the parents only to replace them with their *social* superiors, cultural heroes, is alive and well in Antin's account of the important people—writers, teachers, politicians—who, unlike her parents, enabled her to develop her talents.[25] Her parents, by contrast, helped her most of all by not obstructing her. Americanization initiatives in education and settlement work—from the Massachusetts character factories to Chicago's Hull-House—sought in various ways to negotiate that exchange and reproduce the American family.

Those initiatives were especially important since the state did nothing to discourage the disaffiliation of young immigrants or of the children of older immigrants from their Old World families. Naturalization legislation enacted in 1906 symbolized the state's prerogative to enable and even encourage the immigrants to revise their personal narratives of identity by making a name change, at the court's discretion, a lawful part of the naturalization process. Although designed to document the influx of immigrants, this clause made it possible for an immigrant to exchange the name of an Old World father (or, in some cultures, the hyphenated name of parents) for a name that signaled a new identity. The law itself took the place of the father (or parents) when it conferred that identity—when, that is, it sanctified the immigrant's conversion. This clause in effect allowed the law to negotiate the desire for self-creation—to maintain a proprietorship over the rights and privileges of citizenship, but also to recognize and contend with a subject's impulse to self-definition. The clause allowing for a name change legislated that impulse, providing a controlled outlet.

Yet the very comprehensiveness of this legislation, which now included sample forms, moved toward a more standardized documentation to be used in the making of Americans. Although largely formal rather than substantive, the increasingly prescribed (legally dictated) oaths of allegiance worked against the indeterminacy that Stein dramatized in her text. In the ritualized, performative language of an oath, would-be citizens were asked to abridge themselves of any distinctive voices, at precisely the moment when their *differences* were pronounced by the oath itself. This, like previous naturalization legislation, levied severe penalties against those who in any way tampered with the process, since counterfeiting would call the proprietorship of the law into question. The state had to reserve to itself the transformative power to make citizens. In that sense, the oath-taker occupied a theoretically dangerous position: the danger posed by the mimic, who brings the repressed closest to the surface—in this case, legal proprietorship of the citizen's rights and, by extension, the terms through which personhood is reproduced.

The dominant cultural mandate for the (European) immigrant narrator was to forget, or suppress, the hyphen, to assert his or her successful Americanization. It was a mandate more easily met by some than by others, but most immigrant narratives from this period manifest in varying degrees both the effort to suppress it and the impossibility of fully doing so. Personally as well as historically, the Puritans' Atlantic voyage served as the archetypal moment of Americanization. That voyage constituted an originary moment for a cultural plot onto which European immigrants could superimpose their own journeys to what Mary Antin calls the Promised Land. The prevalence of the verb "to make" (as in the making of Americans) in these accounts and the conspicuous use of the passive voice to describe the moment of transformation imagine American identity as a bestowal, a construction, but also as a miracle that builds on as it replaces spiritual conversion. The immigrants in many such accounts rehearse the Puritans' miraculous genealogy. As the Puritans descended spiritually, through a rhetorical sleight of hand, from the Israelites rather than the English, so the immigrants adopted a spiritual genealogy from the Puritans. The immigrant may never allude to the Puritans directly; Antin, for example, continually invokes her hero George Washington, the subject of her first published poem, rather than any Puritan ancestor. Yet New England's early settlers are the indwelling spirits who formally and meta-phorically legitimate her spiritual conversion to Americanization. She is "transpla[n]ted to the new soil" as the early English colonists established "plantations" on the soil of the New World (*PL,* xxi).[26]

The sea change requires a change of status that manifests the impact of formulations such as Barrett Wendell's or Theodore Roosevelt's. Antin insists on her completed conversion in her widely-circulated immigrant narrative *The Promised Land,* serialized in the *Atlantic Monthly* in 1911–12 and published in 1912 by Houghton Mifflin.[27] The account begins with the writer's dramatic assertion of her own death: "I was born, I have lived, and I have been made over. Is it not time to write my life's story? I am just as much out of the way as if I were dead, for I am absolutely other than the person whose story I have to tell. Physical continuity with my earlier self is no disadvantage. I could speak in the third person and not feel that I was masquerading. I can analyze my subject, I can reveal everything; for *she,* and not *I,* is my real heroine. My life I have still to live; her life ended when mine began" (*PL,* xxii). Antin uses a shift in pronouns to signal the outcome of her being made over, or, to use a word favored by Antin in her narrative, *Americanized.* The narrative that links the speaking subject to the "absolutely other" is a narrative of identity, but one that conspicuously covers up a deliberate discontinuity rather than supplies a forgotten connection.

Antin cannot successfully suppress ambiguous traces of an incomplete conversion. Instead, she expresses a longing to be rid of a double-consciousness that she finds painful: "I long to forget. I think I have thoroughly assimilated my past—I have done its bidding—I want now to be of to-day. It is painful to be consciously of two worlds. The Wandering Jew in me seeks forgetfulness. I am not afraid to live on and on, if only I do not have to remember too much" (*PL,* xxii). Her longing to forget is itself like the clinging garment of a constraining past, straining insistently against her attempts to progress. The tale is to be a "charm" that she tells, "like the Ancient Mariner, . . . in order to be rid of it" (*PL,* xxii). She longs for catharsis, a recitation that will prove a liberation. With reference to the legend of the Wandering Jew, she displays a retention of her culture that betrays an unassimilated past and an incompletely assimilated self. Troubled less by what she has forgotten than by her inability to forget, Antin is haunted by a painful double-consciousness, which, unlike Du Bois, she does not celebrate for its critical potential. Instead, she wishes to exorcize her memories as though they were demons. She longs to cover up her past, a disappearance for which, significantly, she uses the word "assimilated." The passage tells the gruesome, gripping story of the undead who prays for peace through annihilation.

Similar ambivalences and ambiguities are expressed in the less explicitly complicated narrative of Jacob Riis, *The Making of an American* (1901). In an even more obviously archetypal conversion narrative, the Christian Riis is miraculously resurrected to become an American. Recovering from a serious illness while visiting his family in Denmark, Riis languishes, "sick and discouraged," until he catches sight of "the flag of freedom" on a passing ship. Suddenly completely recovered, Riis "thanked God, and, like unto the man sick of the palsy, arose . . . and went home, healed" (JR, 283). Here Riis, a man very much of his time, makes symbolic use of what James C. Malin calls a "nationalistic explosion" registered by the preponderance of centennial celebrations and the increase in patriotic societies and rituals surrounding the flag in the last decade of the nineteenth century. Riis was writing against a backdrop in which, for example, James Bailey Upham used his magazine, the *Youth's Companion,* to publish an early version of the Pledge of Allegiance and to finance a drive to supply every school with a flag.[28] In this personal and cultural moment, the sight of the flag makes Riis recognize himself as an American, and, like Antin, he introduces the moment with a change of pronouns: "*I* have told the story of the making of an American. There remains to tell how *I* found out that *he* was made and finished at last" (JR, 283; emphasis added). Riis's "he" refers not, like Antin's "she," to his prior existence, his preconversion self, but to the moment of his conversion, when he first recalls experiencing himself as an American. "He" is the American Riis believes he has become. Yet the third-person subject thus deployed bears witness to the disavowed alienation of this moment. An exultant Riis unconsciously gives expression to an otherness by which he is apparently untroubled. Americanization in both narratives names an estrangement against which both writers struggle, however unconsciously, and it is an estrangement that both narratives struggle to cover up. Like Du Bois's John Jones at the end of the story, both writers enact the disturbed subjectivity consequent to their Americanization through third-person self-references. The disturbances surface during the act of telling. Each writer indeed seems to embrace an American identity, but the "I" never fully represses—or assimilates—the past. The Ancient Mariner lives to tell his tale again and again.

For Horace Kallen, such apostles of Americanization, among whom he specifically names Riis and Antin, "protest too much, they are too self-conscious and self-centered, their 'Americanization' appears too much like an achievement, a *tour de force,* too little like a growth" (DMP, 193). It is unnatural, concealing, "underneath an excellent writing, a dualism and the strain to overcome it" (DMP, 193). To be too insistently Americanized, argues Kallen, is manifestly not to be American. Kallen's immigrants bring to light the Americanization of all Americans, each generation anew, as many early twentieth-century manuals for the education and Americanization of immigrants were also careful to note. The power (and danger) of Kallen's immigrants lies in their resemblance to native-born Americans. "The same dualism is apparent in different form among the [native-born] Americans," he notes, "and the strain to overcome it seems even stronger" (DMP, 193). The Americanized writer demonstrates a struggle that is even more deeply buried, and more fundamentally troubling, in native-born white Americans.

Stein's work builds on the same premise. In *The Making of Americans* she emblazons the violence inherent in the forgetting, and in the Americanization, and insists on precisely those disturbances feared alike by restrictionists and assimilationists and registered in immigrant narratives, such as Antin's and Riis's, as unsuccessfully repressed discontinuities. As she tells the tale, Stein underscores what Antin and Riis would conceal, and her narrative accordingly becomes the site of pronounced disruptions and highlighted disturbances, registering untold stories. For Stein, this speculative activity happens on the level of language, through the foregrounding of narrative strategies and through words used disjunctively and repetitively. Stein knew that her work prompted more contemplation than an often unsympathetic press conceded. "They always say . . . that my writing is appalling," she remarks in *The Autobiography of Alice B. Toklas*, "but they always quote it and what is more they quote it correctly" (*ABT*, 66). Her work eludes paraphrase but must be cited directly, and the syntactical performance reduces the critic who would have the last word to an explicator who must concede uncertainty.

To be thus quoted is always to remain an *alien* rather than *unassimilated* voice. The difference lies in cultural perception: the alien is recognizably other; the unassimilated is hauntingly among but not of, disturbingly unrecognizable. It is those unassimilated voices that similarly articulate the nuances, or cultural dimensions, of the law. Stein embodies them in the immigrant in whose name always resides a trace of alienation, the memory of a forgetting. "Immigrant" does not distinguish between alien and citizen; an immigrant may be already or not yet naturalized (although the name implies the intention of naturalization). The immigrant, who can be represented but never quite adequately, embodies precisely the irresolution that Stein seeks. She therefore brings immigrant and psychological narratives together in a rewriting of the return of the repressed as a depiction of cultural identity.

In *The Making of Americans,* Stein uses the family as the metaphor and site of socialization to bring psychological and cultural narratives together. The full title of the work explains the terms of her project: "The Making of Americans / being a history of a family's progress." *The Making of Americans* indeed traces the progress of an immigrant family from the

Hersland grandparents' decision to immigrate through several generations of Herslands and Dehnings (the first David Hersland's grandson, Alfred, marries Julia Dehning) in the United States. But an obscure plot and experimental prose more than complicate Stein's use of "history." No one could mistake *The Making of Americans* for an ordinary immigrant narrative. And divorce, despair, and early death among the third generation bespeak a decomposition that adds irony to the word "progress."

Stein's title can also be read as the description of the process of Americanization: the making of Americans is the history of a family's progress. An official narrative of American identity, in other words, is a family narrative. Stein means more by this equation than that the nation has used a familiar—and familial—rhetoric; rather, for her, as Janice Doane has observed, "the middle-class family has produced and structured meaning in ways that have become entrenched by centuries of repetition. Its comfort as an explanatory framework is obvious: . . . one's identity 'explained' by genealogy."[29] If genealogy supplies the logic and language of identity, family relations provide its structure. Identity is marked both by and within the family, which is the cornerstone of socialization.

Stein begins her narrative of immigration with a family struggle. But the genesis and terms of that struggle and its significance to a cultural narrative must be teased out of the two following paragraphs; *The Making of Americans* seems to begin three separate times:

> Once an angry young man dragged his father along the ground through his own orchard. "Stop!" cried the groaning old man at last, "Stop! I did not drag my father beyond this tree."

> It is hard living down the tempers we are born with. We all begin well, for in our youth there is nothing we are more intolerant of than our own sins writ large in others and we fight them fiercely in ourselves; but we grow old and we see that these our sins are of all sins the really harmless ones to own, nay that they give a charm to any character, and so our struggle with them dies away.

> It has always seemed to me a rare privilege, this, of being an American, a real American, one whose tradition it has taken scarcely sixty years to create. We need only realise our parents, remember our grandparents and know ourselves and our history is complete. (*MA*, 3)

Lisa Ruddick reads confusion and ambivalence in what she aptly labels the "unassimilated voices" of the text's beginnings (LR, 57).[30] But each marks a separate strand of Stein's analysis of the making of Americans: a family narrative, a psychological narrative, and a culminating cultural narrative. The apparent discontinuities between each of these paragraphs are tantalizing, calling for connections and drawing attention to the problem of beginning, *"the first step,"* as Edward Said notes, *"in the intentional production of meaning."*[31] Every narrative must begin somewhere, Stein suggests, and that beginning is neither natural nor arbitrary; it represents a choice. In what is anything but a smooth start, Stein makes visible the process of beginning a narrative. Each unassimilated voice of this opening contributes to an aesthetic of disruption through which Stein works to depict as she problematizes the originary moment of any narrative, literary or cultural. In a counternarrative that works, somewhat like Du Bois's, through juxtaposition rather than linear progression, she stresses the gaps, the discontinuities in which, like another contemporary, Sigmund Freud, she finds what has been repressed.[32]

The first paragraph recounts a struggle between father and son, with the implication of violence. The threat of patricide constitutes the pre-text of *The Making of Americans* as it generates civilization in Freud's *Totem and Taboo.* Yet whereas Freud hypothesizes a dispute over leadership of a horde, and especially over possession of its women, as the source of the dispute, Stein describes a dispute with no apparent object. The humor of the parable comes from the reader's surprise, and initial relief, that the son's violence is traditional and that the father fears only that the son will transgress a *physical* boundary marked by "this tree." But the son's threatened transgression would challenge the ritual itself. Ritual offers a controlled outlet for the expression of violence, which the son's potential defiance threatens to unleash.

The second paragraph describes the resignation of self-acceptance. The possibility for change born of recognizing oneself in another gives way to a valorization of one's own sins. With the predictability of this collective drama, Stein again suggests ritualized rather than genuine crisis. The crisis resolves almost magically—"a charm" such as Antin longs for—not only in self-acceptance but, more importantly, in an acceptance of deviant traits as *sins;* that is, in the acceptance of a moral discourse. And it ends in an intact and carefully preserved self conceived as an inheritance: "our sins are of all sins the really harmless ones to own." The juxtaposition of paragraphs tempts us to superimpose the second paragraph on the first, and that superimposition recontextualizes the struggle in the orchard as a struggle over identity. The son sees his "own sins"—including, evidently, his temperament—in his father. He struggles for self-awareness and toward change.

The word "own" links the two paragraphs. A number of meanings converge in the second paragraph when the word "own" is deployed as an adjective (own sins) and as a verb (harmless ones *to own*). To own one's sins is to acknowledge them, or claim possession of them. A *trait*, in effect, is reconceived as a *possession*. One outcome of this transformation is the suggestion that the self-acceptance that marks the end of the struggle to change is related to the reconceptualization of *self* as *owner*. Self-acceptance entails the (unwitting) acceptance of a concept of personhood derived from a prescribed narrative of identity that itself becomes a cultural legacy, transmitted as a psychological (and implicitly legal) inheritance.

This perspective changes the terms of the struggle between the son and the father in the first paragraph, a struggle that may turn on the rhetorical ambiguity of "his own orchard": whose orchard is it, the son's or the father's? The contest between father and son may be a property dispute, but, on a deeper level, Stein subtly casts it as a struggle over the name of "owner," which is to say, over the name of the father that governs inheritance—both property and genealogical relations—and legal and cultural identity. Because their common cultural narrative conceives personhood through ownership, the son struggles against the terms of that narrative represented by his father. In Freud's narrative, civilization originates in taboos put in place in the name of the father to forestall the orgy of fratricidal violence threatening to escalate from a patricide.[33] Stein's implied narrative of culture similarly posits tradition as a defense against violence. In his fear of his son's transgression, then, the father being dragged through the orchard gives vent to an anxiety concerning the premises of the cultural narrative of personhood that supplies the meaningful terms of his existence.

But the son will not transgress the boundaries, as the second paragraph assures us. In fact, his violence is itself traditional, very much in keeping with the spirit of American conquest, such as Woodrow Wilson expresses in his 1897 *Atlantic Monthly* essay, "The Making of the Nation." Wilson lauds the spirit that generates government from plantation, remarking that "it ought to be nothing new and nothing strange to those who have read the history of the English race the world over to learn that conquests have a thousand times sprung out of the initiative of men who have first followed private interest into new lands like speculators, and then planned their occupation and government like statesmen" (MN, 7). The son in Stein's opening is, in two senses, a speculator, one who wants to push past both territorial and psychological boundaries. In the context of Stein's work, the orchard serves as a cultural plot of land, the site of the son's Americanization. Only context determines whether such speculation as Wilson describes enacts, extends, or breaks the law; for its context, hence its comprehensibility, the activity of speculation depends upon a narrative. In Wilson's formulation, a cultural narrative supplies the legal terms of ownership that turn land speculators into governors, or statesmen. Their speculative activity is thereby renarrativized as a conquest leading to ownership, to an extension of geopolitical boundaries through which the cultural narrative is redeployed rather than challenged. Likewise the (psychological) speculators of Stein's second paragraph submit to a collective narrative as owners, seeing that their "own sins are of all sins the really harmless ones to own." Any challenge is thus comprehended through a process of renarrativization. The son does not, and cannot, drag the father "beyond this tree."

Beginning her study of the making of Americans with an analysis of the struggle over ownership and over the patronym, Stein demonstrates the gendering (and, less consciously or explicitly, the racializing) of that drama. Surely she cannot struggle on equal terms over the patronym. The engendering of the American family thus generates her untold—or, in this case, indirectly told—story. Stein represents her own relation to that family, to the terms of an American identity, through the metaphor of her authorship. The law defines authorship, like personhood, through ownership. Stein marks her struggle with the defining terms of the law in an act of plagiarism.[34] She borrows the opening parable, as many readers have noted, from Aristotle's *Nichomachean Ethics* (significantly, his advice to his son).[35] She superimposes her own—or owned—story onto a prior narrative, the genealogical struggle between father and son. The genesis of her act of authorship in an act of theft figures her sense of her intrusion on a governing cultural narrative when she tries to *speculate*, to make visible what the culture has collectively agreed not to see. She steals her way into this work, writing, she suggests, against the law.

Her story—the (conspicuously gendered) family narrative of the making of Americans—emerges from between the cracks, from the actual blank space between the second and third paragraphs on the page in explicit engagement with the written text. In particular, Stein marks the gap in the narrative cover-up through which Americans are made. The space between the second and third paragraphs represents the ocean voyage, the sea change from which Americans emerge—not only immigrants, as Kallen also observes, but all subjects of the nation, who must also be Americanized—who must, that is, exchange personal experience for the comprehensive identity implied by a "complete history." The "complete" history to which the narrator refers in the third paragraph begins, as Antin would like to, by forgetting what preceded the journey to the New World. The space between the second and third paragraphs implies a new beginning, like the immigrant's story in which self-authorizing Americans repossess their pasts, parents, grandparents, even history itself to reach what Sara Smolinsky (in Anzia Yezierska's *Bread Givers*) thinks of as the "bottom starting-point of becoming a person."[36] But it is a forgetting at once analogous to and predicated on an act of violence, the figurative annihilation of one's ancestors tantamount to the "self"-mutilation implicitly evinced by Antin and Riis. It is a violence, moreover, endemic to a nationalist discourse. "Forgetting, . . . even . . . historical error," and in particular forgetting the inevitable originary act of violence, French man of letters Ernest Renan told his Sorbonne audience in 1882, "is a crucial factor in the creation of a nation, which is why progress in historical studies often constitutes danger for [the principle of] nationality."[37] Hence, the narrative cover-up, or renarrativizing, generated by a cultural plot. Stein's narrator "mean[s] to tell" the story of "the old people in a new world, the new people made out of the old, . . . for that is what really is and what [she] really know[s]" (*MA*, 3). But Stein's telling differs from the conventional immigrant narratives because she wants to tell the story of that telling—of the difference between what the narrator *means* to tell and of what she can actually tell. Stein's real crime, as she understands it, is her attempt to analyze official narratives of the making of Americans.

That analysis, for Stein, centers on legal identity: the importance of the patronym and the narrative that confers it. The section on the second-generation David Hersland, who literally inherits the full name of the father and grandfather, begins with the narrator's meditation on illegitimacy: "I do ask some . . . if they would mind it if they found out that they did have the name they had then and *had been having been born* not in the

family living they are then living in, if they had been born illegitimate. I
ask some . . . if they would very much dislike it, if they would make a
tragedy of it, if they would make a joke of it, if they found they had in them
blood of some kind of being that was a low kind to them" (*MA*, 724;
emphasis added). David Hersland is drawn to the patricidal implications
of illegitimacy. All the Hersland children struggle with their father: "It
was against him inside, and strongly always around them, that they had to
do the fighting for their freedom" (*MA*, 45). Yet none achieves that illusory
freedom.[38]

In the wordplay of this passage, Stein embeds an explanation of the
legal construction of personhood and, in particular, its relation to comprehension. The first sentence temporarily dissolves into grammatical
confusion in the string of participles of being and having: "if they found
out that they did have the name they had then and had been having been
born." To make the sentence comprehensible, the reader must punctuate
it, thereby establishing a relation between being and having; a relation
between these terms, articulated as self-ownership, is also the cornerstone
of legal identity in the United States (legal *being* defined through the right
to own). Stein calls attention to the words *have* and *be* through their surfeit,
which makes the sentence hard to read, especially the unnecessary addition of *having been* (had been having been born). In particular, the repetitions underscore the two meanings of *have*, as a verb of possession (have
the name) and auxiliary verb (had been having been born). In this sentence, when the verb of possession (having the name) becomes an auxiliary verb, it marks illegitimacy—or, dispossession. The meaning of the
sentence is clearest if "having" becomes a turning point, working first as a
verb of possession and then an auxiliary verb: "the name they had then
and had been having" *until* the discovery of "having been born not in the
family living they are then living in." With this discovery, "the name they
had then" becomes also "the name they . . . had been," which is to say,
the *name* confers (legal) *being:* the right to possess the name and the right
to possess that is *marked* by the name. The threat of the past participle
("had been having") is the threat of losing the name that confers legal
being ("had been"). Comprehension depends upon defining "having,"
which is, interestingly, also the task of the law. The sentence, like the law,
works out a relation between being and having; in turn, the law, not unlike
this phrase, makes experience comprehensible when it defines being
through (and as) having. The difficulty of Stein's prose, as I have noted,

makes most readers long for comprehension. Many opt out. But if we confront our desire for comprehension, we can begin to understand, by analogy, what is at stake in even the most hypothetical challenge to the familiar terms of a cultural narrative. David, at least, does not drag his father "beyond this tree."

The challenge that David refuses is the challenge that his grandfather, also named David Hersland, must face in *The Making of Americans,* the consequence of a kind of cultural illegitimacy. With that challenge, Stein shows how ownership configures—and genders—identity. For the Old World David Hersland, immigration means dispossession: "he never wanted to lose anything he ever had had around him. He did not want to go to a new world" (*MA*, 37). For his wife, however, immigration represents possibility—economic and social possibility—and it is for her that David agrees to go: "Alright he would go, they would all go and get rich there, Martha could fix it if she wanted so badly to have it, she would be always talking to him about it. Martha could fix it anyway she liked it, yes it would be nice to have all of them get rich there like the neighbors who were writing all the time how rich they had it" (*MA*, 37). Martha takes possession of the neighbors' narratives and writes her family into an American script in which economic success holds forth the possibility for ownership. It is important to understand this desire not as the desire to own but as the desire for the *potential* to own. Martha is more comfortable than David with possibility.

David likes selling his possessions, the human activity of ongoing negotiation, "the feeling of all the doing and the moving and the being important to all of them and everybody always talking" (*MA*, 38). But he does not like the material dispossession that marks the end of the exchange. Without a system that recognizes ownership, outside the law (the immigrant's betwixt and between), David's *potential* to own signifies nothing. His loss of ownership threatens him with a loss of self, an anxiety that runs throughout *The Making of Americans.* He is the figure of unaccommodated man who experiences dispossession as displacement: "It made poor David Hersland very sad to see [another man] standing [in his shop], chopping, talking, selling, wiping his hands on his apron, acting as if it had all always belonged to him, now when there was no place anymore anywhere for Hersland, a place that really belonged to him" (*MA*, 37–38). Stein's interest in this moment stems less from a belief in literal cultural divestment (the historical denial that she spoofs in the third paragraph of

The Making of Americans) than in the male immigrant's *experience* of such a divestment. David's desire to own is a desire to have the potential to participate in the ongoing negotiation of human affairs for which he needs a recognizable position constituted not only by material conditions but by a shared perception of those conditions and a shared mythology about what they mean.

David's patronym, Hersland, inscribes the terms of his conflict. His quest for "a place that really belonged to him" seems futile in light of a name in which "land" is modified by the feminine possessive pronoun, "hers." Significantly, *Hers*land inscribes the possessive pronoun (hers) rather than the possessive adjective (her)—as in Charlotte Perkins Gilman's *Herland*—into David's name, which grammatically complicates the act of possession.[39] The land is not her land; instead, "hers" names the struggle for possession in which David is engaged. The dispossession experienced during immigration brings a man face to face with his own powerlessness, an experience that, in effect, strips him of his patriarchal prerogative. Conversely, the experience of David's dispossession, brought about by Martha, allows for the possibility that she will reverse the terms. If ownership is conceived in male terms—legally, through the patronym— then perhaps, Stein implies, a woman can express herself in relation to those terms most effectively between cultures, in transition. In any case, "hers" signals David's double dispossession: by the outcome of his wife's vision as well as by the fact that immigration to America is *her* vision. The New World will offer him the chance to reclaim a male self as well as the chance to own again, but he must Americanize—which is to say, he must accept the terms of an American self—and his wife and daughters must also, in the end, confirm (and conform to) the terms that enable his and their own recognizability. *The Making of Americans* analyzes the terms and the consequences of that process. Stein considers the relationship between "having" and "being"—among the most common (and certainly most contemplated) verbs in the text's lexicon—as she analyzes the making of Americans.

Narratives of Self-Possession

In David Hersland's experience of dispossession as a losing-*self* sense—as in the father and son's struggle in the orchard—Stein explores the relationship of ownership to the experience of being. *The Making of Americans* posits the centrality of ownership (as a concept) to the experience of self as a source for the anxiety experienced and evoked by David Hersland. Stein's psychological inquiries into the self began when she studied with its foremost American theorist, William James, whose own use of "ownership" to describe the consciousness of self explains David Hersland's response to his dispossession. Significantly, Stein's interest in the questions raised by James led to her analysis, in *The Making of Americans,* of a (cultural) narrative of "self" reinforced by his metaphors. She pursued the philosophical work initiated by James's lectures in the psychological laboratory of Hugo Münsterberg, where she conducted experiments to determine the limits of consciousness. Stein examined how external stimuli—language, physical sensations, even directives—influence the experience and understanding of "self." Her discoveries laid the groundwork both for theories, explored in *The Making of Americans,* of how cultural assumptions shape the experience of self and for the stylistic experimentation of that work through which she analyzed and represented that process.

Ownership is the key term through which James describes the consciousness of self in his *Principles of Psychology*—from which he drew for text and lecture when Stein studied with him. James was a conscientious reformer, liberal pluralist, and avowed anti-imperialist who sought to destabilize normative philosophical notions of selfhood by demonstrating "that we are of one clay with lunatics and criminals."[40] Yet the metaphors of ownership through which he describes the self actually interfere with his inquiry. Gradually becoming traits of the self in the course of his discussion, moreover, those metaphors normalize patriarchal property relations that are consistent with the precepts of overseas expansion that he actively opposed. The inconsistency of these metaphors with James's politics and their interference in his analysis attest to their power.

James offers a psychological analogue to the legal definition of personhood through ownership. What Walter Benn Michaels calls a "Jamesian economy of self-hood" involves the definition of the self through possessions and the experience of selfhood as a feeling of possession.[41] James finds the line "between what a man calls me and what he simply calls *mine* . . . difficult to draw. . . . In its widest possible sense, however, *a man's Self is the sum total of all that he* CAN *call his*" (*PP,* 279). Moreover, an "instinctive impulse drives us to collect property; and the collections thus made become, with different degrees of intimacy, parts of our empirical selves" (*PP*, 281). With "instinctive," James naturalizes both the drive to possess and the possessive quality of self-definition. Once property is naturalized, the self-as-owner cannot be called into question; its legal (and, broadly, cultural) determinants become invisible. But James continually inscribes that self within narratives that betray disturbances and express his discomfort with his own formulations.

James's psychological narrative is a central pre-text for *The Making of Americans*, as Stein establishes when she paraphrases, in the second paragraph, his observation that "it is one of the strangest laws of our nature that many things which we are well satisfied with in ourselves disgust us when seen in others" (*PP*, 299). James understands that disgust as the source of self-regulation, but he remains interested in the discrepancy it expresses. We prefer our own traits and possessions, he explains, because they impart a sense of continuity necessary to the experience of self. The appeal of property is itself a function of the memory and desire it generates: "Our own things are fuller than those others because of the memories they awaken and the practical hopes and expectations they arouse" (*PP*, 311). The familiarity of traits and possessions (of traits reconceived as possessions) constitutes a narrative of identity. Yet, in James's explanation of the consciousness of self, possession and the experience of possession are interchangeable, leaving open the question of what generates the experience of possession.

To address that question, James returns to his descriptive metaphor, a "Self-of-selves" that marks experiences as memories that *belong* to a discrete subject. The Self-of-selves "presides over the perception of sensations, and by giving or withholding its assent . . . influences the movements they tend to arouse," turning attention into motor discharge (*PP*, 285). "Being more incessantly there than any other single element of the mental life," he hypothesizes, "the other elements end by seeming to accrete round it and to belong to it. It becomes opposed to them as the permanent is opposed to the changing and inconstant" (*PP*, 285). James betrays the confusion that underlies his model through a misplaced modifier: "the other elements" rather than (as he intended) the Self-of-selves are "more incessantly there"; the "Self-of-selves" disappears from his sentence at precisely the moment at which it was to assert its supremacy and ownership. This disappearance is in fact more consistent with his subsequent formulation of an endlessly replaced Self-of-selves than is the actual claim of permanence. Yet, in imagining this entity, he cannot seem to decide whether to posit his Self-of-selves as a divine monarch or the man behind the curtain: "it *is* the source of effort and attention, and the place from which *appear* to emanate the fiats of the will" (*PP,* 285; emphasis added). The Self-of-selves is a description through which he increasingly attempts to locate a controlling entity, an agent.

The conventionality—and the confusion—of James's Self-of-selves is apparent in the startling metaphor that he uses to refine and develop the concept. He describes a Self-of-selves that recognizes and "assimilates" the remoter selves of the past through a "glow and a warmth . . . much as out of a herd of cattle let loose for the winter on some wide Western prairie the owner picks out and sorts together, when the time for the round-up comes in the spring, all the beasts on which he finds his own particular brand" (*PP,* 316, 317). Although the concept of ownership causes him problems (it does not quite work as an analogy), James cannot seem to relinquish his investment in it. As Michaels notes, James replaces the question of the agency of the owner—that is, of who has branded the cattle—with a further development of his metaphor in which the "cattle" are already owned. "They are not his because they are branded; they are branded," he explains, "because they are his. . . . [T]he past thoughts never were wild cattle, they were always owned. The Thought does not capture them, but as soon as it comes into existence it finds them already its own" (*PP,* 320–21).[42] This "owner" inherits its title to selves (more precisely, self-feelings) that already cohere. James thus turns to inheritance to solve the problems posed by his metaphor of ownership, and he asserts possession as an irreducible term. In effect, he describes a carefully marked family tree in which inheritance, strictly legislated, contains any challenge to or because of possession.

This readjustment of the metaphor puts ownership rather than an owner at the conceptual center of selfhood: "Each thought is . . . born an owner, and dies owned, transmitting whatever *it realized as its Self* to its own later proprietor" (*PP,* 322; emphasis added). Here owning determines rather than is determined by the name of the owner in a drama such as the one potentially enacted by father and son in the orchard. The legacy that gets transmitted in James's formulation is a *realization* of the Self, an *idea* about the reality of that self. For James, proprietorship imparts the illusion of coherence and continuity on which the integrity—and the health—of the self depends:

> There is no other identity than this in the "stream" of subjective consciousness. . . . Its parts differ, but under all their differences they are knit in these two ways; and if either way of knitting disappears, the sense of unity departs. If a man wakes some fine day unable to recall any of his past experiences, so that he has to learn his biography afresh, or if he only recalls the facts of it in a cold abstract way as things that he is sure once happened; or if, without this loss of memory, his bodily and spiritual habits all change during the night, each organ giving a different tone, and the act of thought becoming aware of itself in a different way; he *feels* and he *says*, that he is a changed person. He disowns his former me, gives himself a new name, identifies his present life with nothing from out of the older time. Such cases are not rare in mental pathology. (*PP,* 319)

A loss of memory or a change in bodily sensation disrupts the experience of coherent selfhood and results in an altered narrative of identity. In his later work, James was intrigued by the nonpathological explanations for radical changes in the experience of selfhood such as a spiritual experience could produce. In this passage, however, the revised narrative offers evidence of mental pathology.

Descriptively, James's healthy self resembles the healthy nation of his contemporary Ernest Renan, the writer and scholar who, according to James, appeared at one time to be "the most exquisite literary genius of France."[43] In 1882, Renan asked his Sorbonne audience to consider "Qu'est-ce qu'une nation?" ("What is a Nation?"). Renan isolates common memory and consent as the nation's two fundamental preconditions:

> A nation is a soul, a spiritual principle. Two things, which in truth are but one, constitute this soul or spiritual principle. One lies in the past, one in the present. One is the possession in common of a rich legacy of memories; the other is present-day consent, the desire to live together, the will to perpetuate the value of the heritage that one has received in an undivided form. The nation, like the individual, is the culmination of a long past of endeavours, sacrifice, and devotion. . . . To have common glories in the past and to have a common will in the present. . . . One loves in proportion to the sacrifices to which one has consented. . . . A nation . . . presupposes a past; it is sum-

marized, however, in the present by a tangible fact, namely, consent, the clearly expressed desire to continue a common life. (ER, 19)

Memory and desire construct and propel Renan's nation as they generate the proprietorship through which James understands self-consciousness. Renan's national self-consciousness, like James's personal self-consciousness, relies on narratives that establish continuity among memories—historical for Renan and (auto)biographical for James—on which the sense of unity relies. For both James and Renan, that continuity inheres in the principle of inheritance: the ownership bequeathed from one Self-of-selves to its successor; the legacy of memories bequeathed from one generation to another. And unity, as Renan observes, "is always effected by brutality" (ER, 11).

A hint of violence—or violation—speaks through James's dominant metaphor in which the act of branding cows, of creating a herd of owned cattle, corresponds to the gathering of experiences into a coherent self. James moves, in his description of ownership, from a "glow and a warmth" of belonging to the branding of cattle without apparent consciousness of any discrepancy. He thus sets the terms for an analysis he never performs, opening the way for Stein to analyze a cultural narrative that conceives of identity through ownership. I make no claim for the literal rewriting of James's metaphor here; rather, Stein perceptively reworks the concept manifested in James's metaphors to disclose the unacknowledged violence—the father and son's struggle—embedded in the branding that marks ownership.

That violence expresses Renan's "brutality"; it is a consequence of the unity he describes. Renan's analogy is actually misleading: a nation is not *like* an individual; rather, the nation and the individual are conjoined in a mutually constitutive process. National narratives supply the terms of personhood, and individuals in turn embody the nation. In the United States at the turn of the century, debates concerning the demography and geography of an expanding nation—of who would be included among We the People—centered on the question of inheritance cast as a threat to social existence (when, in Barrett Wendell's words, "the name of us means something not ourselves"). The ambiguity surrounding "his own" in Stein's opening parable, as I have argued, concerns the conceptual centrality of ownership to personhood. Ownership of the land, the orchard, may prompt a generational conflict, but the ambiguous "his" suggests that the real contest is over a personhood (in this case, a social status) conferred by the name of owner (the title to ownership).

Philosophically, James acknowledged the impossibility of unity. At the end of *A Pluralistic Universe* (1909) he draws an analogy consistent with his politics, especially his anti-imperialism: "The pluralistic world is . . . more like a federal republic than like an empire or a kingdom. However much may be collected, however much may report itself as present at any effective centre of consciousness or action, something else is self-governed and absent and unreduced to unity."[44] An inquiry into the resonant analyses of mental pathology and national crisis might have led him to a more complex and insightful analysis of the imperialism he opposed and of his own metaphors that manifested and sustained the logic of that imperialism. Yet when James describes the Self-of-selves as an "owner," he corporealizes and naturalizes United States property relations; he thus describes selfhood in terms that intrinsically replicate (and normalize) the inequities of those relations. Significantly, James is most imperious when he uses the metaphor of ownership to describe the experience of a self *beyond* a corporeal self (the body's boundaries).[45] The assumptions of his model are literally fleshed out when he casts his Self-of-selves not just as an owner but in particular as a cattle rancher, an important representative figure of the American West. The rancher is not quite a cowboy, precisely because the rancher is an owner, but the rancher partakes of much of the mystique of the cowboy. One might say that the rancher is the captain of industry gone West: the self as an American archetype. "No more fiendish punishment could be devised," James observes, "were such a thing physically possible, than that one should be turned loose in society and remain absolutely unnoticed by all the members thereof" (*PP*, 281). Yet he seems unaware of the significant correspondences between the exclusive experience of selfhood normalized by his metaphor-turned-paradigm and the exclusive social institutions of the United States at the turn of the century that turned many selves loose and refused to notice them.

Stein was interested in analysis not politics, choosing to live in a kind of psychic transit, with America as her "country" and Paris as her "home town" since, she explained, "if you are you in your own civilization you are apt to mix yourself up too much with your civilization."[46] In *The Autobiography of Alice B. Toklas*, she explicitly disavowed any interest in the cause of women or any other cause. Yet it is hard to imagine that her analysis of ownership was not at least intuitively informed and motivated by the masculinist assumptions reflected in James's paradigm. The rights enjoyed by upper- and middle-class white women, although differently distributed and often more extensive than those accorded to colonized, immigrant, and nonwhite men and (especially) women, expressed a complicated relationship to property and access to legal representations.[47] Throughout the nineteenth century, married women's property acts addressed without fully or federally rectifying women's dispossession (and disappearance) within marriage. "Union," for women, meant relinquishing the self. The analogy to the Union is more than figurative; as Linda Kerber notes, "because Americans based their claims to political rights on the Lockean notion that only those who owned a stake in the community properly had a voice in its affairs, the married woman whose control over her property had passed by marriage to her husband had also conceded her political voice."[48] Gradual shifts in women's relations to property both reflected and promoted a changing sense of women's investment in society. Nevertheless, nineteenth-century women, married and unmarried, were in many social contexts invisible and dispossessed. It is important to remember that *The Making of Americans* was completed nearly a decade before the Nineteenth Amendment made it illegal to deny women that most basic definition of United States citizenship, the right to the vote. In James's owner/self as both corporeal entity and rhetorical subject, embedded, as it was, in the culture of its origin, a woman could find neither adequate representation of her body, nor sufficient echo of her voice.

In the broadest sense, Stein's project continued James's. James sought to understand how consciousness worked, positing habits of attention determined by preperceptions: "Men have no eyes but for those aspects of things which they have already been taught to discern. . . . *[T]he only things which we commonly see are those which we preperceive, and the only things which we preperceive are those which have been labelled for us, and the labels stamped into our mind*" (*PP,* 420). The passive voice expresses receptivity, but the agent (the teacher) is again unknown. The minds are stamped as the cattle are branded, and knowing subjects are thus formed, consenting to a "common will." Stein's own analysis of the relationship between consciousness and character set the terms for her analysis of the relationship between preperception and cultural influences and its importance to an understanding of the making of Americans.

James's interest in breaking habits of attention finds its fullest expression in the analysis and literary innovation of *The Making of Americans.*

The evolution of this project is apparent in two essays in which she published the description and results of her experiments in Münsterberg's laboratory. Both appeared in the prestigious *Psychological Review:* "Normal Motor Automatism" in 1896, with her lab partner, Leon M. Solomons (whom James described to Münsterberg as "certainly the *keenest* intellect we ever had, and one of the loftiest characters");[49] and "Cultivated Motor Automatism" in 1898. Solomons and Stein designed the research they conducted in Münsterberg's laboratory to study the relationship between attention and behavior. The *Psychological Review* during these years bears witness to the currency of Solomons and Stein's interest in attention and consciousness, how people see and know, among America's earliest psychologists, but the influence of James's interest in attention in its relation to the experience of self is especially prevalent. Shaped by perceptions, attention in turn prevents experience from being "an utter chaos" (*PP*, 381). James was intrigued by the theories of attention and hysteria offered by Alfred Binet and Pierre Janet; he discussed this work in *Principles of Psychology* and reviewed Janet's *De l'automatisme psychologique* in "The Hidden Self" (1890). Through the use of automatic writing, among other methods, the French psychologists had demonstrated the existence of secondary (or subliminal) consciousness and had shown hysteria to be a disease of attention. Through hypnosis, the hysterical patients manifested different personalities that shed light on the etiologies of the anesthesias for which they were undergoing treatment or investigation. This work, which influenced Freud as well, reinforced James's response to the "Consciousness-Automaton Theory," which saw thoughts and feelings as automatically responsive to rather than productive of motor impulses and which, according to James, maintained "that in everything outward we are pure material machines."[50] James was concerned with attending to attention and with understanding attention as a primary factor in mental pathology.

Solomons and Stein intended their experiments "to determine the limits of normal automatism, and, if possible, show them to be really equal to the explanation of the second personality [the hysteric's "double personality"]; and incidentally to study as carefully as possible the process by which a reaction becomes automatic."[51] To that end they tried to engage the attention of "normal subjects" (themselves) and study their capacity for automatism, beginning with the possibility for unconscious or involuntary movement and including the "unconscious exercise of memory and invention" (NMA, 494). Their discoveries, and the language in which they present them in the report, have explanatory importance for Stein's future work. Solomons and Stein found, for instance, that a recognizable word uttered among nonsensical sounds drew the subject's attention, while repetition of that word could be used to overcome "this habit of attention." Especially interesting in light both of Stein's project in her subsequent literary innovations and of her letter to Mabel Weeks conceding her inability to write the Great American Novel is the experimenters' observation that "the words read must be familiar for the automatism to work well. Dialect stories do not go well at all" (NMA, 504).

The experimenters gave particular attention to the experience of actions performed in the absence of attention, reporting a "feeling of extra personality" (otherness or estrangement) as well as the loss of a sense of self articulated as a loss of a sense of proprietorship (NMA, 495). Experiments with automatic writing, for example, prompt the observation that "the feeling that the writing is *our* writing seems to disappear with the motor impulse" (NMA, 498). An experiment in which the subject read aloud while being read to yielded an experience of estrangement, the sense of the self-as-other: when the subject became aware that he was reading, "his voice seemed as though that of another person" (NMA, 504). What Solomons and Stein call the experience of "extra personality" would be important to Stein's later formulation of a "losing-self sense," and estranging the normal subject from meaningful experience would become central to her literary project.

Despite their professed dissociation of their work from the discoveries of Sigmund Freud, similar preoccupations are evident in Solomons and Stein's report. During this time Freud was using his studies of hysteria to formulate his own understanding of the unconscious. His conviction that a symbolic language governed the symptoms of hysterical patients prompted Freud to investigate the dimension of the self that was inaccessible by conventional means to conscious thought. Following the French psychologists, he used hypnotic suggestion, which, he found, yielded access to the inner logic of the symptom and disclosed an alternative dimension that, he demonstrated, was nevertheless coextensive with the personality of the subject.[52] Solomons and Stein explicitly make "no attempt to answer the vexed question of a so-called 'subliminal consciousness.' . . . The question of consciousness, in all cases where it is not directly experienced," they claim, "is essentially a philosophical one," as it was for James (NMA, 493). And yet, "a reaction becomes automatic" in a process largely compatible with Freud's unconscious processes. Where Solomons and Stein define hysteria as "a *disease* of the *attention*" (NMA, 511), Freud demonstrated its genesis in an act of forgetting. In either case, hysterics could not (or would not) know (or acknowledge) aspects of their own bodies and actions. In that sense, hysterics represented an extreme of what Freud, like Solomons and Stein, came to understand as the normal dimensions of the personality.

The idea that actions were not always directed by conscious knowledge prepared for a theory of preperception. Following James, Solomons and Stein offered a concept of the self that explained earlier theories of demonic possession, as well as the more contemporary theories of "cohabitation" suggested by "second personality," in terms of dissociation (whether "a disease of the attention" or, in Freud's words, "a split consciousness").[53] The "self" of their formulations collected fragmentary experiences into a coherence which, not unlike the moving pictures (or movies) that Stein claimed as a conceptual influence, was largely a function of perceptual illusion. Here we return to James's metaphor, in which the selecting agency of attention (the Self-of-selves) re-members the experiences that constitute the whole self. This "second personality" is not yet Du Bois's double-consciousness, a state of mind brought about by competing affiliations; it was pathological or philosophical rather than political. The young experimenters were interested in describing normal perception and its abnormal distortions rather than a painful response to oppressive *external* conditions.

The habits of attention—and inattention—that Solomons and Stein set out to study became, for Stein, the source of preperceptions and suggestability. In a Jamesian celebration of the will, the experimenters taught themselves "to get control of [their own] attention" (NMA, 498). But this control came, paradoxically, "*whenever the attention [was] sufficiently distracted*" (NMA, 499); the passive voice indicates the *relinquished* agency that their getting control of their attention implies. By demonstrating the existence of motor automatism, Solomons and Stein represented the empowerment of motor impulse by a source other than attention. They found, as James had suggested, that attention to the bodily sensation of converting perception into motor discharge imparted the experience of self: "The motor impulse is necessary for the feeling of personality," and that feeling "always disappears whenever our knowledge of the act is acquired purely by return sensations" (NMA, 506, 511). The sense of personality only emerged, in other words, when they "return[ed] to [them]selves"; it was both contingent upon and defined through a sense of self-possession (NMA, 499). They thus proved the existence of parts of the subject that were not experienced as self and that could literally take "dictation" (unwittingly accept and implement suggestions from external as well as inaccessible internal sources).

Stein continued this investigation in "Cultivated Motor Automatism," expanding her subject pool from herself and Solomons to more than a hundred Harvard and Radcliffe students (still, of course, a select pool). This second report registers Stein's shift from an exploration of attention to a primary interest in character. Outlining different character types that yielded categorically similar responses to her experiments with automatic writing, she observes "that habits of attention are reflexes of the complete character of the individual, and again on habits of attention are dependent the different forms and degrees of automatic writing."[54] By demonstrating the influence of character on how and what a person sees, Stein prepares for a conclusion that forms the basis of *The Making of Americans*: cultural factors determine preperceptions that shape the experience of the self. The first hint of her interest in the impact of environment on character seems almost an intrusion on her data. She interrupts her efforts to classify her observations with a discussion of "the New England character":

> But first a word as to an interesting fact shown in this study. A large number of my subjects were New Englanders, and the habit of self-repression, the intense self-consciousness, the morbid fear of "letting one's self go," that is so prominent an element in the New England character, was a constant stumbling-block. It usually took a New Englander a sitting longer to give a response than the other subjects. I could usually tell them as soon as I began the experiment by their resistance to my guidance. Afterwards I found that Stanley Hall, in his article on Fears, notes the fact that self-consciousness was dreaded by twenty-four boys in Cambridge, Mass., a thing unknown in Trenton or St. Paul. (CMA, 299)

In a report in which interests, habits, and traits define "character," this paragraph, in which region overrides other determinants in the shaping of character, stands out. Her chatty first sentence indicates a problematic transition; Stein seems unsure about what to do with her observation, but it is too "interesting" to omit. It is, in fact, her first step toward the observations of *national* character that will motivate and define *The Making of Americans*. Her use of the expression "letting one's self go" hints at an intuitive grasp of the New England/American understanding of self-possession: the self as both agent and object to be guided.[55] To be guided is to lose the self; the threat posed by the "sense of otherness, of something else pulling or setting the arm going" speaks to an anxiety centered around the loss of the will, and, by implication, the self—a losing-self sense indeed (CMA, 299).[56] While distracted attention explains the sense of otherness experienced during automatism, and, presumably, determines preperceptions and dictated responses, that subliminal consciousness explains people's susceptibility to external (including cultural) influences: what makes "any one of one's period."

This work bears an obvious relation to Stein's writing. First to note the correspondence, at least in a public and critical way, was the influential behaviorist B. F. Skinner, who claimed, in a 1934 *Atlantic Monthly* review, to have found the secret to Stein's style—specifically to the more widely-known *Tender Buttons*—in her early psychological work on automatic writing. Skinner believed that Stein was herself engaged in such a project in her own writing, that this work had been "written automatically and unconsciously."[57] Despite his faulty conclusion, Skinner noted a connection that Stein herself made later the same year in "The Gradual Making of the Making of Americans," one of the lectures, collected in the volume *Lectures in America*, that she delivered during her tour of the United States following the success of *The Autobiography of Alice B. Toklas* in 1933.

Stein enjoyed using the tour to showcase her previously ignored work, as she did in this lecture specifically on *The Making of Americans*. Tracing the genealogy of her masterpiece back through her Harvard experiments, she recalls, "I was supposed to be interested in [my subjects'] reactions but soon I found that I was not but instead that I was enormously interested in the types of their characters that is what I even then thought of as the bottom nature of them."[58] Stein goes on to explain how her concern with "the bottom nature in people" led to her interest "in hearing how everybody said the same thing over and over again with infinite variations but over and over again until finally if you listened with great intensity you could hear it rise and fall and tell all that that there was inside them, not so much by the actual words they said or the thoughts they had but the movement of their thoughts and words endlessly the same and endlessly different" (GM, 138). Repetitions, as she and Solomons had discovered, could have a distracting, a lulling, effect as well as a disruptive one. The reading she advocates will lead, as the experimenters had demonstrated, to an experience of estrangement, but that estrangement in turn will take the reader past the words of a text to an awareness of a story beneath the story. Like Freud, Stein advocates a different kind of attending, a suspended listening in which "the bottom nature in people" emerges in the rhythms and cadences, the repetitions and patterns, rather than the content of their conversations. "Bottom nature" is an untold and conventionally untellable story. With *The Making of Americans*, Stein moved into an exploration of national character, locating subliminal consciousness as the mechanism of its transmission.

To explain the cultural dimension of her work, Stein turned to another early influence, as she remarks in another of her American lectures, "Portraits and Repetition": "I was doing what the cinema was doing, I was making a continuous succession of the statement of what that person was until I had not many things but one thing. . . . I of course did not think of it in terms of the cinema, in fact I doubt whether at that time I had ever seen a cinema but, and I cannot repeat this too often any one is of one's period and this our period was undoubtedly the period of the cinema and series production. And each of us in our own way are bound to express what the world in which we are living is doing" (PR, 177). The movies work basically on the premise, articulated in 1824 by Peter Mark Roget, that the retina retains a ghost image of an object for a brief moment beyond its disappearance.[59] Thus the viewer supplies the continuity between frames that makes the object appear continuously in motion. Zoetropes, Stroboscopes, and Praxinoscopes—simple devices that operated according to Roget's discovery—were staples in mid- to late-nineteenth-century American and European drawing rooms. Although as a device, cinema, which encourages illusion, works against her purposes, Stein uses a cinematic premise to reissue James's challenge to "try, . . . not . . . to arrest, but to notice or attend to, the present moment of time" (*PP*, 573). To do so would be analogous to seeing each frame of a movie as it passed, that is, to resist making the connections that underlie cinematic movement. Stein's style strives to break the laws of perception. In so doing, she hopes to understand how and why one is of one's period. To that end she offers the disruptions of *The Making of Americans*.

The explicit project of *The Making of Americans* is deeply psychological, at least as the narrator describes it. Throughout the work, the narrator articulates the desire to comprehend and classify human types: "I am wishing every one knew every one and wanted to have me make diagrams of all the kinds there are of men and women and the place in this diagram of each one. It would be very contenting to me and I am now not beginning again but going on with my explaining and describing and realising and knowing and being certain. . . . Sometime I will be able to explain the being in each one and make a scheme of relations in kinds of being with each one having in them the way of eating, thinking, feeling, working, drinking, loving, beginning and ending" (*MA*, 595). The narrative voice corresponds significantly to the entries Stein made in the notebooks she kept while at work on *The Making of Americans*. For most readers of Stein, therefore, this narrative voice is comfortably Stein's, and the project of *The Making of Americans* derives from the desire for this comprehension. Central to this project, argue many Stein scholars, was Otto Weininger's *Sex and Character* (1908). Leo and Gertrude discovered this text shortly after its publication and passed it on enthusiastically to their friends in Europe and the United States. *Sex and Character,* which Leon Katz calls "a violent anti-feminist tract," is a fascinating and vitriolic study that Weininger himself calls "anti-feminine" (FM, 268).[60] There is much in Weininger's book that could have intrigued Stein. He argues, for example, for a continuum of masculinity and femininity to replace the binary system of man and woman. Homosexuality, in his view, can be explained as a normal response made abnormal by misguided categories to which society assigns people. Stein surely could have been drawn to that explanation and to his sense of the superiority of masculine women to other women; she could equally have been interested in an observation such as "consciousness and consciousness alone is in itself moral" (*SC*, 182). Yet, it is hard to imagine her sanguine when he reserves the category of genius for *men*, despite her professed anxieties and insecurities about her work during this period of her life.

Although Stein claims affinities with Weininger's work, influences on Stein are always hard to determine. As Katz suggests, Stein was no conventional reader: "Her relations with books and ideas were neither disciplined nor properly attentive" (FM, 269). She typically seized upon something that confirmed her ideas to the extent even of misreading in the process. And scholars have frequently overlooked or underplayed the

apparent—although deceptive—resonances of Weininger with Stein's earlier work. Jayne L. Walker, for example, notes that "Stein's notebooks
reveal that her reading of Otto Weininger's *Sex and Character* in 1908 was
the catalyst for this new project which led her to transform a chronicle of
an American family into a synchronic study of 'kinds,'" yet goes on to
remark on the consistency of Stein's interest in character in *The Making
of Americans* with her earlier laboratory report, "Cultivated Motor Automatism."[61] The form of Stein's work changed during the year she read
Weininger, but the change does not necessarily indicate Stein's uncritical
acceptance of Weininger's terms or his project. On the contrary, my own
skepticism about Stein's uncritical enthusiasm for Weininger, whatever
she may have professed, is supported by her continual undermining of her
own narrator's Weininger-like project. Ultimately, the narrator herself
finds that she cannot accomplish what she has set out to do. The narrator,
who believes that "*everyone* has *their* own being in them," describes "a
solid happy satisfaction to any *one* who has it in *them* to love repeating and
completed understanding" (*MA*, 292–93; emphasis added). As the (underscored) confusion of singular and plural pronouns attests, however, the
multiplicity of experiential subjectivities cannot finally be reduced to a
single subject in the service of "completed understanding."

The continual definition and redefinition of the project counteracts
comprehension and imparts a revisionary quality to *The Making of Americans.* "Perhaps," admits the narrator, "not any one really is a whole one
inside them to themselves or to any one. Perhaps every one is in pieces
inside them and perhaps every one has not completely in them their own
being inside in them" (*MA*, 519). Here the narrator questions both self-
ownership (own and owned being) and certainty—even the certainty that
the project cannot be completed: "I am not certain that I cannot very soon
have finished writing a complete history of all men and all women" (*MA*,
684). At the same time, she dreads completion: "I am not really certain I
am going to be liking to have this as a thing to be completely in me. It
would be an exciting thing to be certain really of this thing having had the
complete history of every one already finished in writing. I will not be
having it as certain this thing, I will go on *being* one every day telling
about *being being* in men and in women. Certainly I will be going on *being*
one telling about *being* in men and women. I am going on being such a
one" (*MA*, 684; emphasis added). Comprehension is the end—in both
senses of the word—of authorship. Since comprehension, as Stein has

shown, means submission to an ordering system, and satiety, then it is also the end of desire, and, therefore, of the author's motivation to continue.

Here Stein's wordplay works against comprehension. Like Freud's interminable analysis, her project will always have new material. The representations of *being* at once underscore the word and obscure its meaning. Existence is as complicated as the use of the word "being" in this passage, and it is finally not comprehensible. The meaning of the passage, like life itself, is richest if the word "being" remains somewhat ambiguous, alternately and sometimes interchangeably a noun and a verb. The narrator will tell "about being being in men and women": about the fact that being is in men and in women or about the fact that she herself is (exists) in men and in women. The meaning of the word is not fixed because, in the end, the narrator cannot say for sure what constitutes being. She cannot finish the complete history of every one, but the incompletion of her task allows her to go on writing—and being.

Stein understood the temptation to seek refuge in a familiar and coherent narrative. The social scientific project of classification evident in the "diagrams of all the kinds there are of men and women and the place in the diagram of each one" that the narrator wishes to make articulates the desire for comprehension. Narrative commentary expresses increasing uncertainty about the outcome of any such project: "Perhaps no one ever will know the complete history of every one" (*MA*, 454). Yet the narrative continues in the face of the impossibility of its project, and Stein sets repetition (the return of earlier assertions of certainty) against the evolving narrative doubt; a hopeful and uncertain narrator places even doubt in doubt. *The Making of Americans* records a writer's struggle with the tantalizing comprehensibility offered by cultural conventions, a struggle played out in the tortured sentences and paragraphs, the fractured narrative that continually re-poses where it cannot repose.

A "Decent Family's Progress": The Melting-Pot and the Marriage Plot

Stein left evidence of the evolution of *The Making of Americans* not only in the notebooks she kept while writing the work, but in the text itself. Stories of two families, the Dehnings and the Herslands, and of their associates are interwoven with the narrator's meditations on her psychological project and on her storytelling. *The Making of Americans* begins with Julia Dehning's marriage to Alfred Hersland, a version of what started out as a fictional account of the failed marriage of one of Stein's New York cousins. But the narrator breaks into that story with a discussion of her authorship, which in turn leads to the account of David Hersland's immigration. The thematic concerns of the work emerge in the juxtaposition. In Julia Dehning's sense of what a man, a marriage, and a home ought to be, in David Hersland's self-definition through ownership, in the narrator's understanding of the story she wants to tell, Stein shows how an unsettling change in status motivates a retreat into familiar (and familial) narratives.

For the narrator, that change grows out of her awareness of the difficulty of telling her story. She enjoins her reader to "listen while I tell you all about us, and wait while I hasten slowly forwards, and love, please, this history of this decent family's progress" (*MA*, 34).[62] With the oxymoron "hasten slowly," she manifests confusion about her task as a storyteller, a confusion amplified by her discussion of her story:

> Yes it is a misfortune we have inside us, some few of us, I cannot deny it to you, all you others, it is true the simple interest I take in my family's progress. I have it, this interest in ordinary middle class existence, in simple firm ordinary middle class traditions, in sordid material unaspiring visions, in a repeating, common, decent enough kind of living, with no fine kind of fancy ways inside us, no excitements to surprise us, no new ways of being bad or good to win us.
>
> You see, it is just an ordinary middle class tradition we must use to understand this family's progress. There must be no aspiring thoughts inside us, there must be a feeling always in us of being in a kind of way in business always honest, there must be in a kind of ordinary way always there inside us the sense of decent enough ways of living for us. Yes I am strong to declare that I have it, here in the heart of this high, aspiring, excitement loving people who despise it,—I throw myself open to the public,—I take a simple interest in the ordinary kind of families, histories, I believe in simple middle class monotonous tradition, in a way in honest enough business methods.
>
> Middle-class, middle-class, I know no one of my friends who will admit *it*, one can find no one among you all to belong to *it*, I know that here we are to be democratic and aristocratic and not have *it*, for middle class is sordid material unillusioned unaspiring and always monotonous for it is always there and to be always repeated, and yet I am strong, and I am right, and I know *it*, and I say it

to you and you are to listen to *it*, yes here in the heart of a people who despise *it*, that a material middle class who know they are *it*, with their straightened bond of family to control *it*, is the one thing always human, vital, and worthy *it*—worthy that all monotonously shall repeat *it*,—and from which has always sprung, and all who really look can see *it*, the very best the world can ever know, and everywhere we always need *it*. (*MA*, 34; emphasis added)

The story of her family is at once complicated and simplified by her need to tell that story as the history of a family's progress, a middle-class narrative. But it is a story that brooks no "aspiring thoughts."

Like the narrator, Stein herself is sincere in her defense of the middle-class tradition. Yet a progressive narrative is, Stein makes clear, only one among other stories that could be told about the Hersland family. The family's progress must be understood in the context of a certain—a middle-class—narrative, the prescriptedness of which finds stylistic expression in the rhythm created by the repetition of the word "it" in the third paragraph cited above. The paragraph comprises a series of clauses that typically end with the word "it." This rhythm becomes so repetitive that the "it" becomes virtually a reflex, even appearing incomprehensibly at the end of the phrase "is the one thing always human, vital and worthy it." The "it" in the following modification, "worthy that all shall monotonously repeat it," could refer to the word "it" as well as to the "material middle class" to which "it" contextually refers. The monotony of the repetition makes it automatic, as Solomons and Stein earlier demonstrated would be the case. Even if the "it" in the first phrase were unintentional, it would demonstrate Stein's point. The meaning of "it" becomes more ambiguous as the word becomes more automatic. The repetition shows how hard it is to tell a story against the reader's expectations. The middle-class narrative colors as it organizes the world. But a misplaced "it" is precisely the kind of disruption that signals the operation of such a narrative, as is the one clause without a concluding "it": "for middle class is sordid material unillusioned unaspiring and always monotonous for it is always there and to be always repeated." The rhetorical and formal disjunctions of this passage point to another story, one about the prescriptiveness of a middle-class narrative.

Families and histories, no less than "honest enough business methods," define this middle-class tradition, which determines the form and content of the stories that can be told. Stein urges her readers to listen to and through her repetitions and disjunctions for the press of untold stories. The repetitions occur on the level of plot as well as in the language, and across as well as within texts. Central to both the immigrant and the middle-class narrative is the marriage plot, an important focus in *The Making of Americans.* For the native-born American, no less than for the immigrant, marriage is a key site of Americanization. As the theorists of race suicide made clear, "America" could reproduce itself only if "Americans" (native-born white Americans) married and began (state-sanctioned) families. For the immigrants, as Werner Sollors notes, marriage was emblematic of the promise of America to replace descent with consent relationships.[63] David Hersland immigrates because of his marriage, but immigration was itself also seen as a marriage, representing, like the name change clause of the 1906 Naturalization Act, the immigrant's conversion to a new identity. Mary Antin, like many immigrants, married into the nation—and out of her faith. Even Jacob Riis, who calls his immigrant narrative a love story about the Danish wife whom he immigrated to win, became an American to earn the name of husband and father, to escape a Danish identity—and the name of a Danish father— deemed insufficient by his wife's family. The love story about him and his wife, Elizabeth, is inseparable from the love story about him and America; Elizabeth's appearances, in fact, are sporadic. Stein's characters similarly seek freedom from the past in marriages that ironically underscore their compulsions to repeat inescapable pasts.

In many fictional immigrant narratives, the immigrant's marriage registers a failed conversion. Often in such works, characters look to marriage as an escape from the past, the means to the forgetting willed by Antin, but with startling regularity these marriages are disturbed by a past that they reiterate. Abraham Cahan's Yekl, for example, rejects his "greenhorn" wife for a more Americanized Russian-Jewish countrywoman, who embodies, for him, the wealth and freedom of his adopted nation, the mobility curtailed by the arrival of his wife and son from Russia. Yet, the end of the novel finds him anything but mobile. Trapped on a cable car with his soon-to-be new bride and her "emissary" on the way to City Hall, he is "painfully reluctant to part with his long-coveted freedom."[64] With each jerk of the car, he "wished the pause could be prolonged indefinitely," and with each resumption of the car's "progress the *violent* lurch it gave was accompanied by a corresponding sensation in his heart" (*Y,* 89). Yekl, or, as he prefers, Jake, thus hastens slowly forwards, forced to recognize the extent to which the economic responsibilities incurred by a marriage—rather than the Old World ways of his wife, Gitl—have ensnared him within a system that leaves him little time to learn new ways. In a final irony, he finds that his new bride's savings have gone toward the divorce settlement that turns his first wife into an entrepreneur and makes Jake more urgently a wage-earner.

In the marriages of Sara Smolinsky's three sisters in Anzia Yezierska's *Bread Givers*, a father bestows his daughters on men who appear willing and able to support him. Having left marriage brokering in the Old World, he nonetheless preserves its structure, and his bad choices attest to the problems of such a transposition. Sara, who watches her father destroy each sister's chance for happiness, prefers the workforce to his tyranny and ends up with an impending, apparently fairy-tale, marriage to Hugo Seelig, the principal of the school where she teaches and himself a Polish-Jewish immigrant. But the novel ends ominously: "Hugo's grip tightened on my arm and we walked on. But I felt the shadow still there, over me. It wasn't just my father, but the generations who made my father whose weight was still upon me" (*BG*, 297). Her "but" suggests that she views Hugo's grip as an alternative to the claim of the generations, yet it is Hugo who has just confirmed—even insisted on—Sara's ambivalent proposal to bring her tyrannical father to live with them. Single, Sara has freed herself from her father; married, she will be his servant once again. He has at last found the daughter from whose sale he can profit, and Hugo's tightening grip bodes ill for Sara's marital expectations. Even her American marriage exerts the force of the grip of generations.

Ironically, the most dramatic depiction of the ambiguity of the marriage plot also popularized the most important metaphor of the nation's assimilationists, that of the melting-pot. Israel Zangwill's *The Melting-Pot* first played to enthusiastic audiences, including Theodore Roosevelt, in Washington's Columbia Theater in 1908. The play revolves around the courtship of its aptly named hero, David Quixano, and Vera, a settlement worker. During this courtship, David is at work on a symphony that explains what America means to him.[65] Orphaned during a pogrom in which he saw his family butchered, David immigrates in order to participate in a new world order that he depicts as a crucible and as "the roaring and bubbling" of "the great Melting-Pot" wherein "the great Alchemist melts and fuses [all] with his purging flame" (*M-P*, 198–99). Despite his evident wish to forget the past, however, David is haunted by his violent

memories, which take the form of seizures and disturb not only his com-
placency but even his most exalted paeans to America. David is possessed
by these memories, a possession amplified by the inescapable irony that
being in the United States is itself predicated on the violence that left
him orphaned. Psychologically, he has incorporated—and embodies—that
violence.

In his own life, as in *The Melting-Pot*, Zangwill advocated mixed mar-
riage as an emblem of the melting-pot and a harbinger of world peace.
Yet, although David quickly overcomes the Russian-born Vera's anti-
Semitism, he subsequently finds himself confronting, in her father, the
Russian soldier who directed the notorious pogrom. Here is the test of his
principles: David must literally face his enemy and triumph over both his
memories and any vestige of belief in traditional kinship that would link
Vera to her father. Vera, in turn, must fully renounce her father to marry
his sworn enemy. Initially, David flees, but *The Melting-Pot* ends with
their reconciliation, which takes place just after the first performance of
his completed symphony at Vera's settlement house, in full view of the
Statue of Liberty.

Yet the reconciliation remains ominous. Vera, agreeing to kiss David
"as we Russians kiss at Easter—the three kisses of peace," inadvertently
summons the Easter massacre of which she fears she will remind him. To
David's response, "Easter was the date of the massacre—see! I am at
peace," Vera rejoins, "God grant it endure!" (*M-P*, 198). Within this
triumph lurk the memories that they must inevitably invoke in each other,
just as within the metaphor of the crucible (the play's original title) lingers an intrinsic violence of Americanization. David's name itself evokes
the much-reduced, disabused Don Quixote. Of the disillusionment that
seethes beneath the play's surface, the audience was, it seems, generally
unaware, as Zangwill himself may have been.

For Stein, however, such disillusionment was of central concern. The
grandchildren of the Herslands and the Dehnings seek freedom from their
pasts in marriages ironically produced by their compulsions to repeat
those pasts. In the marriage choices of the grandchildren, Stein demonstrates how people are shaped by unconscious factors that complicate
their notions of freedom and independence. The family narratives through
which these characters understand their experiences are, broadly speaking, cultural narratives; they facilitate the making of Americans. Stein
uses the marriages of the grandchildren in *The Making of Americans* to

mark the return to familiar narratives in the face of change. She understands that marriage is like a conversion, signaling a change not only in cultural status but, particularly for Stein's characters, in the conception of one's selfhood. The new terms of kinship signaled by "husband" or "wife" make marriage a moment in which one's narrative of identity is especially close to the surface and likely to be rethought—that is to say, identity is likely to be renarrativized in view of the change in status. In her characters' decisions to marry, Stein shows precisely the difficulty of changing any of those terms and the danger of examining them too closely. At the moments when her characters feel most free, and most in flux, Stein insists on the overwhelming reassertion of a familiar narrative of identity and its influence on those characters' perceptions. Not surprisingly, the marriage plot becomes an important site for her contemplation of her own difficulty in telling her story, and of the internal resistance and external constraints that make many stories untellable.

The American contract that Julia Dehning believes her marriage will be—the freedom from the past that she seeks in that marriage—is complicated by psychological and cultural prescriptions foregrounded by Stein. Although not an immigrant, Julia is very much an immigrant figure: "The stamp [of her mother] went deep, far deeper than just for the fair good-looking exterior. . . . Perhaps she was born too near to the old world to ever attain quite altogether that crude virginity that makes the American girl safe in all her liberty" (*MA*, 14–15). The rhetoric of the immigrant experience echoes in the terms of Julia Dehning's betrothal to Alfred Hersland, in "the new world she needed to content her" and in the pretext of the marriage, "their new free life together" (*MA*, 29, 32). Julia's father strenuously opposes her marriage to Alfred Hersland, and she believes that her defiance constitutes freedom; yet, this very defiance is inscribed in her paternal inheritance: "To her father, to know well what one wanted, and to win it, by patient steady fighting for it, was the best act a man or woman could accomplish, and well had his daughter done it" (*MA*, 32).

Everything about Julia's betrothal to Alfred conforms to expectations that attest to a familiar and familial narrative. Explicitly gendered, that narrative yields her conception of manhood: "to a girl like Julia Dehning, all men, excepting those of an outside unknown world, those one reads about in books and never really can believe in . . . for a girl like Julia Dehning, with the family with which she had all her life been living, to her all men that could be counted as men by her must be, all, good strong gentle creatures, honest and honorable and honoring. For her to doubt this of all men, of decent men, of men whom she could ever know well or belong to, to doubt this would be for her to recreate the world and make one all from her own head" (*MA*, 29–30). With the distinction between books and experience on which this passage insists, Stein underscores Julia's belief in the transparency of her experience. She is markedly unaware that the understanding of manhood derived from her family's narrative is no less constructed than the manhood depicted in books. The consequences of questioning that conception are equally explicit in this passage: Julia would have to engage in her own act of authorship, "to recreate the world and make one all from her own head." She is unprepared even to attempt such an act, yet she remains unaware that she bases her marriage on her own family narrative.

Julia ignores anything that contradicts that narrative, such as the concepts of ownership articulated by both her and Alfred that countermand her ideas of freedom. She hopes to "belong to" the kind of man in which, following her family, she believes, and Alfred unwittingly confesses to the patriarchal terms of his desire to marry Julia: "I've got some good schemes in my head, . . . and I mean to do big things, and with a safe man like your father to back me through now I think I can" (*MA*, 32). Alfred's desire for Julia is predicated on a paternal involvement and inheritance that her desire for him ostensibly renounces, but she thinks "more of her ideals . . . than of her man" (*MA*, 30). She does not acknowledge the discrepancies that would expose her having "made [Alfred Hersland], to herself, as she was now making her new house, an unharmonious unreality, a bringing complicated natural tastes to the simplicities of fitness and of decoration of a self-digested older world" (*MA*, 30). The "unharmonious unreality" offers, for the reader, a potential disruption. But for Julia, such disruptions are too threatening to pursue. More palatable, the ambiguous "*self-digested* older world" retains her devotion; she would rather doubt her experiences than challenge her world view. With "self-digested," Stein equally depicts a world that has digested a self and a world that has been digested by a self. In either case, the bodily metaphor suggestively depicts the internalization of cultural prescriptions and the digested (assimilated) self that results.[66] That self is inseparable from, and actually at stake in, the domestic narrative implied by the equation of Alfred and the house. Hence Julia's investment in it. Her belief in the possibility of their "new free life together" comes into conflict with the realities of inheritance, particularly an inherited narrative. Even the "new house" into which she channels her desire for freedom is "in arrangement a small edition of her mother's" (*MA*, 31).

Julia does gain some insight from the competing narratives implied by an "unharmonious reality": "Somehow now it had come to her, to see, as dying men are said to see, clearly and freely things as they are and not as she had wished them to be for her" (*MA*, 33). But she quickly retreats, as, recoiling from the

> sudden sight . . . she dulled her momentary clearing mind and hugged her old illusions to her breast. . . .
>
> "Alfy didn't mean it like that," she said over to herself, "he couldn't mean it like that. He only meant that papa would help him along in his career and of course papa will. Oh I know he didn't really mean it like that, he couldn't mean it like that. Anyhow I will ask him what he really meant."
>
> And she asked him and he *freely* made her understand just what it was he meant. It sounded better then, a little better as he told it to her more at length, but it left her a foreboding sense that perhaps the world had meanings in it that could be hard for her to understand and judge.
>
> But now she had to think that it was all, as it had a little sounded, good and best. She had to think it so else how could she marry, and how could she not marry him. (*MA*, 33; emphasis added)

Julia insistently mishears Alfred until he conforms again to her narrative. Whatever opposition her family, in particular Mr. Dehning, offers to the marriage, the family narrative supplies the definition of manhood into which she fits Alfred and the compulsion to follow through on her betrothal. That narrative gives Alfred the *freedom* ("he freely made her understand") to misrepresent himself; she actually facilitates his misrepresentation. Even when Julia eventually does leave Alfred, she is only enabled to do so by her father. She replaces one figure with another, as she has already done in her marriage; she does not challenge, and in fact she restores, the narrative's patriarchal model of belonging.

The story of Julia Dehning's betrothal segues into the story of Martha and David Hersland's decision to immigrate by way of the narrator's discussion of the middle-class tradition. The narrator's oxymoronic "hasten slowly forwards" explains the logic of the transition: Julia's narrative is informed by a narrative that develops out of the factors and assumptions motivating the Herslands' decision to immigrate. The account of the Herslands' decision, and especially the narrator's interruption, slows the pace of the story of Julia's marriage. Thus the narrator's interruption points to a narrative shaping the telling of *The Making of Americans* and leaving part of that story untold. The narrator must tell her story through and against an appealing prescribed narrative. In the marriage of Alfred's sister Martha Hersland, granddaughter of the Martha Hersland who immigrated to the New World, Stein thinks through her own authorship in an exploration more readily available to the reader with access to Stein's then unpublished manuscripts. This discussion seems to have marked a particularly dramatic insight into her own authorial project.

The language describing Martha Hersland's and Phillip Redfern's courtship and marriage establishes their relationship in archetypally American terms. The couple starts out by asserting their right to "the new world" (*MA*, 433). They meet in college, a "democratic [western] institution" in which no one was especially "conscious of a grand-father" or "held responsible for the father they had" (*MA*, 431)—apparently in this democratic institution, assertions such as Horace Kallen's "men . . . cannot change their grandfathers" hold no sway (DMP, 220). But once Martha becomes Mrs. Redfern, everything changes. She "never understood what had happened to her. In a dazed blind way she tried all ways of breaking through the walls that confined her. She threw herself against them with impatient energy and again she tried to destroy them piece by piece. She was always thrown back bruised and dazed and never quite certain whence came the blow, how it was dealt or why" (*MA*, 434). As Mrs. Redfern, Martha finds herself imprisoned within an identity that, the passive voice suggests, she experiences as imposed by an obscure or obscured source of power. Unaware of the prescribed role she has unwittingly assumed as a wife, and of the apparent liberty she has thereby relinquished, Martha is confined and battered within the walls of her fantasy, like Julia's, a domestic (and domesticating) vision. Again like Julia, Martha returns to her father, with whom she continually replays Phillip's rejection of her: Martha, who "was always full up with desiring beginning," lives with a father who "was full up then with impatient feeling" (*MA*, 471–72). Like Phillip, he is never satisfied with her.

Stein's account of the breakup of Martha's marriage incorporates, with changes, Stein's previously written but unpublished novella *Fernhurst*. Phillip, a professor of philosophy, accepts a position at Farnham College, under the deanship of Hannah Charles, a woman modeled on Martha

Carey Thomas, first the dean and later the president of Bryn Mawr College. At a cocktail party Phillip meets Cora Dounor, a woman described as "completely under [the] control of Hannah Charles" (*MA*, 435). Phillip and Cora's mutual passion for the life of the mind evidently sparks a love affair that takes Phillip away from the wife who, after two years of marriage, had already ceased to interest him. The story is modeled on the scandalous affair between Bryn Mawr philosophy professor Alfred Hodder, a friend of Leo and Gertrude's, and Mary Gwinn, longtime companion of Martha Carey Thomas. Gwinn had lived with Thomas in Germany while Thomas pursued her studies. In 1904, while Stein was fictionalizing the affair in *Fernhurst*, Hodder divorced his wife and married Mary Gwinn in Europe. Leon Katz even notes "a peculiar association with Woodrow Wilson" in Hodder (*FQ*, xxx). Wilson, the archetypal man of letters, had been recruited at the beginning of his career by Thomas with whom he subsequently battled until his departure in 1888.

The story of Martha and Phillip's breakup offers the longest sustained conventionally coherent narrative account in *The Making of Americans*. Katz questioned Alice B. Toklas about the fragment and was told simply that Stein "took [this section] complete from an isolated thing . . . but it was never rewritten. That is why there is such a break in tone and style." He explains Stein's inclusion of the passage as a decision to which she adhered despite finding herself, as he reports, "shocked at the emptiness of its prose style" (*FQ*, xxxvi). For Katz, a juxtaposition of the story told first as a conventional narrative and then in more experimental prose charts Stein's progress as a writer. Alternatively, in my reading, the inclusion of the passage allows Stein to use coherence itself as a kind of narrative disruption. Coherence becomes noticeable and marked rather than the (expected) norm, and the passage offers a key for the overall project. The unremitting wordplay that characterizes most of *The Making of Americans* is used more selectively in this account, more prominently marking digressions from the story line. Through these digressions, Stein pointedly dramatizes the pressure exerted by untold stories on the narrative of *The Making of Americans*. These digressions are effective and revealing even without knowledge of Stein's then unpublished work, although of course that knowledge deepens the reader's understanding of them.

The relationship between Stein's insight into her authorship and the story of the breakup of Martha and Phillip's marriage emerges through a series of displacements that begins when Phillip meets Cora Dounor. A painful description of Phillip's illicit desire, and of Martha's intuition of that desire, is interrupted by a vivid description of a youth at a crossroads:

> It happens often about the twenty-ninth year of a life that all the forces that have been engaged through the years of childhood, adolescence and youth in confused and sometimes angry combat range themselves in ordered ranks, one is uncertain of one's aims, meaning and power during these years of tumultuous growth when aspiration has no relation to fulfillment and one plunges here and there with energy and misdirection during the strain and stress of the making of a personality until at last we reach the twenty-ninth year, the straight and narrow gateway of form and purpose and we exchange a dim possibility for a big or small reality.
>
> Also in our american life where there is no coercion in custom and it is our right to change our vocation as often as we have desire and opportunity, it is a common experience that our youth extends through the whole first twenty-nine years of our life and it is not till we reach thirty that we find at last that vocation for which we feel ourselves fit and to which we willingly devote continued labor. It must be owned that while much labor is lost to the world in these efforts to secure one's true vocation, nevertheless it makes more completeness in individual life and perhaps in the end will prove as useful to the world, and if we believe that there is more meaning in the choice of love than plain propinquity so we may well believe that there is more meaning in vocations than that it is the thing we can first learn about and win an income with. (*MA*, 436–37)

The apparent freedom of choice suggested by "no coercion in custom" is complicated, in this passage, by the use of the passive voice ("have been engaged") in the depiction of psychic struggle. The initiate in this liminal scene struggles unproductively and then submits to the social order with relief.[67] In the predictability of the script—we all reach "our vocational decision at thirty"—Stein implies an invisible cultural directive. William James had labeled "the period between twenty and thirty . . . the critical one in the formation of intellectual and professional habits" (*PP*, 126). Stein's passage, which reflects (and perhaps explores) that assumption, evokes the first two paragraphs of *The Making of Americans*—the scene in the orchard and the gradual acceptance of one's faults—as violence ("angry combat") and uncertainty give way to orderly self-acceptance.

The youth at the crossroads is, of course, Phillip Redfern, but Stein, too, made a vocational commitment, beginning *The Making of Americans* in her twenty-ninth year. Other affinities entwine their stories. The passage, as I have noted, follows Phillip's first encounter with the woman who will become his mistress; it catches him in the first hint of his illicit desire. As such, the scene presents the potential for disruption, a potential quickly deferred by the discussion of Phillip's career choice. In the conjunction of a vocation and a desire experienced as illicit, Stein harks back to the genesis of her own project. Not only did the twenty-nine-year-old Stein begin writing *The Making of Americans* in 1903, but she also expatriated herself and drafted *Q.E.D.*, the story of her illicit desire, which she subsequently misplaced or displaced. In *The Autobiography of Alice B. Toklas* she claims to have rediscovered *Q.E.D.* in 1932, just before writing *Alice B. Toklas.*

Stein wrote *Q.E.D.* in order to understand the painfully unsettling experience of the lesbian love triangle involving her, May Bookstaver, and Mabel Haynes, both fellow students at Johns Hopkins, and she continued to work out the complexities of this devastating relationship in *Fernhurst* and even in "Melanctha." Most interesting and most neglected, however, are the ways her displacements work to foreground issues of composition as well as character. Those displacements are worth rehearsing. To begin with, a triangle among Martha, Phillip, and Cora turns into a less explicit triangle among Hannah Charles, Cora, and Phillip when Hannah enjoins Martha "to keep Mr. Redfern in order" (*MA*, 439). Foiling Martha's desperate attempts to remain in ignorance of her husband's alleged infidelity, Hannah Charles explains that she "cannot allow him to make Miss Dounor the subject of scandalous talk" (*MA*, 439). Phillip has evidently disrupted a proprietary relationship between Hannah and Cora. Stein's choice of names reinforces her interest in dynamic interactions rather than one-to-one correspondences: the act of writing, as she demonstrates, entails reconfiguration rather than representation. *Martha* Carey Thomas becomes Hannah Charles, but *Martha* Hersland inherits her name, as May Bookstaver inherited Thomas's name when she became *Q.E.D.*'s Helen Thomas. *Alfred* Hodder gives his name to Martha's brother, *Alfred* Hersland. More generally, the name Mary resurfaces continually if peripherally in *The Making of Americans.* It is the name not only of Mary Gwinn but also of Mary Garrett, who lived with Thomas at the Bryn Mawr deanery from 1906, and "Mary" is close to "May," Stein's own beloved in the incident that inspired *Q.E.D.*[68] With such displacements, Stein had begun to work out the indirection through which one tells a suppressed story. *Fernhurst* itself functions here as the story Stein *can* tell, the story that displaces the pressing story of *Q.E.D.* Those displacements in turn correspond to the less conscious displacements through which a repressed story (a different kind of untellable story) makes itself felt. Although it is unclear whom she would have expected to understand fully the point of the inclusion of the fragment, one must bear in mind the narrator's quip, in *The Making of Americans*, "I am writing for myself and strangers" (*MA*, 289).

The superimpositions of this passage express Stein's ongoing thematic concerns with the potential disruptions of illicit desire and with the displacements and cover-ups of the bourgeois conventions of nineteenth-century marriages and novels. Where *Q.E.D.* had presented an unconventional theme—the badly ended lesbian affair that arguably began her expatriation—in conventional narrative form, Stein subsequently exchanged thematic for formal unconventionality. Sexual promiscuity and encoded lesbianism surface in the innuendos and implications of *Three Lives*, but, as in many nineteenth-century novels, these transgressions are contained for a white middle-class writer by the protective alterity of race and class. Yet in *The Making of Americans*, the writing itself registers disturbance, the unsettled and unsettling scene of an increasingly insufficient cover-up.

Stein superimposes the desired impact of her own experimentation onto Hannah Carey's insistence that Martha Hersland "gain the knowledge she dreaded to possess" (*MA*, 440). That knowledge comes through "evidence," specifically a letter that Martha finds on Phillip's desk. With Martha's discovery of the letter, the narrative moves from conventional narration to the more characteristic interior prose: "Mrs. Redfern arose and went into his room. She walked up to his desk and opening his portfolio saw a letter in his writing. She scarcely hesitated so eager was she to read it. She read it to the end, she had her evidence. Categories that once to some one had real meaning can later to that same one be all empty. It is queer that words that meant something in our thinking and our feeling can later come to have in them in us not at all any meaning. This is happening always to every one really feeling meaning in words they are saying" (*MA*, 440). Stein brilliantly captures Martha's disorientation in the experience of her own prose. In place of a hackneyed phrase such as "the world seemed emptied of meaning," Stein dramatizes a world emptied of meaning, the unequivocal estrangement of the word. Phillip's behavior challenges Martha's assumptions about the relationship signified by words like "marriage." Stein's disruption of the grammatical structure calls attention to the structures that organize meaning and to the point of her project, which is to estrange the reader from conventional meaning (as Martha has been estranged) and make visible the processes that produce it.

Not only words, but people become strangers at such moments: "there is in each case so complete a changing of experiencing in feeling and thinking, or in time or in something, that something, some one once alive to some one is then completely a stranger to that one, the meaning in a word to that one the meaning in a way of feeling and thinking that is a category to some one, some one whom some one was knowing, these then come to be all lost to that one sometime later in the living of that one" (MA, 441). Not only does Martha no longer recognize the man she thought she knew in Phillip, but the word "husband" has ceased to mean what she had thought it meant. Finally, Stein brings the focus back to herself and her project. The estrangement of language, after all, must affect the writer: "some then have a little shame in them when they are copying an old piece of writing where they were using words that sometime had real meaning for them and now have not any real meaning in them to the feeling and the thinking and the imagining of such a one" (MA, 441). Fernhurst, for example, has changed its meaning as Stein copied it into The Making of Americans.[69] Martha's unsettling, disorienting experience is also the writer's and probably the reader's.

Stein writes on the discomfiting border of public and private, in the language of intrusion, like the language of madness or, to use her own analogy, the "losing-self sense" between waking and sleeping. Her writing is, as Ulla Dydo suggests, more experiential than conventionally narrative.[70] Such is the logic of even Stein's most lucid work, as in The Autobiography of Alice B. Toklas, where her pose does much of the destabilizing work of her prose. And that work most clearly articulates the connection between the threat of lesbianism and the challenge of Stein's experimental writing. The suppressed—or, if we are to believe the untrustworthy narrator of Alice B. Toklas, the repressed—Q.E.D. resurfaces suggestively in the autobiography that Stein tells through Alice's persona. The content of the manuscript is not disclosed, as Toklas and Stein's lesbian relationship remains unspoken, but the resurfaced manuscript nonetheless refigures the story of Stein's lesbianism as itself an inadequately suppressed text, a disruption that may also have generated the narrative.[71] In this context, Stein and Toklas's relationship represents a collaborative subjectivity that envisions the social process by which a self is created. As Cynthia Merrill astutely observes, the persona of "Alice" allows Gertrude to represent the narrating subject as a "mirrored image," a self constructed through the eyes ("gaze") of an other.[72] With the allusion to *Q.E.D.*, Stein analogizes the anxiety evoked by lesbianism and by the paradigm of selfhood offered by this collaborative subjectivity. In her study of contagious madness (*folie à deux*), Terry Castle demonstrates the homophobic discourse (directed especially against two women) resonant within the case studies of pairs who shared in a hallucination, and she argues that the social anxiety generated by female-female relationships is displaced onto the anxiety evoked by shared madness.[73] Those anxieties seem intrinsic to the challenge to conventional ideas of selfhood that Stein depicts in *The Autobiography of Alice B. Toklas*. The collaborative subject that Stein offers in that work corresponds to the logic of her writing, to the losing-self sense that it evokes. The anxiety of identity produced by *The Making of Americans* is likewise generated, in part, by Stein's estrangement of the language of selfhood.

Although Alice is frequently cast as Stein's most enabling reader, the narrator of *The Making of Americans* writes for herself and strangers, where "strangers" summons not only unknown readers but also the alienated that Stein figures in the "niggers and servant girls and the foreign population generally." In a wonderful turn, *The Making of Americans* recasts those strangers of the 1906 Mabel Weeks letter as the mirror images of the most representative "American" self. With the estrangement of the word, the primary experience of Stein's prose, everyone can become a stranger for everyone else—and to themselves. Not only are the estranged never far from "us," but, Stein suggests, we are never far from the experience of estrangement. Although this analysis risks blurring the distinction between the sense of estrangement on the one hand, and social and material marginality on the other, it captures the principal—and motivating—anxiety behind Americanization initiatives, an anxiety that contributes to the construction and perpetuation of those margins.

Stein's performative writing, which represents the (illicit) desire to break through the representational conventions of the nineteenth-century novel, is conveniently superimposed on Phillip Redfern's illicit desire, which threatens the conventions of his nineteenth-century marriage. For

Stein, by analogy, the creative urgency of untold stories expresses illicit desire. And yet, to be "illicit," such desire relies on—and is actually defined by—those conventions. Terms such as "adultery" or "legitimacy," for example, signal the acceptance of cultural prohibitions. By estranging words from their meanings, Stein makes it possible to think about the existence of particular prohibitions: how and why they may have arisen, and how experience becomes comprehensible through them. But her challenge is thereby to meaningful—or, comprehensible—existence.

The author of "Cultivated Motor Automatism" surely understood the psychological forces working against her project. The narrator of *The Making of Americans* follows Martha Hersland's reluctant discovery of the "evidence" of her husband's adultery with a discussion of how each person falls back on a familiar narrative to explain unsettling experiences, no matter how different—to explain loss, for example, or rejection. Her observation, which becomes a kind of refrain in *The Making of Americans,* has cultural as well as psychological implications; she explains how individuals unwittingly create their own demons, which in turn lay the foundation for cultural beliefs. Her formulations anticipate some of the most prescient cultural observations of Sigmund Freud:

> Some out of their own virtue make a god who sometimes later is a terror to them. Out of their own virtue they make a god who sometimes later is a terror to them. Out of their virtue they make a god who sometimes later is a terror to them. Some make some things like laws out of the nature of them, out of the nature of some other one. Some are controlled by other people's virtue, and then it scares them. Listen to each one telling about their own virtue and that grows to make a god for them, grows to be a law for them and often afterwards scares them, some afterwards like it, some forget it, some are it. Some honor what is right to them for them to be doing. Some separate honor from the doing of the thing, have it as a feeling. . . .
>
> Out of their own certain feeling some make a god who sometimes later is a terror to them. That is a kind of feeling that some have about laws of nature as they call them. Many make of their certain feeling a god which later terrifies them. . . .
>
> Some out of their virtue make a god who sometimes later is a terror to them. . . . Some make some things like laws out of the nature of them, out of the nature of some other one. (*MA,* 450, 480)

The word "certain" has two meanings in these passages: *particular* and *sure*. The passages imply a progression from particularity to certainty: how and why a "certain" (particular) feeling becomes a feeling of certainty. The refrains and repetitions trace different configurations to a common source. Science, government, and religion build on the need for "certain feeling." Yet Stein is also concerned with the consequences of this transformation. As Julia seeks refuge in prescribed behavior, the authority of gods, laws, and their incumbent terrors emerge from her readily displaced and ultimately disavowed (hypothetical) act of creation. Julia does not wish "to recreate the world and make one all from her own head." She would rather submit to an illusion of freedom than face the consequences of attempting to challenge such illusions. The god-become-terror, which stems from the sense of passivity before an intact and coherent, although incomprehensible, system (ironically of one's own making) keeps people like Julia from seeing too deeply into the terms of their own creation. A worse terror, it seems, dwells in the possible erosion of cultural authority, and the consequent questions to which incoherence might lead. Stein allows the possibility that "some can just resist and not make their own anything" (*MA*, 443). They are the dispossessed, the particular strangers (or estranged) for whom she most hopefully writes.

Stein assigns literature a principal role in the process of socialization. The narrator of *The Making of Americans* describes another "strange feeling one has in one's later living" that derives from the recognition that one's hard-earned knowledge has already been imparted, although unperceived by the reader, in the "story-books" from one's childhood. The "strange feeling" arises

> when one finds the story-books really have truth in them, for one loved the story-books earlier, one loved to read them but one never really believed there was truth in them, and later when one by living has gained a new illusion and a kind of wisdom, and one reads again in them, there it is, the things we have learned since to believe in, there it is and we know then that the man or the woman who wrote them had just the same kind of wisdom in them we have been spending our lives winning. . . . Yes from their fathers' and their mothers' living [children] can get some wisdom, yes supply them with a tradition by your lives, you grown men and women, and for the rest let them come to us for their teaching. (*MA*, 29)

The storybooks shape their readers' perceptions, which are subsequently converted into beliefs. The writer is therefore a socializing agent. It is a mistake to think of Stein as altogether critical of this project or as opposing either tradition or the cultural practice of literature. The child of immigrants knew the importance, the beauty, of tradition. But she also knew that gods could become terrors, and she was fascinated by the process through which that could happen. Unlike Julia, Stein does set out "to recreate the world and make one all from her own head."

The Making of Americans is not exactly a storybook one loves in one's youth; both may inform, but Stein replaces the conforming of the storybook with her own deforming. She re-presents the group story to expose the cultural plots and thus refocus attention using a writing style that grows out of her efforts to break the "habits of inattention" that, according to James, cause us to pass directly from physical sensations "to their import . . . letting their substantive nature alone" (*PP,* 431). Gertrude Stein did not write stream of consciousness; rather, she wrote against the stream, emphasizing disruptions in order to call attention to the habits of consciousness as shaped and shaping processes. The devices she used to frustrate narrative had the effect as well of deforming the group story. The story of the making of Americans inevitably encounters the plot of that making—the choices determining the direction of attention and the logical progression of events that contributes to a sense of inevitability. But to re-present the unchosen, the gap that narrative conceals, is to risk chaos—or, as Stein's ambivalent reception attests, the consequences of incomprehensibility.

Almost a decade after the publication of *The Making of Americans,* and several decades after its composition, Stein described her project in her lectures in America. "In the three novels written in this generation that are the important things written in this generation," she declares in "Portraits and Repetition," "there is, in none of them a story. There is none in Proust in the Making of Americans or in Ulysses" (PR, 184). She accounts for the popularity of "novels . . . which tell a story" by explaining, presumably with reference to the media, that "anybody literally anybody can hear or read everything or anything about anything or everything that happens every day just as it has happened or is happening on that day," and storytelling novels "are really then more of the same much more of the same, and of course anybody likes more of the same and so a great many novels are written and a great many novels are read telling more of these stories but you can see you do see that the important things written in this generation do not tell a story" (PR, 184–85). Stein refused the story. (Although it is impossible to ignore her self-aggrandizing claims to being the misunderstood genius, it is also impossible to ignore the fact that she was right: her popularity did suffer for her innovation.)

Yet Stein understood the inevitability as well as the distortions of conventional narratives, and her formal innovations reflect her effort to depict and analyze that inevitability. In "The Gradual Making of The Making of Americans," she describes her "struggle . . . to make something as a whole present of something that it had taken a great deal of time to find out." That effort, she explains, "has made [her] try so many ways to tell [her] story." Stylistically, she wrote sentences that dropped "imaginary dependent clauses"—that brought ostensibly less important details into a different relation to ostensibly main ideas—and that relied heavily on present participles and a repetitive interiority characteristic of *Three Lives* (especially "Melanctha") and pushed to an extreme in *The Making of Americans* (GM, 147). Stein had called this stylistic innovation "the continuous present" in "Composition as Explanation," a lecture delivered in England in 1926. She defines it thus: "A continuous present is a continuous present."[74] The continuous present, in other words, is an irreducible equivalence, a writing against the causal or chronological narratives of history. Very much in dialogue with such visual artists as Henri Matisse, Pablo Picasso, and Juan Gris, the young psychologist brought her interests and experiments in perception to bear on the aesthetic concern with perspective. But her own medium was always most pressingly words— words and stories, sentences and paragraphs—and time, in her medium, was paramount. This concern she shared with turn-of-the-century French philosopher Henri Bergson, who argued for a distinction between the perceived or measured time of scientific discourse and the experiential time that he called "*durée réelle*" (real duration). According to Bergson, whose theories also intrigued William James, the attempt to perceive time results in its spatial representation, as a line, that breaks time into successive moments, whereas time experienced (or lived) is simultaneous and whole. The intellect, in other words, works like movies, breaking an experienced totality into successive static images.

Bergson uses this distinction to reconceptualize ideas about human freedom. A person's choices, viewed linearly, appear predetermined; re-situated in real duration, however, choices evolve, making possible freedom of choice—what he calls *"un acte libre"* ("a free act"). A "free act" expresses the fact that "le moi seule en aura été *l'auteur*" (the me alone will have been the *author* of it; emphasis added).[75] With "l'auteur," Bergson chooses a word that forcefully conveys the originary and authoritative locus of the act in the "me." Yet language has no way to convey that freedom; any attempt to explain—or narrate—the act reverts to spatial, and deterministic, conceptualizations. If freedom could be hypothesized, for Bergson, it was more difficult to describe.

The discrepancy between the hypothesis and the description is precisely what interests Stein in *The Making of Americans*. The freedom she conceptualizes defies expression; it has to remain an untold story. Real duration, like repeating, countermands the linear plotting of narration. But the attempt to describe real duration is, like the attempt to legislate freedom, paradoxical. The result, what Stein calls a "space of time," marks a contained and deterministic freedom—a narrative of freedom that describes not a "free act" but an enactment. America, in Stein's formulation, is predicated on a Bergsonian notion of real duration: "In short this generation has conceived an intensity of movement so great that it has not to be seen against something else to be known, and therefore, this generation does not connect itself with anything, that is what makes this generation what it is and that is why it is American" (GM, 166). That denial of connection with the past was precisely what Woodrow Wilson had decried in his 1896 address, "Princeton in the Nation's Service," warning that ignorance of that connection risked making a people "infantile in every generation."[76] For Stein, however, ignorance—or denial—of the past is precisely what makes each generation *repeat* it. The "space of time" is an image of containment: the inevitably of a narrative that preserves the past. Stein calls *The Making of Americans*

an American book an essentially American book, because this thing is an essentially American thing this sense of a space of time and what is to be done within this space of time not in any way excepting in the way that it is inevitable that there is this space of time and anybody who is an American feels what is inside this space of time and so well they do what they do within this space of time, and so ultimately it is a thing contained within. . . . I am always trying to tell this thing that a space of time is a natural thing for an American to always have inside them as something in which they are continuously moving. Think of anything, of cowboys, of movies, of detective stories, of anybody who goes anywhere or stays at home and is an American and you will realize that it is something strictly American to conceive a space that is filled with moving, a space of time that is filled always filled with moving and my first real effort to express this thing which is an American thing began in writing *The Making of Americans*. (GM, 160–61)

In that work, Stein depicts, finally, the paradox of attempting to perceive, or conceive of, real duration—and, conversely, of "attending to attention." To do so, as Bergson acknowledges, is to move into measured, or plotted, time. Stein's "continuous present" invariably becomes emplotted within "a space of time"; history is an inevitable part of human experience: evidence of the will to comprehend and therefore to narrate.

With the "continuous present," Stein imagines an interminable moment of unsated desire in which readers confront their longing for the sentence, for completion and comprehension, and ideally see their complicity as desiring subjects in constructing plots. Many of Stein's readers do not find *The Making of Americans* pleasurable largely because she uses repetition not to defer and thus heighten gratification but to replace it with an insatiable re-visioning, one that suspects pleasure as it refuses comprehension. Through her characters—Julia, Martha, and Phillip, for example—she demonstrates how the desire for comprehension prevails over the desire for freedom as each submits to prewritten scripts. Likewise, the writer (and the reader) cannot resist turning the "continuous present" into "a space of time." The concluding paragraph exemplifies that irresistibility: "Some *being* living and *being* in a family living and coming then to be old ones can come then to be dead ones. Any one can be certain that some can remember such a thing. Any family living can be one *being* existing and some can remember something of some such thing" (*MA*, 925; emphasis added). Context is generally unhelpful in reading this passage, and the reader's decision about parts of speech (whether to read "being" as a verb or a noun, for example) changes its meaning. The irresolution of this passage explains the motivation for cultural prescriptions: we are left unsated; life without the usual laws of grammar, of narration, of historical perception cannot be comprehended. People make sense when the desire to comprehend overpowers the project of attending to attention, as it always does. Sense-making is a fundamentally cultural activity.

In the concluding paragraph, as in the work as a whole, Stein represents the tension between "being" and "a being," the sense-making that turns "being" into "a being" (experience into identity). For her, the immigrant, who is transitional, dramatizes that tension. In *Everybody's Autobiography* (1937), which Stein wrote in part to understand the troubling effect the popularity of *The Autobiography of Alice B. Toklas* had on her writing (when, that is, she could no longer so easily claim the status of genius-outsider), she appears to assert her own innate identity as a writer: "I had always been I because I had words that had to be written inside me."[77] Yet the words, like the identity of writer, preform as they perform that identity. The very title of *Everybody's Autobiography* acknowledges the writer's group identity, which the narrator confirms with the quip, "You are of course never yourself" (*EA*, 68). In *The Making of Americans*, Stein strives to dispossess her readers, to capture, if only for fleeting moments and as if in a dream, the "losing-self sense" that turns them into cultural emigrants and then immigrants who willfully and gratefully conspire, as if with Emerson's Spirit, with what she has identified as a cultural plot.

Mina Loy once remarked that "Gertrude Stein explained the air of cubism to [her] as 'deconstruction preparatory to complete reconstruction of the objective.' "[78] And it is precisely the need to reconstruct that Stein, like Frederick Douglass, Herman Melville, Harriet Wilson, and W. E. B. Du Bois, foregrounds. She does not transcend the cultural activity of sense-making, but she does conceptually engage it through a text that is at once medium and metaphor. *The Making of Americans* turns the immigrant's story into a revisionary narrative. It does not always make for comfortable reading. Yet it performs what was for her the most vital task of art by bringing the unthinkable into dialectical engagement with imagination.

Coda: An American "We"

I return, in conclusion, to the anxiety expressed by Barrett Wendell and cited by Horace Kallen in "Democracy Versus the Melting-Pot": "We are submerged beneath a conquest so complete that the very name of us means something not ourselves" (DMP, 194). Wendell's response to the changing demographics of a nation besieged, to his mind, with immigrants could in fact be the watchword of United States nationalism. The changing "we" of the nation-state makes the very name of any "us" mean "something not ourselves." The task of any official story of the nation is to enable a smooth transition, to accommodate revisions in order simultaneously to transform and preserve "us." It at once builds on and changes prior forms of relatedness and reformulates concepts of personhood and home accordingly.

My study has been about what the poet John Yau calls "the reading of an ever-changing tale."[1] An official story of "a people" invariably lags behind the seismic demographic changes and corresponding untold stories that ultimately compel each revision. A national narrative must make the concept of a "home" for "a people" appear intrinsic and natural rather than contingent and, ultimately, fictive. At the same time, that narrative must make the concept of home able to accommodate both changing and contested frontiers and the mobility within its borders. "Home" must be sufficiently elastic to incorporate the local into the national: it must, in effect, be unhomelike.

I have been interested throughout my inquiry in the excitement generated and risks incurred by authors' efforts to turn attention to untold stories into readings of an ever-changing tale. From Douglass to Stein, these writers risked being thought bad writers; they risked being misunderstood, incomprehensible, and, most of all—to borrow from Stein—being *missable.* Yet they also felt themselves at risk of telling someone else's story. Authorship, for each of those writers, entailed negotiation. And they found in their negotiations the possibility for a dynamic and creative engagement with their own limitations that led to innovations in their art. I have sought to demonstrate how those innovations—the writers' willingness to test the limits and push at the conventions of literary forms—arose from and can in turn contribute to the fashioning and refashioning of official stories: the literariness of the constituting of Americans.

I have argued throughout this study for the creative uses writers have made of cultural anxiety and for the important insights offered by their engagements with it. I end with a recent example from the experimental multigenre narrative of Korean-born performance artist Theresa Hak Kyung Cha. In her haunting and powerful *Dictée* (1982), Cha brings together photographs, calligraphy, poetry, letters, religious and historical texts, political documents, and meditations to present the account offered by a United States immigrant of her inscription into history, and of the difficulty of recounting—of speaking from within—that process. I conclude with an episode in which the narrator transforms a depiction of the anxiety created by her own effort to cross a national border into an analysis of the need for a new story of We the People.

The episode follows a section devoted to the narrator's memory of stories of her mother's exile, when a young girl, in Manchuria and begins with the narrator's meditation on her own naturalization and, in particular, her American passport: "*I* have the documents. Documents, proof, evidence, photograph, signature. One day *you* raise the right hand and *you* are American. *They* give *you* an American Pass port. The United States of America. Somewhere someone has taken *my* identity and replaced it with their photograph. The other one. *Their* signature *their* seals. *Their* own image. And *you* learn the executive branch the legislative branch and the third. Justice. Judicial branch. It makes the difference. The rest is past."[2] Through the naturalization, the narrator stages a drama of identity. An oath turns her into an American, a metamorphosis that calls attention to the performative qualities and transformative powers of language. Yet the passport makes apparent the incompletion of the transformation, which the narrator experiences as an estrangement. She is literally altered, made into "the other one," and experiences her identity as a stolen possession. Cha captures the confusion at the center of this process with the ambiguity of "their photograph" and "their own image": *whose* photograph has replaced her identity? *Whose* image does she see? Presumably, the image in the photograph is the image of her that "they" want to see—that reflects *them*—but the ambiguous "own" underscores the magnitude of the transformation.

The pronouns forcefully dramatize the terms of this naturalization and chart the progress of the passage: "*you*," given a passport, moves through "*my* identity" into "*their* photograph" before reemerging as "you" and, by implication, the "I" with whom the passage begins. From the perspective of the culture into which she is naturalized, the narrator begins as an other ("you"). When the passport confers a legal identity, however, she becomes aware of a split signaled by the first- and third-person possessives, "my" and "their." The possessive pronouns rhetorically envision identity as a possession, a conditional property, which, like the documents that represent it, can be expropriated. The first-person subject "I" is used only to mark her possession of the documents. But, again, the documents reflect their own (and owned) image.

Cha privileges the role of the law in the making of the difference, which is the making of an American. Her new identity inducts her into a legislated (and selective) narrative, into "history," and passes over the "rest." It confers on her the possession that marks (and that is) her identity: the documents themselves and the right to possess those documents, to speak as an American "I." The judicial branch, like the naturalization process in general, "makes the difference" not only in the narrator, but also between history and the "past": the stories that can be told and those that cannot. For her, the naturalization process makes visible the fundamental alienability of any identity—of any "I"—as is evident in her claim that "they" have taken *her identity.* But she is concerned with the inadequacy of the stories that she can tell as an American "I": she resists "disappearing into the whiteness" (*D*, 113).

The narrator underscores that inadequacy in the account of her efforts to use her United States passport to cross national frontiers, which immediately follows the meditation on the naturalization; the anxiety she produces underscores a crisis in the national "we" that the passport does not adequately address:

You return and you are not one of them, they treat you with indifference. All the time you understand what they are saying. But the papers give you away. Every ten feet. They ask you identity. They comment upon your inability or ability to speak. Whether you are telling the truth or not about your nationality. They say you look other than you say. As if you didn't know who you were. You say who you are but you begin to doubt. They search you. They, the anonymous variety of uniforms, each division, strata, classification, any set of miscellaneous properly uni formed. They have the right, no matter what rank, however low their function they have the authority. Their authority sewn into the stitches of their costume. Every ten feet they demand to know who and what you are, who is represented. The eyes gather towards the appropriate proof. Towards the face then again to the papers, when did you leave the country why did you leave this country why are you returning to the country. (*D*, 56–57)

At the border, poised for reentry, the speaker obscures the terms of the return. We do not know whether she is returning to her birth country or to her adoptive one. It does not matter. In either case she is estranged, treated with an indifference that stems from an anxiety provoked by her difference. In fact, what follows does not suggest *indifference;* rather, "they" very insistently want to classify her. But the documents do not do their job; they do not enable the guards to recognize her. The problem lies in the discrepancy between the identity conferred by the documents and the preconceptions of the guards. The narrator disturbs them because they believe they have a clear sense of what a national subject should look like, but she, a Korean American, does not conform to that image ("their own image"). The language suggests an unmasking and a dispossession: "the papers give you away." They believe they have exposed her false claim to her identity, but they have actually dispossessed her of it: "they ask *you* [not your] identity." Identity has become a question rather than a possession.

For American border guards, she embodies a particular anxiety. If she is one of them, then they become unrecognizable to themselves. If she, an American, is excluded, then she embodies a displaced person—the consequences of not belonging and the possibility of their own exclusion as well. The narrator of *Dictée* confronts the contradiction of national narratives at cross purposes; an inclusive narrative comes into conflict with a competing exclusive narrative that brings a nonwhite, foreign-born American's identity into doubt: "they say you look other than you say." The doubt is contagious and destabilizing: "You say who you are but you begin to doubt." She has indeed been given away: dispossessed and betrayed. The process of Americanization has not successfully integrated the speaker into a "we."

"We" is in fact not a word in the lexicon of *Dictée*. For that matter, Cha rarely uses the first-person pronoun in any form. The few uses of "I" are typically reserved for quoted passages and letters (the "I" in the naturalization episode is a notable exception). The border guards and other officials are "they" and the central figures are characteristically "she" and "you." The uni formed world is clothed in indistinction as well as authority: "You see the color the hue the same you see the shape the form the same you see the unchangeable and the unchanged the same you smell filtered edited through progress and westernization the same" (*D*, 57). The stasis of the guards is overwhelming. In a later section, the narrator will recount a story of a wife who is similarly dispossessed by a husband who indisputably "possesses" her; he even touches her only "with his rank. By his knowledge of his own rank. By the claim of his rank" against "her non-body her non-entity" (*D*, 112). The narrator refuses a "we" that is complicated by the whiteness and maleness of those who "own" the images.

The border crossing makes the terms of her exclusion visible to the narrator: "You see the will, you see the breath, you see the out of breath and out of will but you still see the will. Will and will only espouse this land this sky this time this people. You are one same particle. You leave you come back to the shell left empty all this time. To claim to reclaim, the space. Into the mouth the wound the entry is reverse and back each organ artery gland pace element, implanted, housed skin upon skin, membrane, vessel, waters, dams, ducts, canals, bridges" (*D*, 57). More than an act of will speaks "this people" into existence. The use of "espouse" in conjunction with "will" suggests marriage—and the contract signified by marriage. With "I will," the wife takes the husband who will possess her; the immigrant, likewise, consents to the terms specified in the oath of citizenship. At the border, the narrator sees not only an act of will that safeguards identity as it polices national borders, but a corresponding willingness even on the part of the dispossessed. As her body merges into the physical infrastructure of the state at the end of the passage, she literally embodies the terms of the consent: the internalization of frontiers. Bodies thus become representations of the state, normalizing its frontiers. Conversely, the infrastructure becomes coterminous with the body, organic and violable *as a body.* A threat to the integrity of the state can be readily represented in *bodily*—and ontological—terms.

Yet there is no "I" in this passage. The narrator, it will be remembered, has been dispossessed of her representative status. In the guards' narrative, *her* body does not represent this state. Their official story has no place for her, but their efforts at exclusion succeed only in further estranging her, in creating a haunting presence, an emblem of their need for a new, an expanded, official story. Although "not a single word allowed to utter until the last section," the narrator tells her story (*D*, 58). She tells of the need for a revised version of We the People and of the difficulty of those revisions; her telling is evident in her underscored acts of authorship: in the spaces, for example, between "Pass" and "port" or "uni" and "formed" that ask the reader to think anew about words and their function.

The deferred "we" of *Dictée* raises questions that inform all of the works of this study: what are the limits and boundaries of We the People? What is the role of the writer in the constituting of Americans? These remain pressing questions at the close of the twentieth century, and the project of reading and writing ever-changing tales of the nation remains a vital one in law, politics, and literature. *Constituting Americans* has attempted to convey the power of those tales and the urgency of that project.

Notes

······

Introduction

1. W. E. B. Du Bois, *The Souls of Black Folk*, in *W. E. B. Du Bois: Writings* (New York: The Library of America, 1986), pp. 357–547, p. 447. Subsequent text references are designated *S*.

2. Laura [Riding] Jackson, *The Telling* (New York: Harper and Row, 1972), p. 6.

3. For a discussion of American authorship as an effort to define an American "we," see Kenneth Dauber, *The Idea of Authorship in America: Democratic Poetics from Franklin to Melville* (Madison: University of Wisconsin Press, 1990). Dauber sees American authorship as an expression (and sometimes exploration) of democratic politics and a fashioning of "democratic poetics" of which Melville's " 'unreadable' works" represent the extension (xx). I am indebted to Dauber's rhetorical and cultural readings of the formulation of authorship as a concept in America.

4. In the " 'symptomal' analysis" of, for example, Pierre Macherey, Louis Althusser, and Fredric Jameson, literary works manifest the limitations of their own production; silences and breaks mark choices not made—choices that could not be made because of cultural conventions. As Althusser contends "art makes us *see* . . . the *ideology* from which it is born, in which it bathes, from which it detaches itself as art, and to which it *alludes*." See Althusser, "A Letter on Art in Reply to André Daspre," in *Lenin and Philosophy and other Essays*, trans. Ben Brewster (New York: Monthly Review Press, 1971), pp. 221–27, p. 222. The phrase " 'symptomal' analysis" is Jameson's. See Jameson, *The Political Unconscious: Narrative as a Socially Symbolic Act* (Ithaca: Cornell University Press, 1981), p. 57. See also Macherey, *A Theory of Literary Production*, trans. Geoffrey Wall (London: Routledge and Kegan Paul, 1978). Using evidence of untold stories to perform cultural analyses, the authors in this study interestingly anticipate these ideological analyses.

For explorations of the relationship of such reading practices to "the feminine," see, for example, Shari Benstock's "psychogrammanalysis," in *Textualizing the Feminine: On the Limits of Genre* (Norman: University of Oklahoma Press, 1991); and Dale M. Bauer's theories of "conscription" in *Feminist Dialogics: A Theory of Failed Community* (Albany: State University of New York Press, 1988).

5. My assumptions in these readings come closest to what Sacvan Bercovitch calls "the hermeneutics of non-transcendence." See Bercovitch, "Introduction: The Music of America," in *The Rites of Assent: Transformations in the Symbolic Construction of America* (New York: Routledge, 1993), p. 5; see also Bercovitch, "The Problem of Ideology in American Literary History," *Critical Inquiry* 12 (Summer 1986): 631–53. My concerns with the relationship between storytelling and national identity began as an engagement with and response to the arguments put forth by Bercovitch in *The Puritan Origins of the American Self* (New Haven: Yale University Press, 1976), and *The American Jeremiad* (Madison: University of Wisconsin Press, 1978). Finally, in my formulations, I have also been especially challenged by the work of Walter Benn Michaels. See Michaels, *The Gold Standard and the Logic of Naturalism: American Literature at the Turn of the Century* (Berkeley: University of California Press, 1987).

6. Benedict Anderson, *Imagined Communities: Reflections on the Origin and Spread of Nationalism,* rev. ed. (London: Verso, 1991), p. 204; subsequent text references are designated *IC*. Other studies on nationalism I have found especially useful include Hans Kohn, *Nationalism: Its Meaning and History* (New York: Van Nostrand, 1965); Frantz Fanon, *The Wretched of the Earth,* trans. Constance Farrington (New York: Grove Press, 1963); J. A. Armstrong, *Nations before Nationalism* (Chapel Hill: University of North Carolina Press, 1982); Ernest Gellner, *Nations and Nationalism* (Oxford: Oxford University Press, 1983); Anthony D. Smith, *The Ethnic Origins of Nations* (Oxford: Blackwell, 1986) and *National Identity* (Reno: University of Nevada Press, 1991); E. J. Hobsbawm, *Nations and Nationalism since 1780: Programme, Myth, Reality* (Cambridge: Cambridge University Press, 1990); Liah Greenfeld, *Nationalism: Five Roads to Modernity* (Cambridge, Mass.: Harvard University Press, 1992); and especially the essays in Etienne Balibar and Immanuel Wallerstein, *Race, Nation, Class: Ambiguous Identities,* trans. of Etienne Balibar by Chris Turner (London: Verso, 1991); and in Homi K. Bhabha, ed., *Nation and Narration* (London: Routledge, 1990).

Discussions of United States nationalism that I have found especially helpful and resonant with my own work include Anne Norton, *Alternative Americas: A Reading of Antebellum Political Culture* (Chicago: University of Chicago Press, 1986); and Lauren Berlant, *The Anatomy of National Fantasy: Hawthorne, Utopia and Everyday Life* (Chicago: University of Chicago Press, 1991).

My formulations about the national narrative are explicitly engaged with theorists of nation and narrative, especially Anderson, Balibar, Bhabha, and Timothy Brennan. See Bhabha, "DissemiNation: Time, Narrative, and the Margins of the Modern Nation," in *Nation and Narration,* pp. 291–322; and Brennan, "The

National Longing for Form," in *Nation and Narration*, pp. 44–70. My thinking about narrative form has also been shaped in dialogue with and response to a disparate group, including Peter Brooks, *Reading for the Plot: Design and Intention in Narrative* (New York: Vintage Books, 1984); Erich Kahler, *The Inward Turn of Narrative*, trans. Richard Winston and Clara Winston (Evanston, Ill.: Northwestern University Press, 1973); M. M. Bakhtin, "Discourse in the Novel," in *The Dialogic Imagination: Four Essays by M. M. Bakhtin*, ed. Michael Holquist, trans. Caryl Emerson and Michael Holquist (Austin: University of Texas Press, 1981), pp. 259–422; and Hayden White, "The Value of Narrativity in the Representation of Reality," in *On Narrative*, ed. W. J. T. Mitchell (Chicago: University of Chicago Press, 1981), pp. 1–23.

7. Etienne Balibar, "The Nation Form: History and Ideology," in *Race, Nation, Class*, pp. 86–106, p. 93.

8. I typically use cultural identity rather than national identity throughout this study in order to convey a distinction, which was important to the nation-builders treated herein, between a sense of belonging to a community and a recognizable (and legal) political affiliation. That distinction underlay their efforts to press literary authors to depict a latent community that would *justify* national boundaries. These terms, then and now, overlap significantly. I am interested throughout in a *national* cultural identity (American)—shared symbolic systems defined in relation to national frontiers—and in the terms of personhood articulated through narratives of that identity.

9. Sigmund Freud, "The 'Uncanny' " (*Das Unheimliche*), in *The Standard Edition of the Complete Psychological Works of Sigmund Freud*, trans. James Strachey, with Anna Freud, Alix Strachey, and Alan Tyson, vol. 17 (1917–1919), *An Infantile Neurosis and Other Works* (London: Hogarth Press and the Institute of Psycho-Analysis, 1955; reprint, 1986), pp. 217–56, p. 219. Subsequent text references are designated U. My discussion of this essay has benefited from Sam Weber's brilliant analysis in "The Sideshow, or: Remarks on a Canny Moment," *MLN* 88 (December 1973): 1102–33, and from discussions with Alys Weinbaum and Brent Edwards.

10. Even the placement of the note is significant; it ends Freud's discussion of the uncanny experiences associated with allegedly "surmounted" primitive beliefs, and it immediately precedes Freud's distinction between those experiences and the uncanny experiences associated with the return of repressed infantile complexes. Where the former concerns the border between two contradictory systems of belief about reality, the latter involves a psychic boundary between the beliefs of two stages of personal development. Freud goes on to complicate his own distinction between types of uncanny experiences, and the note (in text and context) rests on that "hazy" boundary.

11. The mirror of Jacques Lacan's mirror stage seems to work contrary to Freud's mirror. For Lacan, the mirror stage refers to a developmental period in a child's life (between six and eighteen months) when the mirroring of a child's

body (in an actual or metaphorical mirror) results in the child's identification with the specular image. That identification, for Lacan, transforms the subject. The "Ideal-I" emerges, an illusion of coherent or integral selfhood, which forms the basis for the social selfhood marked by the grammatical subject "I." The mirror stage ends with a move from the specular to the social, elaborated by and through language. Subjectivity, for Lacan, is intrinsically alienating and decidedly social. See "The Mirror Stage as Formative of the Function of the I as Revealed in Psychoanalytic Experience," in *Ecrits: A Selection,* trans. Alan Sheridan (New York: W. W. Norton, 1977), pp. 1–7. I follow the reformulations of Lacan performed by Frantz Fanon and Louis Althusser in reading the mirror stage dynamically as an analysis of the processes that shape cultural identity. See Fanon, "The Negro and Psychopathology," in *Black Skin, White Masks,* trans. Charles Lam Markmann (New York: Grove Press, 1967), pp. 141–209; and Althusser, "Ideology and Ideological State Apparatuses (Notes towards an Investigation)," in *Lenin and Philosophy,* pp. 127–86. Read in this way, Lacan's mirror stage explains why Freud's and Mach's mirrors serve as *dis*orienting media. Freud and Mach discover a specular misrecognition ("meconnaissance" refers to the subject's disavowal of knowledge and feelings); they become aware (although it is not thus formulated) of a discrepancy in their images of themselves. Because of the importance of the mirror (and mirroring) to Freud's, Lacan's, and Fanon's formulations, I read the mirror as a symbolically generative tradition and am less concerned, in my own genealogy, with tracking allusions to *specific* mirrors than with the theoretical development of a concept across cultures and time periods.

12. Horace Kallen cites this remark from his private correspondence with his former instructor, Barrett Wendell, in "Democracy Versus the Melting-Pot: A Study of American Nationality," *Nation* 100 (February 18 and 25, 1915): 190–94 and 217–20, p. 219. For an extended discussion of this statement, see chapter 4 in this volume.

13. Theodore Roosevelt, "True Americanism," reprinted in *The Works of Theodore Roosevelt,* National Edition (New York: Charles Scribner's Sons, 1926), pp. 13–26, p. 26. For an extended discussion of this remark, see chapter 3 in this volume.

14. Sir William Blackstone, *Commentaries on the Laws of England,* 4 vols., vol. 1: *Of the Rights of Persons* (1765) (Chicago: University of Chicago Press, 1979), p. 430. Subsequent text references are designated *BC.*

15. Frantz Fanon, "The Negro and Psychopathology," in *Black Skin, White Masks,* p. 143. Subsequent text references are designated *BS.*

16. Fanon explicitly refers to Lacan's mirror stage for this observation. Fanon's use of "conversely" here—his assertion that the white man is the real Other of the black man—is at odds with the rest of the essay, in which he argues that Antilleans have internalized white images of blackness that make the black man his own Other (the Other's Other is the Other's self).

17. For his full discussion of double-consciousness, see W. E. B. Du Bois, *The Souls of Black Folk*, p. 364.

18. Mina Loy, "Gertrude Stein," in *The Last Lunar Baedeker*, ed. Roger L. Conover (Highlands, N.C.: Jargon Society Press, 1982), p. 26. The whole poem reads:

> Curie
> of the laboratory
> of vocabulary
> she crushed
> the tonnage
> of consciousness
> congealed to phrase
> to extract
> a radium of the word

19. Toni Morrison, *Playing in the Dark: Whiteness and the Literary Imagination* (Cambridge: Harvard University Press, 1992), p. 6. Other studies on how "race" has shaped and misshaped American literature that I have found especially helpful include Aldon Lynn Nielsen, *Reading Race: White American Poets and the Radical Discourse in the Twentieth Century* (Athens, Ga.: University of Georgia Press, 1988); Eric Cheyfitz, *The Poetics of Imperialism: Translation and Colonization from "The Tempest" to "Tarzan"* (New York: Oxford University Press, 1991); Lucy Maddox, *Removals: Nineteenth-Century American Literature and the Politics of Indian Affairs* (New York: Oxford University Press, 1991); Dana D. Nelson, *The Word in Black and White: Reading "Race" in American Literature, 1638–1867* (New York: Oxford University Press, 1992); Kenneth W. Warren, *Black and White Strangers: Race and American Literary Realism* (Chicago: University of Chicago Press, 1993); and Eric J. Sundquist, *To Wake the Nations: Race in the Making of American Literature* (Cambridge, Mass.: Harvard University Press, 1993). These projects are all part of a rethinking of cultural narratives and of the place of literature within those narratives.

For my understanding of the uncanniness of specific groups and practices in the United States, I am especially indebted to Allen Grossman's breathtaking essay, "The Poetics of Union in Whitman and Lincoln: An Inquiry toward the Relationship of Art and Policy," in Walter Benn Michaels and Donald E. Pease, ed., *The American Renaissance Reconsidered: Selected Papers from the English Institute, 1982–83* (Baltimore: Johns Hopkins University Press, 1985), pp. 183–208. Grossman observes that "the refounding of personhood, the historical function of the poet, was the deferred business both of the American Revolution and of American literature" (p. 192). In my own readings, the imperatives of the latter task interfered with the speculations associated with the former. I am also indebted to Grossman's reading of Lincoln in this essay. Ralph Ellison also includes an elegant discussion of the uncanniness of the black American for the white American in "Change the Joke and Slip the Yoke," in *Shadow and Act* (New York: Vintage Books, 1972), pp. 45–59. On the reformulation of personhood in the antebellum United States, see also Karen Sánchez-Eppler, *Touching Liberty: Abolition, Feminism, and the Politics of the Body* (Berkeley: University of California Press, 1993).

1. Neither Citizen Nor Alien

1. On Douglass's relationship with British and United States abolitionists, see especially William S. McFeely, *Frederick Douglass* (New York: W. W. Norton & Company, 1991).

2. Frederick Douglass, *My Bondage and My Freedom*, ed. William L. Andrews (Urbana: University of Illinois Press, 1987), p. 220. Subsequent text references are designated *MB*.

3. See Frances Smith Foster's discussion of white autobiography and black slave narratives in *Witnessing Slavery: The Development of Ante-bellum Slave Narratives* (Westport, Conn.: Greenwood Press, 1979), pp. 5–6.

4. My discussion of these cases and this phenomenon has benefited especially from Alfred H. Kelly, Winfred A. Harbison, and Herman Belz, *The American Constitution: Its Origins and Development*, 6th ed., (New York: W. W. Norton, 1983); Allen Grossman, "The Poetics of Union"; G. Edward White, *The Marshall Court and Cultural Change, 1815–35*, vols. 3–4 of *The History of the Supreme Court of the United States* (New York: Macmillan Publishing Company, 1988), especially pp. 703–40; and James Kettner, *The Development of American Citizenship, 1608–1870* (Chapel Hill: University of North Carolina Press, 1978).

5. James Boyd White, *When Words Lose Their Meaning: Constitutions and Reconstitutions of Language, Character, and Community* (Chicago: University of Chicago Press, 1984), p. 267. For an interesting critique of the deployment of "We the People," see Gayatri Chakravorty Spivak, "The Making of Americans, the Teaching of English and the Future of Culture Studies," *New Literary History* 21.4 (Autumn 1990): 781–98.

6. Abigail Adams to John Adams, March 31, 1776. *The Book of Abigail and John: Selected Letters of the Adams Family 1762–1784*, ed. L. H. Butterfield, Marc Frielaender and Mary-Jo Kline (Cambridge, Mass.: Harvard University Press, 1975), pp. 120–21, p. 121. For a more detailed discussion of this exchange, see Robert Ferguson, "The Limits of Enlightenment," in *The Cambridge History of American Literature, 1590–1820*, vol. 1, ed. Sacvan Bercovitch (Cambridge, MA: Harvard University Press, 1994), pp. 496–537. Ferguson offers the precedent for the exclusion of women from personhood as well as the full rights of citizenship in Blackstone's explanation of *feme-covert*.

7. John Adams to Abigail Adams, April 14, 1776, pp. 121–23.

8. Thomas Jefferson, *Notes on the State of Virginia,* in *Thomas Jefferson: Writings* (New York: The Library of America, 1984), pp. 123–325, p. 289. Subsequent text references are designated *NSV.*

9. As Jeff Rosen points out, theorists of government attempted to resolve this problem by suggesting "that while *the power to control* alienable natural rights may be surrendered to government under certain circumstances, the alienable rights themselves are retained by the people." Rosen finds the distinction "delicate, but . . . essential to social contract theory." A government could not be authorized by rights that it conferred. In my reading, the insistence on making that delicate distinction attests to the anxiety surrounding the question of personhood and embodied by the litigants in these cases. It registers and explains the impossibility of confronting the conventionality of "personhood" itself. See Jeff Rosen, "Was the Flag Burning Unconstitutional?" *Yale Law Review* 100 (1991): 1073–92, p. 1075. Several works in particular have helped me to understand natural rights and the interconnections of freedom, property, and self-ownership in American liberal thought. They include Peter Laslett, ed., *John Locke: Two Treatises of Government* (Cambridge: Cambridge University Press, 1989); C. B. Macpherson, *The Political Theory of Possessive Individualism: Hobbes to Locke* (Oxford: Oxford University Press, 1962); Robert M. Cover, *Justice Accused: Antislavery and the Judicial Process* (New Haven: Yale University Press, 1975); Howard Horwitz, *By the Law of Nature: Form and Value in Nineteenth-Century America* (New York: Oxford University Press, 1991); Eric Cheyfitz, *The Poetics of Imperialism;* and Michael Paul Rogin, *Ronald Reagan, the Movie, and Other Episodes in Political Demonology* (Berkeley: University of California Press, 1987). See especially Cheyfitz's discussion of property and translation in relation to indigenous tribes and Rogin's psychoanalytic reading of the threat that tribal communalism posed to "American" society.

10. Letter from Taney to William M. Beall, March 23, 1836, cited in Carl B. Swisher, *The Taney Period, 1836–1864,* vol. 5 of *The History of the United States Supreme Court* (New York: Macmillan, 1971), p. 37.

11. *Cherokee Nation v. the State of Georgia,* 30 U.S. (5 Peters): 1–80, pp. 16–17; emphasis added. Subsequent text references are designated *CN.*

12. Thomas Jefferson, *Autobiography, 1743–1790, With the Declaration of Independence,* in *Thomas Jefferson: Writings,* pp. 1–101, p. 21. Subsequent text references are designated TJ.

13. This assimilationist strategy represented an ongoing approach that, however progressive at the time, had the effect and the intention of destroying tribal society. As early as 1817, a treaty between representatives of the United States government and of the Cherokee people (signed July 8) contained a provision for the United States government's bestowal of property on any individual "head of any Indian family" wishing to become a United States citizen. That land could not be sold. With the removal of the "owner," the land would revert to the United States government. This offer anticipated the 1887 Dawes Act. Both had the

effect of dispossessing indigenes through legal and, as many of its progressive supporters thought, ethical means.

14. Lucy Maddox, in *Removals* (New York: Oxford University Press, 1991), offers an especially rich analysis of Indian legislation in light of the "persistent otherness of the Indians" who "continued to frustrate white America's efforts . . . to include them within the discourse of American nationalism and, concomitantly, within the structure of the country's laws and institutions" and of how that dilemma shaped early nineteenth-century American culture (8, 7). Robert Berkhofer, Jr. contends that *Cherokee Nation* made the Cherokee the point of reference for this question as well as for removal; see *The White Man's Indian: Images of the American Indian from Columbus to the Present* (New York: Vintage Books, 1979), especially pp. 157–66.

15. Thomas Jefferson to Benjamin Hawkins, February 18, 1803. *Thomas Jefferson: Writings*, pp. 1113–16, p. 1115.

16. Thomas Jefferson, speech to the Chiefs of the Upper Cherokees, May 4, 1808. *The Complete Jefferson: Containing His Major Writings, Published and Unpublished, Except His Letters,* assembled and arranged by Saul K. Padover (New York: Duell, Sloan & Pearce, 1943), pp. 493–95, p. 494.

17. Thomas Jefferson, speech to Captain Hendrick, the Delawares, Mohiccons, and Munries, in *The Complete Jefferson*, pp. 502–4, p. 503.

18. For a discussion of the emergence of Cherokee nationalism and the nationalists' conflict with the separatist traditionalists, see William G. McLoughlin, *Cherokees and Missionaries, 1789–1839* (New Haven: Yale University Press, 1984) and *Cherokee Renascence in the New Republic* (Princeton: Princeton University Press, 1986); and Theda Perdue, "The Conflict Within: Cherokees and Removal," *Cherokee Removal: Before and After,* ed. William L. Anderson (Athens, Ga.: The University of Georgia Press, 1991), pp. 55–74.

19. On Jackson's relation to the Indians, see especially Richard Drinnon, *Facing West: The Metaphysics of Indian-Hating and Empire-Building* (New York: New American Library, 1980); Michael Paul Rogin, *Fathers & Children: Andrew Jackson and the Subjugation of the American Indian* (New York: Vintage Books, 1975); Francis Paul Prucha, *Indian Policy in the United States: Historical Essays* (Lincoln: University of Nebraska Press, 1981); and Richard Slotkin, *Regeneration Through Violence: The Mythology of the American Frontier, 1600–1860* (Middletown, Conn.: Wesleyan University Press, 1973).

20. Letters from Thomas L. McKenney to James Barbour on, respectively 29 Nov. 1827 and 20 Feb. 1827. Cited in McLoughlin, *Cherokees and Missionaries.* The slavery originally practiced by the Cherokee (before Euro-American influence) was a different kind of slavery, entailing the enslavement of an enemy defeated in battle. See especially Theda Perdue, *Slavery and the Evolution of Cherokee Society, 1540–1866* (Knoxville: University of Tennessee Press, 1979).

21. Wilson Lumpkin, *The Removal of the Cherokee Indians From Georgia*

1827–1841 (New York: Dodd, Mead & Company, 1907, reprinted Augustus M. Kelley Publishers, 1971), p. 42. Subsequent text references are designated WL.

22. Georgia compact of 1802, cited in Jeremiah Evarts, *Cherokee Removal: The "William Penn" Essays and Other Writings,* ed. Francis Paul Prucha (Knoxville: University of Tennessee Press, 1981), p. 154.

23. Reprinted in Emmet Starr, *Starr's History of the Cherokee Nation,* ed. Jack Gregory and Rennard Strickland (Fayetteville, Ark.: Indian Heritage Association, 1967), pp. 55–56. Subsequent text references are designated *SH.*

24. Homi Bhabha, "Of Mimicry and Man: The Ambivalence of Colonial Discourse," *October* 28 (Spring 1984): 125–33; p. 126. Subsequent text references are designated MM. The Cherokees function as the colonized in Bhabha's formulation, returning "the look of surveillance as the displacing gaze of the disciplined, where the observer becomes the observed and 'partial' representation rearticulates the whole notion of *identity* and alienates it from essence" (129). The structural contingency of an act of mimicry at least complicates the possibility for critique. In the case of the Cherokees, the mimicry helped to promote dissent in the Cherokee Nation and expedited their removal. Nevertheless, the response of the United States government attests to the Cherokee threat. Reprinted in Homi K. Bhabha, *The Location of Culture* (London: Routledge, 1994), pp. 85–92.

25. Kettner, *The Development of American Citizenship,* pp. 146–47.

26. *Indefeasible* and *inalienable* are synonymous; the Cherokees' use of a word that approaches but is not quite *inalienable* exemplifies the relationship between the two documents. The divergence is especially interesting in light of the importance of the concept of inalienability to the distinction between the documents. It is also interesting to compare the root words, *defeat* and *alien,* in relation to the ways in which each culture conceived of outsiders.

27. Natural rights are invoked, moreover, in the language of the Fifth Amendment, which stipulates that no person shall "be deprived of life, liberty, or property, without due process of law; nor shall private property be taken for public use, without just compensation," and by implication in the Ninth Amendment, which establishes that "the enumeration in the Constitution, of certain rights, shall not be construed to deny or disparage others retained by the people"— natural rights, in other words, did not necessarily have to be enumerated.

28. *Johnson and Graham's Lessee v. William McIntosh,* 21 U.S. (8 Wheaton): 543–605, p. 567. Subsequent text references are designated *JM.* For a more detailed reading of *Johnson* in the context of United States literature and culture, see Eric Cheyfitz, "The Plot Against American Indians in *Johnson and Graham's Lessee v. M'Intosh* and *The Pioneers," Cultures of United States Imperialism,* ed. Amy Kaplan and Donald E. Pease (Durham, N.C.: Duke University Press, 1993), pp. 109–28.

29. Even William Wirt, who argued the case for the Cherokee plaintiffs before

the Supreme Court, "strenuously" counseled Chief John Ross "to go and give up this heart breaking contest" if they could gain lands west of the Mississippi equal to current Cherokee domain and with the assurance of perpetuity. Letter, William Wirt to John Ross, June 4, 1830. *The Papers of Chief John Ross*, Vol. 1, 1807–1839, ed. Gary E. Moulton (Norman: Oklahoma University Press, 1985), pp. 189–90, p. 190.

30. See White's discussion in *The Marshall Court and Cultural Change, 1815–35*, pp. 723–30.

31. In this metaphor, and throughout this study, I draw on the concept of the Name of the Father as explained by Jacques Lacan: "It is in the *name of the father* that we must recognize the support of the symbolic function which, from the dawn of history, has identified his person with the figure of the law." See "Function and Field of Speech and Language in Psychoanalysis," *Ecrits: A Selection*, trans. Alan Sheridan (New York: W. W. Norton & Company, 1977), pp. 30–113; p. 67. For Lacan, the name of the father points to—and exemplifies—the system of language that structures experience. The identification of the name of the father with the law finds expression in the West in the traditional role of the patronym in determining inheritance and legitimacy. I find the cultural implications of Lacan's term convincing for an understanding of western cultures. The importance of kinship relations, and in particular of questions of legitimacy, inheritance, and naming to the nation-builders in this study motivates my use of the term. See also Anne Norton, *Reflections on Political Identity* (Baltimore: Johns Hopkins University Press, 1988).

32. Lydia Maria Child, *Hobomok & Other Writings on Indians* (New Brunswick, N.J.: Rutgers University Press, 1986), p. 136. Subsequent text references are designated *HOB*.

33. John Ross, address to the Cherokees, Head of Coosa C. N., April 14, 1831. *The Papers of Chief John Ross*, pp. 215–19, p. 216.

34. *Samuel A. Worcester v. the State of Georgia* 31 U.S. (6 Peters): 515–675. Subsequent text references are designated *WG*.

35. I refer here to the use of "Indians" to offer a critique of white female sociolegal invisibility in works by such novelists as Child and Catharine Maria Sedgwick (*Hope Leslie*). In both cases, white heroines' encounters with indigenes at once allow for a critique of Puritan society and confirm the heroines in their whiteness.

36. See especially Richard Ellis, *The Union at Risk* (New York: Oxford University Press, 1987).

37. White, *The Marshall Court and Cultural Change, 1815–35*, p. 740.

38. Benjamin Rush, "Of the Mode of Education Proper in a Republic," *The Selected Writings of Benjamin Rush*, ed. Dagobert D. Runes (New York: Philosophical Library, 1947), pp. 87–96; p. 90. Rush hopes that "one general, and uniform system of education, will render the mass of the people more homoge-

neous" and "convert them into republican machines" (88, 92). See also Ferguson, "The Limits of Enlightenment," p. 500.

39. The meaninglessness of personal liberty in the absence of government is, in fact, the justification for government: "where there is no law, there is no freedom," notes Blackstone (*BC*, 122). I am interested here, as throughout, in how (and to what end) liberty is reconfigured as being.

40. Don E. Fehrenbacher explains the context of this "official" opinion in *Slavery, Law and Politics* (New York: Oxford University Press, 1981). Taney offers a long, partisan, and sometimes inaccurate opinion on contradictory aspects of the case (for example, his jurisdictional and territorial rulings may be in conflict). As a result, several of the concurring opinions do not seem fully to concur; nevertheless, the Court's majority concurrence designates Taney's opinion as the "official opinion" of the Court. Fehrenbacher presents convincing evidence that Taney rewrote (and significantly augmented) his opinion in response to Justice Curtis's lengthy and impressive dissenting opinion; the Court records are, therefore, not what was actually heard at the trial (and consented to by the concurring justices); see also Fehrenbacher, *The Dred Scott Case: Its Significance in American Law and Politics* (New York: Oxford University Press, 1978).

41. *Dred Scott v. John F. A. Sandford* 60 U.S. (19 Howard): 395–633, pp. 403–4. Subsequent text references are designated *DS*.

42. Walter Benn Michaels, in "The Vanishing American," *American Literary History* 2 (Summer 1990): 220–41, traces the logical culmination of this process in the official policies through which, by the twentieth century, Indians were viewed as potential citizens and, with the Citizenship Act of 1924, declared citizens. He convincingly reads the act as "at worst a cynical acknowledgment of the ultimate irrelevance of citizenship to the Indians' predicament" (222), and he explains the symbolic process by which "Indians" were appropriated as "American" ancestors and their identity reconceived as a cultural inheritance. I read Taney's contrast between tribal nations and descendants of Africans as an early manifestation of the logic of that policy.

43. On the importance of family imagery to Taney, see Paul W. Kahn, *Legitimacy and History: Self-Government in American Constitutional Thought* (New Haven: Yale University Press, 1992), especially pp. 50–53.

44. In "The Judicial Opinion as Literary Genre," Robert Ferguson conveys the "directed or selective sense of history" through which the judicial opinion obscures its own arbitrariness (215). Legal precedent, as Ferguson suggests, restructures the present in accordance with a presumed (created) past. *Yale Journal of Law and the Humanities*, 2 (Winter 1990): 201–19.

45. Taney goes on to cite directly the first two paragraphs of the Declaration of Independence both to contrast policy toward tribal peoples and African Americans and to preempt the abolitionist appeal to the language of the Declaration.

46. On Curtis's nonpartisanship, see Swisher, *The Taney Period*, pp. 627–30.

47. On the subject of property, Blackstone observes: "the modifications under which we at present find it, the method of conserving it in the present owner, and of translating it from man to man, are entirely derived from society; and are some of those civil advantages, in exchange for which every individual has resigned a part of his natural liberty" (*BC*, 134).

48. The difficulty of marking and identifying "race," the competing biological and phenotypical discourses of blood (genealogy) and color, the alternately synonymous and antithetical concept of "a people," contributed significantly to the anxiety of these cases. On the formulations of race in the early United States, see especially Winthrop D. Jordan, *White Over Black: American Attitudes Toward the Negro, 1550–1812* (New York: W. W. Norton & Company, Inc., 1977). For the development of a discourse of race in the United States, see William Stanton, *The Leopard's Spots: Scientific Attitudes Toward Race in America 1815–59* (Chicago: University of Chicago Press, 1960); George M. Fredrickson, *The Black Image in the White Mind: The Debate on Afro-American Character and Destiny, 1817–1914* (New York: Harper & Row, Publishers, 1971); and Ronald Takaki, *Iron Cages: Race and Culture in 19th-Century America* (New York: Oxford University Press, 1979, 1990).

Of the abundant examples of the binarism and nominalism of difference, the decision in *The People v. George W. Hall* (1854), 4 Cal.: 429–35 is among the most striking. The case, which was heard by the California Supreme Court, concerned whether or not the law permitted the testimony of Chinese witnesses to a murder against a white defendant in a United States court. The decision that they could not turns on two (technically contradictory) interpretations: first, that Columbus's mistake designates "Indian" a generic term that includes Asians; and second, that "the word 'black' may include all negroes, but the term 'negro' does not include all black persons. . . . we understand it to mean the opposite of 'white' " (433). As "Indians" and as "nonwhites," the Chinese witnesses cannot (do not) appear before the bar.

49. "Address at a Sanitary Fair in Baltimore," April 18, 1864, in *Collected Works of Abraham Lincoln*, ed. Roy P. Basler (New Brunswick: Rutgers University Press, 1953), 8 vols., 7:301–3, p. 301. Subsequent text references are designated *AL*.

50. Garry Wills, *Inventing America: Jefferson's Declaration of Independence* (New York: Random House, 1978). Subsequent text references are designated *IA*. Wills develops this claim in *Lincoln at Gettysburg: The Words That Remade America*. Subsequent text references are designated *LG*. See also James M. McPherson, *Abraham Lincoln and the Second American Revolution* (New York: Oxford University Press, 1990).

51. I have taken the phrase "categorical authority" used in this context from Jacques Derrida, who argues that the obscured origins of the law contribute to its "categorical authority." See "Devant la loi," trans. Avital Ronell, in *Kafka and*

the Contemporary Critical Performance: Centenary Readings, ed. Alan Udoff (Bloomington: Indiana University Press, 1987), pp. 128–49.

52. See *We, the Other People: Alternative Declarations of Independence by Labor Groups, Farmers, Women's Rights Advocates, Socialists, and Blacks 1829–1975,* ed. Philip S. Foner (Urbana: University of Illinois Press, 1976).

53. On the logic of the judicial opinion, see Robert Ferguson, "The Judicial Opinion as Literary Genre."

54. Jefferson was a consistently strong advocate of the gradual abolition of slavery, but Lincoln does not address any ambiguities involved with his slaveholding. The status of Thomas Jefferson, and his record opposing the spread of slavery, made him especially valuable political capital for Lincoln. The Louisiana Purchase, which did run counter to Jefferson's political beliefs, can be explained by Jefferson's strategic efforts to establish borders that were not shared with any major foreign military power. See Akhil Reed Arnar, "Some New World Lessons for the Old World," 58 *University of Chicago Law Review* (1991): 483–509.

55. Articles of Confederation in *The Anti-Federalist Papers and the Constitutional Convention Debates* (New York: New American Library, 1986).

56. On the complicated politics of Lincoln's use of ethnicity, see Richard Nelson Current, "Unity, Ethnicity, and Abraham Lincoln," in *Speaking of Abraham Lincoln: The Man and His Meaning for Our Times* (Urbana: University of Illinois Press, 1983), pp. 105–25.

57. Thomas Paine, *Common Sense,* in *Thomas Paine: Political Writings,* ed. Bruce Kuklick (New York: Cambridge University Press, 1989), p. 7.

58. John L. O'Sullivan, *The United States Magazine and Democratic Review* 1.1: 5.

59. *Washington's Farewell Address: In Facsimile, with transliterations of all the drafts of Washington, Madison, & Hamilton, together with their correspondence and other supporting documents,* ed. Victor Hugo Paltsits (New York: New York Public Library, 1935), p. 142. Subsequent text references are designated *GWFA.*

60. Mason L. Weems, *The Life of George Washington,* ed. Marcus Cunliffe (Cambridge, MA: Harvard University Press, 1962).

61. Letter, Abraham Lincoln to Owen Lovejoy, Aug. 11, 1855, *AL* 2:316.

62. The comma in particular has been the source of critical debate. As Don E. Fehrenbacher explains, the speech exists in two versions. It was printed both on June 18 in the *Illinois State Journal* and on June 19 in the *Chicago Tribune,* yet the speeches are not identical. The paragraphs are ordered differently, and the *Tribune* version omits the comma following "endure." The text for the *Journal* speech is thought to be Lincoln's own manuscript, while the *Tribune* printed a reporter's transcription of the speech. But Lincoln kept the *Tribune* version for his scrapbook, and it was that version that provided the official text when the speech appeared as part of the published Lincoln-Douglas debates in 1860. See Don E. Fehrenbacher, "The Words of Lincoln" in *Lincoln in Text and Context: Collected*

Essays (Stanford: Stanford University Press, 1987), pp. 270–86; p. 277. Readers of Lincoln have typically viewed the version with the comma as the more ominous, suggesting that the crisis predicted by Lincoln was already at hand. Don E. Fehrenbacher, "The Words of Lincoln," *Lincoln in Text and Context: Collected Essays* (Stanford: Stanford University Press, 1987), pp. 270–86; p. 277.

63. Stephen Douglas leveled conspiracy charges against Lincoln and his political affiliates as well. Lincoln cites those charges in his July 10, 1858 "Speech in Reply to Douglas at Chicago, Illinois."

64. *The Lincoln-Douglas Debates of 1858*, ed. Robert W. Johannsen (New York: Oxford University Press, 1965), p. 19. Subsequent text references are designated *LDD*. See also David Zarefsky, *Lincoln, Douglas and Slavery: In the Crucible of Public Debate* (Chicago: University of Chicago Press, 1990).

65. Jefferson, *Writings*, p. 1517.

66. Jefferson's *Autobiography* was published by his grandson and executor, Thomas Jefferson Randolph, in 1829 and was reissued by Henry A. Washington, librarian of the Department of State, in 1853–54, following the government's purchase of Jefferson's papers, as part of the nine-volume Congress edition of *The Writings of Thomas Jefferson.*

67. Lincoln makes this point in a "Fragment on Slavery" that Roy P. Basler dates July 1, 1854. Lincoln argues that any justification for enslavement may logically be used to enslave the enslaver (*AL*, 2:222–23).

68. Lincoln explicitly advocated colonization in his June 26, 1857 speech on "The Dred Scott Decision." Lincoln scholars disagree over the extent to which his advocacy of colonization during his presidential years reflected political expediency. Fehrenbacher argues that Lincoln's advocacy was a "dissimulative strategy aimed primarily at the white mind rather than the black population— . . . that he hoped for nothing more than a token emigration of blacks to relieve some of the racial fears engendered by the thought of emancipation"; see "The Deep Reading of Lincoln," *Lincoln in Text and Context*, pp. 214–27; p. 221. Neil Schmitz, by contrast, contends, "To the very end, imagining the future of African Americans in the United States, Lincoln remained a colonizationist, the Clay variety"; see "Refiguring Lincoln: Speeches and Writings, 1832–1865," *American Literary History* 6.1: 103–18; 115. Lincoln was never a radical abolitionist like Garrison, Charles Sumner, or Thaddeus Stevens. In his last address, in April, 1865, he advocated the conferral of the elective franchise "on the very intelligent, and on those who serve our cause as soldiers" among the "freed-people" (*AL*, 8:403). Yet, as ever, his priority was the restoration of "the proper practical relations between these [seceded] states and the Union" (*AL*, 8:403). Salmon P. Chase was not satisfied by the moderation of Lincoln's proposal and, following the speech, wrote to Lincoln, urging him to reconsider: "if you had read what I have [in the New Orleans papers], your feelings of humanity & justice would not let you rest til *all* loyalists are made equal in the right of self protection by suffrage. Once I should have been, if not satisfied, reasonably contented by suffrage for the more intel-

ligent & for those who have been soldiers; now I am convinced that universal suffrage is demanded by sound policy and impartial justice alike" (*AL*, 8:401). See also Eric Foner, *Free Soil, Free Labor, Free Men: The Ideology of the Republican Party before the Civil War* (Oxford: Oxford University Press, 1970).

69. George B. Forgie, *Patricide in the House Divided: A Psychological Interpretation of Lincoln and His Age* (New York: W. W. Norton and Co., 1979). On Lincoln's use of legal and political ancestors, see also Robert A. Ferguson, *Law and Letters in American Culture* (Cambridge, Mass.: Harvard University Press, 1984), pp. 305–17.

70. Proverbs 25:11, "A word fitly spoken *is like* apples of gold in pictures of silver." This fragment is dated January 1861.

71. For a discussion of the drafts and different versions of this speech, see *AL*, ed. Basler, 7:17–23.

72. Paul Kahn offers a related reading in *Legitimacy and History*. He compares Lincoln at Gettysburg to Roger Taney, noting that both argued that the Constitution needed to be *embodied* by individuals who, in turn, transcended the temporality of the body by merging with the state. See especially pp. 52–58. On Lincoln's verbs in this address, see also Andrew Delbanco, *The Puritan Ordeal* (Cambridge, Mass.: Harvard University Press, 1989).

73. Robert Ferguson makes this point in " 'We Do Ordain and Establish': The Constitution as Literary Text," *William & Mary Law Review*, 29 (Fall 1987): 3–25, p. 11. I have also found John Leubsdorf's "Deconstructing the Constitution" especially helpful for my analysis of the structure and presentation of the Constitution. *Stanford Law Review* 40 (Nov. 1987): 181–201.

74. "The Freedmen's Monument to Abraham Lincoln: An Address Delivered in Washington, D.C. on 14 April 1876," *Frederick Douglass Papers*, Series One: Speeches, Debates, and Interviews, ed. John W. Blassingame and John R. McKivigan, vol. 4 (Yale University Press, 1985), pp. 427–40; p. 432. Subsequent text references are designated *FDP*, vol. 00, p. 000. Speeches are identified in text where appropriate. Volumes 1, 2, and 3 are edited by Blassingame. Douglass was not always so measured in his response to Abraham Lincoln; Douglass's own political savviness must also be taken into consideration in assessing his response to Lincoln.

75. Stephen B. Oates, *With Malice Toward None: The Life of Abraham Lincoln* (New York: Harper & Row, Publishers, 1977), p. 412.

76. On the formal influence of African-American oratory, in particular the sermon, on the 1845 *Narrative*, see Robert G. O'Meally, "Frederick Douglass' 1845 *Narrative*: The Text Was Meant to Be Preached" in *Afro-American Literature: The Reconstruction of Instruction*, ed. Dexter Fisher and Robert B. Stepto (New York: The Modern Language Association of America, 1979), pp. 192–211.

77. My discussion of Douglass's struggle with authorizing conventions is indebted to Robert Stepto's reading of Douglass's authorial struggle in the *Narrative* in "Narration, Authentication, and Authorial Control in Frederick Douglass'

Narrative of 1845" in *Afro-American Literature,* pp. 178–91 and *From Behind the Veil: A Study of Afro-American Narrative* (Urbana: University of Illinois Press, 1979), pp. 3–31 and to Valerie Smith's discussion of Douglass's struggle for self-authorization in *Self-Discovery and Authority in Afro-American Narrative* (Cambridge, Mass.: Harvard University Press, 1987), pp. 20–28. See also Rafia Zafar, "The Afro-American as Representative Man" in *Frederick Douglass: New Literary and Historical Essays,* ed. Eric J. Sundquist (Cambridge: Cambridge University Press, 1990), pp. 99–117.

78.   On the textual conventions of slave narratives, see especially Foster, *Witnessing Slavery* and William L. Andrews, *To Tell a Free Story: The First Century of Afro-American Autobiography, 1760–1865* (Urbana: University of Illinois Press, 1986). Subsequent text references to Andrews are designated WA.

79.   Houston Baker, *The Journey Back: Issues in Black Literature, and Criticism* (Chicago: University of Chicago Press, 1980), p. 43. Subsequent text references are designated *JB.* See also Henry Louis Gates, Jr., "Frederick Douglass and the Language of the Self" in *Figures in Black: Words, Signs, and the 'Racial' Self* (New York: Oxford University Press, 1987), pp. 98–124; and Gregory Jay, "American Literature and the New Historicism: The Example of Frederick Douglass," *boundary 2* 17 (Spring 1990): 211–42. For a reading of the *Narrative* as a reconciliation of public and private selves, see Donald Gibson, "Reconciling Public and Private in Frederick Douglass' *Narrative,*" *American Literature* 87 (December 1985): 549–69.

80.   See Andrews, *To Tell A Free Story;* Eric J. Sundquist, *To Wake the Nations: Race in the Making of American Literature* (Cambridge, Mass.: Harvard University Press, 1993); and William S. McFeely, *Frederick Douglass* (New York: W. W. Norton, 1991). Subsequent text references to Sundquist are designated ES.

81.   James McCune Smith, Introduction (to 1855 edition), *My Bondage and My Freedom,* pp. 9–23, p. 14. Subsequent text references are designated *MB.*

82.   Theodore Parker, "The American Scholar," in *The American Scholar,* vol. 8, *The Centenary Edition of Theodore Parker's Writings,* ed. George Willis Cooke (Boston: American Unitarian Association, 1907), pp. 1–53, p. 37. Delivered first at Colby College, Maine. Subsequent text references are designated TP.

83.   Ephraim Peabody, "Narratives of Fugitive Slaves," *Christian Examiner* 47 (July 1849): 61–93, p. 62.

84.   *The Liberator* 15, no. 21 (May 23, 1845): 82.

85.   *The Liberator* 15, no. 23 (June 6, 1845): 89–90, p. 90. Subsequent reference in text is to the same page.

86.   For an in-depth discussion of the triangulation of this scene, see George P. Cunningham, " 'Called Into Existence': Desire, Gender, and Voice in Frederick Douglass's *Narrative* of 1845," *differences* 1.3 (1989): pp. 108–35.

87.   "For Douglass," notes Henry Louis Gates, Jr., "the bonds of blood kinship are the primary metaphors of human culture. See "Binary Oppositions in Chapter One of *Narrative of the Life of Frederick Douglass an American Slave, Written by*

Himself," in *Figures in Black: Words, Signs and the 'Racial' Self* (New York: Oxford University Press, 1987), pp. 80–97, p. 91.

88. The quotation in parentheses is from a description of a speech delivered by William Lloyd Garrison from *The Liberator* 25, no. 2 (January 12, 1855): 8. For a discussion of the context of the comparison and of what it overlooked, see Karen Sánchez-Eppler, *Touching Liberty.*

89. It is interesting to consider the possibility of the influence of Douglass's widely-circulated *Narrative* on Hawthorne's choice of his heroine's name.

90. On the use of quotation marks to underscore Douglass's symbolic identity, and the space between the name and the author, see Cunningham, "Called Into Existence."

91. The phrase is from William L. Andrews, *To Tell A Free Story.* Andrews refers similarly to Douglass's struggle with the abolitionists. On the issue of Douglass's freedom to tell his story, see also Baker, *The Journey Back;* Thad Ziolowski, "Antitheses: The Dialectic of Violence and Literacy in Frederick Douglass's *Narrative* of 1845," in *Critical Essays on Frederick Douglass,* ed. William Andrews (Boston: G. K. Hall, 1991), pp. 148–65; and Wilson J. Moses, "Writing Freely?: Frederick Douglass and the Constraints of Racialized Writing," in *Frederick Douglass: New Literary and Historical Essays,* ed. Sundquist, pp. 66–83.

92. On the use of slavery as a critique of labor and as a means of *uniting* a white working class, see David R. Roediger, *The Wages of Whiteness: Race and the Making of the American Working Class* (London: Verso, 1991). The equation was also a cornerstone of the analysis of the economic and social relations of capitalism in the work of Karl Marx and Friedrich Engels. See especially Engels, *The Origin of the Family, Private Property, and the State, in the Light of the Researches of Lewis H. Morgan* (1942; New York: International Publishers, 1972).

93. Isaiah 1:17, "Learn to do well; seek judgement, relieve the oppressed, judge the fatherless, plead for the widow."

94. Sacvan Bercovitch, *The American Jeremiad.*

95. See discussions of this choice in Peter F. Walker, *Moral Choices: Memory, Desire, and Imagination in Nineteenth-Century American Abolition* (Baton Rouge: Louisiana State University Press, 1978), pp. 252–54, Waldo E. Martin, Jr., *The Mind of Frederick Douglass* (Chapel Hill: University of North Carolina Press, 1984), pp. 4–5; and Deborah E. McDowell, "In the First Place: Making Frederick Douglass and the Afro-American Narrative Tradition," *Critical Essays on Frederick Douglass,* ed. William L. Andrews (Boston: G. K. Hall & Co., 1991), pp. 192–214. I am especially indebted to McDowell's discussion of the masculinist assumptions evident in the "interpretive history" of Douglass's *Narrative* (193). Subsequent text references to McDowell are designated DM.

96. If he was troubled by the exclusion of his mother, however, he seems less bothered by that of his wife, Anna Murray Douglass. On the formal conventions that led to Douglass's minimizing his personal life and especially the importance

of his first wife to his work, see especially Foster, *Witnessing Slavery*, pp. 111–14; and Nellie Y. McKay, "The Souls of Black Women Folk in the Writings of W. E. B. Du Bois," in *Reading Black, Reading Feminist: A Critical Anthology*, ed. Henry Louis Gates, Jr. (New York: Meridian, 1990), pp. 227–43. On the class and gender implications of Douglass's "preoccupation with manhood," see David Leverenz, *Manhood and the American Renaissance* (Ithaca: Cornell University Press, 1989), Chapter 4: "Frederick Douglass's Self-Refashioning," pp. 108–34, p. 109.

97. The words *white* and *black* in this quotation are italicized in *My Bondage and My Freedom*.

98. *Letters of Noah Webster*, ed. Harry R. Warfel (New York: Library Publications, 1953), p. 4. Subsequent text references are designated *NWL*.

99. Noah Webster, *A grammatical institute of the English language, comprising an easy, concise, and systematic method of education, designed for the use of English schools in America. In three parts*, part 1, Speller (Hartford, Conn.: Hudson and Goodwin, 1783), p. 4. Subsequent text references are designated NWS.

100. Webster's is one among a group of related projects to create a new national language. Projects included dictionaries, spellers, and even a proposed National Language Academy. Among those most prominently associated with these movements are Webster, John Adams, Benjamin Franklin, and John Pickering. See Denis E. Baron, *Grammar and Good Taste: Reforming the American Language* (New Haven: Yale University Press, 1982); Christopher Looby, "Phonetics and Politics: Franklin's Alphabet as a Political Design," *Eighteenth-Century Studies*, vol. 18 (1984), pp. 1–34; David Simpson, *The Politics of American English, 1776–1850* (Oxford: Oxford University Press, 1986). On Webster and the legacy of his work, see especially Kenneth Cmiel, *Democratic Eloquence: The Fight Over Popular Speech in Nineteenth-Century America* (New York: William Morrow and Company, 1990), pp. 82–90.

101. In his introduction James McCune Smith calls attention to Douglass's "mimicry" to suggest his forced imitation of abolitionist prescriptions. For Douglass, however, the necessity of mimicry opens into a possibility of critique.

2. "As From a Faithful Mirror"

1. On the earliest uses of the phrase, see Julius W. Pratt, "The Origin of 'Manifest Destiny,'" *American Historical Review* 32 (October 1926–January 1927): 795–98. Pratt points to O'Sullivan's use of the phrase "destined to manifest" in "The Great Nation of Futurity." The concept was commonly evoked by O'Sullivan particularly in regard to the annexation of Texas (as, forcefully, in "The Texas Question," vol. 14 [March 1844]: 423–31). But the phrase as such first appeared in 1845. On the popularity of the phrases "Manifest Destiny" and "Young America" in American culture in the 1840s, see Michael Paul Rogin,

Subversive Genealogy: The Politics and Art of Herman Melville (New York: Knopf, 1983), pp. 70–76; and George B. Forgie, *Patricide in the House Divided*. As Rogin notes, the Young Americans eventually abandoned the name when a political faction (that included Stephen Douglas) made it synonymous with militant expansion. I see the Young Americans as somewhat more ambivalent about national expansion than Rogin does.

2. Perry Miller's *The Raven and the Whale: The War of Words and Wits in the Era of Poe and Melville* (New York: Harcourt, Brace & World, 1956) documents the political context of literary nationalism. Miller makes clear that the Whigs no less than the Democrats sought a coherent literary program for the emerging nation. While the contexts of those programs differed markedly (the Whigs more comfortably and explicitly accepted English—and European—standards of literary excellence, for example), both sides were engaged in encoding a national culture. My discussion of the literary nationalists has benefited greatly from Miller and from John Stafford, *The Literary Criticism of Young America: A Study in the Relationship of Politics and Literature, 1837–1850*, vol. 3, *English Studies* (Berkeley: University of California Press, 1952). Unless otherwise specified, I have agreed with Miller's and Staffords' attributions of authorship for unsigned *Democratic Review* essays. Subsequent text references to Miller are designated *RW*.

On the importance of literature to the nationalist imperative in the antebellum period and, conversely, the shaping of literature by that imperative, see especially Larzer Ziff, *Literary Democracy: The Declaration of Cultural Independence in America* (New York: Viking Press, 1981); Brook Thomas, *Cross Examinations of Law and Literature: Cooper, Hawthorne, Stowe, and Melville* (Cambridge: Cambridge University Press, 1987); and David S. Reynolds, *Beneath the American Renaissance: The Subversive Imagination in the Age of Emerson and Melville* (New York: Alfred A. Knopf, 1988).

3. The quotation is from Richard Brodhead, *Hawthorne, Melville, and the Novel* (Chicago: University of Chicago Press, 1976), pp. 189–90.

4. I do not disagree with these autobiographical readings, but I would advocate a shift in the interpretations they frequently produce. Autobiographical readings of both works frequently underplay the author's craft, the distance from and commentary on the fictionalized account of the life, and the fictionalizing process itself. That process actually lends itself to the authors' meditations on storytelling and on the limitations on which stories can be told.

5. Letter to Sophia Hawthorne, *The Letters of Herman Melville*, ed. Merrell R. Davis and William H. Gilman (New Haven: Yale University Press, 1960), p. 146.

6. It is difficult to compare the politics of New York literati in the 1830s and 1840s to the politics of an Illinois politician in the 1850s and 1860s. Lincoln himself, as I have shown, changed his positions as political experience and national crisis matured him. Young America's alliance with O'Sullivan itself eventually foundered on political grounds. While O'Sullivan was a Jacksonian

Democrat, the Young Americans were uncomfortable with a number of party positions. Their position on annexation, although they professed opposition, was murky; international copyright, opposed by O'Sullivan and passionately supported by Young America, was central to their final break. Nonetheless, they agreed on the urgent need for a recognizably American cultural identity and on the importance of enlisting literary authors in the project of articulating that identity.

7. *The United States Magazine and Democratic Review,* 1.1:15. Subsequent text references are designated by volume, number, and page, with *DR* and author's name where necessary.

8. For an analysis of how the European settlers materialized themselves by materializing the continent, "by becoming flesh in the body of the American continent" (4), see Myra Jehlen, *American Incarnation: The Individual, the Nation, and the Continent* (Cambridge, Mass.: Harvard University Press, 1986).

9. For a related reading with a different emphasis, see Jehlen's discussion of Manifest Destiny in *American Incarnation,* pp. 24–27. On Manifest Destiny, see also Norman Graebner, *Manifest Destiny* (Indianapolis: Bobbs-Merrill, 1968); and Reginald Horsman, *Race and Manifest Destiny: The Origins of Racial Anglo-Saxonism* (Cambridge, Mass.: Harvard University Press, 1987).

10. Ralph Waldo Emerson, "The Young American: A Lecture read before the Mercantile Library Association, Boston, February 7, 1844," *Ralph Waldo Emerson: Essays and Lectures* (New York: Library of America, 1983), pp. 210–30, p. 215. Subsequent text references are designated YA.

11. This characterization begins the entry on Choate in the Duyckincks' literary history, *Cyclopaedia of American Literature.* See Evert A. Duyckinck and George L. Duyckinck, *Cyclopaedia of American Literature: Embracing Personal and Critical Notices of Authors, and Selections From Their Writings. From the Earliest Period to the Present Day. With Portraits, Autographs, and Other Illustrations.* 2 volumes. (New York: Charles Scribner, 1856), 2:286. Subsequent text references are designated *CAL.*

12. Rufus Choate, "The Importance of Illustrating New-England History by a Series of Romances Like the Waverley Novels," *The Works of Rufus Choate with a Memoir of His Life,* ed. Samuel Gilman Brown (Boston: Little, Brown and Company, 1862), pp. 319–46, p. 344.

13. On the racial exclusions and racist implications of Manifest Destiny, see Reginald Horsman, *Race and Manifest Destiny*; and Alexander Saxton, *The Rise and Fall of the White Republic: Class Politics and Mass Culture in Nineteenth-Century America* (London: Verso, 1990).

14. William Gilpin, *The Cosmopolitan Railway, compacting and fusing together all the world's continents* (San Francisco: The History Co., 1890). Subsequent text references are designated *CR.*

15. On the relationship of masculinity and national expansion in the context of United States imperialism, see Amy Kaplan, "Romancing the Empire: The

Embodiment of American Masculinity in the Popular Historical Novel of the 1890s," *American Literary History* 2 (Winter 1990): 659–90.

16. Edmund Burke, "The Thirteen Resolutions," *Two Speeches on Conciliation with America and Two Letters on the Irish Questions,* 2nd ed. (London: George Routledge & Sons, 1889), pp. 99–196, p. 120. Subsequent text references are designated TR.

17. See, for example, Rufus Griswold, preface to *Prose Writers of America* (New York: Garrett Press, 1969). A similar use of "Young" was employed by nationalist groups throughout western Europe.

18. See Bernard Bailyn, *Pamphlets of the American Revolution* (Cambridge, Mass.: Harvard University Press, 1965).

19. Prominent southern writer and Young America associate William Gilmore Simms sounded the warning for the readers of the *Southern and Western Magazine.* European imitation or influence, he argued, would "denationalize the American mind" and "enslave the national heart." The political implication of this cultural treason speaks through his assertion that those writers place the American people "at the mercy of the foreigner." See "Americanism in Literature" (review of an oration published under the same title by Alabama politician, poet, and historian Alexander B. Meek in 1844) originally in *Southern and Western Magazine* 1 (January 1845): 1–14, and reprinted in *Views and Reviews in American Literature, History and Fiction,* ed. C. Hugh Holman (Cambridge, Mass.: Belknap Press of Harvard, 1962), pp. 7–29. I am citing the reprint.

20. The *North American Review* was itself founded in the early nineteenth century to promote an American national culture distinct from European cultures, although the promotion of national unity was never the imperative that it was at the *Democratic Review.* It thrived under the early editorship of two lawyers, Alexander H. and Edward Everett (the invited orator at the dedication of the cemetery at Gettysburg). See Frank Luther Mott, *A History of American Magazines,* vol. 1: *1741–1850* (Cambridge, Mass.: The Belknap Press of Harvard, 1930, revised 1958, 1966).

21. James Russell Lowell, review of Henry Wadsworth Longfellow's *Kavanagh, a Tale* in the *North American Review* 69. 144 (July 1849): 196–215.

22. It is not surprising that the Duyckincks added an anthology, their 1856 *Cyclopaedia of American Literature,* to the growing number of such projects during this period. This work was consistent with their literary nationalism insofar as it sought to manifest the expression of an American culture in its literary (broadly defined) production: "The history of the literature of the country involved in the pages of this work, is not so much an exhibition of art and invention, of literature in its immediate and philosophical sense, as a record of mental progress and cultivation, of facts and opinions, which derives its main interest from its historical rather than its critical value. It is important to know what books have been produced, and by whom; whatever the books may have been or whoever the men" (1:v).

23. Cornelius Mathews, Preface, *Arcturus*, vol. 1. Cited in Stafford, p. 47. *Arcturus* was the first venture of Young America; it ran from December 1840–May 1842.

24. Cornelius Mathews, Address to the University of New York, *Broadway Journal* 2 (July 19, 1845): 26–27. Cited in Frank Luther Mott, *A History of American Magazines*, p. 391.

25. Jay Leyda, *The Melville Log: A Documentary Life of Herman Melville, 1819–1891*, vol. 1 (New York: Gordian Press, 1969), p. 292. Subsequent text references are designated *ML*.

26. The point of this signature is not clear. Brook Thomas offers the possibility of a political motivation. Writing in the year in which the Fugitive Slave Law was passed, he suggests, this signature could be meant to express Melville's understanding of a southern point of view or the masquerade of such an understanding. See *Cross Examinations of Law and Literature*, p. 151. Melville could also be evoking Edgar Allan Poe, whose reviews of Hawthorne, including one in 1847 after the publication of Hawthorne's *Mosses* (1846), were well known to Young America. Poe describes the reader's response to originality such as Hawthorne's as either embarrassment at not having already had the idea *him*self or joy at the bond of sympathy between them. Writes Poe, "They two, he fancies, have, alone of all men, thought thus. They two have, together, created this thing." The exclusion of women from this vision, and the homoerotic undercurrent, is amplified by Melville in the language with which the Virginian describes his response to Hawthorne. In a milder echo of Poe's collaborative fantasy, moreover, the Virginian refers to "a parity of ideas . . . between a man like Hawthorne and a man like me" ("Hawthorne and His Mosses," 1169). "Hawthorne and His Mosses," *The Literary World* 7 (Aug. 17 and Aug. 24, 1850): 125–27, 145–47. Reprinted in *Herman Melville* (New York: Library of America, 1984), pp. 1154–71. I have taken page references from this reprint. Subsequent text references are designated HHM. Poe also uses a birth metaphor rather than a dissemination metaphor for authorship. Poe, *The Works of the Late Edgar Allan Poe with a Memoir by Rufus Wilmot Griswold and Notices of His Life and Genius by N. P. Willis and J. R. Lowell*, vol. 3: *The Literati* (New York: Redfield, 1857).

27. Leyda has compiled excerpts from a number of reports of this venture. See *The Melville Log*, pp. 383–85. See also Perry Miller, *The Raven and the Whale*, chapter 4, "A Berkshire Idyl," pp. 280–91.

28. HHM, 1161. Reading *Pierre* as a continuation of rather than break from (or disillusionment with) the sentiments of "Hawthorne and His Mosses," I am reading against the critical grain. For other readings of this essay in a political context, see Reynolds, *Beneath the American Renaissance* and Rogin, *Subversive Genealogy*. Rogin calls the essay Melville's "own Young America literary manifesto" (74). Melville may well not have been aware of the extent of the disillusionment with Young America that I see reflected in the essay.

29. *The Letters of Herman Melville*, p. 128.

30. Herman Melville, *Pierre: or, The Ambiguities* in *Herman Melville*, pp. 1–421; p. 319. Subsequent text references are designated *P.*

31. Emory Elliot similarly traces Pierre's inability to write to his inability to escape his social bonds: he is afraid of self-loss. "Art, Religion, and the Problem of Authority in *Pierre*," in *Ideology and Classic American Literature*, ed. Sacvan Bercovitch and Myra Jehlen (Cambridge: Cambridge University Press, 1986), pp. 337–51. For readings that see Pierre as rebelling unsuccessfully against sentimentalism and domesticity, see Gillian Brown, *Domestic Individualism: Imagining Self in Nineteenth-Century America* (Berkeley: University of California Press, 1990), chapter 5: "Anti-sentimentalism and Authorship in *Pierre*;" and Paul Royster, "Melville's Economy of Language," in *Ideology and Classic American Literature*, pp. 313–36.

32. Nina Baym, "Melville's Quarrel with Fiction," *PMLA* 94 (Oct. 1979): 909–23, p. 919.

33. Brodhead, *Hawthorne, Melville, and the Novel*, pp. 189–90. See also Ann Douglas's claim that Melville "allows his readers no way into the novel" in *The Feminization of American Culture* (New York: Alfred A. Knopf, 1977), p. 373. From its earliest contemporary reviews into the early 1980s, *Pierre* was, for the most part, accounted a failure. In the 1940s, F. O. Matthiessen called the text a "great failure" (*American Renaissance: Art and Expression in the Age of Emerson and Whitman* [New York: Oxford University Press, 1941, 1961], p. 487). In the early 1960s, Richard Chase labelled it "a ranting melodrama" (Introduction, *Melville: A Collection of Critical Essays* [Englewood Cliffs, N.J.: Prentice-Hall, 1962], p. 9); and Newton Arvin called it "one of the most painfully ill-conditioned books ever to be produced by a first-rate mind" (*Herman Melville* [New York: Viking Press, 1964]). Those more inclined to regard the book as a success often do so because of its psychological sophistication. Among the earliest of such readers, Raymond Weaver called the work "a book to send a Freudian into ravishment" (*Herman Melville: Mariner and Mystic* [New York: Doran, 1921], p. 63). E. L. Grant Watson, in 1930, wrote of the psychic struggle captured by Melville in Pierre ("Melville's Pierre," *New England Quarterly* 3 [April 1930]: 195–234). And psychologist Henry A. Murray saw in Pierre an anticipation of Jungian depth analysis (Introduction to *Pierre, or the Ambiguities* [New York: Hendricks House, Farrar Straus, 1949], pp. xiii–ciii).

Edgar Dryden's *Melville's Thematics of Form: The Great Art of Telling the Truth* offers one of the earliest efforts to consider the writerly themes of the text, separating *Pierre* from both Melville and the narrator and regarding the "failure" as Pierre's rather than Melville's (Baltimore: Johns Hopkins University Press, 1968). Many of the most recent evaluations, including those by Brown, Elliot, Rogin, Royster, Jehlen (in *American Incarnations*), Thomas (in *Cross Examinations of Law and Literature*), Sundquist, Bercovitch, and Wai-chee Dimock, have re-read *Pierre* as a more successful text, a cogent response to the complex politics of the antebellum United States. Sundquist, *Home as Found: Authority and Gene-*

alogy in Nineteenth-Century American Literature (Baltimore: Johns Hopkins University Press, 1979), "'At home in his words': Parody and Patricide in Melville's *Pierre*" (pp. 143–85); Bercovitch, "*Pierre*, or the Ambiguities of American Literary History," *The Rites of Assent: Transformations in the Symbolic Construction of America* (London: Routledge, Chapman and Hall, Inc., 1993), pp. 246–306; Dimock, *Empire for Liberty: Melville and the Poetics of Individualism* (Princeton, N.J.: Princeton University Press, 1989), pp. 140–75.

34. The *Literary World*, August 21, 1852, pp. 118–20, p. 118. There has been significant disagreement about the identity of the reviewer. Many readers, beginning with Perry Miller, have attributed the review to Evert Duyckinck (*RW*, 309). Others, including John Stafford, Jay Leyda, and Hugh W. Hetherington, assign authorship to *George* rather than Evert. See Hetherington, *Melville's Reviewers: British and American, 1846–1891* (New York: Russell & Russell, 1961), p. 231. I follow Bercovitch in assigning the review to both Duyckincks. On the relation of *Pierre* to the literary nationalists, see especially Miller and Bercovitch. In particular, Bercovitch notes Pierre's "inability to distinguish . . . between mirror and reflection" (*Rites* 267). Subsequent text references to this review are designated *LW*.

35. See Thomas Mallon, *Stolen Words: Forays into the Origins and Ravages of Plagiarism* (New York: Ticknor & Fields, 1989).

36. Edgar Allan Poe, "The Fall of the House of Usher," *Edgar Allan Poe: Poetry and Tales* (New York: Library of America, 1984), pp. 317–36, p. 323. Subsequent text references are designated FHU.

37. For a discussion of psychoanalysis and horror in a different context but with important implications for these readings, see Ann Douglas, "The Dream of the Wise Child: Freud's Family Romance Revisited in Contemporary Narratives of Horror," *Prospects* 9 (1984): 293–348.

38. See Forgie, *Patricide in the House Divided*. See also Jehlen's discussion of Pierre's revolutionary legacy in *American Incarnation*, pp. 202–3.

39. Matthew Sorin, *The Domestic Circle: or, Moral and social duties explained and enforced on scriptural principles, in a series of discourses* (Philadelphia: J. Harmstead, 1840), p. 59.

40. Edgar Allan Poe, "William Wilson," in *Edgar Allan Poe: Poetry and Tales*, pp. 337–57, p. 356. Subsequent text references are designated WW.

41. *The Works of Edgar Allan Poe*, p. 191; and Lowell, review of Longfellow's *Kavanagh*, p. 209.

42. This, at any rate, is the myth that Isabel creates about herself. She has vague memories of places—a ship, a madhouse, a farm—for which she has no name and so she cannot document their existence. Yet she is subjected before her birth to an identity that, however unconventional her upbringing, nonetheless marks her as human and in relation to norms of personhood. The extent to which Isabel is an outcast, a madwoman, or a brilliant storyteller is not knowable in

Pierre. Her own description of her acquisition of language is, regardless, an extraordinary cultural analysis.

43. Marc Shell, noting the uncertainty of all consanguineous relations and their importance for cultural continuity, points to the centrality of figural kinship relations to the imagined community. *Pierre* is a key text in his analysis. *Children of the Earth: Literature, Politics, & Nationhood* (New York: Oxford University Press, 1993), "The Judgement of Solomon, or An American Introduction to the Study of Brothers and Others," pp. 3–23.

44. For a fascinating and extended discussion of incest in *Pierre,* see Fred G. See, *Desire and the Sign: Nineteenth-Century American Fiction,* chapter 3: "Incest and Language in *Pierre*" (Baton Rouge: Louisiana State University Press, 1987). See also Marc Shell, *Children of the Earth.*

45. Nathaniel Hawthorne, "My Kinsman, Major Molineux," *Nathaniel Hawthorne: Tales and Sketches* (New York: Library of America, 1982), pp. 68–87. Subsequent text references are designated MK.

46. Miller, *The Raven and the Whale,* p. 306.

47. For a discussion of the deployment of slavery in the shaping of the labor movement in the mid-century United States, see David R. Roediger, *The Wages of Whiteness.*

48. Michael Rogin draws a parallel between Melville's literary and Shaw's legal formalism but notes that they worked conversely: "Melville's formalism exposed institutional fragility; it was the shadow side of Shaw's"; see *Subversive Genealogy,* p. 158.

49. This is Melville's version of the transparent eyeball of Emerson's "Nature" (1836). Emerson makes this point even more forcefully in later essays, such as "Experience" (1844), written after the death of his son, or the later "Nature" (1849).

50. Harriet E. Wilson, *Our Nig, or Sketches from the Life of a Free Black* (London: Allison & Busby, 1984), p. 3. Subsequent text references are designated *ON.*

51. Henry Louis Gates, Jr., Introduction to *Our Nig,* pp. xi–lix, p. xxxvi.

52. As Mark Rose notes, copyright laws originally protected booksellers rather than authors. "The Author as Proprietor: *Donaldson v. Beckett* and the Genealogy of Modern Authorship," *Representations* 23 (Summer 1988), pp. 51–85. See also Cathy N. Davidson, *Revolution and the Word: The Rise of the Novel in America* (New York: Oxford University Press, 1986).

53. See David Ames Curtis and Henry Louis Gates, Jr., "Establishing the Identity of the Author of *Our Nig,*" in *Wild Women in the Whirlwind* (New Brunswick: Rutgers University Press, 1990), pp. 48–69; and Barbara A. White, " 'Our Nig' and the She-Devil: New Information about Harriet Wilson and the 'Bellmont' Family," *American Literature* 65 (March 1993): 19–52. Subsequent text references to White are designated BW.

54. Hazel Carby reads Wilson's plea as an effort to marginalize a white audience. See *Reconstructing Womanhood: The Emergence of the Afro-American
Woman Novelist* (Oxford: Oxford University Press, 1987), pp. 43–45. Eric Gard-
ner has wonderfully documented the actual readership of *Our Nig* in " 'This
Attempt of Their Sister': Harriet Wilson's *Our Nig* from Printer to Readers," *New
England Quarterly* 66 (1993): 226–46. Whatever her intentions, Wilson seems
primarily to have drawn a young white readership. On Wilson's metaphoric use of
the market, see John Ernest, "Economies of Identity: Harriet E. Wilson's *Our
Nig*," *PMLA* 109 (May 1994): 424–38; Karla Holloway, "Economies of Space:
Markets and Marketability in *Our Nig* and *Iola Leroy*" in *The (Other) American
Traditions: Nineteenth-Century Women Writers*, ed. Joyce W. Warren (New Bruns-
wick, N.J.: Rutgers University Press, 1993), pp. 126–40; Carla L. Peterson, "Capitalism, Black (Under)development, and the Production of the African-American
Novel in the 1850s," *American Literary History* 4 (Winter 1992): 559–83.

55. Claudia Tate, "Allegories of Black Female Desire; or, Rereading Nineteenth-Century Sentimental Narratives of Black Female Authority" in *Changing
Our Own Words: Essays on Critical Theory and Writing By Black Women*, ed.
Cheryl A. Wall (New Brunswick, N.J.: Rutgers University Press, 1989), pp. 98–
126, pp. 114–15.

56. On the relation of sentimental and slave narratives, see Gates, Introduc-
tion to *Our Nig;* Gates, "Parallel Discursive Universes: Fictions of the Self in
Harriet E. Wilson's *Our Nig*," in *Figures in Black*, pp. 125–63, p. 138; and Hazel
Carby, *Reconstructing Womanhood*, pp. 43–45.

57. Harriet A. Jacobs, *Incidents in the Life of a Slave Girl, Written by Herself*
(Cambridge, Mass.: Harvard University Press, 1987), p. 62. Jacobs, unlike Mag,
recants when her child actually becomes ill. Subsequent text references are
designated HJ.

58. See Karen Sánchez-Eppler's discussion of writing and virtue in Jacobs in
Touching Liberty, chapter 3: "Righting Slavery and Writing Sex: The Erotics of
Narration in Harriet Jacobs's *Incidents*," pp. 83–104.

59. See Eva Saks, "Representing Miscegenation Law," *Raritan*, 8 (1988): 39–
69, p. 51.

60. Nina Baym both delineates and documents this plot in *Woman's Fiction: A
Guide to Novels By and About Women in America 1820–70* (Ithaca, N.Y.: Cornell
University Press, 1978). Gates applies Baym's categories to *Our Nig* in his pref-
ace to the text. See also Beth Maclay Doriani, "Black Womanhood in Nineteenth-
Century America: Subversion and Self-Construction in Two Women's Autobiogra-
phies" *American Quarterly* 43 (June 1991): 199–222.

61. See especially the discussion of this phenomenon in Willie Lee Rose,
Slavery and Freedom (New York: Oxford University Press, 1982); and Paula
Giddings, *When and Where I Enter: The Impact of Black Women on Race and Sex
in America* (New York: Bantam Books, 1984).

62. White also notes the complicity of Mr. Bellmont, p. 39.

63. For a different reading of this scene, see Ernest, p. 433.

64. W. E. B. Du Bois's definition of "double-consciousness" from "Of Our Spiritual Strivings," the first chapter of *The Souls of Black Folk*.

65. The full text of Ecclesiastes 1:9 reads "The thing that hath been, it *is that* which shall be; and that which is done *is* that which shall be done: and *there is* no new *thing* under the sun" (*The Holy Bible*, New York: New American Library).

3. "The Strange Meaning of Being Black"

1. Du Bois, *Black Reconstruction* (New York: Harcourt, Brace, 1935), p. 718. Subsequent text references are designated PH.

2. The Thirteenth, Fourteenth, and Fifteenth amendments are the Civil War Amendments. On the transformation of the United States legal system represented and achieved by these amendments, see especially Bruce Ackerman, *We the People: Foundations* (Cambridge, Mass.: Harvard University Press, 1991).

3. These included literary histories. On the national narrative disseminated through the histories of American literature written (in many cases, commissioned) at the turn of the century, see Nina Baym, "Early Histories of American Literature: A Chapter in the Institution of New England," *American Literary History* 1 (Fall 1989): 459–88. As Baym argues, these histories stressed the British ancestry of United States culture and, responding to the influx of Southern and Eastern European immigrants, were designed to be part of the Americanizing process. I read these literary histories as part of the general historical project that, in the effort to articulate an American identity, continued the project of the literary nationalists.

4. John W. Burgess, *Reconstruction and the Constitution: 1866–1876* (New York: Charles Scribner's Sons, 1902), p. vii. Subsequent text references are designated *RC*.

5. William Archibald Dunning, *Reconstruction: Political and Economic, 1865–1877* (New York: Harper & Brothers, 1907), p. 213. Subsequent text references are designated *RPE*.

6. Justin Winsor, "The Perils of Historical Narrative," *Atlantic Monthly* 66 (September 1890): 289–97.

7. Peter Novick, *That Noble Dream: The "Objectivity Question" and the American Historical Profession* (Cambridge: Cambridge University Press, 1988).

8. Du Bois's insistence on the propagandistic function of art must be understood in the context of his conviction that "all Art is propaganda and ever must be." See "Criteria of Negro Art," *Crisis* (October 1926): 290–97, the published version of an address delivered by Du Bois at the Chicago Conference of the NAACP that year. The statement is part of Du Bois's analysis of the "racial prejudgement" that "a white public today demands from its artists, literary and pictorial," an analysis of literary production that he continues in *Black Recon-*

struction. During that same year, Du Bois also sponsored an ongoing symposium in the *Crisis* entitled "The Negro in Art: How Shall He Be Portrayed." See also Darwin T. Turner, "W. E. B. Du Bois and the Theory of a Black Aesthetic," in *Critical Essays on W. E. B. Du Bois,* ed. William L. Andrews (Boston: G. K. Hall & Co., 1985), pp. 73–92. Turner maintains that Du Bois anticipated the Black Arts movement in his proposal of "a theory of art from the perspective of black Americans" (74).

9. Du Bois, *Dusk of Dawn: An Essay Toward an Autobiography of a Race Concept* in *W. E. B. Du Bois: Writings* (New York: Library of America, 1986), pp. 549–802, p. 612. Subsequent text references are designated *DD.*

10. *The Souls of Black Folk* in *W. E. B. Du Bois: Writings,* pp. 357–547, p. 521. Subsequent text references are designated *S.*

11. Franklin H. Giddings, *The Principles of Sociology: An Analysis of the Phenomenon of Association and of Social Organization* (New York: Macmillan, 1896), p. 292. An important theorist of the self for Du Bois was William James, of whom Du Bois described himself as "a devoted follower at the time he was developing his pragmatic philosophy." See Du Bois, *The Autobiography of W. E. B. Du Bois: A Soliloquy on Viewing My Life from the Last Decade of Its First Century* (New York: International Publishers, 1968), p. 133. Yet the importance of James's formulations about the self are more apparent in the work of Gertrude Stein than in that of Du Bois. See my discussion of James and Stein in Chapter 4. On the history of sociology and the development of the social sciences, see especially, Thomas L. Haskell, *The Emergence of Professional Social Science: The American Social Science Association and the Nineteenth-Century Crisis of Authority* (Urbana: University of Illinois Press, 1977); Robert C. Bannister, *Sociology and Scientism: The American Quest for Objectivity, 1880–1940* (Chapel Hill: University of North Carolina Press, 1987); and Dorothy Ross, *The Origins of American Social Science* (Cambridge: Cambridge University Press, 1991). Susan Mizruchi applies the development of sociology as a discipline to writerly concerns in "Cataloguing the Creatures of the Deep: 'Billy Budd, Sailor' and the Rise of Sociology," *boundary 2* 17 (Spring 1990): pp. 272–304.

12. For a detailed discussion of these sources, see Dickson D. Bruce, Jr., "W. E. B. Du Bois and the Idea of Double Consciousness," *American Literature* 64 (June 1992): 299–309. See also Arnold Rampersad, *The Art and Imagination of W. E. B. Du Bois,* (New York: Schocken Books, 1976, 1990), p. 74; Werner Sollors, "Of Mules and Mares in a Land of Difference; or, Quadrupeds All?" *American Quarterly* 42 (June 1990): 167–90, p. 182; Kimberly Benston, "I Yam What I Am: The Topos of (Un)naming in Afro-American Literature," in *Black Literature and Literary Theory,* ed. H. L. Gates, Jr. (New York: Routledge, 1984), pp. 151–72; Anita Haya Goldman, "Black Nationalism: The Contradictory Claims of Rights and Race in the Writings of W. E. B. Du Bois" (Presented at the convention of the American Studies Association, Baltimore, November 1991).

Goldman is particularly insightful about the complicated relationship of race and nation in both Emerson and Du Bois configured in this concept.

David Levering Lewis attributes the source of Du Bois's expression of "two-ness" to "his beloved Goethe's words in *Faust* and even possibly those of Ralph Waldo Emerson in 'The Transcendentalist'" in *W. E. B. Du Bois: Biography of a Race, 1868–1919* (New York: Henry Holt, 1993), p. 281. See also Lewis's reading of Du Bois and William James, pp. 86–96. Subsequent text references are designated DLL.

For an essay that stresses the relationship between alienation and second-sight, see Thomas C. Holt, "The Political Uses of Alienation: W. E. B. Du Bois on Politics, Race, and Culture, 1903–1940," *American Quarterly* 42 (June 1990): 301–23.

13. For a more extended discussion of Stein's psychological work in this context, see Chapter 4.

14. Ralph Waldo Emerson, "The Transcendentalist," in *Emerson: Essays and Lectures* (New York: Library of America, 1983), pp. 191–209, pp. 205–6. Subsequent text references are designated T. Melville satirizes Emerson's divisions in Plotinus Plinlimmon's pamphlet, entitled "Chronometricals and Horologicals," in *Pierre*, pp. 247–52.

15. Ralph Waldo Emerson, "Fate," in *Emerson: Essays and Lectures*, pp. 941–68, p. 966. Subsequent text references are designated F.

16. *Narrative of the Life of Frederick Douglass, an American Slave*, p. 52.

17. Du Bois's use of the word "singular" to mean "odd," although not in itself remarkable, in this context at least hints at a grammar of oppression—and Du Bois's political analysis of language and, conversely, analysis of politics at the level of language. It is interesting to consider John's Greek lessons, and their outcome, in light of Mikhail Bakhtin's discussion of dialogics. John's discovery corresponds to the "verbal-ideological decentering" that, Bakhtin argues, "will occur only when a national culture loses its sealed-off and self-sufficient character, when it becomes conscious of itself as only one among *other* cultures and languages" in "Discourse in the Novel," *The Dialogic Imagination: Four Essays by M. M. Bakhtin*, ed. Michael Holquist, trans. Caryl Emerson and Michael Holquist (Austin: University of Texas Press, 1981), pp. 259–422, p. 370.

18. Cited in Lewis, p. 135. Albion Tourgée also uses this text in his 1895 brief for the famous legal test of segregation laws, *Plessy v. Ferguson*. Tourgée compares the white "unhappiness" at a black presence to Haman's unhappiness at the sight of "Mordecai the Jew sitting at the King's gate." *The Thin Disguise: Turning Point in Negro History (Plessy v. Ferguson: A Documentary Presentation [1864–1896])*, ed. Otto H. Olsen (New York: Humanities Press, 1967), p. 90.

19. "The Minister's Black Veil," in *Hawthorne: Tales and Sketches*, (New York: Library of America, 1982), pp. 371–84, pp. 378, 372, 374. Subsequent text references are designated MBV. In an elegant reading, Anita Haya Goldman

offers Hawthorne's story as "an influence on the development of Du Bois's symbolic method" ("Black Nationalism").

20. J. Hillis Miller, *Hawthorne and History: Defacing It* (Cambridge, Mass.: Basil Blackwell, 1991), p. 73.

21. Du Bois describes black America as "the spiritual world in which ten thousand thousand Americans live and strive" (*S,* 359), a phrase that recurs throughout *Souls* and could be an echo of Jefferson, suggesting the embodiment of the guilt that white America does not wish to remember or confront.

22. On the difference between Jefferson's attitudes toward African Americans and indigenes, see Francis Paul Prucha, "The Image of the Indian in Pre–Civil War America," *Indian Policy in the United States: Historical Essays* (Lincoln: University of Nebraska Press, 1981), pp. 49–63. For my analysis of this passage, I am indebted to Rebecca Garden and John Matteson.

23. Lewis reports, for example, Du Bois's impatient response to a student at the religious Wilberforce University who, when Du Bois wandered into a religious gathering, announced that the new professor would lead them in prayer. Du Bois was never comfortable with the administration or, for the most part, students at Wilberforce and was particularly troubled by the religious revivals. See *W. E. B. Du Bois: Biography of a Race,* pp. 150–78.

24. See Eric Sundquist's reading of "John," with a different reading of the use of *Lohengrin,* in *To Wake the Nations,* pp. 521–25.

25. Campaigns against and analysis of the practice of lynching were an important part of Du Bois's work, particularly following the brutal burning of Sam Hose in Atlanta in 1899, while Du Bois was a professor at Atlanta University. In *Dusk of Dawn,* Du Bois describes Hose's death and explains how it disrupted his work: "one could not be a calm, cool, and detached scientist while Negroes were lynched, murdered and starved" (603).

26. Michael G. Cooke, *Afro-American Literature in the Twentieth Century: The Achievement of Intimacy* (New Haven: Yale University Press, 1984).

27. James Weldon Johnson, *The Autobiography of an Ex-Coloured Man* (New York: Alfred A. Knopf, 1970), p. 204. Subsequent text references are designated JWJ.

28. E. M. Fairchild, "Society's Need of Effective Ethical Instruction in School and Church, and the Suggestion of an Available Method," *American Journal of Sociology,* 4 (January 1899): 433–39, p. 438.

29. It is hard to know how "self-conscious" Du Bois was in his conventional and generic use of "manhood." He was, however, committed to women's rights, especially suffrage. On the acknowledged influence of women—especially African-American women—on Du Bois, see Nellie McKay, "The Souls of Black Women Folk in the Writings of W. E. B. Du Bois," pp. 227–43; on Du Bois's use of the feminine to represent the integrity of racial culture, see Paul Gilroy, *The Black Atlantic: Modernity and Double Consciousness* (Cambridge: Harvard University Press, 1993), pp. 135–46.

30. August Meier, *Along the Color Line: Explorations in the Black Experience* (Urbana: University of Illinois Press, 1976), p. 52.

31. William T. Alexander, *History of the Colored Race in America* (New York: Negro Universities Press, 1968).

32. Edward Augustus Johnson, *A School History of the Negro Race in America* (New York: AMS Press, 1969), p. 111.

33. Arnold Rampersad, "Slavery and the Literary Imagination: Du Bois's *The Souls of Black Folk*," in *Slavery and the Literary Imagination,* ed. Deborah E. McDowell and Arnold Rampersad (Baltimore: Johns Hopkins University Press, 1989), pp. 104–24, p. 105. Rampersad goes on to call *The Souls of Black Folk* "a direct, parodic challenge to certain forms and assumptions of the slave narrative (in all their variety) which had so aided Booker T. Washington's arguments" (106). Subsequent text references are designated *SLI.*

34. "Comment on Recent Books in American History," *Atlantic Monthly* 74 (April 1897): 559–69, p. 560.

35. William Sharlip and Albert A. Owens, *Adult Immigrant Education: Its Scope, Content and Methods* (New York: Macmillan, 1925), pp. 171–72.

36. Woodrow Wilson, "The Making of the Nation," *Atlantic Monthly* 80 (July 1897): 1–14, p. 1. Subsequent text references are designated MN.

37. Woodrow Wilson, "Princeton in the Nation's Service," *The Papers of Woodrow Wilson,* ed. Arthur S. Link (Princeton: Princeton University Press, 1971), vol. 10: *1896–98,* pp. 11–31; p. 24, p. 23. Delivered October 21, 1896. Interestingly, Wilson cites the same speech by Edmund Burke that Duyckinck cites in "The Great Nation of Futurity." In this speech, Wilson opposes "newness" to "growth" and "progress." He blames the "scientific spirit of the age," which, he argues, must be tempered by the knowledge and vision imparted by the humanities (29). Nonetheless he shared with many of the most exuberant among the social scientists the sense that the universities had to be enlisted in the national project, that "the school must be of the nation" (31). In an outline of an address entitled "The Teacher as Citizen," Wilson writes, "there is *a national spirit,* and *study* should be conducted *in that spirit.*" *The Papers of Woodrow Wilson,* vol. 11: *1898–1900,* 1971, pp. 104–5, p. 104.

38. Emil G. Hirsch, "The American University,"*American Journal of Sociology* 1 (Sept. 1895): 113–31, p. 114. Subsequent text references are designated EH.

39. Barrett Wendell, *A Literary History of America* (New York: Charles Scribner's Sons, 1925), p. 524. Subsequent text references are designated *LHA.* Rampersad, writing on Du Bois's relationship with Wendell, notes that "The biased opinions of Wendell's *Literary History of America* (1900) may have set back scholarship in American literature by at least several years" (*The Art and Imagination of W. E. B. Du Bois,* p. 39).

40. G. Stanley Hall, ed., *Methods of Teaching History,* 2nd ed. (Boston: D. C. Heath, 1898).

41. George S. Morris, "The Philosophy of the State and of History," in *Methods of Teaching History*, pp. 149–66, p. 159.

42. Emil G. Hirsch uses the metaphor of the Gulf Stream to make the same point in "The American University."

43. Wilson cites Turner's essay "Western State-Making in the Revolutionary Era," *American Historical Review* 1 (October 1895): 70–87.

44. Haskell, *The Emergence of Professional Social Science.*

45. Wilson, "The Significance of American History," *The Papers of Woodrow Wilson*, vol. 12 (1900–1902), 1972, pp. 179–84, p. 183; it appeared as the preface to *Harper's Encyclopaedia of United States History* (10 volumes, New York, 1902), vol. I: xxvii–xxxii. Subsequent text references are designated SAH.

46. Walter Bagehot, *Physics and Politics, or Thoughts on the Application of the Principles of "Natural Selection" and "Inheritance" to Political Science* (Boston: Beacon Press, 1956), pp. 90–91; see especially the chapters on "Nation-Making."

47. Franklin Giddings, *The Elements of Society* (New York: Macmillan, 1898; reprint, 1900), pp. 122, 63. Subsequent text references are designated FG.

48. William Graham Sumner, *Folkways* (New York: Ayer and Company, n.d.).

49. On the use of race in the creation of a new American identity during this period, see Walter Benn Michaels, "The Souls of White Folk," *Literature and the Body: Essays on Population and Persons*, ed. Elaine Scarry (Baltimore: Johns Hopkins University Press, 1988), pp. 185–209.

50. Newspaper Report of a Lecture in Lancaster on Bagehot, *The Papers of Woodrow Wilson*, vol. 9, pp. 381–83, p. 382.

51. Those who, on the contrary, insisted on the newness of "the American man"—his discontinuity from a European heritage—were equally racialist. Historian H. G. Cutler, in an 1893 *New England Magazine* essay, "The American Not a New Englishman, But a New Man," for example, leaves no room for a separate but equal community when he advocates "the amalgamation of Northern and Southern temperaments, amid the most favorable of surroundings" and asserts that "in the United States are being chemically united the best traits of the Northern and Southern characters; that, since our civil and racial convulsion, we have had a destiny within our grasp which is immeasurably grander than could be evolved from any English or New English type of man." Cutler's use of "amalgamation" presumes mutually assimilable groups; the "racial convulsion" refers to the contest between cultures—North and South. His language also anticipates and explains the tension of unassimilable groups (descendants of Africans, for example) inevitably summoned with the evocation of this new man. Narratives that relied on the language of mixing and blending were especially troubled, explicitly or otherwise, by unassimilable groups. See H. G. Cutler, "The American Not an Englishman, But a New Man," *New England Magazine* 9 (September 1893): 24–30, p. 30.

52. N. S. Shaler, "European Peasants as Immigrants," *Atlantic Monthly* (May 1893): 646–55, p. 647. Subsequent text references are designated NS.

53. Thomas Dixon, *The Leopard's Spots: A Romance of the White Man's Burden 1865–1900* (New York: Doubleday and Page, 1902), p. 148.

54. Theodore Roosevelt, "True Americanism," pp. 13–26, p. 26. Subsequent text references are designated TA.

55. John Dewey, speech delivered to National Education Association, 1902, cited in Robert A. Carlson, *The Quest for Conformity: Americanization Through Education* (New York: John Wiley and Sons, 1975), p. 112.

56. "Preamble of Act No. 111, the Laws of Louisiana, July 10, 1890," in Otto H. Olsen, ed., *The Thin Disguise: Turning Point in Negro History: Plessy v. Ferguson, A Documentary Presentation (1864–1896)* (New York: Humanities Press, 1967), p. 54. See also Tourgée's 1895 brief. Subsequent text references to documents in this collection are designated OO.

57. *Homer Adolph Plessy v. J. H. Ferguson*, 163 U.S. 537–64, p. 555. Subsequent text references are designated *PF.*

58. Franz Boas, Letter to Professor J. W. Jencks, December 31, 1909, *A Franz Boas Reader: The Shaping of American Anthropology, 1883–1911*, ed. George W. Stocking (Chicago: University of Chicago Press, 1974), p. 212.

59. This "our" accounts for the critical assumption that Du Bois intends to advocate an African-American nation in *The Souls of Black Folk*. On that advocacy, see especially August Meier, *Along the Color Line;* Herbert Aptheker, introduction, W. E. B. Du Bois, *Against Racism: Unpublished Essays, Papers, Addresses, 1887–1961*, ed. Aptheker (Amherst: University of Massachusetts Press, 1985); and Wilson J. Moses, "The Poetics of Ethiopianism: W. E. B. Du Bois and Literary Black Nationalism," in *Critical Essays on W. E. B. Du Bois*, ed. Andrews, pp. 92–106. Rampersad revises the traditional idea of cultural nationalism as it applies to Du Bois in *The Art and Imagination of W. E. B. Du Bois*, pp. 87ff. On Du Bois's validation of an African diaspora, see Gilroy, *The Black Atlantic.*

60. Du Bois, "The Conservation of Races," in *Du Bois: Writings*, pp. 815–26, p. 817, emphasis added. Subsequent text references are designated COR.

61. Anthony Appiah, "The Uncompleted Argument: Du Bois and the Illusion of Race," *Race, Writing, and Difference*, ed. Henry Louis Gates, Jr. (Chicago: University of Chicago Press, 1986), pp. 21–37. Subsequent text references are designated AA. Appiah offers a (slightly revised) version of this essay in Kwame Anthony Appiah, *In My Father's House: Africa in the Philosophy of Culture* (London: Methuen, 1992), which includes a comparison of Du Bois and philosopher of cultural pluralism Horace Kallen. See also Houston A. Baker, Jr.'s response to Appiah's piece in "Caliban's Triple Play," *Critical Inquiry* 13 (Autumn 1986): 182–96. Thomas C. Holt argues for the visionary formulation that I also see at the center of Du Bois's apparent contradictions; double-consciousness affords an insight into culture to which most whites historically had less direct access. See "The Political Uses of Alienation," especially pp. 304 and 320.

62. "The moon was at the full and the waters of the Atlantic lay like a lake. All the long slow afternoons as the sun robed herself in her western scarlet with veils

of misty cloud, I had seen Africa afar" (*DD*, 640). The language of the passage insists on the mediation of the place through an idea and a vision from which Du Bois derives his identity.

63. W. E. B. Du Bois, "The Freedmen's Bureau," *Atlantic Monthly* 87 (March 1901): 354–65, p. 356. Subsequent text references are designated FB.

64. Du Bois wrote two short pieces on Lincoln for the *Crisis*, the second in response to the outcry raised by the first. In both, he praises Lincoln for his greatness and for his inconsistencies. An intolerance of inconsistencies and imperfection leads to a tendency to "whitewash" a "great man" upon his death, argues Du Bois. Yet he finds Lincoln "the most human and lovable" of the "five masters" of the nineteenth century precisely because he was not perfect "and yet triumphed. . . . The world is full of people born hating and despising their fellows. To these I love to say: See this man. He was one of you and yet he became Abraham Lincoln." These two essays, "Abraham Lincoln" and "Again, Lincoln," appeared in the *Crisis* in May and September of 1922 and are reprinted in *W. E. B. Du Bois: Writings*, pp. 1196–99.

65. Mary Taylor Blauvelt, "The Race Problem: As Discussed by Negro Women," *American Journal of Sociology* 6 (March 1901): 662–72, p. 668; emphasis added.

66. In a passage from *Dusk of Dawn* beginning "What is Africa to me?" Du Bois qualifies the answer of "fatherland" or "motherland" that he once might have given by underscoring his dependence on an ever-changing "concept of race." Africa is a "fatherland" that "neither my father nor my father's father ever saw . . . or knew [the] meaning [of n]or cared overmuch for it." Instead, his tie to Africa is based on a feeling that is in turn tied to culturally determined signification: "The mark of their [his ancestors'] heritage is upon me in color and hair. These are obvious things, but of little meaning in themselves; only important as they stand for real and more subtle differences from other men. Whether they do or not, I do not know nor does science know today" (639).

67. In a similar strategy, Frantz Fanon advocates a national consciousness—which he distinguishes from nationalism—designed to culminate in a global vision: "If man is known by his acts, then we will say that the most urgent thing today for the intellectual is to build up his nation. If this building up is true, that is to say if it interprets the manifest will of the people and reveals the eager African peoples, then the building of a nation is of necessity accompanied by the discovery and encouragement of universalizing values. Far from keeping aloof from other nations, therefore, it is national liberation which leads the nation to play its part on the stage of history. It is at the heart of national consciousness that international consciousness lives and grows. And this two-fold emerging is ultimately only the source of all culture"; see "On National Culture," in *The Wretched of the Earth*, pp. 206–48, pp. 247–48.

68. Sarah E. Simons, "Social Assimilation," *American Journal of Sociology* 6 (May 1901): 790–822, pp. 799, 808.

69. Du Bois, "The Freedmen's Bureau," p. 354; Mark Twain, *Pudd'nhead Wilson.* In the *Plessy* decision, Justice Henry Billings Brown acknowledges the legal fiction of race when he confirms that "the question of the proportion of colored blood necessary to constitute a colored person, as distinguished from a white person, is one upon which there is a difference of opinion in the different States. . . . [T]hese are questions to be determined under the laws of each State" (*PF,* 552). See Evan Carton, *"Pudd'nhead Wilson* and the Fiction of Law and Custom," in *American Realism: New Essays,* ed. Eric J. Sundquist (Baltimore: Johns Hopkins University Press, 1982), pp. 82–94; Eric J. Sundquist, "Mark Twain and Homer Plessy" (pp. 46–72), and Susan Gillman, " 'Sure Identifiers': Race, Science, and the Law in *Pudd'nhead Wilson"* (pp. 86–104), in *Mark Twain's "Puddn'head Wilson,"* ed. Susan Gillman and Forrest G. Robinson (Durham, N.C.: Duke University Press, 1990).

70. Du Bois, "The Souls of White Folk," in *Du Bois: Writings,* pp. 923–38, p. 923.

71. August Meier, *Along the Color Line,* p. 267; John Higham, *Send These to Me: Immigrants in Urban America,* rev. ed. (Baltimore: Johns Hopkins University Press, 1984), p. 212.

72. Du Bois, *"The Souls of Black Folk," Independent* (November 17, 1904), p. 1152, cited in Arnold Rampersad, *The Art and Imagination of W. E. B. Du Bois,* p. 69.

73. Robert B. Stepto, *From Behind the Veil,* p. 61.

74. Albert Bushnell Hart, *National Ideals Historically Traced, 1607–1907,* in *The American Nation: A History,* vol. 26 (New York: Harper and Brothers, 1907), p. xiv.

75. *Downes v. Bidwell* (1901) 182 U.S. 244–392, p. 339. Subsequent text references are designated *DB.* The Supreme Court was almost evenly divided in this case, with four dissenting opinions. In *Downes v. Bidwell* the Court sought to reconcile the politics of overseas imperialism with republican ideals. Condemning the Taney Court's refusal to grant civil rights to descendants of Africans, the Court insisted on the *civil* rights of the inhabitants of overseas territories but refused to grant them *political* rights, including the right to citizenship. In the end, the Court's decision most resembles that of *Cherokee Nation* in its attempt to find a moral solution to an immoral political dilemma.

76. See Sundquist on Du Bois's use of the spirituals, especially in relation to race and nationalism, "Swing Low: *The Souls of Black Folk,*" in *To Wake the Nations.*

77. I have taken the term "symbolic geography" from Stepto. See *From Behind the Veil,* p. 61.

78. Herbert Adolphus Miller, "Science, Pseudo-Science and the Race Question," delivered at the annual conference of the NAACP in June 1925; reprinted in *Crisis* (October 1925): 287–91, p. 289.

4. A "Losing-Self Sense"

1. I have found Wendy Steiner's discussions of Stein's laboratory work especially useful. See Steiner, "The Steinian Portrait: The History of a Theory," in *Exact Resemblance to Exact Resemblance: The Literary Portraiture of Gertrude Stein* (New Haven: Yale University Press, 1978). Steiner is interested in the relationship of Stein's evolving theory of identity to her portraiture. See also "Gertrude Stein in the Psychological Laboratory," appended to Michael Hoffman's *The Development of Abstractionism in the Writings of Gertrude Stein* (Philadelphia: University of Pennsylvania Press, 1965).

2. William James, *The Principles of Psychology* (Cambridge, Mass.: Harvard University Press, 1983), p. 279. Subsequent text references are designated *PP*. One thinks here of Thomas Jefferson's claim that "mankind are more disposed to suffer while evils are sufferable, than to right themselves by abolishing the forms to which they are accustomed" (*TJ*, 19).

3. William James, "The Chicago School," in *William James: Writings, 1902–1910* (New York: Library of America, 1987), pp. 1136–40, p. 1137. The essay identifies a philosophical school of thought associated with John Dewey and colleagues and students at the University of Chicago. Originally published in *The Psychological Bulletin*, January 15, 1904.

4. For an example of *The Making of Americans* in an American cultural context—read as a generational narrative—see Mary Dearborn, *Pocahontas's Daughters: Gender and Ethnicity in American Culture* (New York: Oxford University Press, 1986).

5. "Portraits and Repetition," in *Lectures in America* (Boston: Beacon Press, 1985), pp. 163–206, p. 177. Subsequent text references are designated PR.

6. Gertrude Stein, *The Making of Americans, being a history of a family's progress* (New York: Something Else Press, 1966), p. 5. Subsequent text references are designated *MA*.

7. Ellen Berry, "On Reading Gertrude Stein," *Genders* 5 (Summer 1989): 1–20, pp. 13–14. Berry advocates "being more attentive to the ways in which narrative as a structure itself may act to obscure difference" (17).

8. Scholars attempting to document the dates of the text's composition have had to contend both with Stein's conflicting claims—notably, on the title page of the first edition where she describes the work as having been "written 1906–1908" and in "The Gradual Making of The Making of Americans," a lecture she gave in the United States in 1934, where she claims to have worked on the narrative over three years—and with the multiple revisions that the manuscript underwent. In "The Making of *The Making of Americans*," Donald Gallup posits 1903 as the beginning, 1906 as the recommencement (after Stein had finished *Three Lives*), and 1911 as the date of completion. Leon Katz, who originally claimed 1902 as the beginning, later decided that while Stein may have begun work on the narrative in 1902, she did not begin to write until 1903. The note-

books Stein kept as she drafted the manuscript show a marked change in style in 1908, the year she read Otto Weininger's *Sex and Character*. See especially Katz's "The First Making of *The Making of Americans:* A Study Based on Gertrude Stein's Notebooks and Early Versions of Her Novel (1902–1908)" (Ph.D. dissertation, Columbia University, 1963); and Katz's introduction to *Fernhurst, Q.E.D., and other early writings by Gertrude Stein* (New York: Liveright, 1971), pp. ix–xlii. Subsequent text references are designated FM and *FQ* respectively. Gallup's "The Making of *The Making of Americans*" is included as an appendix to *Fernhurst, Q.E.D., and other early writings by Gertrude Stein.* It is also interesting that Stein dates the *end* of her composition 1908, as though, she might say, beginning writing is an ending.

9. Letter, Gertrude Stein to Mabel Weeks, early 1906, Yale Collection of American Literature, Beinecke Rare Book and Manuscript Library, Yale University. For discussions of this letter, see John Malcolm Brinnin, *The Third Rose: Gertrude Stein and Her World* (New York: Addison-Wesley, 1987), pp. 99–100; and Katz, "The First Making of *The Making of Americans*," p. 76.

10. Stein's wordplay in this letter is, typically, tantalizing. Although the word "publia" has conventionally been cited as "public," my own analysis of Stein's handwriting yields "publia." Stein's general linguistic playfulness, as exhibited in this letter, cannot preclude sheer nonsensical wordplay, part of her jouissance. Yet the sexuality frequently associated with Stein's wordplay offers a tempting alternative. "Publia" is richly evocative, suggestive perhaps of "publica," literally "public woman"—or prostitute. The American public in this image, made pretentious by the Latinate term, is readily flattered and easily swayed, coquettish more than professional and subject to blandishments. Stein knows that she will present to the public—or publia—an image that "she," the public, does not wish to confront in her mirror; hence, an ill-fitting selfhood.

11. Of all the Lovetts living and writing during this period, Robert Morss Lovett seems the most likely candidate. Not only was he at Harvard (as a student and professor) while Leo and Gertrude Stein were there, but he was also in Europe—and a particular friend of Stein intimate Bernard Berenson—at the end of the nineteenth and again at the beginning of the twentieth centuries. During this time Lovett coauthored the *History of English Literature,* the kind of book the Steins could very well have been sent—perhaps in manuscript. Lovett's coauthor, William Vaughn Moody, was Stein's English composition instructor (she seems, in fact, to have made use of a few of her compositions in *The Making of Americans;* see note 35). Gertrude and Leo could also have read a manuscript that was never published and subsequently lost. In his autobiography, *All Our Years* (New York: Viking Press, 1948), Lovett describes a (much later) debate with Gertrude Stein, in which he acknowledges having "fared badly," about property and literature (93). (In *The Autobiography of W. E. B. Du Bois,* Du Bois describes Lovett as "perhaps the closest white friend I made at Harvard" [p. 288].) Another possibility is Eva Lovett, who wrote *The Making of a Girl* (1902), a manners guide for

young ladies published by J. F. Taylor and Company. While this work offers intriguing possibilities for spoof on the part of both Leo and Gertrude, I have found nothing that links Eva Lovett or her book to the Steins.

12. See especially Katz, introduction to *Fernhurst, Q.E.D.;* Catharine R. Stimpson, "The Mind, the Body, and Gertrude Stein," *Critical Inquiry* 3 (1977): 489–506; and Lisa Ruddick, *Reading Gertrude Stein: Body, Text, Gnosis* (Ithaca, N.Y.: Cornell University Press, 1990). Subsequent text references to Ruddick are designated LR.

13. Toni Morrison, *Playing in the Dark,* p. 17.

14. See especially Sonia Saldívar-Hull, "Wrestling Your Ally: Stein, Racism, and Feminist Critical Practice," in *Women's Writing in Exile,* ed. Mary Lynn Broe and Angela Ingram (Chapel Hill: University of North Carolina Press, 1989), pp. 182–98.

15. *The Autobiography of Alice B. Toklas,* in *Selected Writings of Gertrude Stein,* ed. Carl Van Vechten (New York: Vintage Books, 1962), pp. 2–237, p. 38. Subsequent text references are designated *ABT.*

16. Jacob Riis, *The Making of an American* (New York: Macmillan, 1928). Subsequent text references are designated JR.

17. Horace Kallen, "Democracy Versus the Melting-Pot," p. 219. Subsequent text references are designated DMP.

18. On Wendell as the source for Kallen's quotation, and on Kallen's relationship with Wendell, see Werner Sollors, "A Critique of Pure Pluralism," in *Reconstructing American Literary History,* ed. Sacvan Bercovitch (Cambridge, Mass.: Harvard University Press, 1986), pp. 250–79.

19. John R. Commons, "Racial Composition of the American People: Amalgamation and Assimilation," *Chautauqua* 39 (May 1904): 217–25, p. 218. Subsequent reference in this paragraph is to this essay.

20. Theodore Roosevelt first wrote these words in a letter to Mrs. Bessie Van Vorst, October 18, 1902. See *Works: Presidential Addresses and State Papers,* part 2, vol. 14, Statesman Edition (New York: Review of Reviews Co., 1904), pp. 508–10, p. 510. Roosevelt wrote in response to Van Vorst's article, "The Woman who Toils."

21. Day Allen Willey wrote about Character Factories in "Americans in the Making: New England's Method of Assimilating the Alien," *Putnam's Monthly and the Reader* 5 (January 1909): 456–63; pp. 462–63. Subsequent reference in this paragraph is to this essay.

22. Jacob A. Riis, *How the Other Half Lives: Studies Among the Tenements of New York* (New York: Dover, 1971), p. 83.

23. John Dewey, "The School as Social Centre," in *John Dewey: The Middle Works, 1899–1924,* vol. 2: *1902–1903,* ed. Jo Ann Boydston (Carbondale: Southern Illinois University Press, 1976), pp. 80–93, p. 85, originally delivered as an address to the National Council of Education, Minneapolis, Minnesota, July 1902.

In their efforts to address the problem described by Dewey, progressive settlement workers like Jane Addams came up with such projects as the Hull-House Labor Museum to illustrate the evolution of modern industry from Old World crafts and thereby offer children "a dramatic representation of the inherited resources of their daily occupation." In her exuberance, Addams overlooked the extent to which seeing one's parents displayed in an Old World setting reinforces the distance from the past conveyed by "museum." See *Twenty Years at Hull-House* (New York: New American Library, 1981), p. 172.

In their study of the development of adolescence as a concept, John and Virginia Demos trace the noticeable development of a "youth culture" in the urbanization of the late-nineteenth-century United States. According to the Demoses, the rapid changes introduced by industrialization disrupted the structure of the American family and promoted children's identification with agemates rather than with the generations of their families. Arguing that "immigrant families presented an especially dramatic case in point," the Demoses explain the logic governing the changes so forcefully decried by many social commentators (638). Familial disruption was particularly evident in immigrant families, where factors such as language and education made children's adjustment to and identification with the new culture easier than the adults'. The immigrant family became a paradigm for the kinds of changes characterizing United States society at large—hence, the anxiety evoked by the immigrant family, which was in turn blamed for those changes. See John Demos and Virginia Demos, "Adolescence in Historical Perspective," *Journal of Marriage and the Family* 31 (November 1969): 632–38.

24. Mary Antin, *The Promised Land* (New York: Houghton Mifflin, 1925), pp. xix, xx. Subsequent text references are designated *PL*.

25. Sigmund Freud, "Family Romances," 9: 235–41. The fantasy allows the child to replace either both parents or the father with others who are more powerful or famous. It avenges and corrects the child's disappointment in parents who are not as all-powerful as the child had at one time believed.

26. On Antin's use of familiar Puritan formulations and the Exodus story that underlay them, and on the immigrants' use of Puritan metaphors and formulations in general, see Sollors, *Beyond Ethnicity*, especially pp. 40–65. For a different reading of the Puritan legacy of the immigrant experience, see Delbanco, *The Puritan Ordeal*, especially pp. 235–52. Immigration, for Delbanco, offers "a paradigm for human experience" in American literature (p. 243); he focuses on the longing for the suspended self as an escape from history rather than the anxiety surrounding this experience.

27. On Houghton Mifflin's especially aggressive role in the promotion of Americanization in the schools through the publication and dissemination of literary histories, see Nina Baym, "Early Histories of American Literature."

28. James C. Malin, *Confounded Rot About Napolean* (Lawrence, Kans.: Coronado Press, 1961), pp. 1, 7.

29. Doane, *Silence and Narrative: The Early Novels of Gertrude Stein* (Westport, Conn.: Greenwood Press, 1986), p. 91.

30. Stein characterizes "real thinking" as "aiming again and again, always going back to the beginning and aiming again." Cited, from Stein's notebooks, in the introduction to *A Stein Reader*, ed. Ulla Dydo (Evanston, Ill.: Northwestern University Press, 1993), p. 21.

31. Edward Said, *Beginnings: Intention and Method* (New York: Columbia University Press, 1975), p. 5.

32. Unlike Du Bois, however, Stein comes to her incremental style as a result of her psychological project, her interest in character. How that concern leads to her interest in narrative disruption is in part the subject of the second section of this chapter. On *The Making of Americans* and Freud's theories of repression and repetition, see Lisa Ruddick, *"The Making of Americans:* Modernism and Patricide," in *Reading Gertrude Stein.*

33. See *Totem and Taboo*, 13: 1–162, especially pp. 140–46; and *Civilization and Its Discontents* 21: 59–145, especially pp. 99–107. Freud draws on Darwin's theory of a primal horde in which a violent and jealous patriarch keeps the women for himself by driving his older sons from the horde. In Freud's narrative, the sons return, kill the father, and ultimately resurrect him—or, his authority— through taboos against fratricide and incest that enable them to continue to live communally. This is the foundation of the law.

34. Harriet Chessman notes similarly, although in a different context, that Stein "suggests a link between narrative plot and the national plots—the making of 'history'—leading to war. The nationalistic assertion of power, grounded in a rhetoric of priority and ownership, finds disturbing reflection within the authorial claim to originary power and possession of one's creation." See Harriet Chessman, *The Public Is Invited to Dance: Representations, the Body and Dialogue in Gertrude Stein* (Stanford, Ca.: Stanford University Press, 1989), p. 116.

35. See, for example, Louis Zukofsky's "A-12," in *A-12* (Berkeley: University of California Press, 1978), p. 168; Dearborn's *Pocahontas's Daughters*, p. 166; Richard Bridgman's *Gertrude Stein in Pieces*, pp. 66–67; Brinnin, *The Third Rose*, p. 93, and Doane's *Silence and Narrative*, pp. 92–3. Both Bridgman and Doane view Stein's departure from Aristotle's theme as largely unintentional. See also Rosalind S. Miller, *Gertrude Stein: Form and Intelligibility* (New York: The Exposition Press, 1949), for another source of this passage in a Radcliffe writing assignment (*The Radcliffe Manuscripts*, p. 120). On Stein's December 4, 1894 submissions, "There is nothing we are more tolerant of than our own sins writ large in others," an instructor has written, "Montaigne or Confucius." Elsewhere in *The Radcliffe Manuscripts*, however, Stein is explicit about her intellectual debt to "Professor James." Stein's use of Aristotle would not be a legal but an ethical breach.

36. Anzia Yezierska, *Bread Givers: A struggle between a father of the Old World and a daughter of the New* (New York: Persea Books, 1925), p. 159.

Subsequent text references are designated *BG*. This phrase becomes something of a refrain in *Bread Givers*.

37. Ernest Renan, "What is a Nation?" trans. Martin Thom, in *Nation and Narration*, ed. Bhabha, pp. 8–22, p. 11. Subsequent text references are designated ER. Benedict Anderson generates his discussion of the relationship between forgetting and the national narrative from Renan's speech in a chapter he has added to the revised edition of *Imagined Communities:* "having to 'have already forgotten' tragedies of which one needs unceasingly to be 'reminded' turns out to be a characteristic device in the later construction of national genealogies" (*IC*, 201). These narratives impose national unity by means of what Anderson calls the "reassuring fratricides" of a "family history" (*IC*, 201); they are written and disseminated through such cultural institutions as the education system.

38. The language of patricide in the name of freedom suggests what Donald Pease calls "the revolutionary mythos," the fictive break from the father(s), by which the early Republic defined itself. David's patricidal impulses, like Pierre's, are in the name of the father(s). See Donald Pease, *Visionary Compacts: American Renaissance Writings in Cultural Context* (Madison: University of Wisconsin Press, 1987), p. x.

39. Gilman's *Herland* describes a utopian female collective, a land owned by women. Stein's possessive, I argue, suggests something different. Janice Doane gives it yet another reading: it "suggests both 'her land' (a strong matriarchy), and the German word 'herz,' meaning heart or courage," the latter of which Doane sees becoming increasingly ironic. See *Silence and Narrative*, p. 133.

40. *William James on Exceptional Mental States: The 1896 Lowell Lectures*, reconstructed by Eugene Taylor (New York: Scribner's, 1983), p. 5. The lectures are reconstructions not transcriptions. James used *Psychology (Briefer Course)* as a classroom text. On the influence of James's psychology on Stein, see Lisa Ruddick's *Reading Gertrude Stein*. The imperialistic traces that, unlike Frank Lentricchia, I see in James inhere in how he writes (his metaphors, his sentence structures) rather than in what he *explicitly* professes. See Lentricchia, "On the Ideologies of Poetic Modernism: The Example of William James, 1890–1913," *Reconstructing American Literary History*, ed. Sacvan Bercovitch (Cambridge, Mass.: Harvard University Press, 1986), pp. 220–49 and *Ariel and the Police: Michel Foucault, William James, Wallace Stevens* (Madison: University of Wisconsin Press, 1988). It is important to note that James was an *active* anti-imperialist, a member of the Anti-Imperialist League. In this section I argue that Stein offered a sustained and radical analysis of the metaphors and rhetorical assumptions of an imperialist self; her analysis, however, did not translate into activist politics. James was much more of a political activist than Stein. In the discussion that follows, I do not wish to minimize James's important political commitments and analyses, such as his December 1903 "Address on the Philippine Question," nor to suggest that Stein's analyses are more important than James's political

activism. In fact James's career demonstrates that political activism can be effective despite unwittingly contradictory assumptions, and Stein's career demonstrates that radical analysis does not necessarily lead to political activism. For a rich discussion of pragmatism that uses James's philosophy to locate Stein in an Emersonian tradition, see Richard Poirier, *Poetry & Pragmatism* (Cambridge, Mass.: Harvard University Press, 1992).

41. Walter Benn Michaels, *The Gold Standard and the Logic of Naturalism: American Literature at the Turn of the Century* (Berkeley: University of California Press, 1987), p. 9. Subsequent text references are designated *GS*. Tom Lutz also notes James's "imperialist conception of the self and consciousness"; see *American Nervousness, 1903: An Anecdotal History* (Ithaca: Cornell University Press, 1991), p. 95.

42. See Michaels's discussion of this metaphor in *The Gold Standard*, pp. 7–9. It is interesting to note the role played by herds of cattle in nineteenth-century narratives of the origins of society. In *The Origin of the Family, Private Property, and the State*, for example, Friedrich Engels argues that the source of wealth created by the breeding of herds resulted in new forms of social relations, including the division of labor and patriarchal inheritance. James's contemporary and countryman Thorstein Veblen analyzes the conjunction of women, slaves, and cattle as the basis of "the institution of ownership," which in part arises "as evidence of the prowess of their owner," in *The Theory of the Leisure Class* (1899; reprint, New York: Penguin Books, 1987), p. 53.

43. James made this remark in an 1876 review of Renan's *Dialogues et fragments philosophiques*, a work that James felt registered Renan's inability to live up to his potential and marked his "mental ruin." See William James, "Renan's 'Dialogues,'" in *Collected Essays and Reviews* (New York: Russell and Russell, 1920, reissued 1969), 36–39, p. 36.

44. James, *A Pluralistic Universe: Hibbert Lectures at Manchester College on the Present Situation in Philosophy*, in *William James: Writings 1902–1920*, pp. 625–819; this quotation is from "Lecture VII: Concisions," p. 776.

45. For a discussion of the boundaries of the self in William James, see David E. Leary, "William James on the Self and Personality: Clearing the Ground for Subsequent Theorists, Researchers, and Practitioners," in *Reflections on The Principles of Psychology: William James After a Century*, ed. Michael G. Johnson and Tracy B. Henley (Hillsdale, N.J.: Lawrence Erlbaum Associates, 1990).

46. Gertrude Stein, *What Are Masterpieces* (1940; reprint, New York: Pitman, 1970), pp. 62, 63.

47. Although traditionally granted access to citizenship, these women were deprived of the vote until 1920. Women were not consistently granted legal representation and were often excluded from inheritance throughout much of the nineteenth century.

48. Linda Kerber, "From the Declaration of Independence to the Declaration of Sentiments: The Legal Status of Women in the Early Republic, 1776–1848,"

in *Women, the Law, and the Constitution: Major Historical Interpretations*, ed. Kermit L. Hall (New York: Garland, 1987), pp. 397–413, p. 400.

49. James, Letter to Hugo Münsterberg, March 13, 1900, in *The Letters of William James*, ed. Henry James (William's son), vol. 2 (Boston: Atlantic Monthly Press, 1920), pp. 119–20, p. 119.

50. James, "Are We Automata?" in *The Works of William James: Essays in Psychology* (Cambridge, Mass.: Harvard University Press, 1983), pp. 38–61, p. 38.

51. Gertrude Stein and Leon M. Solomons, "Normal Motor Automatism," *Psychological Review* 3 (1896): 492–572, p. 493. Subsequent text references are designated NMA.

52. Freud and Josef Breuer first publicized their study of hysteria in a paper delivered in 1893, "On the Psychical Mechanism of Hysterical Phenomena: Preliminary Communication." It subsequently became the first chapter of *Studies in Hysteria* (2:3–17).

53. Freud first used this term in "On the Theory of Hysterical Attacks," one of the *Sketches for the "Preliminary Communication" of 1893* (1:145–54, p. 151). The concept of repression so critical to Freud's theory of the unconscious distinguishes that theory from James's subliminal (or secondary) consciousness. James was particularly troubled by Freud's "dream theories" and he called " 'symbolism' a most dangerous method." See Ralph Barton Perry, *The Thought and Character of William James: As Revealed in Unpublished Correspondence and Notes, Together With His Published Writings* vol. 2 (Boston: Little, Brown and Company, 1935), p. 122. On Stein's turn from James to Freud, see Lisa Ruddick, *Reading Gertrude Stein*, especially pp. 92–104. My own understanding of the complex resemblances and differences among Stein, James, and Freud has benefited greatly from conversations with Ann Douglas and from her *Terrible Honesty: Mongrel Manhattan in the 1920s* (New York: Farrar Straus, 1995); see chapter 11: " 'The Necessary Angel': Skyscrapers, Airplanes, and Airmindedness."

54. Gertrude Stein, "Cultivated Motor Automatism; A Study of Character in its Relation to Attention," *Psychological Review* 5 (1898): 299–306, p. 299. Subsequent text references are designated CMA.

55. Stein cites a common expression in "letting oneself go," one that was especially important to Henry James, whose journal entries several times record his injunctions to himself to learn to let himself go and whose Lambert Strether in *The Ambassadors* echoes this concern.

Stein, unlike James, was never at home in New England; she considered herself, alternately, southern and western. Donald Sutherland suggests that her disconnection from "any native or local context is . . . partly a Jewish situation and partly the accident of being born in Pennsylvania, traveling in France and Austria, and living in California and Baltimore, all before turning up for college work at Radcliffe, in the deliquescence of New England and the Puritan tradition"; see his *Gertrude Stein: A Biography of Her Work* (New Haven: Yale University Press, 1951), p. 8. Perhaps what Sutherland calls Stein's general "delocalization" was in fact a distance from *New England* and from its inhabitants' tendency to claim its equation with "America."

56. It is easy to imagine New England as the locus of development of a character motivated by fear of losing the self both because of the Puritan legacy that privileged self-possession and because it was the first region to industrialize and urbanize extensively—that is, to impose a markedly external experience of fragmentation on the family. Although Stein's move from regional to national observations is not evident in this work, her observations dovetail with extrinsic cultural concerns. The immigrant narratives, for example, attest to the facility with which this psychological concept of self-possession attaches to, and extends, the liberal postulate of the self-as-owner, an extension that is, in part, the subject of *The Making of Americans.*

57. B. F. Skinner, "Has Gertrude Stein a Secret?" *Atlantic Monthly* 153 (January 1934): 50–57.

58. Gertrude Stein, "The Gradual Making of The Making of Americans" in *Lectures in America* (Boston: Beacon Press, 1935, 1985), pp. 133–61, p. 137. Subsequent text references are designated GM.

59. Arthur Knight, *The Liveliest Art: A Panoramic History of the Movies* (New York: New American Library, 1957).

60. Katz later published the section of his dissertation that treats Weininger as "Weininger and *The Making of Americans,*" *Twentieth-Century Literature* 24 (Spring 1978): 8–14. Otto Weininger, *Sex and Character* (New York: AMS Press, 1975); subsequent text references are designated *SC.*

61. Jayne Walker, *The Making of a Modernist: Gertrude Stein from Three Lives to Tender Buttons* (Amherst: University of Massachusetts Press, 1984), p. 47.

62. This address, and "the decent family's progress" that the narrator sets out to recount, were part of the original narrative about the ill-fated marriage of Stein's cousin Bird, the model for Julia Dehning. By the final version, the stories of the Dehnings and Herslands had melded into one story about the making of Americans. See Ulla E. Dydo, introduction to *A Stein Reader.*

63. Sollors, in *Beyond Ethnicity,* notes a tension between genealogy (descent) and the melting-pot (consent) at the center of American ideology. For Sollors, the "contrastive strategies—naming and name-calling among them—[that] become the most important thing about ethnicity" constitute attempts to negotiate the conflicts between organicist and consensual conceptions of personhood (28). Marriage, with its implications of consent as well as of a change of status and, for the woman, of name, marks the (emblematic and often actual) site of these conflicts.

The Naturalization Act of 1906 demonstrates the social importance of the institution of marriage; the would-be citizen must swear to a disbelief in polygamy. That clause was certainly directed against the Mormons, who advocated not only polygamy but also property held in common, as opposed to the Union's common *concept* of property (and property relations). In addition, the triangulated desire that a second wife would surely introduce runs a greater risk of complicating the contractarian model that suppresses "unassimilated voices." The United States is a jealous spouse, requiring the would-be citizen "to renounce absolutely and forever all allegiance and fidelity to any foreign prince, potentate, state, or sovereignty." Choosing to live outside United States boundaries, an option available to a native-born American, is, for an immigrant, tantamount to renouncing citizenship.

64. Abraham Cahan, *Yekl and the Imported Bridegroom and Other Stories of the New York Ghetto* (New York: Dover, 1970), p. 89. Subsequent text references are designated *Y.*

65. Israel Zangwill, *The Melting-Pot* (New York: Arno Press, 1975; c. 1914). Subsequent text references are designated *M-P.* See Sollors's discussion of Zangwill's play and of the history of the term "melting-pot" in *Beyond Ethnicity,* pp. 66–101.

66. In his "Address on the Philippine Question" (delivered in December 1903), James uses the metaphor of digestion to describe the assimilation of imperialism: "In the physiologies which I studied when I was young, the function of incorporating foreign bodies into one's organism was divided into four stages—prehension, deglutition, digestion and assimilation. We prehended our prey, or took it into our mouth, when President McKinley posted his annexation edict, and insalivated with pious phrases the alternative he offered to our late allies of instant obedience or death. . . . [I]f the swallowing took three years, how long ought the process of digestion, that teaching of the Filipinos to be 'fit' for rule, that solution of recalcitrant lumps into a smooth 'chyle,' with which our civil commission is charged—how long ought that to take?" See "Address on the Philippine Question," in *William James: Writings 1902–1910,* pp. 1130–35, p. 1130.

67. On the evolution and development of the concept of liminality, see especially Victor Turner, "Betwixt and Between: The Liminal Period in *Rites de Passage,*" in *The Forest of Symbols: Aspects of Ndembu Ritual* (New York: Cornell University Press, 1967), pp. 93–111. In Turner's thesis, the terror of liminality evoked by the exposure to formlessness compels the initiate's grateful acquiescence in the terms of the social order. Liminality makes any alternative to a given social order appear to be anarchy rather than an alternative social order. Turner's formulations are central to my understanding of the anxiety of identity.

68. Ulla Dydo argues that Toklas's discovery of the manuscript of *Q.E.D.*, and of Stein's relationship to May Bookstaver, so enraged her that she became "paranoid about the name May" (30). Toklas's paranoia resulted in Stein's stylistic and rhetorical contortions, including the pervasive substitutions in *Stanzas in Meditation* of the word "can" for the word "may." Dydo shows also how many of Stein's slips resulted in the revelation of what she had putatively sought to conceal. See Dydo, *"Stanzas in Meditation:* The Other Autobiography," *Chicago Review* 35 (Winter 1985): 4–20. Although the discovery took place long after Stein wrote

The Making of Americans, similar stylistic and rhetorical concerns operate in the narrative.

69. For other discussions of these changes, see Katz, introduction to *Fernhurst, Q.E.D.,* and Dydo, introduction to *A Stein Reader.*

70. Ulla Dydo, "*Stanzas in Meditation:* The Other Autobiography"; and "Words as Pieces Words in Pieces," *West Coast Line* 24 (Winter 1990).

71. Stein's stylistic indirection may well have begun, as Catharine Stimpson suggests (in "The Mind, the Body, and Gertrude Stein"), as lesbian encoding, and the idea of an alternative system of communication gave rise to a radically experimental poetics of secrecy. For Stein, all meaning is a kind of encoding, a way of defining an inside and an outside that is not unrelated to the machinations of secrecy. Indeterminacy, for her, marks the outsiders' experience of secrecy. (The code could have any number of meanings and therefore verges on—but isn't—meaninglessness.) Indeterminacy is, then, the poetics of outsiders, those who, finally, refuse the "secrecy" of meaning. In other words, we can look for codes, but those codes are as like as not to be *unconscious*—hence, the reader may have a more privileged insight into Stein's mind than Stein has herself. Stein invites the reader into her own unconscious associations. I shift Stimpson's claim somewhat to suggest that Stein's lesbianism contributed to a desire to write in general, and a desire to write against conventions in particular. On the poetics of secrecy, see also Elizabeth Fifer, "Is Flesh Advisable? The Interior Theater of Gertrude Stein," *Signs* 4 (Spring 1979): 472–83. See also Catharine R. Stimpson, "Gertrude Stein and the Transposition of Gender," in *The Poetics of Gender,* ed. Nancy K. Miller (New York: Columbia University Press, 1986), pp. 1–18.

72. Cynthia Merrill, "Mirrored Image: Gertrude Stein and Autobiography," *Pacific Coast Philology,* 20 (November 1985): 11–17.

73. Terry Castle, "Contagious Folly: *An Adventure* and Its Skeptics," *Critical Inquiry* 17 (Summer 1991): 741–72.

74. Stein, "Composition as Explanation," in Dydo, ed., *A Gertrude Stein Reader,* pp. 493–503, p. 498.

75. Henri Bergson, *Essai sur les données immédiates de la conscience* (Geneva: Editions Albert Skira, 1945), p. 131; emphasis added. *Time and Free Will: An Essay on the Immediate Data of Consciousness,* trans. F. L. Pogson (London: Swan Sonnenschein and Company, Limited, 1910), p. 165. Pogson translates "le moi" as "the self." I have left it as the more suggestive and literal "the me" to convey the particular idea of the self thereby connoted.

76. Woodrow Wilson, "Princeton in the Nation's Service," p. 24. For a more sustained discussion of this speech, see Chapter 3.

77. Gertrude Stein, *Everybody's Autobiography* (1937; reprint. New York: Random House, 1959), p. 64. Subsequent text references are designated *EA.*

78. "Phenomenon in American Art," *Last Lunar Baedeker,* pp. 300–302, p. 300.

Coda

1. The phrase is a title of a poem that has appeared in several volumes, the first taking its name from the poem: *The Reading of an Ever-Changing Tale* (Clinton, N.Y.: Nobodaddy Press, 1977); *Sometimes* (New York: Sheep Meadow Press, 1979), p. 17; *Corpse and Mirror* (New York: Holt, Rinehart & Winston, 1983), p. 72; *Radiant Silhouette: New and Selected Work, 1974–1988* (Santa Rosa, Calif.: Black Sparrow Press, 1989), p. 20.

2. Theresa Hak Kyung Cha, *Dictée* (New York: Tanam Press, 1982), p. 56; emphasis added. Subsequent text references are designated *D*.

Selected Bibliography

Ackerman, Bruce. *We the People: Foundations*. Cambridge, Mass.: Harvard University Press, 1991.

Addams, Jane. *Twenty Years at Hull-House*. New York: New American Library, 1981.

Alexander, William T. *History of the Colored Race in America*. New York: Negro Universities Press, 1968.

Althusser, Louis. "Ideology and Ideological State Apparatuses (Notes towards an Investigation)." In *Lenin and Philosophy and Other Essays*, trans. Ben Brewster, 127–86. New York: Monthly Review Press, 1971.

———. "A Letter on Art in Reply to André Daspre." In *Lenin and Philosophy and Other Essays*, trans. Ben Brewster, 221–27. New York: Monthly Review Press, 1971.

Amar, Akhil Reed. "Some New World Lessons for the Old World," *University of Chicago Law Review* 58 (1991): 483–509.

Anderson, Benedict. *Imagined Communities: Reflections on the Origin and Spread of Nationalism*. Rev. ed. London: Verso, 1991.

Andrews, William L. *To Tell A Free Story: The First Century of Afro-American Autobiography, 1760–1865*. Urbana: University of Illinois Press, 1986.

Antin, Mary. *The Promised Land*. New York: Houghton Mifflin, 1925.

Appiah, Kwame Anthony. *In My Father's House: Africa in the Philosophy of Culture*. London: Methuen, 1992.

———. "The Uncompleted Argument: Du Bois and the Illusion of Race." In *Race, Writing, and Difference*, ed. Henry Louis Gates, Jr., 21–37. Chicago: University of Chicago Press, 1986.

Armstrong, J. A. *Nations before Nationalism*. Chapel Hill: University of North Carolina Press, 1982.

Arvin, Newton. *Herman Melville*. New York: Viking Press, 1964.

Bagehot, Walter. *Physics and Politics, or Thoughts on the Application of the Principles of "Natural Selection" and "Inheritance" to Political Science.* Boston: Beacon Press, 1956.

Bailyn, Bernard. *Pamphlets of the American Revolution.* Cambridge: Harvard University Press, 1965.

Baker, Houston. *The Journey Back: Issues in Black Literature and Criticism.* Chicago: University of Chicago Press, 1980.

Bakhtin, Mikhail M. "Discourse in the Novel." In *The Dialogic Imagination: Four Essays by M. M. Bakhtin,* ed. Michael Holquist, trans. Caryl Emerson and Michael Holquist, 259–422. Austin: University of Texas Press, 1981.

Balibar, Etienne, and Immanuel Wallerstein. *Race, Nation, Class: Ambiguous Identities,* trans. of Etienne Balibar by Chris Turner. London: Verson, 1991.

Bannister, Robert C. *Sociology and Scientism: The American Quest for Objectivity, 1880–1940.* Chapel Hill: University of North Carolina Press, 1987.

Baron, Denis E. *Grammar and Good Taste: Reforming the American Language.* New Haven: Yale University Press, 1982.

Bauer, Dale. *Feminist Dialogics: A Theory of Failed Community.* Albany: State University of New York Press, 1988.

Baym, Nina. "Early Histories of American Literature." *American Literary History* 1.3 (Fall 1989): 459–88.

———. "Melville's Quarrel with Fiction." *PMLA* 94.5 (October 1979): 909–23.

———. *Woman's Fiction: A Guide to Novels By and About Women in America, 1820–70.* Ithaca: Cornell University Press, 1978.

Benstock, Shari. *Textualizing the Feminine: On the Limits of Genre.* Norman: University of Oklahoma Press, 1991.

Benston, Kimberly. "I Yam What I Am: The Topos of (Un)naming in Afro-American Literature." In *Black Literature and Literary Theory,* ed. Henry Louis Gates, Jr. New York: Routledge, 1984.

Bercovitch, Sacvan. *The American Jeremiad.* Madison: University of Wisconsin Press, 1978.

———. "The Problem of Ideology in American Literary History." *Critical Inquiry* 12 (Summer 1986): 631–53.

———. *The Puritan Origins of the American Self.* New Haven: Yale University Press, 1976.

———. *Rites of Assent: Transformations in the Symbolic Construction of America.* London: Routledge, Chapman and Hall, 1993.

Bergson, Henri. *Essai Sur les Données Immédiates de la Conscience.* Geneva: Editions Albert Skira, 1945.

Berkhofer, Robert, Jr. *The White Man's Indian: Images of the American Indian from Columbus to the Present.* New York: Vintage Books, 1979.

Berkson, Isaac B. *Theories of Americanization: A Critical Study with Special Reference to the Jewish Group.* New York: Teacher's College, Columbia University, 1920.

Berlant, Lauren. *The Anatomy of National Fantasy: Hawthorne, Utopia, and Everyday Life.* Chicago: University of Chicago Press, 1992.

Berry, Ellen. "On Reading Gertrude Stein." *Genders* 5 (Spring 1989): 1–20.

Bhabha, Homi K. "DissemiNation: Time, Narrative, and the Margins of the Modern Nation." In *Nation and Narration,* ed. Homi K. Bhabha, 291–322. London: Routledge, 1990.

———. "Of Mimicry and Man: The Ambivalence of Colonial Discourse." *October* 28 (Spring 1984): 125–33.

Blackstone, Sir William. *Commentaries on the Laws of England.* 4 vols. Chicago: University of Chicago Press, 1979.

Blauvelt, Mary Taylor. "The Race Problem: As Discussed by Negro Women." *American Journal of Sociology.* 6.5 (March 1901): 662–72.

Boas, Franz. *A Franz Boas Reader: The Shaping of American Anthropology, 1883–1911,* ed. George W. Stocking. Chicago: University of Chicago Press, 1974.

The Book of Abigail and John: Selected Letters of the Adams Family, 1762–1784. Edited by L. H. Butterfield, Marc Frielaender, and Mary-Jo Kline. Cambridge, Mass.: Harvard University Press, 1975.

Brennan, Timothy. "The National Longing for Form." In *Nation and Narration,* ed. Homi Bhabha, 44–70. London: Routledge, 1990.

Bridgman, Richard. *Gertrude Stein in Pieces.* New York: Oxford University Press, 1970.

Brinnon, Malcolm. *The Third Rose: Gertrude Stein and Her World.* New York: Addison-Wesley, 1987.

Brodhead, Richard. *Hawthorne, Melville, and the Novel.* Chicago: University of Chicago Press, 1976.

Brooks, Peter. *Reading for the Plot: Design and Intention in Narrative.* New York: Vintage Books, 1984.

Brown, Gillian. *Domestic Individualism: Imagining Self in Nineteenth-Century America.* Berkeley: University of California Press, 1990.

Bruce, Dickson D., Jr. "W. E. B. Du Bois and the Idea of Double Consciousness." *American Literature* 64.2 (June 1992): 299–309.

Burgess, John W. *Reconstruction and the Constitution: 1866–1876.* New York: Scribner's, 1902.

Burke, Edmund. "The Thirteen Resolutions." In *Two Speeches on Conciliation with America and Two Letters on the Irish Questions*, 2d ed., 99–196. London: George Routledge & Sons, 1889.

Cahan, Abraham. *Yekl and the Imported Bridegroom and Other Stories of the New York Ghetto.* New York: Dover, 1970.

Carby, Hazel. "On the Threshold of Woman's Era: Lynching, Empire, and Sexuality in Black Feminist Theory." *Critical Inquiry* 12.1 (1985): 262–77.

———. *Reconstructing Womanhood: The Emergence of the Afro-American Woman Novelist.* Oxford: Oxford University Press, 1987.

Carlson, Robert A. *The Quest for Conformity: Americanization Through Education.* New York: John Wiley, 1975.

Carton, Evan. "*Pudd'nhead Wilson* and the Fiction of Law Custom." In *American Realism: New Essays*, ed. Eric J. Sundquist. Baltimore: Johns Hopkins University Press, 1982.

Castle, Terry. "Contagious Folly: *An Adventure* and Its Skeptics." *Critical Inquiry* 17 (Summer 1991): 741–72.

Cha, Theresa. *Dictée.* New York: Tanam Press, 1982.

Chase, Richard, ed. *Melville: A Collection of Critical Essays.* Englewood Cliffs, N.J.: Prentice-Hall, 1962.

Chessman, Harriet. *The Public Is Invited to Dance: Representations, the Body and Dialogue in Gertrude Stein.* Stanford: Stanford University Press, 1989.

Cheyfitz, Eric. *The Poetics of Imperialism: Translation and Colonization from "The Tempest" to Tarzan."* New York: Oxford University Press, 1991.

Child, Lydia Maria. *Hobomok & Other Writings on Indians.* New Brunswick, N.J.: Rutgers University Press, 1986.

Choate, Rufus. "The Importance of Illustrating New-England History by a Series of Romances Like the Waverley Novels. *The Works of Rufus Choate with a Memoir of His Life*, ed. Samuel Gilman Brown, 319–46. Boston: Little, Brown, 1862.

Cmiel, Kenneth. *Democratic Eloquence: The Fight Over Popular Speech in Nineteenth-Century America.* New York: William Morrow and Co., 1990.

"Comment on Recent Books in American History." *Atlantic Monthly* (April 1897): 559–69.

Commons, John R. "Racial Composition of the American People: Amalgamation and Assimilation." *Chautauqua* 39 (May 1904): 217–25.

Cover, Robert. *Justice Accused: Antislavery and the Judicial Process.* New Haven: Yale University Press, 1975.

Cunningham, George P. "Called into Existence: Desire, Gender, and Voice in Frederick Douglass's *Narrative* of 1845." *differences* 1.3 (1989): 108–35.

Current, Richard Nelson. "Unity, Ethnicity, and Abraham Lincoln." In *Speaking of Abraham Lincoln: The Man and His Meaning for Our Times*, 105–25. Urbana: University of Illinois Press, 1983.

Curtis, David Ames, and Henry Louis Gates, Jr. "Establishing the Identity of the Author of *Our Nig.*" In *Wild Women in the Whirlwind: Afra-American Culture and the Contemporary Literary Renaissance*, ed. Joanne M. Braxton and Andrée Nicola McLaughlin, 48–69. New Brunswick: Rutgers University Press, 1990.

Cutler, H. G. "The American Not a New Englishman, But a New Man." *New England Magazine* 9.1 (September 1893): 24–30.

Dauber, Kenneth. *The Idea of Authorship in America: Democratic Poetics from Franklin to Melville*. Madison: University of Wisconsin Press, 1990.

Davidson, Cathy N. *Revolution and the Word: The Rise of the Novel in America*. New York: Oxford University Press, 1986.

Dearborn, Mary. *Pocahontas's Daughters: Gender and Ethnicity in American Culture*. New York: Oxford University Press, 1986.

DeKoven, Marianne. *A Different Language: Gertrude Stein's Experimental Writing*. Madison: University of Wisconsin Press, 1983.

Delbanco, Andrew. *The Puritan Ordeal*. Cambridge: Harvard University Press, 1989.

Demos, John, and Virginia Demos. "Adolescence in Historical Perspective." *Journal of Marriage and the Family* (November 1969): 632–38.

Derrida, Jacques. "Devant la loi." Trans. Avital Ronell. In *Kafka and the Contemporary Critical Performance: Centenary Readings*, ed. Alan Udoff. Bloomington: Indiana University Press, 1987.

Dewey, John. "The School as Social Centre." In *John Dewey: The Middle Works, 1899–1924*, vol. 2: *1902–1903*, ed. Jo Ann Boydston, 80–93. Carbondale: Southern Illinois University Press, 1976.

Dimock, Wai-chee. *Empire for Liberty: Melville and the Poetics of Individualism*. Princeton: Princeton University Press, 1989.

Dixon, Thomas. *The Leopard's Spots: A Romance of the White Man's Burden, 1865–1900*. New York: Doubleday and Page, 1902.

Doane, Janice. *Silence and Narrative: The Early Novels of Gertrude Stein*. Westport, Conn.: Greenwood Press, 1986.

Doriani, Beth Maclay. "Black Womanhood in Nineteenth-Century America: Subversion and Self-Construction in Two Women's Autobiographies." *American Quarterly* 43.2 (June 1991): 199–222.

Douglas, Ann. "The Dream of the Wise Child: Freud's Family Romance Revisited in Contemporary Narratives of Horror." *Prospects* 9 (1984): 293–348.

———. *The Feminization of American Culture*. New York: Knopf, 1977.

———. *Terrible Honesty: Mongrel Manhattan in the 1920s*. New York: Farrar, Straus & Giroux, 1995.

Douglass, Frederick. *Frederick Douglass Papers*. Vols. 1–3, ed. John Blassingame. Vol. 4, ed. John Blassingame and John R. McKivigan. New Haven: Yale University Press, 1985.

———. *Life and Times of Frederick Douglass: His Early Life as a Slave, His Escape from Bondage, and His Complete History*. 1892. Reprint. New York: Collier Books, Macmillan Publishing Co., 1962.

———. *My Bondage and My Freedom*, ed. William L. Andrews. Urbana: University of Illinois Press, 1987.

———. *Narrative of the Life of Frederick Douglass, an American Slave, Written by Himself*, ed. David W. Blight. New York: St. Martin's Press.

Drinnon, Richard. *Facing West: The Metaphysics of Indian-Hating and Empire-Building*. New York: New American Library, 1980.

Dryden, Edgar. *Melville's Thematics of Form: The Great Art of Telling the Truth*. Baltimore: Johns Hopkins University Press, 1968.

Du Bois, W. E. B. *The Autobiography of W. E. B. Du Bois: A Soliloquy on Viewing My Life from the Last Decade of its First Century*. New York: International Publishers, 1968.

———. *Black Reconstruction*. New York: Harcourt, Brace, 1935.

———. "The Conservation of Races." In *W. E. B. Du Bois: Writings*, 815–26. New York: Library of America, 1986.

———. "Criteria of Negro Art." *Crisis* (October 1926): 290–97.

———. *Dusk of Dawn: An Essay Toward an Autobiography of a Race Concept*. In *W. E. B. Du Bois: Writings*, 549–802. New York: Library of America, 1986.

———. "The Freedmen's Bureau." *Atlantic Monthly* 87 (March 1901): 354–65.

———. *The Souls of Black Folk*. In *W. E. B. Du Bois: Writings*, 357–547. New York: Library of America, 1986.

———. "The Souls of White Folk." In *W. E. B. Du Bois: Writings*, 923–38. New York: Library of America, 1986.

———. *W. E. B. Du Bois: Against Racism*, ed. Herbert Aptheker. Amherst: University of Massachusetts Press, 1985.

Dunning, William Archibald. *Reconstruction: Political and Economic, 1865–1877*. New York: Harper & Brothers, 1907.

Duyckinck, Evert. "Nationality in Literature." *The United States Magazine and Democratic Review* 20.105 (March 1847): 264–72.

Duyckinck, Evert A. and George L. *Cyclopaedia of American Literature: Embracing Personal and Critical Notices of Authors, and Selections From Their Writ-*

ings. From the Earliest Period to the Present Day, With Portraits, Autographs, and Other Illustrations. 2 vols. New York: Scribner's, 1856.

Dydo, Ulla. "*Stanzas in Meditation:* The Other Autobiography." *Chicago Review* 35 (Winter 1985): 4–20.

——. "Words as Pieces Words in Pieces." *West Coast Line* 24.3 (Winter 1990).

Elliot, Emory. "Art, Religion, and the Problem of Authority in *Pierre.*" In *Ideology and Classic American Literature,* ed. Sacvan Bercovitch and Myra Jehlen, 337–51. Cambridge: Cambridge University Press, 1986.

Ellis, Richard. *The Union at Risk.* New York: Oxford University Press, 1987.

Ellison, Ralph. "Change the Joke and Slip the Yoke." In *Shadow and Act,* 45–59. New York: Vintage Books, 1972.

Emerson, Ralph Waldo. "Fate." In *Ralph Waldo Emerson: Essays and Lectures,* 5–49. New York: Library of America, 1983.

——. "Nature." In *Ralph Waldo Emerson: Essays and Lectures,* 3–49. New York: Library of America, 1983.

——. "The Transcendentalist." In *Ralph Waldo Emerson: Essays and Lectures,* 191–209. New York: Library of America, 1983.

——. "The Young American: A Lecture Read Before the Mercantile Library Association, Boston, February 7, 1844." In *Ralph Waldo Emerson: Essays and Lectures,* 210–30. New York: Library of America, 1983.

Engels, Friedrich. *The Origin of the Family, Private Property, and the State, in the Light of the Researches of Lewis H. Morgan.* 1942. New York: International Publishers, 1972.

Ernest, John. "Economies of Identity: Harriet E. Wilson's *Our Nig.*" *PMLA* 109.3 (May 1994): 424–38.

Evarts, Jeremiah. *Cherokee Removal: The "William Penn" Essays and Other Writings,* ed. Francis Paul Prucha. Knoxville: University of Tennessee Press, 1981.

Fairchild, E. M. "Society's Need of Effective Ethical Instruction in School and Church, and the Suggestion of an Available Method." *American Journal of Sociology* 4.4 (January 1899): 433–39.

Fanon, Frantz. *Black Skin, White Masks,* trans. Charles Lam Markmann, 141–209. New York: Grove Press, 1967.

——. *The Wretched of the Earth: The Handbook for the Black Revolution That Is Changing the Shape of the World,* trans. Constance Farrington. New York: Grove Press, 1963.

Fehrenbacher, Don E. "The Deep Reading of Lincoln." In *Lincoln in Text and Context,* 214–27. Stanford: Stanford University Press, 1987.

——. *The Dred Scott Case: Its Significance in American Law and Politics.* New York: Oxford University Press, 1978.

————. *Slavery, Law, and Politics.* New York: Oxford University Press, 1981.

————. "The Words of Lincoln." In *Lincoln in Text and Context: Collected Essays,* 270–86. Stanford: Stanford University Press, 1987.

Ferguson, Robert. "The Judicial Opinion as Literary Genre." *Yale Journal of Law & the Humanities* 2.1 (Winter 1990): 201–19.

————. *Law and Letters in American Culture.* Cambridge, Mass.: Harvard University Press, 1984.

————. "The Limits of Enlightenment." In *The Cambridge History of American Literature, 1590–1820,* ed. Sacvan Bercovitch, vol. 1. Cambridge: Cambridge University Press, 1994.

————. " 'We Do Ordain and Establish': The Constitution as Literary Text." *William & Mary Law Review* 29.1 (Fall 1987): 3–25.

Fifer, Elizabeth. "Is Flesh Advisable? The Interior Theater of Gertrude Stein." *Signs* 4.3 (Spring 1979): 472–83.

Foner, Eric. *Free Soil, Free Labor, Free Men: The Ideology of the Republican Party before the Civil War.* Oxford: Oxford University Press, 1970.

Foner, Philip S., ed. *We, the Other People: Alternative Declarations of Independence by Labor Groups, Farmers, Women's Rights Advocates, Socialists, and Blacks 1829–1975.* Urbana: University of Illinois Press, 1976.

Forgie, George B. *Patricide in the House Divided: A Psychological Interpretation of Lincoln and His Age.* New York: W. W. Norton, 1979.

Foster, Frances Smith. *Witnessing Slavery: The Development of Ante-bellum Slave Narratives.* Westport, Conn.: Greenwood Press, 1979.

Fredrickson, George M. *The Black Image in the White Mind: The Debate on Afro-American Character and Destiny, 1817–1914.* New York: Harper & Row, 1971.

Freud, Sigmund. *Civilization and Its Discontents,* 59–145. Vol. 21 of *The Standard Edition of the Complete Psychological Works of Sigmund Freud,* trans. James Strachey with Anna Freud, Alix Strachey, and Alan Tyson. 1955. London: Hogarth Press and the Institute of Psycho-Analysis, 1986.

————. "Family Romances." In *Complete Works,* 9:235–41.

————. "On the Theory of Hysterical Attacks." *Sketches for the 'Preliminary Communication' of 1893.* In *Complete Works,* 1:145–54.

————. *Totem and Taboo.* In *Complete Works,* 13:1–162.

————. "The Uncanny." In *Complete Works,* 17:217–48.

Freud, Sigmund, and Josef Breuer. "On the Psychical Mechanism of Hysterical Phenomena: Preliminary Communication." In *Complete Works,* 2:3–17.

Gardner, Eric. "'This Attempt of Their Sister': Harriet Wilson's *Our Nig* from Printer to Readers." *New England Quarterly* 66 (1993): 226–46.

Gates, Henry Louis, Jr. "Binary Oppositions in Chapter One of *Narrative of the Life of Frederick Douglass an American Slave, Written by Himself.*" In *Figures in Black: Words, Signs and the "Racial" Self,* 80–97. New York: Oxford University Press, 1987.

——. "Frederick Douglass and the Language of Self." In *Figures in Black,* 98–124. New York: Oxford University Press, 1987.

——. "Parallel Discursive Universes: Fictions of the Self in Harriet E. Wilson's *Our Nig.*" In *Figures in Black,* 125–63. New York: Oxford University Press, 1987.

Gellner, Ernest. *Nations and Nationalism.* Oxford: Oxford University Press, 1983.

Gibson, Donald. "Reconciling Public and Private in Frederick Douglass' *Narrative.*" *American Literature* 87.4 (December 1985): 549–69.

Giddings, Franklin. *The Elements of Sociology.* New York: Macmillan, 1898. Reprint, 1900.

——. *The Principles of Sociology: An Analysis of the Phenomenon of Association and of Social Organization.* New York: Macmillan, 1896.

Giddings, Paula. *When and Where I Enter: The Impact of Black Women on Race and Sex in America.* New York: Bantam Books, 1984.

Gillman, Susan. " 'Sure Identifiers': Race, Science, and the Law in *Pudd'nhead Wilson.*" In *Mark Twain's "Pudd'nhead Wilson,"* ed. Susan Gillman and Forrest G. Robinson. Durham, N.C.: Duke University Press, 1990.

Gilpin, William. *The Cosmopolitan Railway, Compacting and Fusing Together All the World's Continents.* San Francisco: History Company, 1890.

Gilroy, Paul. *The Black Atlantic: Modernity and Double Consciousness.* Cambridge, Mass.: Harvard University Press, 1993.

Goldman, Anita Haya. "Black Nationalism: the Contradictory Claims of Rights and Race in the Writings of W. E. B. Du Bois." Paper Presented at the Convention of the American Studies Association, Baltimore, Md., November 1991.

Graebner, Norman. *Manifest Destiny.* Indianapolis: Bobbs-Merrill, 1968.

Grant, Percy Stickney. "American Ideals and Race Mixture." *North American Review* 195 (April 1912): 513–25.

Greenfield, Liah. *Nationalism: Five Roads to Modernity.* Cambridge: Harvard University Press, 1992.

Griswold, Rufus. *Prose Writers of America.* New York: Garrett Press, 1969.

Grossman, Allen. "The Poetics of Union in Whitman and Lincoln: An Inquiry toward the Relationship of Art and Policy." In *The American Renaissance Reconsidered,* ed. Walter Benn Michaels and Donald E. Pease, 183–208. Baltimore: Johns Hopkins University Press, 1985.

Hall, G. Stanley. Introduction. *Methods of Teaching History,* ed. G. Stanley Hall. 2d ed. Boston: D. C. Heath, 1898.

Hart, Albert Bushnell. *National Ideals Historically Traced, 1607–1907.* New York: Harper and Brothers, 1907.

Haskell, Thomas L. *The Emergence of Professional Social Science: The American Social Science Association and the Nineteenth-Century Crisis of Authority.* Urbana: University of Illinois Press, 1977.

Hawthorne, Nathaniel. "The Minister's Black Veil." In *Hawthorne: Tales and Sketches,* 371–84. New York: Library of America, 1982.

Hetherington, Hugh W. *Melville's Reviewers: British and American, 1846–1891.* New York: Russell & Russell, 1961.

Higham, John. *Send These to Me: Immigrants in Urban America.* Rev. ed. Baltimore: Johns Hopkins University Press, 1984.

———. *Strangers in the Land: Patterns of American Nativism, 1860–1925.* 1955. New York: Atheneum, 1963.

Hirsch, Emil G. "The American University." *American Journal of Sociology* 1.2 (September 1895): 113–31.

Hobsbawm, E. J. *Nations and Nationalism since 1780: Programme, Myth, Reality.* Cambridge: Cambridge University Press, 1990.

Hoffman, Michael. *The Development of Abstractionism in the Writings of Gertrude Stein.* Philadelphia: University of Pennsylvania Press, 1965.

Holloway, Karla. "Economies of Space: Markets and Marketability in *Our Nig* and *Iola Leroy.*" In *The (Other) American Traditions: Nineteenth-Century Women Writers,* ed. Joyce W. Warren, 126–40. New Brunswick: Rutgers University Press, 1993.

Holt, Thomas C. "The Political Uses of Alienation: W. E. B. Du Bois on Politics, Race, and Culture, 1903–1940." *American Quarterly* 42.2 (June 1990): 301–23.

Horsman, Reginald. *Race and Manifest Destiny: The Origins of Racial Anglo-Saxonism.* Cambridge: Harvard University Press, 1987.

Horwitz, Howard. *By the Law of Nature: Form and Value in Nineteenth-Century America.* New York: Oxford University Press, 1991.

Irigaray, Luce. *This Sex Which Is Not One,* trans. Catherine Porter with Carolyn Burke. Ithaca: Cornell University Press, 1985.

Jackson, Laura (Riding). *The Telling.* New York: Harper and Row, 1972.

Jacobs, Harriet A. *Incidents in the Life of a Slave Girl.* Cambridge: Harvard University Press, 1987.

James, William. "Address on the Philippine Question." In *William James: Writings, 1902–1910.* New York: Library of America, 1987.

——. "Are We Automata?" In *The Works of William James: Essays in Psychology*, 38–61. Cambridge, Mass.: Harvard University Press, 1983.

——. "The Chicago School." In *William James: Writings, 1902–1920*. New York: Library of America, 1987.

——. "Renan's Dialogues." In *Collected Essays and Reviews*, 36–39. 1920. New York: Russell & Russell, 1969.

——. *The Letters of William James*, edited by his son Henry James. Vol. 2. Boston: Atlantic Monthly Press, 1920.

——. *A Pluralistic Universe: Hibbert Lectures at Manchester College on the Present Situation in Philosophy*. In *William James: Writings, 1902–1920*, 625–819. New York: Library of America, 1987.

——. *The Principles of Psychology*. Cambridge, Mass.: Harvard University Press, 1983.

——. *William James on Exceptional Mental States: The 1896 Lowell Lectures*. Reconstructed by Eugene Taylor. New York: Scribner's, 1983.

Jameson, Frederic. *The Political Unconscious: Narrative as a Socially Symbolic Act*. Ithaca: Cornell University Press, 1981.

Jefferson, Thomas. *The Complete Jefferson: Containing His Major Writings, Published and Unpublished, Except His Letters*. Assembled and arranged by Saul K. Padover. New York: Duell, Sloan & Pearce, 1943.

——. *Thomas Jefferson: Writings*. New York: Library of America, 1984.

Jehlen, Myra. *American Incarnation: The Individual, the Nation, and the Continent*. Cambridge: Harvard University Press, 1986.

Johnson, Edward Augustus. *A School History of the Negro Race in America*. New York: AMS Press, 1969.

Johnson, James Weldon. *The Autobiography of an Ex-Coloured Man*. New York: Knopf, 1970.

Jones, William Alfred. "Democracy and Literature." *The United States Magazine and Democratic Review* 11.50 (August 1842): 196–200.

Jordon, Winthrop D. *White Over Black: American Attitudes Toward the Negro, 1550–1812*. New York: W. W. Norton, 1977.

Kahler, Erich. *The Inward Turn of Narrative*. Translated by Richard and Clara Winston. Evanston: Northwestern University Press, 1973. Reprint, 1987.

Kahn, Paul W. *Legitimacy and History: Self-Government in American Constitutional Thought*. New Haven: Yale University Press, 1992.

Kallen, Horace. "Democracy Versus the Melting-Pot." *Nation* 100.2509-91 (February 18 and 25, 1915): 190–94, 217–20.

Kaplan, Amy. "Romancing the Empire: The Embodiment of American Masculinity in the Popular Historical Novel of the 1890s." *American Literary History* 2.4 (Winter 1990): 659–90.

Katz, Leon. "The First Making of *The Making of Americans:* A Study Based on Gertrude Stein's Notebooks and Early Versions of Her Novel (1902–1908)." Ph.D. dissertation, Columbia University, 1963.

———. "Weininger and *The Making of Americans.*" *Twentieth-Century Literature* 24.1 (Spring 1978): 8–14.

Kelly, Alfred H., Winfred A. Harbison, and Herman Belz. *The American Constitution: Its Origins and Development.* 6th ed. New York: W. W. Norton, 1983.

Kerber, Linda. "From the Declaration of Independence to the Declaration of Sentiments: The Legal Status of Women in the Early Republic, 1776–1848." In *Women, the Law, and the Constitution: Major Historical Interpretations,* ed. Kermit L. Hall, 397–413. New York: Garland, 1987.

Kettner, James. *The Development of American Citizenship, 1608–1870.* Chapel Hill: University of North Carolina Press, 1978.

Knight, Arthur. *The Liveliest Art: A Panoramic History of the Movies.* New York: New American Library, 1957.

Kohn, Hans. *The Idea of Nationalism.* Toronto: Macmillan, 1944.

———. *Nationalism: Its Meaning and History.* New York: Van Nostrand, 1965.

Lacan, Jacques. "The Function and Field of Speech and Language in Psychoanalysis." In *Ecrits: A Selection,* trans. Alan Sheridan, 30–113. New York: W. W. Norton, 1977.

———. "The Mirror Stage as Formative of the Function of the I as Revealed in Psychoanalytic Experience." In *Ecrits,* 1–7. New York: W. W. Norton, 1977.

Leary, David E. "William James on the Self and Personality: Clearing the Ground for Subsequent Theorists, Researchers, and Practitioners." In *Reflections on The Principles of Psychology: William James After a Century,* ed. Michael G. Johnson and Tracy B. Henley. Hillsdale, N.J.: Lawrence Erlbaum Associates, 1990.

Lentricchia, Frank. *Ariel and the Police: Michel Foucault, William James, Wallace Stevens.* Madison: University of Wisconsin Press, 1988.

———. "On the Ideologies of Poetic Modernism: The Example of William James, 1890–1913." In *Reconstructing American Literary History,* ed. Sacvan Bercovitch, 220–49. Cambridge: Harvard University Press, 1986.

Leubsdorf, John. "Deconstructing the Constitution." *Stanford Law Review* 40 (November 1987): 181–201.

Leverenz, David. *Manhood and the American Renaissance.* Ithaca: Cornell University Press, 1989.

Lewis, David Levering. *W. E. B. Du Bois: Biography of a Race, 1868–1919.* New York: Henry Holt, 1993.

Leyda, Jay. *The Melville Log: A Documentary Life of Herman Melville, 1819–91*. Vol. 1. New York: Gordian Press, 1969.

Lincoln, Abraham. *Collected Works of Abraham Lincoln*, ed. Roy P. Basler. 8 vols. New Brunswick: Rutgers University Press, 1953.

The Lincoln-Douglas Debates of 1858, ed. Robert W. Johannsen. New York: Oxford University Press, 1965.

Locke, John. *John Locke: Two Treatises of Government*, ed. Peter Laslett. Cambridge: Cambridge University Press, 1989.

Looby, Christopher. "Phonetics and Politics: Franklin's Alphabet as a Political Design." *Eighteenth-Century Studies* 18 (1984): 1–34.

Lovett, Robert Morss. *All Our Years*. New York: Viking Press, 1948.

Lowell, James Russell. Review of Henry Wadsworth Longfellow's *Kavanagh, a Tale*. *North American Review* 69.144 (July 1849): 196–215.

Loy, Mina. *The Last Lunar Baedeker*. Edited by Roger L. Conover. Highlands, N.C.: Jargon Society Press, 1982.

Lumpkin, Wilson. *The Removal of the Cherokee Indians from Georgia, 1827–1841*. New York: Dodd, Mead, 1907. Reprint, New York: Augustus M. Kelley Publishers, 1971.

Lutz, Tom. *American Nervousness, 1903: An Anecdotal History*. Ithaca: Cornell University Press, 1991.

McDowell, Deborah E. "In the First Place: Making Frederick Douglass and the Afro-American Tradition." In *Critical Essays on Frederick Douglass*, ed. William L. Andrews, 192–214. Boston: G. K. Hall, 1991.

McFeely, William S. *Frederick Douglass*. New York: W. W. Norton, 1991.

Macherey, Pierre. *A Theory of Literary Production*, trans. Geoffrey Wall. London: Routledge, 1978.

McKay, Nellie Y. "The Souls of Black Women Folk in the Writings of W. E. B. Du Bois." In *Reading Black, Reading Feminist: A Critical Anthology*, ed. Henry Louis Gates, Jr., 227–43. New York: Meridian, 1990.

McLoughlin, William G. *Cherokees and Missionaries, 1789–1839*. New Haven: Yale University Press, 1984.

———. *Cherokee Renascence in the New Republic*. Princeton: Princeton University Press, 1986.

Macpherson, C. B. *The Political Theory of Possessive Individualism: Hobbes to Locke*. Oxford: Oxford University Press, 1962.

McPherson, James M. *Abraham Lincoln and the Second American Revolution*. New York: Oxford University Press, 1990.

Maddox, Lucy. *Removals: Nineteenth-Century American Literature and the Politics of Indian Affairs*. Oxford: Oxford University Press, 1991.

Malin, James C. *Confounded Rot About Napolean.* Lawrence, Kans.: Coronado Press, 1961.

Mallon, Thomas. *Stolen Words: Forays into the Origins and Ravages of Plagiarism.* New York: Ticknor & Fields, 1989.

Matthiessen, F. O. *American Renaissance: Art and Expression in the Age of Emerson and Whitman.* 1941. New York: Oxford University Press, 1961.

Meier, August. *Along the Color Line, Explorations in the Black Experience.* Urbana: University of Illinois Press, 1976.

Melville, Herman. "Hawthorne and His Mosses." In *Herman Melville,* 1154–71. New York: Library of America, 1984.

———. *The Letters of Herman Melville,* ed. Merrell R. Davis and William H. Gilman. New Haven: Yale University Press, 1960.

———. *Pierre, or the Ambiguities.* In *Herman Melville,* 1–421. New York: Library of America, 1984.

Merrill, Cynthia. "Mirrored Image: Gertrude Stein and Autobiography." *Pacific Coast Philology.* 20.1–2 (November 1985): 11–17.

Michaels, Walter Benn. *The Gold Standard and the Logic of Naturalism: American Literature at the Turn of the Century.* Berkeley: University of California Press, 1987.

———. "The Souls of Black Folk." In *Literature and the Body: Essays on Population and Persons,* ed. Elaine Scarry, 185–209. Baltimore: Johns Hopkins University Press, 1988.

———. "The Vanishing American." *American Literary History* 2.2 (Summer 1990): 220–41.

Miller, Herbert Adolphus. "Science, Pseudo-Science and the Race Question." *Crisis* (October 1925): 287–91.

Miller, J. Hillis. *Hawthorne and History: Defacing It.* Cambridge: Blackwell, 1991.

Miller, Perry. *The Raven and the Whale: The War of Words and Wits in the Era of Poe and Melville.* New York: Harcourt, Brace & World, 1956.

Miller, Rosalind S. *Gertrude Stein: Form and Intelligibility.* New York: Exposition Press, 1949.

Mizruchi, Susan. "Cataloguing the Creatures of the Deep: 'Billy Budd, Sailor' and the Rise of Sociology." *boundary 2* 17.1 (Spring 1990): 272–304.

Moody, William Vaughn, and Robert Morss Lovett. *A History of English Literature.* New York: Scribner's, 1906.

Morris, George S. "The Philosophy of the State and of History." In *Methods of Teaching History,* ed. G. Stanley Hall, 149–66. 2d ed. Boston: D. C. Heath, 1898.

Morrison, Toni. *Playing in the Dark: Whiteness and the Literary Imagination.* Cambridge: Harvard University Press, 1992.

Moses, Wilson J. "The Poetics of Ethiopianism: W. E. B. Du Bois and Literary Black Nationalism." In *Critical Essays on W. E. B. Du Bois,* ed. William L. Andrews, 92–106. Boston: G. K. Hall, 1985.

———. "Writing Freely?: Frederick Douglass and the Constraints of Racialized Writing." In *Frederick Douglass: New Literary and Historical Essays,* ed. Eric J. Sundquist, 66–83. Cambridge: Cambridge University Press, 1990.

Mosse, George L. *The Crisis in German Ideology: Intellectual Origins of the Third Reich.* 1964. New York:

———. *Nationalism and Sexuality.* Madison: University of Wisconsin Press, 1985.

Mott, Luther. *A History of American Magazines.* Vol. 1: *1741–1850.* 1930. Rev. ed., Cambridge: Harvard University Press, 1966.

Murray, Henry A. Introduction to *Pierre, or the Ambiguities.* New York: Hendricks House and Farrar, Straus, 1949.

"Nature—A Prose Poem." *The United States Magazine and Democratic Review* 1.3 (February 1838): 319–29.

Nelson, Dana D. *The Word in Black and White: Reading "Race" in American Literature, 1638–1867.* New York: Oxford University Press, 1992.

Nielsen, Aldon Lynn. *Reading Race: White American Poets and the Racial Discourse in the Twentieth Century.* Athens: University of Georgia Press, 1988.

Norton, Anne. *Alternative Americas: A Reading of Antebellum Political Culture.* Chicago: University of Chicago Press, 1986.

———. *Reflections on Political Identity.* Baltimore: Johns Hopkins University Press, 1988.

Novick, Peter. *That Noble Dream: The "Objectivity Question" and the American Historical Profession.* Cambridge: Cambridge University Press, 1988.

Oates, Stephen B. *With Malice Toward None: The Life of Abraham Lincoln.* New York: Harper & Row, 1977.

Olsen, Otto H., ed. *The Thin Disguise: Turning Point in Negro History (Plessy v. Ferguson): A Documentary Presentation (1864–1896).* New York: Humanities Press, 1967.

O'Meally, Robert G. "Frederick Douglass' 1845 *Narrative:* The Text Was Meant to Be Preached." *Afro-American Literature: The Reconstruction of Instruction,* ed. Dexter Fisher and Robert B. Stepto, 192–211. New York: Modern Language Association of America, 1979.

O'Sullivan, John L. "The Great Nation of Futurity." *The United States Magazine and Democratic Review* 6.23 (November 1839): 426–30.

———. Introduction. *The United States Magazine and Democratic Review* 1.1 (October 1837): 1–15.

Otis, D. S. *The Dawes Act and the Allotment of Indian Lands*, ed. Francis Paul Prucha. Norman: University of Oklahoma Press, 1973.

Paine, Thomas. *Common Sense*. In *Thomas Paine: Political Writings*, ed. Bruce Kuklick. New York: Cambridge University Press, 1989.

Parker, Theodore. "The American Scholar." In *The Centenary Edition of Theodore Parker's Writings*, ed. George Willis Cooke, vol. 8: *The American Scholar*, 1–53. Boston: American Unitarian Association, 1907.

Peabody, Ephraim. "Narratives of Fugitive Slaves." *Christian Examiner* 47 (July 1849): 61–93.

Pease, Donald. *Visionary Compacts: American Renaissance Writings in Cultural Context*. Madison: University of Wisconsin Press, 1987.

Perdue, Theda. "The Conflict Within: Cherokees and Removal." In *Cherokee Removal: Before and After*, ed. William L. Anderson. Athens: University of Georgia Press, 1991.

———. *Slavery and the Evolution of Cherokee Society, 1540–1866*. Knoxville: University of Tennessee Press, 1979.

Perloff, Marjorie. *The Poetics of Indeterminacy: Rimbaud to Cage*. Princeton: Princeton University Press, 1981.

———. "Six Stein Styles in Search of a Reader." In *A Gertrude Stein Companion: Content With the Example*, ed. Bruce Kellner, 96–108. New York: Greenwood Press, 1988.

Perry, Ralph Barton. *The Thought and Character of William James*. 2 vols. Boston: Little, Brown, 1935.

Peterson, Carla L. "Capitalism, Black (Under)development, and the Production of the African-American Novel in the 1850s." *American Literary History* 4.4 (Winter 1992): 559–83.

Poe, Edgar Allan. "The Fall of the House of Usher." In *Edgar Allan Poe: Poetry and Tales*, 317–36. New York: Library of America, 1984.

———. "William Wilson." In *Edgar Allan Poe: Poetry and Tales*, 337–57. New York: Library of America, 1984.

———. *The Works of the Late Edgar Allan Poe with a Memoir by Rufus Wilmot Griswold and Notices of His Life and Genius by N. P. Willis and J. R. Lowell*. Vol. 3: *The Literati*. New York: Redfield, 1857.

Poirier, Richard. *Poetry & Pragmatism*. Cambridge: Harvard University Press, 1992.

Pratt, Julius W. "The Origin of 'Manifest Destiny.'" *American Historical Review* 32 (October 1926–January 1927): 795–98.

Prucha, Francis Paul. "The Image of the Indian in Pre-Civil War America." In *Indian Policy in the United States: Historical Essays*, 49–63. Lincoln: University of Nebraska Press, 1981.

Rampersad, Arnold. *The Art and Imagination of W. E. B. Du Bois.* 1976. New York: Schocken Books, 1990.

———. "Slavery and the Literary Imagination: Du Bois's *The Souls of Black Folk.*" In *Slavery and the Literary Imagination*, ed. Deborah McDowell and Arnold Rampersad, 104–24. Baltimore: Johns Hopkins University Press, 1989.

Renan, Ernest. "What Is a Nation?" trans. Martin Thom. In *Nation and Narration*, ed. Homi K. Bhabha, 8–22. London: Routledge, 1990.

Reynolds, David S. *Beneath the American Renaissance: The Subversive Imagination in the Age of Emerson and Melville.* New York: Knopf, 1988.

Riis, Jacob. *How the Other Half Lives: Studies Among the Tenements of New York.* New York: Dover, 1971.

———. *The Making of an American.* New York: Macmillan, 1928.

Roediger, David R. *The Wages of Whiteness: Race and the Making of the American Working Class.* London: Verso, 1991.

Rogin, Michael Paul. *Fathers & Children: Andrew Jackson and the Subjugation of the American Indian.* New York: Vintage Books, 1975.

———. *Ronald Reagan, the Movie, and Other Episodes in Political Demonology.* Berkeley: University of California Press, 1987.

———. *Subversive Genealogy: The Politics and Art of Herman Melville.* New York: Knopf, 1983.

Roosevelt, Theodore. "True Americanism." In *The Works of Theodore Roosevelt*, 13–26. National Edition. New York: Scribner's, 1926.

———. *Works: Presidential Addresses and State Papers.* Parts 2, 14. Statesman Edition. New York: Review of Reviews Co., 1904.

Rose, Mark. "The Author as Proprietor: *Donaldson v. Beckett* and the Genealogy of Modern Authorship," *Representations* 23 (Summer 1988): 51–85.

Rosen, Jeff. "Was the Flag Burning Unconstitutional?" *Yale Law Review* 100 (1991): 1073–92.

Ross, Dorothy. *The Origins of American Social Science.* Cambridge: Cambridge University Press, 1991.

Ross, John. *The Papers of John Ross.* Vol. 1: *1807–1839*, ed. Gary E. Moulton. Norman: Oklahoma University Press, 1985.

Royster, Paul. "Melville's Economy of Language." In *Ideology and Classic American Literature*, ed. Sacvan Bercovitch and Myra Jehlen, 313–36. Cambridge: Cambridge University Press, 1986.

Ruddick, Lisa. *Reading Gertrude Stein: Body, Text, Gnosis.* Ithaca: Cornell University Press, 1990.

Rush, Benjamin. "Of the Mode of Education Proper in a Republic." In *The Selected Writings of Benjamin Rush,* ed. Dagobert D. Runes, 87–96. New York: Philosophical Library, 1947.

Said, Edward. *Beginnings: Intention and Method.* New York: Columbia University Press, 1975.

Saks, Eva. "Representing Miscegenation Law." *Raritan* 8.2 (1988): 39–69.

Saldívar-Hull, Sonia. "Wrestling Your Ally: Stein, Racism, and Feminist Critical Practice." In *Women's Writing in Exile,* ed. Mary Lynn Broe and Angela Ingram, 182–98. Chapel Hill: University of North Carolina Press, 1989.

Sánchez-Eppler, Karen. *Touching Liberty: Abolition, Feminism, and the Politics of the Body.* Berkeley: University of California Press, 1993.

Saxton, Alexander. *The Rise and Fall of the White Republic: Class Politics and Mass Culture in Nineteenth-Century America.* London: Verso, 1990.

Schmitz, Neil. "Refiguring Lincoln: Speeches and Writings, 1832–1865." *American Literary History* 6.1 (Spring 1994): 103–18.

See, Fred G. *Desire and the Sign: Nineteenth-Century American Fiction.* Baton Rouge: Louisiana State University Press, 1987.

Shaler, N. S. "European Peasants as Immigrants." *Atlantic Monthly* (May 1893): 646–55.

Sharlip, William, and Albert A. Owens. *Adult Immigrant Education: Its Scope, Content, and Methods.* New York: Macmillan, 1925.

Shell, Marc. *Children of the Earth: Literature, Politics, and Nationhood.* New York: Oxford University Press, 1993.

Simms, William Gilmore. "Americanism in Literature." In *Views and Reviews in American Literature, History, and Fiction,* ed. C. Hugh Holman, 7–29. Cambridge: Harvard University Press, 1962.

Simons, Sarah E. "Social Assimilation." *American Journal of Sociology* 6.6 (May 1901): 790–822.

Simpson, David. *The Politics of American English, 1776–1850.* Oxford: Oxford University Press, 1986.

Skinner, B. F. "Has Gertrude Stein a Secret?" *Atlantic Monthly* 153 (January 1934): 50–57.

Slotkin, Richard. *Regeneration Through Violence: The Mythology of the American Frontier, 1600–1800.* Middletown, Conn.: Wesleyan University Press, 1973.

Small, Albion W. "The Era of Sociology." *American Journal of Sociology* 1.1 (July 1895): 1–15.

Smith, Anthony D. *The Ethnic Origins of Nations.* Oxford: Blackwell, 1986.

——. *National Identity.* Reno: University of Nevada Press, 1991.

Sollors, Werner. *Beyond Ethnicity: Consent and Descent in American Culture.* New York: Oxford University Press, 1986.

——. "A Critique of Pure Pluralism." In *Reconstructing American Literary History,* ed. Sacvan Bercovitch, 250–79. Cambridge, Mass.: Harvard University Press, 1986.

——. "Of Mules and Mares in a Land of Difference; or, Quadrupeds All?" *American Quarterly* 42.2 (1990): 167–90.

Sorin, Matthew. *The Domestic Circle; or, Moral and social duties explained and enforced on scriptural principles, in a series of discourses.* Philadelphia: J. Harmstead, 1840.

Spivak, Gayatri Chakravorty. "The Making of Americans, the Teaching of English, and the Future of Culture Studies." *New Literary History* 21.4 (Autumn 1990): 781–98.

Stafford, John. *The Literary Criticism of Young America: A Study in the Relationship of Politics and Literature, 1837–1850.* Vol. 3: *English Studies.* Berkeley: University of California Press, 1952.

Stanton, William. *The Leopard's Spots: Scientific Attitudes Toward Race in America 1815–59.* Chicago: University of Chicago Press, 1960.

Starr, Emmett. *Starr's History of the Cherokee Nation,* ed. Jack Gregory and Rennard Strickland. Fayetteville, Ark.: Indian Heritage Association, 1967.

Stein, Gertrude. *The Autobiography of Alice B. Toklas.* In *Selected Writings of Gertrude Stein,* ed. Carl Van Vechten, 2–237. New York: Vintage Books, 1962.

——. "Composition as Explanation." In *A Stein Reader,* ed. Ulla E. Dydo, 493–503. Evanston: Northwestern University Press.

——. "Cultivated Motor Automatism." *Psychological Review* 5 (1898): 299–306.

——. *Everybody's Autobiography.* New York: Random House, 1959.

——. *Fernhurst, Q.E.D., and other early writings by Gertrude Stein.* New York: Liveright, 1971.

——. *Lectures in America.* Boston: Beacon Press, 1985.

——. *The Making of Americans, Being a History of a Family's Progress.* New York: Something Else Press, 1966.

——. *What Are Masterpieces.* New York: Pitman, 1940; rprt. 1970.

Stein, Gertrude, and Leon M. Solomons. "Normal Motor Automatism." *Psychological Review* 3 (1896): 492–572.

Steiner, Wendy. *Exact Resemblance to Exact Resemblance: The Literary Portraiture of Gertrude Stein.* New Haven: Yale University Press, 1978.

Stepto, Robert B. *From Behind the Veil: A Study of Afro-American Narrative.* Urbana: University of Illinois Press, 1979.

——. "Narration, Authentication, and Authorial Control in Frederick Douglass' *Narrative* of 1845." In *Afro-American Literature,* ed. Dexter Fisher and Robert B. Stepto, 178–91. New York: Modern Language Association of America, 1979.

Stimpson, Catharine R. "Gertrude Stein and the Transposition of Gender." In *The Poetics of Gender,* ed. Nancy K. Miller, 1–18. New York: Columbia University Press, 1986.

——. "The Mind, the Body, and Gertrude Stein." *Critical Inquiry* 3 (1977): 489–506.

Sumner, William Graham. *Folkways.* New York: Ayer and Company, n.d.

Sundquist, Eric J. "Frederick Douglass: Literacy and Paternalism." In *Critical Essays on Frederick Douglass,* ed. William L. Andrews, 120–32. Boston: G. K. Hall, 1991.

——. *Home as Found: Authority and Genealogy in Nineteenth-Century American Literature.* Baltimore: Johns Hopkins University Press, 1979.

——. "Mark Twain and Homer Plessy." *Mark Twain's "Puddn'head Wilson,"* ed. Susan Gillman and Forrest G. Robinson, 46–72. Durham, N.C.: Duke University Press, 1990.

——. *To Wake the Nations: Race in the Making of American Literature.* Cambridge: Harvard University Press, 1993.

Sutherland, Donald. *Gertrude Stein: A Biography of Her Work.* New Haven: Yale University Press, 1951.

Swisher, Carl B. *The Taney Period, 1836–1864.* Vol. 5 of *The History of the United States Supreme Court.* New York: Macmillan, 1971.

Takaki, Ronald. *Iron Cages: Race and Culture in Nineteenth-Century America.* 1979. New York: Oxford University Press, 1990.

Tate, Claudia. "Allegories of Black Female Desire; or, Rereading Nineteenth-Century Sentimental Narratives of Black Female Authority." In *Changing Our Own Words: Essays on Critical Theory and Writing By Black Women,* ed. Cheryl A. Wall, 98–126. New Brunswick, N.J.: Rutgers University Press, 1989.

Thomas, Brook. *Cross Examinations of Law and Literature: Cooper, Hawthorne, Stowe, and Melville.* Cambridge: Cambridge University Press, 1987.

Turner, Darwin T. "W. E. B. Du Bois and the Theory of a Black Aesthetic." In *Critical Essays on W. E. B. Du Bois,* ed. William L. Andrews, 73–92. Boston: G. K. Hall, 1985.

Turner, Victor. *The Forest of Symbols: Aspects of Ndembu Ritual.* Ithaca: Cornell University Press, 1967.

Veblen, Thorstein. *The Theory of the Leisure Class.* New York: Penguin Books, 1987.

Walker, Jayne. *The Making of a Modernist: Gertrude Stein from Three Lives to Tender Buttons.* Amherst: University of Massachusetts Press, 1984.

Warren, Kenneth W. *Black and White Strangers: Race and American Literary Realism.* Chicago: University of Chicago Press, 1993.

Washington's Farewell Address: In Facsimile, with Transliterations of All the Drafts of Washington, Madison, and Hamilton, Together with Their Correspondence and Other Supporting Documents. Edited by Victor Hugo Paltsits. New York: New York Public Library, 1935.

Watson, E. L. Grant. "Melville's *Pierre.*" *New England Quarterly* 3 (April 1930): 195–234.

Weaver, Raymond. *Herman Melville: Mariner and Mystic.* New York: Doran, 1921.

Weber, Sam. "The Sideshow, or: Remarks on a Canny Moment." *MLN* 88 (December 1973): 1102–33.

Webster, Noah. *A grammatical institute of the English language, comprising an easy, concise, and systematic method of education, designed for the use of English schools in America. In three parts.* Part I, *Speller.* Hartford: Hudson and Goodwin, 1783.

———. *Letters of Noah Webster,* ed. Harry R. Warfel. New York: Library Publications, 1953.

Weems, Mason L. *The Life of Washington,* ed. Marcus Cunliffe. Cambridge, Mass.: Harvard University Press, 1962.

Weininger, Otto. *Sex and Character.* New York: AMS Press, 1975.

Wendell, Barrett. *A Literary History of America.* New York: Scribner's, 1925.

White, Barbara A. " 'Our Nig' and the She-Devil: New Information about Harriet Wilson and the 'Bellmont' Family." *American Literature* 65.1 (March 1993): 19–52.

White, Edward. *The Marshall Court and Cultural Change, 1815–35.* Vols. 3 and 4 of *The History of the Supreme Court of the United States.* New York: Macmillan, 1988.

White, Hayden. "The Value of Narrativity in the Representation of Reality." In *On Narrative,* ed. W. J. T. Mitchell, 1–23. Chicago: University of Chicago Press, 1981.

White, James Boyd. *When Words Lose Their Meaning: Constitutions and Reconstitutions of Language, Character, and Community.* Chicago: University of Chicago Press, 1984.

Willey, Day Allen. "Americans in the Making: New England's Method of Assimilating the Alien." *Putnam's Monthly and the Reader* 5 (1909): 456–63.

Wills, Garry. *Inventing America: Jefferson's Declaration of Independence.* New York: Random House, 1978.

——. *Lincoln at Gettysburg: The Words That Remade America.* New York: Simon and Schuster, 1992.

Wilson, Harriet E. *Our Nig, or Sketches from the Life of a Free Black.* London: Allison & Busby, 1984.

Wilson, Woodrow. "The Making of the Nation." *Atlantic Monthly* 80.377 (July 1897): 1–14.

——. "Newspaper Report of Lecture in Lancaster on Bagehot." In *The Papers of Woodrow Wilson,* ed. Arthur S. Link, vol. 9: *1894–96,* 381–83. Princeton: Princeton University Press, 1966.

——. "Princeton in the Nation's Service." In *The Papers of Woodrow Wilson,* ed. Arthur S. Link, vol. 10: *1896–98,* 11–31. Princeton: Princeton University Press, 1971.

——. "The Significance of American History." In *The Papers of Woodrow Wilson,* ed. Arthur S. Link, vol. 12: *1900–1902,* 179–84. Princeton: Princeton University Press, 1972.

——. "The Teacher as Citizen." In *The Papers of Woodrow Wilson,* ed. Arthur S. Link, vol. 11: *1898–1900,* 104–5. Princeton: Princeton University Press, 1971.

Winsor, Justin. "The Perils of Historical Narrative." *Atlantic Monthly* 66.395 (September 1890): 289–97.

Yau, John. *The Reading of an Ever-changing Tale.* New York: Nobodaddy Press, 1977.

Yezierska, Anzia. *Bread Givers: A Struggle Between a Father of the Old World and a Daughter of the New.* New York: Persea Books, 1925.

Zafar, Rafia. "The Afro-American as Representative Man." In *Frederick Douglass: New Literary and Historical Essays,* ed. Eric J. Sundquist, 99–117. Cambridge: Cambridge University Press, 1990.

Zangwill, İsrael. *The Melting-Pot.* 1914. New York: Arno Press, 1975.

Zarefsky, David. *Lincoln, Douglas, and Slavery: In the Crucible of Public Debate.* Chicago: University of Chicago Press, 1990.

Ziff, Larzer. *Literary Democracy: The Declaration of Cultural Independence in America.* New York: Viking Press, 1981.

Ziolowski, Thad. "Antitheses: The Dialectic of Violence and Literacy in Frederick Douglass's *Narrative* of 1845." In *Critical Essays on Frederick Douglass,* ed. William L. Andrews, 148–65. Boston: G. K. Hall, 1991.

Index

······

About the Author

Priscilla Wald is Assistant Professor of English at
Columbia University and a contributing editor to
American Literary History.

Library of Congress Cataloging-in-Publication Data

Wald, Priscilla.

Constituting Americans : cultural anxiety and narrative form /
Priscilla Wald.

p. cm. — (New Americanists)

Includes bibliographical references and index.

ISBN 0-8223-1550-5 (cloth). — ISBN 0-8223-1547-5 (paper)

1. Group identity—United States—History. 2. Narration
(Rhetoric)—Political aspects—United States. 3. Political culture—
United States—History. 4. American literature—19th century—
History and criticism. 5. American literature—20th century—
History and criticism. I. Title. II. Series.

E169.1.W25 1995

973′.01′9—dc20   94-32227   CIP